A LIGHT IN THE TUNNEL

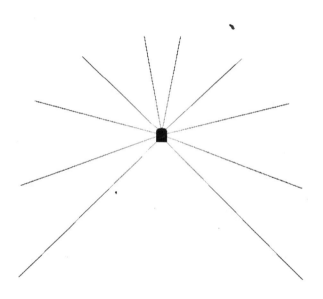

a novel by

ABRAHAM GORDON

ISBN: 1537465082
ISBN 13: 9781537465081
Library of Congress Control Number: 2016914756
CreateSpace Independent Publishing Platform
North Charleston, South Carolina
www.alightinthetunnel.com
@alightinthetunnel (instagram)
@thabrahamgordon (twitter)
A Light in the Tunnel (facebook)
Cover design by Sebastian Alappat @seabats16 (instagram)
www.theartofsebastianalappat.com
Editors: Christian Berry, Stephen Cobb

Message to the reader: "A Light in the Tunnel" can be categorized as a *philosophical novel*. It is a unique method of writing, and therefore will be a unique reading experience.

This novel was not created to serve as a distraction from real life. This is real life. My only request is that you bring awareness to potentially becoming too attached to storyline and characters. This fiction is a glue that holds together something larger. What's inside counts for more.

Thank you to music, family, games, airplanes, meditation, friends, pets, and medicine (including food). Thank you to kindness, water, computers, snowboarding, books, laughter, gravity, dreaming, the sun, and yoga. Thank you to the expression of writing—you have served my need to create.

"Enter with an open mind, and your mind might be changed forever."

– M.G.

Siaynoq

CONTENTS

PREFACE

His five-year-old mind was sucking up new abilities like a powerful magnetic force. That seemed right to him—how it was supposed to be. For little Peter, learning how to swim was the latest in his rapidly growing arsenal of amazing human capacities for action.

Presently, he found himself sitting on the edge of the water participating in his weekly indoor swimming class at the local YMCA. There were two other boys in the class, along with their teacher. On this particular evening, these four individuals found that they had the entire pool of water to themselves. It was night time. Around seven o'clock.

Although his teacher was only sixteen, she seemed to be far older than Peter could ever imagine being himself. She was pretty to him—with blond hair, a small nose, hazel eyes and a big wide smile. He even liked her name...*Carly.*

The three boys were given permission to enter the pool, and Peter soon found himself able to pick up where he had left off the previous week. He sloppily began navigating the warm liquid with the motions his body remembered being taught.

Carly blew the whistle, and he swam over to the side to join the other boys along the wall.

"Today," she said, "I'm going to take you into the deeper end of the pool." Peter looked outward toward the other side. It was massive in appearance. At his young age, he still had a tendency to focus on his immediate surroundings and block out that which was further away. A sense of dread tickled his senses as he cast his gaze over the entirety of the room—its' huge vaulted ceiling.

However, Peter had already begun learning the satisfaction that comes from suppressing fear, overcoming it, and completing challenges. He had learned no reason so far, to see challenge as anything but excitement; so he trusted. The boy readied his small body once again.

His teacher kicked herself back off the wall and encouraged them to swim toward her. Together they moved up along the length of the pool—staying close to the side. Eventually they stopped well into an area he had never been before. Peter clutched the white pale blue tiled railing. He saw the numbers change from three, where they had started, to eight where they now found themselves to be. He had an intuitive notion of what the numbers meant.

Between himself and the other two boys, Peter had the early lead on strongest swimmer. Therefore, Carly called him out first. When they had new skills to learn, she would work with them one at a time. Peter quickly pushed himself off the wall and grabbed onto the safety of her arms extending out before him.

"Very good," she said. "Peter, I'm going to let you go now. Keep up the same movement that you were doing in the shallow end, and just keep swimming until you reach the other wall. I'll stay next to you. Look at you go! Great. You're a natural."

He kept doing exactly what she told him. The encouragement felt intoxicating. *I can do it—I can do it.*

It was hard, but he struggled right along across the deep width of the pool; kicking his legs and extending his arms with power. He felt his teacher beside him, and her presence supported his movements. After a few more strokes, he saw her effectual departure back toward the other boys from the periphery of his sight. *She thinks I can do the rest by myself,* he thought quickly. *Oh boy!* He was so close to completing his goal, but he still wished he hadn't seen her leave. So life moves.

Little Peter continued on a bit farther; maintaining the habit of motion. Then, he suddenly felt a stab of panic grab hold of his mind.

After all, his safety net had just disappeared—it was a blow he was currently struggling to contend with. He lost his stroke and swallowed a small bit of chlorinated water. For a brief moment he kept control by treading water in place, then found himself looking toward the wall ahead as his legs and arms worked madly. It suddenly didn't seem so close at all. The distance scared him even more than losing his teacher had. His body was now questioning his capacity to complete what just a moment ago was certain success. *Can I make it?* He kept his arms moving, leveling out his body, and tried to start swimming forward again.

This all happened fast. His shoulders felt instantly like bricks as his legs dropped again below his torso. In a flash, his mouth was struggling to stay above the waterline. Then his head went under as well.

Suddenly Peter found that his eyes were searching the distorted world below the air. Although he didn't give up with his effort, he felt his body continue moving downward. Quickly he became aware of the incredible danger he was in. He thought about how he had not yelled out when he had the chance. His body yearned for that opportunity now. *Hadn't dad warned me about doing that?* He hadn't made noise, he instinctively knew, because he didn't want to disappoint his teacher. *I'm good at things,* he had told himself within that struggling moment. *Aren't I?*

As he found himself approaching the floor of the pool, Peter tried to think of ways to be successful again—tried desperately moving his limbs in varying motions, tried moving his mind as well. But no method gave him confidence. Fear and water pressure were so strongly wrapped around his awareness that there wasn't room for much else.

The boy tilted his head back and looked up. He saw the distant light coming from the ceiling fixture high above. Then, abruptly, he felt something inside his mind begin to crackle—on the verge of snapping. Although he had never experienced the feeling before, he intuitively knew what it meant. *It's over. This is me breaking.*

Instantly, a kind of acceptance moved into the space that panic had been previously holding. *I can't believe it's over this quickly,* he thought to himself philosophically. *Hadn't it just begun?*

Surprisingly, it didn't feel bad to him. It simply was what was happening—his karma.

Then, amidst that sentiment of acceptance, he felt hands wrap around his body and jerk him upward.

He broke the surface and gasped for breath after breath of delicious and necessary air. He had forgotten how good it felt to operate the lungs.

Quickly following the shock of what had just occurred, and as he was being escorted out of the pool—he experienced feelings of jubilation consuming his entire body. The feelings were well beyond anything he had previously believed to be possible. He was only bliss.

His teacher helped him over to the bench on the side. When she wrapped a towel around him, and asked if he was alright, Peter could only nod his head. He looked up at her with a piercing gaze that vibrated with relaxed seriousness. Somehow, she knew by that look, that he was telling the truth.

Little did he know at the time, Peter was having the most spiritual moment of his life. *As I was letting go, I was saved*, he thought. He couldn't believe it! Still, somehow it felt right to him. As if he had learned something that he'd never be able to define.

Afterward, he made almost no fuss regarding the incident. He didn't even tell his father or his sister. In fact, Peter didn't share the happenings with anyone. He moved on with his life and completely forgot about the entire incident himself!

Well, at least consciously.

PART I

FAMILY

DANIEL

D aniel Sol was born in a different, much quieter time than his children. With cherished space to create understanding, he firmly divided the world into two groups of people: those who appreciated the capacities of the mind, and those who thought, but tried not to. As a young man, he decided to plant himself firmly into that first group. He wasn't sure why, but as soon as he had this realization, exploring the bandwidth of 'thinking,' became the theme of his life.

Daniel's thirst for creative thought allowed him to probe subject matter freely and deeply. It was hard for him to grasp how he might have fit in as a child in the current age of information and exposure he now found himself existing in as an adult. *Would I still have been able to develop this love for peaceful thought? Probably not. But maybe.*

Regardless, he viewed his body as a vessel to be used however he should choose, and he chose to use it to think. Sometimes he would have little silly thoughts: a desire to watch people driving on the television screen in his home. No action, no accidents, no drama—simply the view of the road through the drivers' perspective as they calmly navigated their vehicle through the turns of space-time. Daniel wanted a whole television station devoted just for that. He felt that he could watch that sort of thing for hours.

Other times he'd have deeper thoughts. He'd picture the planet sitting on its' holdings of gravity in Space, and imagine all the forms of life moving around on it—imagine them doing a countless number of activities, while at the same time taking their actions way too seriously. That kind of imagery made him smile because he was certain it was a quite laughable phenomenon. However, it also made him sad. In fact, he couldn't help but look at the entire human species (himself included), and feel deep compassion for the immensity of the combined confusion. Somehow a few important pieces of the puzzle seemed to be missing. His gut told him that humans knew less than they boasted.

He had grown up in a small farm town in southern Oregon. His family owned a winery, and he and his brother were as instrumental in its success as their parents were. From an early age, Daniel and Brian learned how to perform almost every element of the operation. They were sharp boys and quickly adapted to the circumstances presented before them—toiling in the fields with the vines, sorting the grapes during harvest, and operating the tasting room in the summer. As they got older, the two of them developed a master understanding of the most important factor to their success—weather.

They were fanatical about keeping track of temperature, rain, and sunshine. Timing was everything to their business, and the decision of when the grapes would be at their peak and ready to be harvested was a constant consideration. Daniel would lie awake at night contemplating it; wondering if they were right to wait for tomorrow or whether they should have seized the opportunity today. It felt only natural for him to be included in this decision-making, and his family respected his often idealistic point of view.

Although he was the youngest, he was aware of his ability to cut through to the source of almost any given problem. *First I have to take the time to understand, and then the answer comes. It seems to work that way.* He didn't think about trusting his mind—he just did.

One of the earliest conclusions Daniel found, was that how you started your day mattered. He had begun doing fifty push-ups every morning at eight years old and hadn't stopped since. No matter what, this was his first practice of the day. *It reminds my body of its own strength and propels me forward with increased energy*, he reflected years later.

His parents were good-hearted people with strong values, but it was really Brian who set him on his life's course of being a "thinker." For whatever reason (perhaps because he was five years older or because their parents were somewhat clueless), Brian took it upon himself to train Daniel. He sought to harden him and to foster his growth toward his own set of ideals for what "being capable" meant.

One day, when Daniel was twelve and Brian seventeen, they were driving together in their father's old truck. They were heading into town to make a delivery and were stopped at a light. All of a sudden, Brian turned toward Daniel and looked at him mischievously. Then, he slowly lifted his arm into the air before swiftly bringing his tightly clenched fist down onto his brother's innocent thigh.

Daniel cried out in shock, "What the hell did you do that for?!" His leg was throbbing with pain.

Brian replied simply, "I'm making you tough. You've always gotta be ready. Don't you know that?"

It was kind of insane and perhaps wrong, but Daniel couldn't help but see that there was a certain amount of sense in his brother's words. Soon it became a game for him to see how ready he could make himself. That single event changed his relationship with external forces.

But more impactful than the unsuspecting physical assaults, was the fact that Brian taught his younger brother how to be good at things. There was no denying that Brian was an amazingly capable person and Daniel not only respected it, he tried to emulate him. In certain areas he could never match his brother, in others it was the other way around. They both saw that. The only downfall was the presence of jealous competition between them.

Still, great physical progress was made as a result of their arduous relationship. Brian taught Daniel to investigate challenge, and see the body through a different sort of lens. They'd learn a new skill, and as soon as they were somewhat proficient, he'd say: "OK, now let's do it the hard way." They'd throw a frisbee to each other using their left arm, snowboard down a mountain with the opposite leg forward, pour wine with the weaker hand. The drive toward ambidexterity had profound effects.

Daniel had thought to himself, *it's a way of saying…let's make sure we're well rounded before we start getting big ideas about our abilities. Plus, it's sort of satisfying. After all, being awkward is usually pretty funny; which is the perfect starting point for progress.*

Even looking back on his life now as a grown man, Daniel still believed that the correct form for a human to take was that of a boulder in a raging river—standing firm with your beliefs, even as the waters of doubt pass into and beside you. *Brian saw it more in the physical sense,* he thought. Although Daniel also knew the importance of having a strong, healthy body—he had found himself searching for something with more stability. Perhaps that was still just another way of him trying to be better. Perhaps.

What if ten soldiers are faced down by a thousand? What if you have a terribly unlucky accident and become paralyzed? There are sensible limits to the emphasis of physical strength… are there not? But the mind…how far can that be taken? He guessed much further.

Through these matters of deduction, he decidedly placed his greater interest in growing the mind muscle instead. It seemed like the element that had the best chance to sustain success regardless of the circumstance. *A sharp, reflective mind means that I can be ready for anything to happen on any given day.* It meant he would have the ability to deal with disaster, joy, conflict, and responsibility. He adopted an attitude of fearlessness about experiencing any feeling of life because he knew it would only add to his preparedness. His mantra became "A strong mind cannot be afraid to have any kind of experience." Daniel constantly repeated that to himself. The message drove him on a path to becoming a professor of philosophy at one of the most prestigious universities in the country.

At Princeton, he took great pride in creating a classroom environment where exploring truth was promoted, not feared. "The more questions the better," he'd say to his students. "Question everything. You aren't too small for it. Contrary to popular belief, philosophy is not about dropping out. The exact opposite in fact. Philosophy is about plugging in! It can bring us to conclusions like this:"

He stood in front of his class, nice and tall with his arms by his sides—closing his eyes and speaking words as in prayer. "I'm allowed to feel anything I want, and I don't have to tell anyone about it. Now that that's straight, I ask myself: 'what is it that I want to feel?' Hatred, paranoia, lack of appreciation, lack of faith? Nope, not for me—not at all. Let's try the other way around."

Although his career was steady, Daniel spent years of life without an intimate partner. He couldn't have it. He couldn't help but find most relationships to be a constant trading of whose roll it was—trying to bridle the other in order to pacify insecurity. After so many instances of bewilderment and startle, he simply gave up. He was tired of trying to figure out whether or not it was his fault. It was a shame, really, as the union of male and female absolutely fascinated the man. There was something so obviously philosophically brilliant about sex to Daniel, and he wondered why humans didn't focus more attention on the majesty of it. He had no problem with homosexuality. In fact, he once published an essay entitled 'we are all bi-sexual.' The overall premise being that no one could say how much they might crave intimate physical touch, if stranded on a dessert island for years with the company of the same sex. Regardless, his metaphysical mind found itself quite fascinated with the act of fitting together puzzle pieces in order to create new life forms.

Who could deny the brilliance of our creation? No one reasonable, he thought. *Not just for humans, but for all animals. We're constructed together so expertly. We don't have to understand what the force is in order to acknowledge and respect the genius behind it.*

Although he gave up on marriage, he didn't give up on having kids. After years of bumming around about not finding a partner, on his forty-second birthday, Daniel Sol clasped a firm hold on the theory of adoption.

There are children that do not have a home. I have a home with empty rooms, as well as the means to take care of them. I want children—there are children who want a father. I can be a good father. What am I doing not embracing this opportunity? What a harmonizing way for humans to support each other in community! If you were a kid who didn't have a home...wouldn't you hope for someone decent to show you the ropes, give you a chance? Man, being a kid is hard enough already—even for parents who've accepted their responsibility.

Thinking about it now, I'm not so sure if it even makes sense for people who are so similar to all be living together the way most families do. Often, it doesn't seem to be such a good idea to have too much of any one thing in the same place. Oh well, it won't be something for me to worry about.

He settled on Peter and Jo rather quickly; his basic requirements being that they were as little as possible, and that he could get them at the same time. Jo was only three and a half months when he took guardianship over her. He wanted to start from scratch with them, and he also wanted each of his children to have the company of a sibling. Daniel thought it wise to see this undertaking as a joint adventure for three separate humans at once. And so their journey together began.

As Peter and Jo grew, he sought to provide them with tools that could sustain the strength of their minds regardless of external circumstance. Much of Daniel's life exposure was to individuals who were utterly confused and not in the least bit grounded. *As if the mechanisms of their mind are something just happening; a secret, unrealized power stored in the basement and locked away.* As a result of seeing what kind of terrifying effect an unhealthy upbringing could have, he inspired himself to probe the limitations of the opposite extreme as a method of parenting. So, from an early age he began teaching his children the lessons of *honoring thought.*

As they matured, so did his pride in their behavior. Daniel was rewarded with positive feedback to continue styling his parenting in his own colors. They not only absorbed the concepts of his philosophy at an astounding rate but also put them into practice far better than he had ever been able to himself. Daniel's thoughts and ideas had proven impactful for him, but he knew that he had also been held back by years of social conditioning in a system of more traditional parenting. He found too much of his attention occupied with whether or not he was liked by others, and whether or not he was 'doing enough.' He had reservations—a kind of filter that his children did not.

He knew as well as anyone (and preached to all of his students) that so many of the problems of the world would be solved if people stopped caring so much about the impressions and comparisons they made in regard to trying to rank themselves with other humans. He thought back to what his parents used to say to him all the time; "Do you know how much we sacrifice for you?!" He always disliked it when they said that, but he never understood why until he became an adult himself—until he took the time to investigate sacrifice.

I never want to be objectified, and I never want to objectify my children, he firmly decided. He found himself believing that parents who boasted about the sacrifices they made for their children, were actually doing the complete opposite. He thought they were making it all about their own aspirations toward impressive self-imagery. *The translation is this: look at how great of a parent I am…I don't even care about myself! Whoa me!*

When he considered the concept even further and asked—*would I want someone to sacrifice their happiness in order to please me?* The answer came to him in the form of a massive mind-opening awakening. *No way…that's disgusting! What a terrible way to live.*

Nonetheless, like many things, it had proven easier said than done not to objectify his own children. *Action is the step after thought,* he discovered again and again. *While I try to undo some of the brainwashing, Peter and Jo fly ahead with fewer barriers. Good for them. Let them see an example of someone who is openly working toward improving the happiness of their own life while simultaneously wanting the best for others.*

The desire to be a hard-working parent is completely selfish, he realized. *Selfish in the right kind of way. There is no sacrifice when we give. Giving, gives back to us...as long as we don't believe in sacrifice as a method which drains our energy.*

HOME

It was nearing the end of April, and Daniel was driving from campus to his personal residence. It was a beautiful early-spring day—one that naturally tends to fill the body with an appreciation for the heat of the sun and the color green itself. He knew that the depth of this feeling could only be reached after having recently experienced the coldness of winter. That's why he liked the seasons. *If I had it all year long, I couldn't possibly appreciate it as much.*

Today was Thursday, *Jo's day,* he thought. As Daniel drove through the familiar streets of his neighborhood, he let out a deep breath. The stillness at the end of the exhale gave him some clarity and focus as he turned onto his street. As he approached the house, he saw his son lying out on the grass of the front lawn with his arms and legs sprawled out in varying angles of comfort. Peter Sol was tall, lean, and muscular. Although they were not biologically related, Peter had similar dark-brown hair and eyes as his father.

There was a certain easiness and fluidity about his son. His demeanor said to those around him, "I'll accept you for you with kindness; just don't underestimate my ability to behave very differently if I choose." He seemed to express these words without having to say much of anything at all. Peter would take in his observations of the world as if he had every right to do so, every right to mold himself to any particular situation. He had been growing into himself so securely that Daniel now often looked to his son for answers.

As soon as Peter saw the car round the corner, he slowly stood up. Daniel pulled into the driveway, put the car in park, turned off the ignition, and unbuckled his seat belt. He turned his head and locked eyes with his son. They smiled at each other slyly. Daniel opened the door handle, slammed the door behind him quickly, and immediately took off running down the street. After a few minutes of sprinting, Daniel allowed Peter to catch up, and the two of them resumed regular, steady pace.

This was their Thursday ritual, and his daughter Jo was the one who had started it. She had directed the two men in her life firmly, "We run to the Plainsboro Reserve, and we rest for ten minutes at the fountain. Then we circle the water before taking off back home again." It was three miles there and three more back. They had begun the practice on Jo's eighth birthday.

There seemed to be a weight in the air as they stopped for their usual break at the lavish fountain dominating the man made construction at the center of the preserve. The fountain was inlaid with chiseled marble and fantastical mythical gods. In the center was a woman with a crown—mouth open, water spewing out. Beside her was a bearded man brandishing a cudgel. *What is it about these kind of scenes that is so appealing to humans?* Daniel found himself pondering.

He decided to save the answer for another time. He felt that today was one of life's moments when being present mattered a great deal. The weight of a deeper reality came into focus for both him and his son simultaneously. Perhaps it was the sound of the rushing water combined with the heightened awareness that can come after physical exertion. More likely it was the fact that they recently had their most favorite person ripped out of their lives.

Peter stood leaning against the railing that circled the fountain. Daniel knew his son would speak a millisecond before saying his first word. Intuition was a mystery to him, yet Daniel often found traces of its truth. *We are connected, and the energy of our thoughts does radiate out into the world somehow. We notice it but can't do more than that. We're not supposed to make decisions based on the supernatural place. Instead, we exist in the realms of what we know more solidly. Superstition is a childish distraction. The true adult knows better. If you glimpse absurd connections...consider yourself on the right path and then continue to move right along on your path of objective decision making. Some games are over our heads. We need not play at them.*

"Dad, I want to say thank you. I know I don't say it enough." Daniel started to interrupt, but Peter lifted his hand before continuing. "Not so much for all the things you've done for me but more for just being the person you are. For having done the personal work yourself. I look around at my friends' parents, and they seem to have no clue what they're doing. I see them setting their children up to expect everything from life. They're forming this pattern of striving and striving forever—never defining what they're actually trying to get. Money, power, acceptance? The truth is, I don't think they really know. That's scary. But you, Dad. You're not like that. You taught us to consider first and to simplify our desires. I couldn't be more thankful for that reality. Happy doesn't come close to describing how I feel about it. I just wanted to tell you that. That I see some of it. Maybe I wanted to say it more for me than for you. And I think that should be okay too."

Daniel allowed the words to have their time. He let them impact him with strength. Then he spoke softly. "The world is divided into two kinds of people, Peter—those who think and those who try not to. Consider yourself a strong member of the first camp. Stay there."

He was always proud, but sometimes there were bubbles of pride felt more fully. This was one of those times. He had no idea what his son would do with his life, but standing there with the last rays of light beginning to descend behind, he glimpsed the depths of how unordinary it had the potential to be. *He's a seeker. Confident in his own interpretations. That will place him outside of the social fabric. He won't stop listening to himself.*

Daniel wasn't sure what made him connect to God in this moment, but the connection came and flooded him with energy. He was overtaken by the blissful feeling of surrendering to something higher. He had developed a firm grasp on his own personal concept of God somewhere in his mid-twenties. He held it to be true ever since. It was a very unordinary definition.

Daniel believed nature and God to be one and the same. What he saw in humans was a beautiful growth of nature—a significant formation to be sure—but still a form of the same essence. Not so different from a flower or the laws of gravity. A special and more intelligent part perhaps but still made up of the same truth fabric—the same magic matter that comprised the universe itself. He even saw a beautiful manifestation of this in his own children. He found it a shame that early, unrealistic, and childish definitions of the word 'God' now made people feel uncomfortable using it. *It's entwined with a slew of religious history that is difficult to see past and get to the real point of its necessity. What is the point?* He asked himself often. *Answer...acknowledge limitation.*

Daniel found himself responding to his son in an unexpected way. He never had to worry about going down into the depths with him, and he allowed himself to do that now. Trying to understand what was happening in the world and to them personally seemed natural to his family—philosophical conversation one of the most gratifying parts of life. They knew it was irregular, but they didn't care. It was fun for them to question and feed off each other's ideas in the safety of accepting individuality.

"I'm sorry, Pete. I'm sorry that we have to be so strong against this opposition. It's unnecessary really. What's going on with humans is a sickness of the mind that's been passed down from generation to generation. But it's also just a phase of evolution. Never forget that. When the weight of reality becomes too negative, that's when it's time to find the deeper truth always there to smile at."

Peter considered for a moment. "What do you mean exactly—that it's a phase? How can you be so sure of it?"

"What I mean is that eventually humans will start to understand better the nature of time itself. Right now we're confused and scared, so we do the natural thing that comes of fear—we separate and distract ourselves. Just like the example you gave about your friend's parents before. Through our fear we maintain and hold on to an illusion of control. We dive into the planning of our lives and develop fleeting pride in thinking that we can take credit. We forget so easily that we were created and are part of a much larger force than simply our aspirations. How many events beyond your control had to happen in order to give birth to your existence, to this moment itself? It's not deep, but concrete true. We feel the need to take credit for ourselves when it's not ours to take. The fact that you and I are having this conversation is proof of evolution. When fear stops being so prominent, we'll start improving our relationship with control. We'll see that our drives at targets themselves are small pieces in a much larger system of operation."

Peter nodded and reflected before responding. "So you think there's hope then?" He looked up from the ground with a blank, open face. Daniel had a sneaky feeling his son had already been through all of this before in his mind. *Sometimes you just need to hear the words coming from another source though. I get that.*

"Yes, of course. It's only a matter of time. I don't know how long it'll take. I'm not sure if it'll happen in our lifetimes. Perhaps yours. All of this fighting, all of this bickering—it makes no logical sense. Just look at how much humans have accomplished together. It makes no difference that most of us don't stop to realize what great teammates we've been throughout the years. We focus on the negative—on the conflict instead, on the differences. Like the news. We think we've been fighting, and that's true—we have—but we've also been constantly establishing more and more beautiful partnerships. We each choose how much of the truth we want to see. You know that. We're afraid of how positive the truth might be. We're afraid to see that we are standing on the shoulders of giant loving creatures of the past, Peter. Those giants are other human progressions. We will be the same giants for the future generation. We can improve greatly, of course, but one of the ways to do it, is by fessing up to our goodness." He shook his head and moved around some gravel with his foot.

This deeper line of thinking was fresh and new to Peter. He had not gone to this particular place before and often found himself harboring on the negative side of human direction. *Sometimes a new thought can have dramatic effects on perspective,* he considered. This happened to him as he stood there with his arms folded across his chest. *We're great teammates but don't know it. Interesting. It feels real and right. Imagine what would be possible if more of us saw it?*

He nodded his head before speaking. "It seems as though almost everyone is completely consumed with how they're seen though. They care about what they're owed and whether or not they're liked. And I can feel that pull myself, Dad. Especially in school. It's as if they're trying to get me to be like them too. I don't know if they realize it, but that's still what they're doing. They think that if they keep making me feel crazy, that I'll give in. But to me, giving in is the crazy. I'm just worried about what might happen when I don't." He laughed a brief, sharp chuckle considering the inevitability of it.

Daniel looked and watched his son relax himself. *That was really well said, worked out, and true. I'm glad he used the word 'when.' His understanding of his own tendencies is perhaps his best attribute. Our over emphasis on age causes adults to initiate our children. As if the idea of them knowing better in certain ways than we do is impossible. Perhaps experience feeds us with wisdom, but perhaps there is a lot more grey area than we choose to acknowledge.* This train of thought caused Daniel to open up more fully to his son and express vulnerability. "I remember being your age and it makes me feel both happy and sad. I told myself I would never forget what it was like to be a kid, and I haven't. What I think of the most is the pressure I felt to subscribe to mating practices. Wow did I fall so deeply into that game," he said with a smile. "I have done a lot of work and am fine with taking chances now as an adult—asking a lady out on a date and being totally comfortable with whatever the result of that exchange is. But I also remember the boy. The boy who wanted the girl friend, wanted the experiences, so badly. That boy didn't have the teachings, didn't have the understanding of life. I still care about him. To be scared shitless of taking a misstep is no way to live. Playing gender roles overtook me as a boy and in that way I wasn't free. There was too much the boy had to do—had to get."

Daniel took a moment to stare out into space and really remember what his previous self had felt like. Then he took a step toward Peter and placed one hand on his shoulder. He looked his son in the eyes with all the courage he could muster sending out, then pulled him in, and hugged him tightly. He allowed for the natural radiation of love to seep out and take effect. *Strong and soft*, he thought intuitively. *Both at the same time. That's the message.*

"Don't worry, it'll all be how it's supposed to be. That I'm sure of. Somehow," he whispered. Daniel let go and stepped back. "Come on. Ten minutes are up. Jo wouldn't want us to dawdle."

JO

"There are no bad thoughts." These were the first words Jo remembered her father speaking to her. "Allow yourself to think about anything you want. Every ounce of you is good when you're trying to decide what makes sense."

Daniel wanted his children to feel empowered. He wanted them to develop tools that would allow them to easily combat the pressure of feeling guilty—of ever questioning whether or not they were good enough. Therefore, he talked to them incessantly about themselves, about the tendencies of humans. He taught them that control had everything to do with understanding what was happening inside the body.

As Jo grew in years, her father's teachings became more specific. "It's as if you go through constant waves of thoughts: *nothing much, nothing, nothing...oh! There's something. Let me play with that worthwhile nugget for a bit.* And that leads to the next one and the next. An impossible chain to break, and we all go through it. If a problem does exist, it's when the nothing refuses to believe what it is. The nothing thoughts get trapped in feelings of importance. They forget that everything is nothing and that we all just go from here." There was much of that that Jo didn't quite grasp, but she felt the truth all the same. She looked forward to understanding more.

In the current world, Daniel knew they needed these skills of philosophy. He knew their sense of worth would be attacked from more directions than he could think of. Therefore, he planned ahead. Every morning each member of the family stood in front of the mirror and spoke aloud: "I'm not scared. I accept myself the way I was created." Then they closed their eyes and allowed fear to leave the body before moving along with their day.

There were many other nonconventional parenting practices that Daniel instituted. He taught them, "We don't ask for gifts or ever expect them. If someone wants to give something, that's up to them. Giving a gift should be completely voluntary. Otherwise it defeats the purpose." Or, "I want you to find three times every day to close your eyes while staying awake. Notice the difference in how you feel when your eyes are closed and open. Settle down and simply sense your surroundings—sense the workings of your mind. Does some of the nervousness disappear? Maybe now if you're up for it, send beams of love and healing out into the world. You can."

He would send them out on missions in public. "Find someone who is doing something you admire or someone who is doing something dangerous. Then come back and tell me about it." They came to agree that you could tell a lot about someone just by taking the time to truly inspect their face. He told them not to search for opinions, but instead allow them to arrive naturally with patience.

Like many other parents, Daniel was wary of predators. However, his solution was not to shelter or keep his children by his side at all times. Instead, when he felt they were old enough to explore on their own, he communicated with them as honestly and openly as possible. "Some adults are ill and confused. They might try to take advantage of a person they can physically overwhelm. Most of them have been harmed themselves. Often these behaviors are linked to their own traumatic experiences as children. Don't be angry or fear them; just know that they are troubled and seek to drag others down to their own place. They might seem kind and friendly, but many people are very good actors. So good that they don't even realize that they're pretend-ing. Always look in their eyes and use your best judgment. Listen to the tone as much as the words themselves. If you see or hear lust—if it looks like they want something from you, move away calmly with confidence. Search in their eyes and then come back and tell me what you sense is true. Also, try to always make sure there are other people around. If it comes down to it, don't hesitate to scream as loudly as you possibly can. Why not? Anything to stay safe. Don't forget your priorities."

Jo knew there were certain things that her father had to decide for her (after all, she was still a little girl), but as soon as he thought she was capable of deciding for herself, he usually allowed it. He'd ask the question, give his opinion, and then let her choose. For in-stance; he didn't just tell her to wear a helmet when she rode her bike—getting high on the power of authority like so many parents do. Instead he asked, "why would you want to?" Then they'd have a whole conversation about reasonably protecting the safety of the body.

"Will you commit to having dinner as a family every night? It would be nice to count on each other for certain things. Personally, I'd like to count on seeing my children for dinner."

"Of course," Jo had said, before Peter had a chance to respond. Her father's requests were almost never unreasonable. In fact, she found it quite funny how anxious asking seemed to make him. As if it were one of the hardest things he had to do. She didn't understand why, but it was still funny to her—especially considering how much she craved being around him.

Although Jo loved and appreciated Daniel's teachings and wisdom, there was one practice she had started long ago that became her very own. On her fifth birthday, she developed an obsession with never allowing what she considered to be "important feelings" slip away from her memory. In fact, she gave these moments a name— *stayers. Stayers* were simply times of your life that were too good or too important to be forgotten. By naming them she was better able to hold them.

The process of creating *stayers* started on the day she turned six. It felt to her like the most amazing day of her life. They had a huge party with animals, friends, bubbles, and balloons. Plus, she was wearing her most favorite bathing suit in the world. She had just gone down the Slip'N Slide for the seventh time in a row and was in line for number eight. As she stood there behind her friends, something subtly dramatic occurred. In that glorious moment of happy anticipation, she suddenly stopped like a statue as a bolt of thought stabbed through her and penetrated her deeper awareness. As thoughts often do, it seemingly arrived from another place. It made her ask one question... *what did I do for my birthday last year...my fifth one?* She felt that it was fun but for the life of her, she couldn't remember any of the details. She tried and tried but came up with nothing.

It bothered her so much that she took herself out of line, and walked to her favorite spot in their backyard, underneath a big oak tree. She felt so happy to be outside—with each passing day she became more in love with the freedom and beauty of nature. It was as if her eyes were telling her how lucky she was to be looking at all this "stuff"—the uniqueness of every object, the plethora of colors and the variety of life. The beauty was so immense and never-ending for her. She couldn't believe she got to wake up to it every day and that the days and the new discoveries within them kept coming. Jo was a child who had yet to be told that life was supposed to be anything but a miraculous adventure.

But in that fleeting instant, standing and staring at the swirling bark of the tree, there came a moment when distraction came close to causing Jo to forget what the purpose of her movement was. Luckily something in her quickly developing and determined mind reminded her of the message she had sent to herself moments before. *There's a reason I came over to this place, and it's important. I have to remember.* She sat for a few moments pulsing with both anger and focus. Anger that she could be distracted so easily and focus to overcome it and find her answer. She didn't know why, but she found herself clearing her mind—closing her eyes, taking a deep breath, and relaxing. And there it was! In the instant of nothingness, it all came back. *I came over here because I couldn't remember last year's birthday. How can that be? How can I possibly forget a day as wonderful as today?* In the moment of the experience, it seemed completely unforgettable, but then—it was forgotten.

It was her first insight into the power of time and the substantial role it played. She made a vow to herself and hugged her friend, the oak, to seal the pact. *I refuse to let the same thing ever happen to a day like today or any other great moment of my life. What does happy matter if I can't remember?*

Without thinking, she picked up a green leaf off the top of the grass and started to examine it. It was the middle of summer, and nature was at its peak cycle. She looked at all the veins running through and marveled at the faint passageways that led from the main artery through the middle. She traced her finger along the outer edge, feeling its texture and appreciating its sharpness. She looked at the changes of color—the different shades of green. Then she slowly started walking toward the house, went upstairs to her room, and put the leaf on the bookshelf next to her bed. She had a feeling it would help her remember.

"Hold on to them, Jo," she whispered to herself, as she ran back down the stairs. She dashed out through the back door, sprinted over to the front of the line, and dived forward onto the Slip'N Slide. It was the first time in her life she'd ever cut the line. *How can I forget doing that?* she thought.

Soon she developed a ranking system that maintained effectiveness all the way into her teenage years. Any memory, idea, or thought that she deemed "worthy of retaining" was a *stayer* she'd rank on a scale from one to ten. Then she'd write down an explanation of why she gave it that ranking. She saw no reason why thoughts should require less organization than anything else.

As she gained more experience, she was better able to put the importance of this process into word thoughts:

In the same way that I get dressed piece by piece, I also construct my attitude. I may find that one day I have an incredibly powerful thought, but if I don't write it down, return to it again and again…its ability to affect me is minimal. Feeling something is important does not mean I'll remember or that it will have as large of an effect on my life as I desire. After all, there are more than enough distractions to sidetrack me from a beautiful truth seen one day.

It took work and concentration for her to follow this path. It was her little system of disciplined philosophy. The powerful moments of life were enough to get Jo through anything. When extreme happiness grasped her, she not only allowed herself to get swept away in its glory, she also made sure to implant the feelings as firmly as possible into her soul. Then she'd write them down—returning to read them over and over. She was obsessive, but it was chosen and concentrated obsession. Unknowingly, this was what was occurring as a result of her father's parenting style.

Spending time with her family allowed for plenty of happy moments. Daniel encouraged them to balance the time they spent alone with the time they spent with others. He claimed that spending time alone would allow for greater appreciation for being with others, and also in the reverse. It made sense to her, and she tried to split her days up as evenly as possible.

Sometimes the three of them would all sit together silently listening to music one of them had chosen. When she looked at her brother and father it made her feel proud to be a part of this family. She saw both of them as being exceptional men. Their specialness was unavoidable. Not as much a result of their words, but more for their presence itself. When they did have discussions, she'd often sit listening to the two of them pull out whatever was on their minds.

"Peter, tell me, what do you want most out of your life?" They were spread out in a broken circle, lounging in their favorite chairs outside sipping on hot cocoa and listening to George Harrison on the deck. It was a few hours after the sun had gone down.

"I don't know, Dad. I guess if I had to say, it would be that I want to reach my potential—whatever that means."

"Nice! I love that answer, Peter. You will. Anything you do, you already are. If you have faith that it's the way it's supposed to be, and if you're not scared. That goes for both of you." He looked over at his daughter and smiled. "There are no repeats. At least we're not supposed to think that there are."

Jo caught Peter sitting up a little straighter and lifting his chin—looking up at the fat yellow moon in the black sky. She saw incredible strength but also something else in her brother. *What is that? Sadness?* It was if in that moment, he was understanding how much work it was all going to take—how much resilience.

He responded sincerely. "Dad, why do I feel that as I get older, more and more worries start to creep into my head? When I was a little kid, I just did. There was almost no hesitation. Now I start to wonder whether I should do something other than what I've decided. I wonder if people expect something different out of me—if I should bend myself to please them."

They sat there together in silence for what seemed like a long while. Jo waited patiently, wondering how long it would take to get an answer. Finally, it came.

"All I can say to you is that knowing what you just said makes a difference," her father said. "I can't give you knowledge of the future, but I can give you the truth of that. Continue down the path of honest thought, because it's the only way to go. Many people don't believe in honesty being the best policy. What they have done is severely crippled themselves and impeded their ability to experience life fully. Believing in honesty doesn't mean that you have to share everything you think. However, it does mean that you see no reason not to if it feels like the right thing to do. You see, exposing our true thoughts and feelings is what we have to offer the world most. It creates relationships, love and loyalty—all good things. If someone dislikes you for your vulnerability, well then that's their problem. Do you know what I mean? It's most likely a result of your comfort intimidating them and is a result of a lifestyle that constantly tries to weigh 'who is better?' If I know anything, it's that competition goes very deep. Remember that your real self is your best self. Never believe anyone who tells you differently. Honor your inner knowledge and do what it says. Then everything will fall easily into place. That's just how it works. Trying to act a way, instead of being it, is a very slippery slope. It creates illusions of success that are a result of short term rewards. Oh, and one more thing my beautifully intelligent children—only question what needs questioning. Don't let doubt creep in when you're certain."

The look on Peter's face told Jo how seriously he took those words. It was almost as if she were watching him embrace a new layer of armor that he never planned on taking off. It was nice for her to see the effect that people could have on each other.

As the years went by, Jo continued to develop more insights into the character of her father. He seemed to have unlimited amounts of patience for others but not always for himself.

Once she overheard him talking on the phone to a friend. She had just come home from school, put her bag down next to the stairs, and sat down. She knew instantly by his tone that he was upset and confused.

"I was born, and slowly all this garbage got put into my head, Tom!" She knew Tom was one of the other professors he worked with. "Tomorrow? What do I know about tomorrow? Tomorrow is just an idea in my mind—a concept. Don't you see what's wrong? I can plan—there's nothing wrong with that—but what happens when planning becomes my way of life? It's a distraction from the weight of appreciation is what it is. It's like this: someone is healthy in his body, but he complains about the lack of jobs. He gets a job, but then he starts to worry about not having a partner. The day he gets engaged, he's already planning his wedding. He gets married, and he wants children. Something's still missing, so he gets divorced. He can't help himself. On and on forever passing time until death. I don't want to do that. I want to watch my kids. Love them, now...*today*."

She didn't know exactly what he meant, but she was glad she was overhearing. She thought she might have a feeling as to what he was getting at. She didn't ask him about it and decided it best to wait until understanding more. Then of course she'd see if she could help.

Similar to Peter, Jo tried to take pride in everything she did. Winning and losing didn't interest her very much. Although the truth was—she rarely lost. It still didn't matter. Winning was only a byproduct of quality produced. When she did lose, she laughed and joked around as much or more as when she won.

As she got older, she developed a deep love for the sport of soccer. She'd compete with all her strength, lose, and then give the opposing players hugs while telling them how great they did. On the field, she would turn to her rival during stoppages in play and say, "How great is this? There's nothing I'd rather be doing right now." Then the whistle would blow, and she'd turn around and run as hard as she could for the ball.

Although she loved playing sports, there was something about them that troubled her. She couldn't help but feel that when she was having success she seemed to be hurting the girls on the other team. Somehow she felt that she might be deflating their feelings about themselves. Perhaps it had something to do with the disappointment she saw on their parents' faces when they lost. Daniel didn't do that to her. He only cared about how she played.

The outstanding games where she scored multiple goals and dominated were found to be the most uncomfortable for her. Afterward people would treat her coldly or give fake, plastic smiles and compliments. It was as if they were putting her up on a pedestal in their minds and could now start throwing things at her to bring her down. They spoke well, but in Jo, Daniel had created a truth detector. She often doubted the sincerity of their words. Most certainly they would do everything they could to make sure she didn't stay on top for too long.

But the feeling went even deeper than the games. Often she would observe her own demeanor and see how it affected her surroundings. The times when she was the most positive and outgoing (those she felt should be spreading joy) often seemed to have the opposite effect on others. *Somehow my confidence and spirit comes off as threatening.* When she was sad and sulking, she saw that it encouraged joyfulness and security—made the people around her happier and more relaxed. She caught a certain kind of light in their expressions as they asked her what was wrong. For an enlightened eye like hers, being meek and ordinary seemed to be the most beneficial thing to give to others. This utterly confused her. Sometimes, as a young teenager, she thought to herself, *you want sad, I'll show you sad.* She would sit and look and listen, not saying a word. Most people let her be. Their fleeting comparisons were allowing them to finally take a breath of fresh air in the space of superiority. *It doesn't matter what they think, because they'll forget about me anyway. Even if they care now, tomorrow it'll be back to themselves. Or maybe it never stopped being about that.* Her training with memory allowed her to see and understand these patterns.

Her own family never felt the need to fill space with empty words. Perhaps that was one of the reasons why Jo liked being around Peter and Daniel so much. They didn't have any issues with awkwardness. Things just were however they were. She would listen to her friends babble on and on and hear the conversations people were having in public, in restaurants, and in their own homes. They didn't stop talking—pretty much ever. The meaning behind the words didn't seem to matter very much. *They just want to fill space,* she realized one day. *Somehow it's making them feel more comfortable. They're afraid of silence.* She didn't understand it because silence was the space where she'd made most of her great discoveries. She loved silence and felt that everyone else should too. She thought that perhaps it was the same issue that Daniel was getting at that one day on the phone. It was as if being quiet around each other would show people a reality they were trying to hide from.

Jo saw that people would often have beautiful things to say but wouldn't stop after saying them in order to give their listeners (or themselves) a chance to integrate the information. Constantly she witnessed great substance followed by great meaninglessness. *Both are said in the same tone and pace. They quickly continue on until their gift is gone— forgetting a deeper truth...that we're meant to be each other's teachers.*

PUBLIC SCHOOL

She didn't invest very much time in her schoolwork. Perhaps it had something to do with her father's outrage with what school chose to do with its time.

"They don't understand the basic nature of humans," he poured forth one day in the car after picking her up. She had just given a report of another typical, monotonous day filled with loads of pressure and minimal opportunity for participation. It was not unusual for him to go off the rails with emotion, and she listened closely from the passenger's seat.

However, much of it was said with an overly dramatic voice of humor and exaggerated gesturing. It was a habit of his to never *not* be trying to make her laugh. Especially when it was just the two of them. Regardless, she thought that sometimes he wanted her to draw out the truth behind his playfulness. He struggled with that balance, but she thought he did well enough.

"Without choice you can only be led, Jo. Don't you see? Artistic expression, mental creativity—these are the things human beings do best. To plug into that brilliance requires a certain amount of freedom to be as you wish and explore your own desires. They just don't get it, do they, my bristling fire starter?" He was prone to calling her ridiculous names that didn't make much sense. Jo nodded her head grinning. He continued. "Take reading. Do you know how many people are driven away from the natural joy that comes from reading books because it's a mandatory activity for years of their lives? It's hard for me to even meet adults anymore who like to read, and the disparity will be even more severe for your generation. It's most tragic simply because of how worthwhile becoming enthralled in fiction is. Take something objectively great—make someone do it; destroy the activity. We're still trying to force each other to our ways with whips and rods, and it's seriously holding back the progression of our species." He mimicked the motion of snapping her with a whip and made a terrifying face. "But seriously, it makes me very sad when wonderful activity is drained of its' natural value because of unnecessary pressure. Your teachers probably don't want me to say this stuff to you, but you deserve to know the truth. They claim to be helping and that they know what's best— I truly wish that they did. They know very little kiddo. Taking away choice is so incredibly simpleminded and psychologically counterproductive that someone should put a stop to it immediately. How can the population support such an institution? What kind of people do we want our children to be? Sometimes I wonder if folks ever even ask themselves that question. They probably don't. They follow, and that's all they do. I know that teachers' jobs are accomplished best if parents support them, but I guess I just don't put much value in the goal of the entire thing. I don't know if it has a goal." He shook his head from side to side and then dropped the whole subject, turning up the music on the radio and beginning to sing along to some Billy Joel. Daniel had gotten too serious for himself in the presence of his daughter.

Later that night Jo marked the speech down as a *stayer* worthy of a ten. She did not want to forget his words. She knew there was some real truth in them, knew how to prize the times when dad was most open.

Although not able to make the connections as he had, at school she often felt what he spoke about. Most of the time, she chose to obey their rules as best she could—but sometimes she couldn't bring herself to sit down and take a test. She simply didn't feel like taking on that task. When this happened, she was usually sent to the office to sit in a chair and wait. Sometimes she would sit there for hours. All she could do was try and creatively observe both her inner and outer surroundings and patiently deal with the frustration of being unable to freely move her body. *Some punishment this is,* she thought. She wanted to refuse to go to the office. There were times she wished she could just walk outside to the playground, sit, and be with nature. *Who cares what they do to me anyway? Being in class isn't very much fun. Plus, I don't mind thinking. I just wish I had a better place to do it in than this boring square room.*

But she knew if she walked out, it would cause such a commotion that it wouldn't be worth it. They'd call her father, and that would make him even more upset.

Truth be told, most of the time she was fine with going through the motions. Overall, she was too happy about living in general to let the worst parts of school bother her. She joked around a lot and made friends easily. School may not have always been her favorite of times, but she was also sure there could be a lot worse situations to be in. She was an avid reader, and many of the stories she read had told her of that truth.

She and Peter would often read the same books together. Jo was only two years younger and could usually keep up. They went back and forth with who got to choose. They read countless stories of times in the past that were horribly bad. The two siblings enlightened themselves to places in the world that were currently in turmoil. Suffering seemed to be a thing humans did in abundance. *Why?* Jo wondered. *Why don't people want to help each other?* Zooming out, humans seemed incredibly immature to her. *Why don't they listen to the better books about adventures, real heroes, good deeds, and systems that make sense? There's so much wisdom in words,* she thought. *But even in those books, there is almost always a villain of sorts. I seldom hear stories without bad guys in them. Maybe that's the problem,* she considered. *Maybe people feel that there's always bad guys even when there isn't?*

She was fourteen and sat on the floor of her room. Peter sat in an old rocking chair beside her. They had been reading silently for about an hour when a thought occurred to her. She instantly decided to share.

"Peter, why is it so hard for us to figure out that working together makes the most sense? Is that really such a ridiculous concept?"

She considered her own words pensively. Often she had the habit of answering her own questions—letting loose her stream of consciousness. Daniel always told them that no answers were out of reach, so they often tried offering up their own within a few breaths of the inquiry.

"I've been thinking that maybe that's the problem. We don't have a common goal yet. We don't know what actually makes sense to do with our time. Therefore, we just keep distracting ourselves by fighting against each other. How silly is that!"

Peter smiled and looked up from his book. "That's smart, Jo, really smart—and sad too. I think you just hit a very fat nail on the head. Maybe we don't know because most people haven't been taught? And not only are they not being taught, but have been learning something else completely different and opposite."

She considered for a moment before speaking again. "Yes, it seems obvious that you would become exhausted if you didn't even have a firm understanding of what it was you were going for—if you didn't realize how you actually wanted to be spending your time. I don't want to be tired, Peter, but perhaps the desire to fit in is stronger than we realize? Perhaps there's something we're missing that's valuable in it? Do you think that people just move along without thinking because they're afraid of how much the answers might set them apart if they take the time to find them? Maybe that makes sense." She quickly continued without giving much thought to her words. "Should I get better at following? Maybe it is smarter to be more like a sheep. Maybe that's the safest place? Otherwise people won't like me very much, and that can be much harder. It doesn't seem very fun, but I can see how it can protect."

Her brother slowly closed his book, pushed himself out of the chair, and took a step toward her. He towered over her for a second, before kneeling down and meeting her at eye level. Peter's face had an expression of steel and his eyes a determination that was fire in form. He didn't say anything but simply held her gaze for a few moments and investigated the darkness of her inner pupil. She looked away, but when Jo turned back—he was still there with the exact same expression. Then he finally stood up and went back to his seat. He didn't use words to get his point across, and as a result it had a much more intensifying effect.

That was a stupid thing to say, she realized instantly. *He's trying to tell me that I know better. Could I really even turn off my mind and stop doing what I thought made sense if I wanted to?* She brought her thumb and pointer finger to her chin. She turned her head to look up at her brother. "You're right, Peter. I'm sorry for saying that."

He nodded. "Not a problem. I know how you feel."

PETER

Although he was older, in many ways he felt that Jo was the more mature one between the two of them. Regardless, it was clear they existed as a team. Outside of school, when they weren't spending time alone, they were hanging out together. She may have been a girl, but she held her own against Peter in almost any activity or topic of conversation. He saw her as ferocious in both her actions and opinions. He taught her many things, but there was no doubt that the flow of learning slid in both directions. He heard some of his friends talking about their annoying little sisters and wondered why he didn't feel the same way. In fact, Jo was his favorite person in the world, and second place wasn't close. There was an energy about her that called for him to continuously unleash his best.

Like most kids, the two of them did not particularly love the institution of learning where they spent so much of their time. Getting by wasn't difficult, but neither put forth much more than a fraction of their creative potential. When the school bell rang, they'd rush home to follow their own schedule.

Being raised by a single father may have changed things for them, but they never felt deprived in any way. As a parent, Daniel instituted two major rules: take turns making decisions and be kind. It might have seemed odd that a person who was so in favor of promoting freedom would create any rules at all. But Daniel was aware of the fine balances of structure. Structure was a tool just like anything else (to be used for good or bad). If best utilized, he believed, it could actually have the potential for allowing for even greater amounts of freedom.

The first rule manifested itself in the ownership of days. Monday and Wednesday were Peter's, Thursday and Friday were Jo's, Tuesday was a day spent solo, and Saturday and Sunday were Daniel's. You could of course switch any days you liked in a given week (in fact, all rules were subject to change with a majority vote), but on your day it was your time to make the decisions. If you wished not to participate, that was your choice as well (but that hardly ever happened). They had incredible amounts of fun doing just about anything. It became a friendly competition to see whose choices would lead to the most amount of fun and fulfillment. The designation of days gave each of them a chance to be both a leader and a follower and to understand how to adeptly play at each role. To Daniel, finding comfort in these two positions was absolutely vital to his parenting game plan.

Another substantial part of Daniel's philosophy was that change itself was a healthy experience to seek out in reasonable amounts. They constantly searched for ways to shake things up and Daniel promoted this kind of thinking. The family even decided to take on the practice of switching bedrooms once a year.

It was Peter's idea that every fall they'd rotate rooms in their single story ranch. They would all clear out everything and move all their personal possessions into the next room in a clockwise direction. Daniel would know, *okay next year I'll be in Jo's room.* It was also a great way to take on often neglected cleaning duties. Most parents would be averse to giving up the master bedroom with a walk-in closet and personal bathroom. In fact, the majority of adults never even considered the possibility. But Daniel wasn't most parents. He didn't have many material possessions anyway and also didn't believe in the concept of age alone entitling one to more. His priorities were differently aligned, and he rarely chose not to engage in the games of his children's manifestations.

Their system of chores was very simple. Daniel knew that organization was key to being successful at most anything. Therefore, he hung on the refrigerator a notepad with a constant list of what needed doing in and around the house.

"Any one of us can add to this list if we notice something which could use improvement," Daniel had told them when they were still quite young. "It is not only up to me to dish out all of the responsibility for our household. We all live here, and we should all feel pride in the quality of our space. Each set of eyes sees something different. Write down a new chore yourself, or take on doing what has already been noticed by someone else. Either way, cleaning or fixing can be as fun as anything."

Throughout his childhood Peter found sports to be the primary outlet for concentrating both his physical and mental aptitude. It was hard to say whether or not he loved playing sports because he was good at them, or was good at them because he loved to play. Regardless, it didn't really matter. Peter possessed the necessary balances between strength, aggressiveness, overview and fluidity. These skills served him well in all sports. He was a point guard for his high-school basketball team in the winter, a catcher for the baseball team in the spring, and a cross-country runner in the fall.

When he faced opponents, he didn't concern himself with getting pulled into the drama of their stories. There was no personality for him to focus on and get hung up with. He didn't care what it meant for them to win or lose. His competitors were merely moving entities that were challenging obstacles within the layout of game. In fact, Daniel taught him to be thankful for their effort, which provided a growth inducing opportunity for him.

"Hit your target, but be sure to choose your target well. If beating another kid is your target, your attention moves away from what you need to do to score. Scoring becomes your secondary focus instead of the primary one. Play the ball not the player, Peter. Be aware that they'll try to pull you into their obsession of caring about who's better. Don't allow it. It's the hardest thing not to get swept into the energy of others. Challenge yourself to play your own way."

He was made captain of the basketball and baseball teams as a junior and led them both to state titles in the same year. Winning a state title in both sports was something that hadn't been done at Lawson High for more than thirty years. Needless to say, in the swirling waters of social life—it was a big deal to be him.

Years later he reflected that his experience in receiving high social standing in his youth allowed for him to care about it less as an adult. He knew that it wasn't the case for many, but he experienced what it meant to be admired, and then chose to shrug his shoulders at it. *Admiration will not become my addiction*, he decided.

Although he was captain, Peter wasn't a very forceful leader. However, he did have a way of lifting up his teammates. When it was time to give the captain's speech, he would often choose not to say anything at all or leave it at a few simple words. Before the baseball state championship, he stood up in the dugout with a face that was both relaxed and determined. He waited patiently for his teammates to settle down and listen.

"Try," he told them once they did. And that was it. Even though he loved Yoda, he wasn't a believer in the whole "do instead of try" nonsense. *That's an example of people taking their actions too seriously,* he figured out one day. *What else is there to do besides try? You can 'try,' or you can 'really try.' That's a different story. Trying as hard as you want is plenty.*

He could remember vividly sitting back down and continuing to put on his equipment after speaking just that one word. Perhaps if he hadn't already built up trust they would have laughed at him. But his teammates were well aware of what Peters' definition of 'try' meant. He called them to focus themselves on what was most important. They won the game twelve to three.

In the winter of his senior year, he made a move that shocked most of the student body at his school, as well as many athletes in other schools within their same conference too. Three weeks before the basketball season began, he told his coach he would be quitting to join the wrestling team. His coach was furious. Nearly everyone from last year's squad was returning, and with Pete at the helm, there was no reason to think they wouldn't have a superb chance to defend their title. Eventually, the anger transitioned into pleading. "You have a real chance of getting a scholarship to a top college for basketball, and you're going to give that up—for what—for wrestling! No one cares about wrestling!"

But Peter held his ground. When it came down to it, he could be as stubborn as anyone. His mind had been made up, and he was ready for the change. Even all his teammates' pleas and guilt trips were not enough to sway him. *This is my life. Do I owe them something? I don't see it that way.*

His father's sport had been wrestling when he was younger, and Peter felt an urge to experience its value for himself. He had a feeling that it had much to do with the man that Daniel had become, and he wanted to know why.

Competing on the mat quickly became one of the most gratifying experiences of his life. Almost immediately he recognized it to be one of the best decisions he had ever made. He thrived in the simplicity of facing off one-on-one, with no reliance on anyone but himself. For too long he had felt burdened by the weight of those outside of his immediate control. *No fraction of the bounce of a ball to decide matches and no cheap fouls.* In wrestling, the better wrestler almost always won. It was simple, intense, and pure.

Practices were like nothing he had ever experienced before. He had taken pride in always being in good shape, but this was another level of body conditioning. Sweat poured down his face every day, and his muscles rapidly became leaner and stronger. Even the way Peter walked down the hallways and carried himself morphed into something different. He wasn't exactly conscious of it, but he moved with the confidence of someone who felt entirely comfortable with his body. His muscles would ache, and he would walk slowly, but all of that could change in an instant if necessary—and he knew it. His body had become a weapon; expertly conditioned to control itself.

His new coach told him at the end of the season, "I never in my whole career have seen someone make as much progress as you have in just one season. If only you would have started as a freshman Peter."

"That's OK; thank you, Coach. It's meant a lot to me. More than the amount of wins I was able to stack up." Regret was not something Peter allowed for. *If there are lessons to learn, take them—that's it.*

In his final year at school, he felt both his mind and body growing in maturity. He saw the same happening for his sister in her second year. He knew that a lot of it had to do with who their father was. Outside of school Daniel made sure that they spent their time how they actually wanted, and in no other way. Often he would remind them to answer the question, "What do you feel like doing right now, in this moment?"

"Answering that question makes all the difference," he'd say. "Not 'what do I *have* to do?' but 'what does my body *feel* like doing?' Perhaps something that might feel challenging in the beginning, but satisfying at the end? That very well could be the case—or not. Regardless, inspect what might serve, and be easy with your choices."

They were their own type of family. Little emphasis was given to what others might think of their unusual practices. Daniel made it clear that tapping into your true self was each person's primary objective for life. Peter and Jo bought into that philosophy with vigor simply because it made sense to them, and because they trusted their father. These two factors were plenty. How others reacted to their vulnerability was simply what they saw out of the corner of their eye as they kept a firm view on their personal roads of creation.

NATURE

It was a Monday morning in early April that Timothy Walsh chose for his day. It had been exactly one year ago that he had set himself on fire with this particular course of action. The day had finally arrived. *I'm ready*, were the first words he thought to himself as soon as he opened his eyes.

It wasn't one thing that made Tim come to the decision to do the things he was about to do. Rather, it was a culmination of years of buildup. *The lies and the games. The lack of sense in this world. So much pressure. I despise it all,* he told himself repeatedly.

That so many people couldn't see—that they were actually dumb enough to enjoy their lives—outraged him to no end. *All of those ignorant, pretty girls at school with their social standing and fancy clothes—they walk around as if they actually know something about being strong. I'll show them what it means.*

He was woken up by his mother at seven o'clock as usual. He took a shower and got dressed but decided not to brush his teeth. He knew why. He packed up everything he needed and went downstairs for breakfast. His father was the cook in the house and a good one at that. Tim felt that both of his parents were extremely ordinary. Their attempts at fitting in made him sick. They preached to him about the importance of schoolwork and college and doing what was right. They told him life wasn't supposed to be easy—that you had to make sacrifices. They were consumed by their own images and acted completely differently in public than they did at home; his mother especially. *She's all about facade. She won't make a decision until she's seen five of her friends make it before her. She doesn't live by her own set of rules; she lives by what she's told. A travesty.*

He concluded that any semblance of his parents individuality or character had been driven out of them long ago. They claimed to love him, but he didn't think they even knew the meaning of the word. *How can they love someone else when they don't even like who they are themselves? Pathetic…it's all so pathetic.*

He didn't say anything to them that morning. They were used to his coldness and brushed it off as being typical of teenage growing pains. He grabbed his lunch and the keys to the car they had bought him for his seventeenth birthday. He took a few deep breaths as he sat in the seat, hands on the steering wheel, and focused himself before turning on the ignition.

This is it. There was no more time left for thinking about his parents he realized. He vibrated with nervous energy. He was scared but also determined. He had practiced this moment so many times before in his head…*but this is for real.* Of course that made a difference.

As he drove to school, he started to gain some calmness. He pulled into the parking lot at 7:38 a.m. *Perfect,* he thought. He parked next to the curb and the parking spot of Mrs. Jones, his biology teacher from last year. He opened the door to his car, and he caught a smell of pavement mixed with morning dew. He looked around at the campus—at the trees, at the buildings and the fields, at the other kids walking with their heavy backpacks on and their heads down. He read the words 'Lawson High School' painted on the stones in front of him.

Just another day at school, he thought. *No one wants to be here. Little do they know this isn't going to be just another day. Today is different. Today is for me.*

Tim had such a yearning to separate himself. Everything in the culture told him that he must stand out. In all the conventional ways like schoolwork or sports, he always felt completely ordinary. The actions of this day were all his mind seemed able to come up with in order to break away from how well he seemed to fit in. He wanted to be the troublemaker in class, or even the student who asked hundreds of questions. Instead, all he ever seemed able to do was exactly as he was told. Today was the result of the escalating pressure.

And there she was, pulling into the lot in her big red minivan. He waited until she parked—for her to grab her things and get out of the car. Now was the time, the moment; *no hesitation*. Boom, that was it. He allowed himself to be flung into the continuous action of his previously visualized training. He felt his feet moving as he ran over to his former teacher and spoke his rehearsed line. "Good morning, you bitch!" Then he pulled the shotgun out from behind his back and shot her in the face. It seemed to all happened in slow motion for him. The crack of the gun rang hard in his ears, as he watched the bullets take her in a stunned face. He saw the blood spurt out the back of her head as the movement of her eyes came to an abrupt halt.

After she fell, he stood there for a moment looking at her mangled face lying on the cold hard pavement. He had dreamed of this moment, yearned for it. But staring at her now, he felt only confusion. He was not experiencing the relief or elation that he thought would arrive. He figured he'd be at the very least satisfied, but he didn't feel that way either. He realized that he still felt scared. *Same as before*, he admitted. He forced himself to move past it—suppressing the feeling and pushing it down.

He had decided that he didn't care much about what happened after this. Mrs. Jones was the one he really wanted. She was the one who had made the experience of being a student such a nightmare for him. She was the one who looked at him and saw nothing but weakness, and sought to exploit it. She had the power to make him do what she wanted, and somehow he knew that someday he would flip that power around on her. *Today I have.* That produced a small smile; a tiny trickle of satisfying revenge.

There were only two people he had to make sure to kill...Beth Jones and Tim Walsh. However, he did have other plans.

So he ran into the side entranceway of his school and took a hard right into the athletic wing. He ran down the flight of stairs moving swiftly—*be like a soldier,* he chided to himself. *They never had any idea what I was capable of. Now I'm showing them.*

As soon as he reached the bottom step and put out his hand for the door handle, the door began to swing open from the opposite side. Entering into the stairwell was someone he hadn't seen or thought about in quite a while—Jo Sol.

This would be the real test for him, and he knew it when the moment came. He had gone to elementary and middle school with Jo but they had never shared a class at their current institution of learning. Once in a while, they'd pass each other in the halls, and she would wave and smile. But they hadn't spoken in years. Deep down he felt that perhaps she wasn't that bad—*not like the others,* he thought. They had played together as friends when they were much younger, and she had been kind to him. But his mind reminded itself that none of them were actually good. He reminded himself that life sucked for everyone. He felt that even she was a part of something that he hated. *Even her...weak and afraid of death. She probably thinks that this life means something. How stupid. Just like all the rest.*

He moved back a few paces to let her step in. He watched her soft smile turn into confusion and shock as she saw what he held in his hands.

"Holy shit!" she blurted. "Tim, what are you doing?"

"This is it. I'm sorry. Say your good-bye, Jo."

He was so serious it made a deep chill run through her body. She saw the look in his eyes and stared right back at him. She saw the anger, the horror, and the sadness—she saw it all at once. *This boy who so desperately needs a hug and doesn't know how to ask for it.*

The sound and the feeling took her together as one. A sharp pain was driven into her ears and a hot burning into the middle of her chest. She staggered backward, still staring at him as she took a seat on the floor.

Jo sat there for what felt like an eternity—her back against the wall, head tilted to the side. She looked out the window as she listened to the door open and close behind him. She watched a bird perched on the limb of a tree and chose to inspect the structure of its' wings. *So intricate*, she thought.

AFTERMATH

The carnage on that day carried five people from this world into whatever comes next. Timothy continued into the girls' locker room, killing two more of his classmates. Then he walked to the mirror by the sinks, looked at his own face one last time, and handed life the greatest insult.

Peter had just taken his seat in first-period American History when he heard a far-off scream followed shortly by the principal coming onto the PA system to announce that there was a code orange. "Everyone stay in your classrooms and lock the doors." The honest nervousness was evident in his leader's voice.

Peter sat there wondering what it could be. *Was this a drill?* For some reason, it didn't feel like one to him. Although a dread rippled through his bones, he had no way of knowing what it meant.

After an hour of waiting, they came for him; two policemen. They took him into the hallway and told him that his sister had been hurt and was being rushed to the hospital. "There's been an attack. Come with us."

When they told him what happened while sitting in the backseat of their car, he was too shocked to cry or really have much of any reaction at all. But when he saw her lying there with tubes and gadgetry running all over her body he wept and screamed. Then he wept and screamed more—experiencing sensations of unfamiliar pain that colored his being with horrifying torture. He felt it was as if his body was decomposing, and he wondered why he was still living at all. *This can't be happening…it's not possible.* The reality was too heavy for him. If this was a video game, it would be the moment he pulled the chord in frustration. *What can I do? There has to be something.*

Jo was dying, but she wasn't dead yet. Peter clasped her hand and kissed her forehead. Daniel had yet to arrive. It was just the two siblings together.

"Please don't feel sorry for me, Pete," she managed to whisper through her tears. "I really don't want you to. My life has been incredible. Because of you. Because of Dad. As much as I can't believe what's happening, my body is telling my mind to start accepting it. Somehow I'm sure the point is not to be afraid—even now. I'm sure of it," she said as she closed her eyes, squeezed his hand, and moved into the next level of release. "All of us who think we're owed ninety-some-odd years at least." He saw the pain overcome her as her face turned even more pale and she struggled to maintain composure. He wanted her to be quiet—she struggled to press upon him her point. *Just listen Peter. Whatever she's trying to say is very important to her. Take it in.*

She coughed as she spoke. "We're missing it. We're not thinking the right way. We can't keep making this mistake. It's unacceptable. I saw his eyes Peter. Something terrible is happening to people. They don't realize that we aren't owed anything. They don't realize that life itself is a risk. If they did, everything would be much safer I think.

"Do you know what I mean?" She smiled at him as she looked and saw total focus in the expression on his face. "Please help them see it. You can be that big. I know you can."

He watched as she let go, and also felt a loosening—as life energy flowed out of her beautifully crafted hand.

PART II

INTO ADULTHOOD

TRAVEL

After his sister's death, Peter began training himself rigorously. Exactly how, why, and what for he couldn't exactly put into words. It was more of a feeling that guided him towards areas that he felt would be wise to investigate. He saw his relationship to himself in both clarity and mystery. He saw that he was one with the will of nature but also responsible for trying to make rational decisions. *Part of rational decision making tells me to hold onto the reigns of life with only so much grip. It also tells me to question how I truly want to grow. Not how others think I should. How I do, and how Jo would want to as well.*

His best answer regarding the focus of his training was the same he had given his father long ago—a large philosophical concept that offered him the necessary direction. *Program myself to reach potential.* It might have seemed dispassionate to view yourself as a 'programmable machine,' but Peter questioned whether or not the programming itself couldn't have greater bandwidth than we tended to believe. *Can a program not inspire me to be more emotional, more passionate, more human?*

He was most definitely his own man, but Peter had adopted many of his father's interests. One was the topic of education. As he grew in years the issue of how to best raise young humans became more and more of a rock solid key to Peter. He remembered the weight of being a boy and dreading having to go to school in the morning—of days filled with being told what to do. He was able to like a great many variety of activities, but he could never imagine himself enjoying a day filled with unkind direction. *It's almost as if they're scared of what will happen if they allow humans to be their natural selves,* he realized one day. *This is an extremely telling and fundamental flaw in the current status of our culture.*

He saw a clear divide in the mentality people took. *The first path says that our natural selves are knowing and good...that left to our own devices we'll do the right thing. The second path says that humans are inherently bad and therefore we must stop one another from having the freedom to explore the world. Why? Because we're bound to cause destruction...our very nature is perilous.*

He made a connection with how he had been forced to curb so much of himself at school. *Our current structure of education is based on the second path. That's crystal clear to me now. What a travesty—mostly because it's based on such a falsehood. The flaw is not that there is anything wrong with us, but that we think that there is. All the horror comes from that mentality.* Peter was sure.

As many children do, he realized that he had mistakenly grouped learning and school together. Perhaps less so because he was raised by Daniel, but he had still gotten roped into the distasteful practice of taking on new information. He saw that in many ways he hadn't even developed a true love for learning until after he had graduated from college.

After he was free to spend time however he chose, he had an epiphany. He saw that it wasn't the quest for knowledge that he despised but rather the system that claimed to know so much about it. He questioned why more people didn't have this realization as well; his instinct told him that more were starting to. He thought to himself, *the freedom of becoming an adult must be too overwhelming for some. Even if you have the freedom to do anything you want with your life, you'll still put yourself in chains, because it's what you know—because of the habit. The schools breed fearful minds. Perhaps if the habit of listening to others telling you what to do grows so strong, it becomes a safe place of familiarity. Even if it doesn't make sense, and even if it's the least safe practice imaginable.*

He didn't think it was really a part of some master plan or super conspiracy of the elite, but rather just the way that things happen to have been worked out over time. Regardless, there was a part of him that was disgustingly impressed with the ability of the system to cause people to willingly give up the greatest gift in the world; the freedom to explore important questions—and live by—their own conclusions.

Fortunately, Peter had the ability to live what he believed. He knew it meant everything to practice his conclusions, and he had the strength of his sister to increase the motivational waters within his spiritual well. *That well goes deep,* he told himself thankfully.

Sometimes the grief of losing Jo overwhelmed him with feelings of injustice. *Why does life have to be so unfair? It doesn't make sense! She could have done so much more good with her time.*

But then he'd remember her final words, and serve himself feedings of strength that connected to the limitations of human understanding.

Seeing no reason why he couldn't live with feelings of living for two people at once—when he was old enough to cease being told, Peter became free to decide. Daniels guidance was a tremendous gift that put him far ahead on his path of exploration, but it was still not enough for him. He wanted more—he knew his own personal adventure would be vitally important to the good he would one day be able to accomplish. So, he began traveling more broadly upon the planes of his planet.

What he discovered immediately was that he wasn't afraid to work. In fact, he mostly enjoyed it and was a far better worker than he had ever been a student. Why? Because the motivation was clear—*do a good job.* He didn't grasp common conception of work. *People not only accept work as necessary suffering; they also place it into the most important category of their lives. What a pair to content with! Sometimes we even enjoy it while we're complaining about it. Oh us humans; how can we possibly take on the burden of participating in such stupefying methods of activity?*

He saw it as a road where insanity was the destination. *To so many, it's an excuse for being stressed out and overly anxious; yet the action is continued as if we have a right to our grumpiness. We don't. There is a choice beyond the path of the follower. The words "I'm sorry; I've just been so busy at work," are thrown around as if they can justify and be a reasonable excuse for any kind of inconsiderate method of behavior. Nope, not for me.*

To Peter, work was an experience not much different from anything else. Other rules didn't cease to apply because he was being paid—he wasn't one way sometimes and other ways other times. Wherever he was, he tried focusing on how to best be being. That was it. Work was simply another environment for him to try and have fun doing that.

We're not forced to do anything; we just think that we are. The mentality that keeps us down is the one that embraces this unnecessary desire for so much material comfort—not to have it, but simply to be accepted. Shift your priorities to where you truly want them to be; toward bettering the health of the mind and body, he told himself. *I think you might find that you don't need nearly as much money or material as you've been using. You also don't have to feel guilty about what you've been doing for so long. The past doesn't matter. We don't have to hang onto it because the shock of fessing up would be too painful. It's more painful to hold out on ourselves,* he thought. *All variety of experience are simply unique chunks that make up our path. A life focused on the new discovery of simple desires, can be so completely satisfying. After that, then I can start using my money for smarter things—the things I care about...if I have it.*

Considering his skepticism concerning the functionality of the school system, it was surprising that Peter found himself working as a teacher. Being abroad and in possession of the English language made it easy to find work in that role. Teaching children who didn't speak the same language opened his eyes to seeing how much communication existed beyond the limitation of words. Often he found himself as the only adult in a classroom filled with thirty Chinese children who barely knew the ABCs. That left him in quite the predicament. *Teaching five-year-olds is hard enough. Teaching five-year-olds that don't understand you...almost laughable in the immensity of the challenge.*

So he was forced to use every tool at his disposal. Hand gestures, drawings, music, and especially tone of voice became his arsenal of accomplishment. He learned quickly that words themselves are less important than the energy in which they are voiced.

Standing in front of these classrooms displayed for him proof of the awesome power of attitude. If he was funny one day, it would cause the children to let loose. If he was serious, it encouraged focus. If he was tired—well, let's just say that those were the most trying of days. Regardless, he saw the power of his energy and the effect that it had on those around him. Sometimes that knowledge overwhelmed and put pressure on him to be his best self (perhaps too much), but he also knew that he had to accept the inconsistency of mood as an inevitability of life. *Can't be the same all the time.*

Embracing multiple ways of being led him to develop a new level of confidence and belief in his skills as a leader. In fact, he began to feel a responsibility to foster his own ability to speak up. *There are so few people who can actually do it well,* he thought…*without getting sidetracked by the power involved in other people agreeing with what you have to say.*

As a teacher, he developed even firmer beliefs that life as a student was unnecessarily painful. Much of why teaching was a more pleasant experience, was because he was the one making most of the decisions. He tried to implement as much choice as he could for his students, but there was only so much he could do in the system he was in. The students still had to listen to him, and most of them would rather have been doing something else. He wished for more leeway. A different kind of environment to lead within.

Looking back on this experience years later, he felt that there couldn't have been any better training for him. The task of teaching children demanded focus, confidence, and personal conviction. He took being a role model and guiding youth seriously. *Few people can understand better than the teacher the importance of being present. Chance of success when distracted or inauthentic is virtually impossible. The only way to succeed is by actually being confident.*

From this place, he saw how drastic the conundrum was. It was not just the schools that were the problem—it was the psychological box of shelter and safety adults attempted to place their children inside of. They tried to carve out a life for them by limiting their exposure to reality—choosing schools with other wealthy families in order to place them firmly within their conceived blueprint for life. *Understandable for the people you've birthed but a tragic mistake nonetheless. It's not for us to plan others' lives. Even our own kids'. Squeeze them too hard, and they'll burst. There's an art to guiding gently—all while acknowledging the limitations of your strategy.*

Peter taught for five years in four different countries—China, Singapore, Poland, and Brazil. Although there were of course plenty of peculiarities, he still found that overall school was school and people were people. The acceptance of life as a difficult journey was pervasive everywhere, and throughout the world children were being forced to spend their time more harshly than he felt necessary. *If only we could better introduce people into this world, so many of our problems would vanish.* His experiences firmed this belief to the core.

He didn't think much on the change he was personally effecting. *Assessing your impact on the world outside of yourself is a tricky thing.* He felt it was impossible to understand even to a small extent his influence on mentoring countless children or on his relationships with women, friends, or even strangers for that matter. That was whatever it was—something for the gods to weigh and for him to try at. *Sometimes in life the best intentions are taken the wrong way. The only thing that's important is that I intend what's best and accept the path as it unfolds before me. Simple really.*

As he lived and traveled from place to place, he began to understand the intimate relationship that he had with himself. Eventually he reached a point of greater understanding of what his father had told him throughout his childhood. He constantly considered how to become as close to his genuine and natural self as possible. He decided that his relaxed self was indeed his favorite one. He realized that it wasn't going to be easy to always be it, but that everything was also *it* anyway. When he put that final piece together, it was as if this huge weight had been lifted from his shoulders. He was free to be real and knew that nothing else was possible. *What a fine balance*, he marveled.

With this personal freedom of the mind, he decided to spend his time having the experiences he really wanted to have. He only had to answer one question: *what to do with my time…now?* Teaching was great, but he also felt an itch to explore so many other ways of spending time. It was hard for him to choose which experiences he wanted to have, but he knew he had to choose regardless.

It was not that he felt there was anything wrong with choosing a single passion and sticking to it, but one specific activity had yet to grab him so strongly, and he also knew that he was somehow appropriately addicted to change. He had plenty of interests, and to him there was nothing wrong with jumping from one to the next. *As long as I can keep at bay the voices that question my ability to commit, I can see value in having a variety of experiences.*

"All of life is beautiful without fear," Jo had told him. He believed her. In fact, it felt right and made sense for him not to get locked down in his prime years. *The responsibility of the future may very well not allow for it.* He was a young man, and he didn't plan on having regret later on.

He felt the pressure that others were going through, but he fought against the desire to fit in with them. He considered what would make sense in order to improve himself, and then he did that thing with resolve. If he felt there was more to be taken from an experience, he continued doing it. If it was time to move on to something else, so be it. With the weight of building a résumé and the forceful choice of a career gone—with an unbreakable conviction that life was not meant to be suffering—he freed himself to the joys of experience.

Peter worked in retail, became a recruiter, and worked in marketing and management. He became a bartender, a sports referee, a massage therapist, and experienced the life of farming as well. He even graded standardized tests for a short period of time. This experience gave him a behind the scene glimpse at the true absurdity of the system. The company tried to turn individuals into machines by believing the grading of state writing exams could be uniform across the board. It did not play out. The grades that children studied so hard to obtain were dependent on whether or not he or the person next to him received their test, how strict the moderator of his table happened to be, or if he was trying to get out of the building for lunch.

All of this experience before Peter turned thirty-five. He met a multitude of people and had deep, honest relationships. He made friends easily and joined communities all over the world. He found himself by the ocean, in the mountains, and in the heart of the city. His life was adventure because that's how he saw it. He would save money, go home to spend time with his father and regroup—and then set out once more. As he did all of these things, he felt himself getting stronger and stronger with each new experience. He saw more and more proof that his most valuable assets weren't material objects but rather the things that he always carried with him—his mind, his voice, his honesty. It amazed and saddened him how far away from this reality most people seemed to be living. It was a truth he felt called to share.

He worked and was able to provide for himself. Sometimes he asked for help, but he had great success in giving far more than he received. He allowed one event to flow naturally into the next. *Like they're supposed to.* A suggestion that came from a friend might determine what he would do next. He saw the truth of it and didn't see an issue with embracing the weight. It was just life. Of course he would have to like the suggestion in order to push forward, but he might not have thought of it without this other person. In this way, Peter didn't take much credit for the circumstances of his life.

Spending time abroad gave him a certain sense of easiness when he came back to his home country. He could remember times being lost on his motor scooter on the outskirts of Shanghai—being late for work and having to ask strangers who didn't speak his language for help. He remembered well those feelings of weakness and of having no choice but to place himself in the hands of destiny.

Those experiences now give me power—because I always made it through. They were often the memories that hung around his mind the longest and changed his mood when he found himself in a rut. He'd consider events in his past and use them to bring on feelings of ease; as well as cosmic acceptance. He'd smile at the absurdity of the whole thing— most especially, the realness of his present mood.

In every job, he witnessed the split between those who were con-formers and those who were rebellious. He found that it wasn't even about the circumstances of the jobs themselves—it was about some-thing more. It was about the relationship to the self within a system.

Although a natural rebel, the experience of teaching gave Peter a new found appreciation for those who saw value in following a path that had already been laid out. However, he also saw that most con-formists did not allow themselves to truly dive into the importance of questioning the quality of what was happening. They did not zoom out enough to see the cultural necessity for every human to be willing to risk it all.

A SNEEZE

Peter sat on the floor of his small studio on the Upper East Side of Manhattan. New York made him a bit uneasy, but living there was undeniably a valuable experience. He had turned thirty-one a few days earlier. It had been about thirteen years since the death of his sister. Someway, somehow, he had continued moving forward through the action of his life. There seemed to be no other choice for him as he felt he owed it to her.

He sat in the middle of a large circular rug slightly lifted on top of a cushion with his legs crossed, spine extended straight, head and neck relaxed. He stilled himself into meditation as he closed his eyes and noticed how his body was feeling. *Thoughts are not the enemy...but just like anything else they do need to rest. Once they've had a break, their quality will drastically improve. I'm sure of it.*

He allowed his mind to wander back and forth between emptiness and thought, training his mind to rest and his body to feel. *Time—time is everything. The more time spent doing something, the more ingrained the habit. Everything we do is a habit. Choose to create the right ones, and you're on your way. First we have to decide which ones we want.* He often repeated these thoughts to himself as a mantra—the constant acknowledgment of the power of customs becoming the most important custom itself.

Reflection and writing became two of his core habits—both taken from Jo. Reflection, he felt, led to conscious change and improvement. It astounded him how many people seemed to be moving so fast they couldn't possibly be taking time to reflect on all their life happenings. *They just move—giving away what it means to be human.* Without reflection, it was clear to him that the same mistakes would continue on in a vicious cycle of frustration.

For him, doing that wasn't an option. Most people were too sensitive to shed light on their unhealthy habits; Peter searched to find more of them.

It's only possible if you don't take yourself too seriously, he reflected one day. *Otherwise you care too much about how good you are. What a frivolous analysis!*

Writing felt both freeing and necessary to him. It came naturally as he continued to enjoy the process of recording more and more of his observations.

Writing puts me in a good mood. It makes me feel productive. I think that might be the most valuable feeling in life. I imagine it's the same for all art forms—whether it's parenting, painting, or playing billiards. Art, work, life. It's all doing what we think matters. It's not what we're good at...it's what pumps us up and sets us off. I don't think we should be wasting our time getting strung along into things—wasting our time because we don't want to take ownership of our choices. We have to get rid of the bullshit from our lives. And there's always more of it. Doubt in my ability to write, doubt in my goodness as a person...BULLSHIT!

Even if no one else read his words, the action of getting his ideas down on paper felt extremely valuable. He knew that the process planted the ideas more firmly into his memory, and that was his objective. He knew that Jo had been a master at this. Peter sought to carry on the torch of creating art with words.

Forming these habits left the path for improvement clear and open. *Growth is simply the great game of life.* Patience, focus, letting loose, feeling good, and accepting ambiguity were all a part of that same game. On occasion he could see paths split before him—see a seemingly small decision and feel the weight it might have on his life.

Presently he found himself remembering something significant that he used to do when he was a child. As a boy, he would naturally let his mind wander deep down whatever path it was choosing to go. *Just like I'm doing right now,* he thought. One night lying in his bed—for whatever reason—he stopped the stream of thoughts to ask one question. That question would drastically alter the course of his life. He had asked himself simply...*how did I get here, to this very thought I'm now engulfed in?* He remembered what seemed like moments before being in a completely different area of focus. The only thing that seemed sensible to do was to follow back the chain of linking thoughts to find out how he got to where he was. The thoughts went as follows:

Right now I was just thinking about what it would be like to learn how to play an instrument. Before that I was wondering what music was like hundreds of years ago. Before that—what it was like to live in a time when everyone carried weapons. Before that, that hockey sticks would make good weapons...except in close quarters. Before that, the feeling I had when I scored a goal in gym class earlier today. Before that, what I have to look forward to tomorrow. Gym again!

Following the experience of that ordinary night, it became a little game for him to try and stop—follow the chain of thoughts to see how he had gotten where he was from where he had begun. The practice improved his intimacy with his own mind, and made him a scientist of his own being. He would often be amazed at how the smallest detail, once focused on, led to an entire new platform of thought. *Our minds really do have a life of their own. I think it's good to allow them to fly around.*

Thinking about these memories as he sat there reflecting in his small box in the midst of one of the most impressive cities ever built, the preciousness of his life overwhelmed him. *It's so beautiful and can be so short. How can we insult it by not appreciating, by choosing to suffer with feelings of failure? It's insane. We control these bodies and can take them where we will. We operate our own real-life video-game character—what a gift! We just have to realize it—again and again and again.*

If any worry over the things he didn't have existed, it was completely swept away in that moment. *This is what she wanted me to see,* he knew.

Later that night, sleeping in bed, Peter was woken up by a sneeze of his roommate. For whatever reason, he wasn't able to fall back asleep. He sat lying awake thinking about the potential consequences of that sneeze. *I've been lying here for what seems like an hour. Now my sleep will be different, my energy tomorrow on another track. I was planning on waking up and going for a run, but I might sleep later now instead. If I'm being honest...as a result of the sound of one sneeze; it's very possible, and even likely, that my entire day tomorrow, and therefore my entire life will be different. Maybe better, maybe worse. Who knows? Not me! Definitely different though. I know it's crazy to think about stuff like this, but is it really? It actually feels practical to me. Can't run away from reality. Simple acts do have the potential to alter the entire course of our lives. Maybe I'll now cross paths and form a friendship with someone whom I wouldn't have otherwise. Maybe that friendship will take me to new places and change my life. Can I not look back on my life and see plenty of examples of small events having dramatic implications?*

I understand why we avoid the immensity of how it all works—but truth is truth. Perhaps the unwillingness to acknowledge it is another example of the ego trying to make believe it has more control than it really does? Oh that silly little ego!

No matter how uncommon these thoughts were, he knew that to turn away would be to fight against his truer nature. *Can't do it.*

"I could write a book called, 'The Implications of a Sneeze'," he chuckled to himself.

Eventually that night, when his mind had had its' fill of play, Peter brought his attention to the imprint of the cotton sheets surrounding his body. *When we're lying in these safe little boxes of security, in our built-for-comfort beds...it's a little piece of heaven, is it not? I don't need anything else right now. Most of us amazingly get to experience peaceful comfort every night. What luxury! Those that don't...well I can think about them later.*

He then let go of his thoughts, allowed that knowledge to be the last realization of the day, and finally fell into the mysterious state of dreams.

MAYA

S he carried her body through the busy streets of Manhattan like a painter composing a mural. She went through speedy phases of movement and would then stop abruptly to take a seat on a bench or step off to the side of the crowd to look through a storefront. To Maya Frankel, movement itself was an art form. There were moments of precise determination and moments of seamless wandering. *Isn't that what all art is a combination of—the play between feeling and focus?*

She was prone to find bliss in the simple act of walking and it was perhaps her favorite part of life in New York. She didn't concern herself much with the swarms of other humans surrounding her. Sometimes she would give a smile, and sometimes she would search through the faces technically—not knowing what she'd find. Often she'd glimpse things that confused her—an angry man in a Ferrari driving by a smiling woman on a bicycle—strangeness that made you question and wonder about priority.

Maya had pitch-black hair and darkened skin. Her eyes were big, brown, and slightly oval. The well-aligned proportions of her body became secondary once one became aware of the pleasantness of looking into her face.

The way that men leered usually made her uncomfortable—as if not being able to have her was causing them some kind of physical pain. She despised that. *They don't even know me, but still almost every one of them would make the mistake of bending themselves out of their beliefs in order to impress me.*

The public has an unhealthy relationship not only with sex, but with a fakeness, a certain formula associated with the games leading up to it, she thought. *It tends to objectify the other person involved. As if...here is a time where we can allow selfish planning to supersede the evidence of a separate individual with their own personal desires, their own heart which breaks.*

Not that the dance can't be the most beautiful and powerful of experiences... it can, she knew. *But in order for it to be that way, we have to remember how to tame our lust. Anyone who knows anything about actually making love knows that it is in the honest trading of pleasure that can make the experience godlike. Giving and receiving—back and forth in focus without a semblance of guilt to be found anywhere. That, and that alone carries us to the place we hope to go.*

Maya Frankel was born in a far off land to most of her friends and even to herself now—the suburbs of Buenos Aires, Argentina. Her grandmother Juliet was a Jewish Hungarian and a champion survivor of Auschwitz. She had been one of the few Jews from Hungary to survive the war and her character represented her life's challenges. Maya recalled being younger, hearing small tidbits of detail, and questioning to herself: *Because they were Jewish? Really? Kill people for something they don't even control. If you're going to hate, wouldn't you at least want to find a better reason for it?*

Her grandfather was an Argentine businessman. Unfortunately, he suffered from a fatal heart attack when she was just four and now all she childishly remembered was his solid hands and distinct smell.

Her grandmother Juliet, however, was as influential a presence in her life as anyone. When Maya was nine, her mother acquired a job as a curator at a prestigious museum in New York City, and they decided to move to a country which called itself "the home of the free."

"It'll be an adventure," Juliet had told her to ease her nervousness. *She certainly hasn't been wrong,* Maya reflected.

Her father continued working as a pharmacist, and both of her parents spent long hours accumulating enough to pay their hefty rent. That left a good deal of time for Maya and Juliet to spend together—getting used to a new life, complaining about parts of American culture, and being vulnerable regarding the challenge of the experience. These components made the two of them sister like. It was a beautiful relationship that happens quite often between first and third generations.

Although Juliet showered Maya with unconditional love, she also tried to instill in her granddaughter a rigid discipline. Her parents were also compliant in adding to this pressure. Because Maya was her parents' only child and her grandmother's only grandchild, much of the time it seemed as though the hope for all three of their futures' rested squarely on her delicate shoulders. It was as if her success could satisfy them with continued justification for their hefty move north of the equator.

One of the most important practices Juliet taught Maya was the way to eat her food. "You'll notice the way most people eat," her grandmother said as the two of them sat at their dinner table side-by-side with two full plates in front of them, "is thinking about the next bite as soon as the first one has just entered the mouth. Most of us do this again and again, until all the food is gone; barely taking in a fraction of the majesty the taste has to offer—and then finding ourselves full and sad at the end. I want you to take one bite at a time, and I want you to experience that bite of food all the way through—for all the changes that happen in your mouth and in your mind—until there is absolutely nothing left. It isn't annoying or hard; it's fun. Think about the feeling, look forward to the next bite, and only then pick up your fork again."

Years later Maya better understood the specialness of her grandmother. *It was not merely that she loved me. People can love in all sorts of nasty ways. It was the flavor of kindness which deeply penetrated my heart.*

Her families chief ambition was seeing Maya excel in school. They firmly adopted the belief that it was the path for opening doors of opportunity. They constantly questioned her about her studies—made sure that homework was the first thing she did when she got home, and that she was clear in making school her ultimate priority. Maya found no reason not to comply. It made sense to her. It was pressure, but she hardly knew of any other way. She wanted to make them happy and committed herself to meeting, and exceeding their expectations.

Socially, Maya transitioned similar to the way most foreigners might—keeping more to herself in the first year and then slowly emerging from her tortoise shell as she gained comfort and confidence. She slowly and carefully gathered friends but never lost sight of what she was at school to do. *Perhaps my family puts pressure on me because they know I can handle it,* she had secretly and continuously chided herself. *I can.*

Her favorite aspect of being born into the Frankel family was the experience of observing, and participating in, incredibly engaging debates. Perhaps it had something to do with their Jewish and South American combination of heritage, or perhaps it simply was the result of their own uniqueness as a family. Regardless, dinner usually consisted of fiery dialogue about politics, art, and even the individual habits of each person at the table. What she learned most importantly, was the ability to turn off the switch when time was up and love was bustling to have its' say. After a heated argument between her father and grandmother, it was common for Juliet to walk over to her son-in-law and kiss him gently on the crown of his head. He'd reach out and squeeze her hand and they'd move right along to laughing and focusing on something completely different. This made Maya smile and feel happy about the world. They were experts at not crossing the line of conflict, but very much enjoyed playing around close to the edge.

Unsurprisingly, Maya graduated first in her high-school class— perhaps mostly as a result of her keen focus on her objective. Early on, she had seen that it was not as much a matter of learning the actual material, but rather a game to learn what each teacher *believed* to be the material. The same small insight carried her through four years of academic success at Columbia University as an undergraduate, and three more years at their law school as well. She identified what needed to get done and then made sure to place that work on her top shelf of priority. Once it sat there, there was no longer a choice in the matter of completion. She input blocks of time into the calendar on her phone, and if she wasn't able to complete the work in the time she originally planned, she would add in another slot. She had her own standards of quality completion, and they served her just fine. *I only wish the rest of my life were as clearly defined as my school work,* she often dreamed.

This was now all a part of her past. Presently, Maya was nearing her seventh year working for one of the top real-estate law firms in the country. She was excelling at her work to a similar degree she had achieved success as a student. She was meticulous concerning detail and demanded excellence from the team of lawyers working beneath her. Her annual salary was now over half a million dollars.

But all the academic, professional and financial success didn't stop Maya from feeling that her life had now found its' way into some sort of a standstill. She felt the desire for dramatic change but wasn't sure how to go about getting it. *I've done all the right things. Am I supposed to be experiencing these feelings of emptiness? No one told me about this…about what comes after doing everything that I'm told.* She saw that the acquisition of money was similar to the acquisition of grades in school. *It's not about the value of what the money can bring, or of the learning to be had…it's about having a clear goal that allows our lives to feel comfortably focused. A matter of psychology really.*

Something was missing, and she felt thirsty for a part of life she couldn't quite put her finger on. She reflected on her job and her years of being a student. *There's a lack of logic to the system. It doesn't address some of our deeper longings,* I think.

When she stopped to consider it more fully, she realized that hardly any of the subject matter she learned in school transferred into the working world. It was a whole new separate set of information necessary. Although her drive and organization came from a similar mindset, the methodology to the system was totally out of whack. This disturbed her. While she was busy memorizing loads of information at school, she had figured it would be needed for future work. She was not happy when she discovered that virtually none of it applied. All those thousands of facts that were poured over and put on a pedestal of 'vital information,' slowly dissipated from her memory after being unused for so long. *School and the working world like to think of themselves as connected...but really they are two entities desperately in need of productive dialogue.*

Maya was one to use both her creativity and logic to solve problems. As she completed more and more challenges others set for her, she began developing her own distinguished enlightened eye. As she grew in confidence she began to see problems on a larger scale. She didn't think outside of the box; there was no box at all. There were only ideas, and problems needing solving.

It was the second day in the month of December that reached out and planted itself significantly into her life. She had just come from dinner with her family and was on her way to meet up with some friends for drinks. Surprisingly, she found it to be pleasantly chilly for this time of year. *Slightly cold but not brutal.*

Plenty of happiness was found for her in building loyal relationships. As a friend, however, Maya demanded a certain kind of open-mindedness. She enjoyed the process of combining different groups of people and shaking up the dynamics. When she had been younger, sometimes she would be afraid certain friends wouldn't get along and would choose to split her time between them. Now she ignored that kind of over controlled attempt at perfected separation. She found it fun to see what happened when different types of people were brought together. Maya was exposing them to those they might not have encountered without her intervention and she believed the risk to be worthwhile. Sometimes she would make dinner plans with a coworker, a friend she met at dance class, and her grandmother. Conversation was unpredictable and entertaining. Her friends grew to love this about her. The way she saw it, expectations often needed to be stamped out. It was something she was working on.

Maya could be serious, but most people would never say that she wasn't fun. Although they usually didn't tell her, people felt that things were somehow different when she was around. She created an air of purpose by sticking up for the little man. She gave strength to those who often stayed cooped up in their protective shell by encouraging them to honestly explore their attributes. It made a difference.

Talking badly about others was something she found to be horribly monotonous, and she usually tried to steer the conversation away from superiority chatter. She was all about having the most possible fun now, in this moment. Sometimes she would sit silently, falling into the background just to see what would happen. She enjoyed the practice of becoming more of a listener too, but found people to be much more sullen and negative when she didn't assert herself. It caused her to feel both proud to be the person she was, and also pressurized to proactively inflate her environment by taking on leadership over and over.

Others would often confide in her and feel no worry that the conversations they had would be repeated. It was obvious that she had no interest in betrayal or gossip. However, it didn't always go both ways. More and more Maya was grappling with the fact that she could often be taken advantage of by those who were closest to her. Her open and calm demeanor often led others to unknowingly develop competitive behaviors with her—trying to make impossible and unfair comparisons between them. What they failed to see was how much strength it took to be what she was—how much persistence of thought was required to really care about others. They tried to compete, but failed to realize that they were playing on an entirely different field.

Recently she began to feel that obsession of the sensitive ego was running more rampant than ever before. It depressed her to see so many people she loved overcome with its nagging voice. She also couldn't deny that there was some of it in her too. *And it really is a sickness—no matter how many other people share it. It's a sickness of skewing reality to put down the self.*

What made it hardest was the fact that it was extremely socially acceptable to state your insecurities; especially for women. *If you aren't worried about how you look or what people think about you, then how can you connect with others? What else is there?* The hordes of people in New York seemed to be constantly shouting, "Me, me, me, look at me. I'm something! Right? Aren't I?"

Because everyone around was doing it, it seemed to be OK. *It isn't!* She was realizing it to be a monumental problem needing fixing. Particularly that last little question at the end.

Maya's eyes darted up from the ground, bringing her out of her thoughts and into the present reality. *Be here now. Nothing else is as important.* That was her new mantra taken from the great spiritual teacher Ram Dass. He was a Harvard psychology professor who at some point got hip to the limits of the game. He changed his name and began following a much more adventurous path. His mantra reminded her to focus on the exquisiteness of any given moment. She enjoyed considering the past or imagining the future, but understood them as merely different flavors of being present.

The place she was headed was just around the corner. She moved briskly to the entrance. Before she went in, she stopped and looked at the door—at the structure of the building surrounding it—the brick within the lines of mortar, and the pattern of the design. In that moment she realized something...*I don't want to go in here.* She wasn't in her most social mood, and when she wasn't, those scenes tended to exhaust her. *I know I can try to change my mood...but do I really want to?* She took a deep breath, remembered that she was trying to be more kind to herself—and turned around and walked away. She texted her friend to let her know she wouldn't be coming. She did feel badly about that, but it simply wasn't what she wanted to be doing. *If that's the case, does it really make much sense to do it? Maybe, maybe not. No right answer...only a feeling.* She was starting to gain more and more confidence in listening to what her natural desires for action were. *What I want in this moment is to keep walking.* She did that.

After a while, she turned off of an avenue and onto a quiet side street. She found a small bar in the middle of it. Going into a bar by herself was something Maya had never done before. But as of late she was prone to take on new experiences—beginning to get an enhanced thrill in them. It wasn't that she was depressed or un-happy or didn't like other people—she was simply growing, and in that growth starting to prefer spending more and more time alone. Again it was that question, that desire for something more to show up in her life. She needed change—was so thirsty for it. This was how she was trying.

All of that aside, there was something else pecking at her core. If she was being completely honest, she had to admit that she was burst-ing with a love that was needing to be contained. Although she had family and friends, she did not have someone to share life with as intimately as she secretly yearned. Maya was single. She was young, independent, and primed for partnership. She deeply wanted to start a journey with a man—to take care of him and have him desire to take care of her as well. She knew it could never be just anyone and refused to settle out of a compulsion to ease her discomfort. Her eyes were open, and she was witness to too many troubled and dangerous rela-tionships. Too many people who dreaded going home. She wouldn't have any part of that. *Either it will be beautiful, or it won't be at all. I don't need company that badly, and life is too remarkable to go ahead and make it willingly worse. I'm not even sure if I approve of the institution of marriage. I can know how I feel in this moment, and perhaps I do not expect that to change, but aren't I different today than I was five or ten years ago...or even yesterday? Does it really make sense to start making promises for the rest of my life? Is that whole conception not based on self-conscious fear regarding the future? I don't want my partner to stay with me simply because he made a promise. I want him to stay because that's how he feels...now.*

The most difficult part for her was not getting swept away in all of the conversations about men. She saw that the majority of women wanted deeply intimate relationships with their partners, but then they would betray those relationships by sharing what should not be shared. She knew they did it in order to impress their friends. They did it as a result of getting swept up in the desire to be interesting within any given moment. By doing so, they unknowingly were transferring their allegiances to places outside of their union. She saw how joking complaints repeated often enough eventually turned into real problems. The habit of needing to gossip meant that conflict could be secretly sought. *We need a place to talk about these things,* she thought. *To get ourselves straight. But in the mode of problem solver, not of complainer. Oh how much better things would be if we spent our time solving problems instead of complaining about them.*

She turned the knob of the door that was suddenly before her and walked in. The bar was softly lit with fancy booths lining the wall, as well as a smooth onyx bar that glowed from lights underneath. The place was about half-full of patrons, with only one bartender working. It was old in style and didn't hold many people. She liked that. She found a seat on the stool farthest away from the door. The bartender smiled at her and laid out a black napkin before her.

"How's it going?"

"Oh, not so bad at all."

"What can I get for you?"

"Hmm, I don't know. Would you mind choosing for me? I don't really care tonight."

He smiled at her again. He was handsome, with a full beard and strong jaw. "Any preference on the spirit?"

"Anything but vodka please."

"You got it."

She took a sweep of the place—gauging what kind of bar it was and who the people were. It was only a few blocks from her apartment, and she wondered why this was the first time she had been here. New York was like that though—always small new places to be discovered. She felt it was one of those spots where the history of it was almost palpable, making her instantly content.

It seems to have a purpose...a class that allows you to let go and feel like you are where you need to be. Whoever designed it did so with care.

She watched the bartender as he made her drink. He moved fast but without much stress in his movements. He peeled an orange, he dashed some bitters, and he sprayed a splash of soda into the glass before snatching a muddler to bring out the aroma and combine ingredients. He chose rye and stirred the drink a few times before placing it down as a finished product. She recognized this as a craft and the man as someone who enjoyed practicing it. For some reason it was uplifting to watch him. It naturally brought about a shift in her mood. She was trying to get better at witnessing those around her who deserved admiration. *Only possible if we stop trying to decide who's better,* she realized.

She took notice of not just how he made his drinks but also how he interacted with the other customers. There was quality in what this man was doing—a surety of self. *Not arrogant but definitely confident.* He spoke to others passionately, but even more than that, he listened with an almost ferocious amount of focus. *You could justify his behavior by saying he's simply trying to make the most tips, but to a keen eye, genuineness isn't a quality to be faked.* It seemed almost as if he were giving his customers a gift by taking from them whatever they chose to offer up. *For some,* she considered, *it means the world simply for their voices to be heard. I think maybe that kind of respect is hard to come by these days.*

She sat quietly, as she slowly took small sips of her drink. She had tasted plenty of old-fashions before but none as well balanced as this one. As she politely chatted with the man sitting next to her, she experienced a mental tugging. This bartender had latched onto her awareness in a way that can only come from the magnetic forces of romantic attraction. She felt both hesitant and excited simultaneously. She sat there for about an hour considering her feelings. When she finished her drink, she thanked him and left.

I'll do something, she decided. *But not just yet.*

LITTLE PETER

Although Peter grounded himself in his own disciplined training of positivity, it still didn't completely prevent him from having his share of deeply depressing moments. They usually came about when he got sucked into the swirling enigma of thinking about his future. His life existing on the periphery of a typical trajectory played games with his emotions.

At the worst of times it made him feel like a failure. Voices in his head spoke of "settling down" and questioned his ability to make commitments. These feelings confused him and made him uncertain—made him interested in the value of the path well-traveled. *If the general population is anywhere close to sane in how they structure their ambitions, I have something to worry about. I've spiraled so far away,* he realized. *Value in planning—I can hardly see it. Apathy has taken hold. A willingness to do anything but no clue what to do. I've made myself too sane,* he realized. *Ambition—I don't have it. They make me feel like a loser, like there's something wrong with me. But I have no desire to attempt to gain control over my life in such a delusional kind of way. How can I go backwards?*

It was Saturday night, and he was visiting his father back in New Jersey. He had gone out earlier to meet up with a friend, drink a few beers, and watch the hockey game. When he came back to the house, Daniel was still out. He sat down to watch some TV and started falling asleep. He managed to lift himself off the couch, went upstairs, brushed his teeth, washed his face, and crawled into his old bed from childhood. But in those few moments of movement, he had lost his drive for sleep. He tried to push past it—to clear his mind and allow his body to relax. Suddenly he had a flash of realization into the depths of how sad he really felt. Maybe it was the beer, or maybe it was the food he ate. Regardless—right then everything felt horrible. It was one of those moments that grab hold so powerfully that permanency feels inevitable.

What's the point of it all? How many experiences do I need to have before it's over? When does this end?

Depressing questions bombarded him like snowballs. He couldn't see that he was depressed—he just was. He thought of Jo and how short her life had been. It made him feel even worse to disrespect time this way.

To fit in, he was expected to think about his future—to spend a large majority of his time in the present planning for something else. But he didn't believe in any of that. By not buying into it, he couldn't be included or even connect with other people and how they were experiencing reality. Desperately he wanted to help, but he was exhausted from the effort of letting others fall into traps that he saw clearly. He was exhausted from seeing so far down the rabbit hole and not being able to make changes on a larger scale. He was tired of living on the outskirts without much support for the things he believed to make sense. He was tired of taking on notions of superiority which others projected onto him. He wanted the world to get better already. He was tired of questioning whether or not he believed it, or instead wanted to be right. He wanted to team up with someone; to do true work of value. He thirsted for the responsibility he knew he could carry—the purpose to add meaning to his life without getting lost in questioning his worth. He wanted it so badly it hurt.

The pressure he felt at the possibility of something working out with a woman was too much—always trying, always hoping. But his way, his unique path, made it hard to find a partner who saw similarly. Most women were scared of his attitude and perspectives. Others might have had similar opinions, but Peter was living those opinions. That took him to a place others were hesitant to follow.

Most recently he was decidedly getting sick of searching and initiating possibility. He told himself he wasn't going to do it anymore, and it was a huge burden lifted off his shoulders. He saw the depths of the pressure put on males to aggressively go after their prey like hunters (women were taught to enjoy their role as prey).

I might want it, but maybe now's not the right time. He had enough self-value to realize that it was indeed possible for someone to see and want what he had to offer. *In the chase I lose my clarity,* he realized. *I can't do that anymore.*

He wanted a person who respected how he lived and understood even to a small extent what he was capable of. He didn't feel that he should need exorbitant amounts of money or a prestigious title to prove his worth. All that he needed was a pair of eyes that could see and assess true value. The game of valuing the external was a terrible trap most fell into. It was a game for lazy eyes. Unfortunately, the tendencies of the people in the age in which he was living left him with few possibilities. For a person who didn't buy into many of the rules, it was hard to relate to the way most people were prioritizing their lives. *Most people want to fit in—they don't want to truly think.* It caused him to remember the two categories of people his father split the world into. He was starting to feel that everyone fell into that second category. *They've been told so often what they should be looking for that they no longer remember how to decide what they want.*

Lying there in bed, he sought a place of peace. *It doesn't matter what happens. I can let the world come to me in my way, and it will be fantastic.* He put on some music. Even though it didn't completely alter his mood, there was still something soothing in it, and the sound itself was friend like. He could focus his mind on following the noise, and it gave him the distraction he was yearning for.

He didn't really want life to end (although he often wondered how much time was really necessary). What he did wish was that he could shut off his mind and take a break from being with it for a while. Not meditation but a true shutting off. Not losing memory, but a simple re-booting which would bring about a wash of freshness. Sleep was great, but dreams could often feel more exhausting than real life.

It was not to be. He had to deal with what was. *Thinking doesn't ever really stop.* He thought about Jo. He wished he could go back to being a little boy, just for one day, or even to have one hour to spend with her again. *Time is cruel in its concreteness*, he thought. *How amazing would it be if my whole life were recorded and I could go back and watch myself move through past days? Recording is a beautiful way humans have discovered to harness time. Why can't they implant a camera into our foreheads when we're born and give each of us the only key to access our recordings? We would improve so much faster by watching ourselves. The video would allow us to see proof of how we really are. It would be impossible to deny what...*

Finally, his string of waking thoughts came to an abrupt end. He was so tired. When he fell asleep, he dreamed.

They sat together at a table in a busy restaurant he had been to once during his travels in Cambodia. It was nighttime. All the other tables were filled with people talking, laughing, drinking, and eating. The intense traffic could be heard outside, and the smell of food permeated his awareness. There were palm trees inside of a large old greenhouse converted into a restaurant. Small statues and large rugs decorated the dimly lit room almost in a Grecian sort of way. His little sister stared at him across the table.

"What are you doing?" she asked.

"I don't know. I'm lost," he replied instantly.

"Are you scared of the end?"

"No, but what if I'm wrong? What if people are beyond my help? What if they're right? What if you were right? Maybe I should just play the game like all the rest? It feels too hard sometimes—trying to make change and living my own kind of life. I'm trapped in my mind, and I can't get out, Jo. Maybe ignorance is bliss?"

His sister reached across the table and slapped him hard across the face all in one quick motion. She sat back in her chair and waited a moment. He felt bewildered as he rubbed his cheek. It was not in her character to do something like that, but it had the effect of stilling his whining.

"Peter, why do you think there's an end? People like to jump to the worst-case scenario and be overly dramatic. Yes, you can't be sure, but that's part of the whole *real* game of life—not being sure. Part of playing it well is choosing not to assume the worst. Do you see that? Be aware of your limitations, aware of the rules. It's something most are not very good at. You're trying to find all the answers when all you need to do is accept where you are. Simple. Very, very simple."

He looked up into her eyes, and she gave him a smile that brought the energy of life back into him. He was so happy to see her the feeling of crying overcame him with the absence of tears. It was that feeling deep within the heart that simply experiences emotion with joy.

In a flash they were no longer in the restaurant but driving in an automobile back in America. Jo was at the wheel, and for some reason Peter found himself sitting in the backseat.

"Are you excited to see him?" she asked without taking her attention from the road. After all these years, he realized that he had somehow lost sight and underestimated the extent of his sisters outgoing demeanor. It was almost as if there were a bounce to her words themselves.

His dream body sent a message to his waking body not to forget. The way in which her memory lived on within him was extremely important to Peter. The message was transmitted.

"See whom?" he asked, half-interested.

No answer. She turned up the music on the radio and started humming along. They drove for what seemed like a long while. They said nothing, and Peter peered out the window looking at the trees, the road, and all the creations of the earth—feeling content.

After a while Jo started speaking. "People like to separate elements of nature and things that are man-made, but really it's all the same— what we build, what we are." She turned around and looked at him quickly. "Humans tend to think we are something different. But we're made of the earth just like the flowers, trees, oil, and all the rest of it. We are bound to our home planet. Yes, we have the ability to go up in the air and even out to space for a time. Perhaps we have a greater ability to love and discipline ourselves. But we must always come back to what we are—a fascinating growth of earth."

They were suddenly parked in a driveway. Peter didn't realize they had stopped. He looked up at a house unfamiliar to him. Jo turned her head around from the front seat.

"Well, are you going to sit there all day or say hi?"

He looked out the window and this time saw whom she was talking about. There he was. He stared at a child that was in fact himself at what looked to be about three years old. Little Peter. *Dreams are crazy.*

The boy sat on the grass playing with some toys—creating a kingdom of his own imagination. Peter opened the door of the car and went over to him. He stood simply watching for a few moments, noticing the brilliance of the play. There seemed to be no rush at all in his actions. As he watched, his love for this boy grew and grew.

Finally, he swept his little-self up in his arms and squeezed him with all the power of love he could ever imagine having to give. He just did it—because he wanted to.

Little Peter smiled and giggled like it was all a part of the wonderful world he found himself playing in. The joy was so pure it made Peter explode with the emotion of youthful memory. There was only happiness in that boy—no thought of life being anything but play. He realized, then, the degree to which he had allowed himself to be corrupted. *I'm not trying to think differently; I'm trying to think right.*

He looked at his younger version and saw again. *Other people are simply tools for his joy. He doesn't disrespect them by feeling that way...he honors them.*

And then, as if the current emotions of the dream were too magnetic to continue, Peter opened his eyes and found himself back in bed. It was the morning of the waking world. *This life,* he realized. He blinked and adjusted himself to the transition. *Did that happen? Should I really write that off as a crazy dream and move on,* were his first thoughts. He knew he had received a gift that very few people ever experience. He felt ten times better than the night before. *What I needed was given to me and then some. It did happen—and I can't forget how changed they've made me feel.*

The lesson is crystal clear...that little boy still exists inside me. If he didn't, I wouldn't have dreamt it. He hasn't gone anywhere. Remember.

ATTRACTION

The days passed in a regular type of fashion after that. Peter went back to his apartment in the city and continued on with the life he had gently constructed. He enjoyed being a bartender as much as any work he'd taken on before. The movement of his hands, the exercise of memory, and the steady concentration needed was gratifying for him. Sometimes the bar would get packed and he would not stop moving at top speed for hours. He would go home feeling satisfyingly exhausted and well used up.

At first he had difficulty finding purpose in his work, but then he began focusing more on his interactions with customers. Even though a bar was supposed to be a place to let go and relax, he found that most people had a difficult time doing so—no matter how much wealth they had accumulated, no matter how hard they worked that day. Even walking into a place created for enjoyment, most people still weren't able to shed the layers of anxiety and animosity that they carried with them everywhere. Instead, they often focused their energy in the direction of those giving them service—not letting go of their need to constantly judge and assess.

They often challenged Peter's knowledge of recipes, liquor, customer service—anything to catch him up in their critical net and lower his feelings of self-worth. After all, he was just the bartender. *How many times do they have to do it until they believe that they're better?* It troubled him how worked up they could get about things of such little importance. *Is this how they go about their lives—in constant angst of how right they are? Taste your drink and enjoy it, damn it!*

If he was being honest, interacting with these characters was rapidly becoming the most meaningful part of the job. He made a game of trying to turn them around. He focused on transmitting the message that there wasn't a place for all of that baggage here with him. He wasn't always successful, but often his demeanor and his ability to joke around—to look a person directly in the eye—made them realize how silly they were being. They saw how much he truly didn't give a shit. He was more interested in trends than individual people. That was where he directed his own assessments—to the trends.

Soon after becoming a bartender, Peter seriously cut down on his alcohol consumption. From his stance behind the bar, he couldn't help but see a deeper reality of what was happening. *Alcohol is an outlet for getting really happy and then really sad. It's a way to get confused by the swing of emotions and then disregard the whole thing…ready to repeat the process.* The way he saw it, people were dying to let loose and be rid of their self-contained boxes. Alcohol gave them the opportunity to launch themselves free for a few breaths—to disregard all the confinement they were compounding inside of their minds. *It's almost as if the body insists on at least experiencing spontaneous freedom for a short while. Even at its own detriment.*

The issue as he saw it, was that extreme living was dangerous for the health of the mind. *Ideally we want to get to a place of greater consistency. People are giving way too many fucks in their sober lives, so that when they get drunk, their behavior takes on outrageous forms of the opposite extreme. Although perhaps freer…their drunk selves are not their best form. They may be letting loose, but many of them are letting loose an ugly and confused side that their better selves would never condone.*

The answer Peter arrived at was that people desperately needed to lose their filters, but had to start learning how to do it while sober. *Only the right support system can overcome that hurdle.*

When she came and sat at the bar for the first time, he didn't have much of a reaction. There were beautiful women who moved within his vision often. What he usually found in them (after he was able to peel away their camouflage) was a group of people deathly frightened of truth. The prettiest ones wondered all the time whether or not their beauty was real. They obsessed over their appearance as if it was everything in the world. *We don't make ourselves...what are they so proud of?*

No matter how many times he had tried forming deeper relationships, he found he was unable to convince most pretty women to accept the bodies they were born into and leave it at that. Like many obsessed people, they couldn't turn their attention away from the topic of fascination. Therefore, the truth only became hazier. It frustrated him that the logic of accepting the concrete wasn't easily acknowledged. *What a travesty.*

Sometimes I feel sincere compassion for those who are good-looking, Peter realized. *From their point of view, it's easier to fall into the trap...thinking that it matters.*

When Maya came in for the second night, he couldn't help but begin to form that nervous sensation in the pit of his stomach that comes by way of magnetic attraction. *Sometimes your heart chooses what to feel and there's nothing to be done but go with it.*

Her beauty was overwhelming. Not just the beauty of her appearance but more importantly the peaceful way in which she carried her body. *Strong...but also soft.*

He tapped into his training to calm himself. *Relax; be present. Keep moving and allow the universe to tell you what to do.* He felt into the sensations of his own body and embraced the nervousness. It helped.

"Back again?" He asked.

"Yeah, this place isn't too bad. There's something about the way it feels that transports me back in time."

"Agreed. That's one of the reasons I like working here. What's your name?"

"I'm Maya. And yours?"

"Peter."

He extended his hand to her across the barrier. She looked directly at him and smiled as she shook it.

"What can I get for you, Maya?"

"Do you remember what you made me last time?"

"Sure do. The same?"

"Please."

From his vantage point, he often sat as a spectator watching the games of courting unfold before him. One of the things he wished he could change was exactly what his father had taught him as an adolescent—the acceptance of the roles and responsibilities that men and women often adopted for each other. He would see a woman watching a man, develop an interest, and then do absolutely nothing about it. He knew it was the little voice in her head saying, "It's his job, not mine." That deep belief in the existence of rules prevented them from taking otherwise reasonable action. The man, wrapped up in conversation or the game on TV, would be ambivalent to this woman's interest in him; or simply be too tired of trying. He would do nothing even though he may have been hoping for just her distinguished type of presence in his life. The woman would do nothing; nothing would happen. This was a kind of insanity to him. *If you see something you want in life, how does it make any sense not to try to get it? Because of some rule you were told to believe in as a child? Fairytales and expectations destroy our propensity for happiness.*

Furthermore, if he was generalizing about the sexes, he felt that women were even better than men at knowing what might be a suitable match for them. However, they'd wait and wait, holding to the rules they'd been taught. They'd get impatient and hornier—their vision growing cloudy. Then that overly aggressive type of male who believed in working percentages, would push through their thin barrier in order to acquire his objective. Peter didn't have to be with them the next morning to know what the feeling was destined to be like as they walked home cold and confused.

Regardless, he presently found himself wearing those courting shoes himself. Except...*I'm aware. I also think she might be different. Is it too much to hope? Probably.*

He made her a drink, trying to focus on the work and not what he might or might not say next. He placed the short heavy rocks glass on the napkin in front of her and looked forward. She was staring right back at him. In that moment, none of his courting analysis truly mattered at all. He had nothing to do but smile and hold his focus steady. As he was about to form words, she thankfully beat him to it.

"I like you," she said.

He moved his eyes left to right jokingly and smiled again. "Is that right? Just like that?"

"Yeah, you'll probably disappoint me once I get to know you, but I still think I'll go for trying this time."

Honesty is the most attractive quality, Peter's mind fluttered quickly.

"Wow—that's pretty insightful there. I'm not sure whether to be impressed or conclude that you're a pessimist. Then again, I do have some kind of idea what it's like out there." He swept his hand out in front of him abstractly. "Men can be vile creatures, but the superficiality of women is perhaps an even more severe sickness. Hard to tell which is more frustrating."

Assessing her reaction, he wasn't sure whether or not she liked that. She gave him a half smile and took a sip of her drink. As he was about to move away, she spoke again.

"So what's next, Mr. Peter?"

He smiled fully from ear-to-ear, and felt a puff of laughing air escape from his nose. "That's a good question. Anything we want, I think. Your move. I chose your drink."

"I think perhaps a date might be in order, funny man."

CHANGE

One of the most attractive qualities she admired in him was his ability to connect easily with anyone. The amount of time he knew them did not produce the automatic barrier of distance that it did for most people. Within minutes, he'd be asking waitresses at restaurants, or passengers sitting next to them on the train, questions which quickly sparked greater sharpness into their days. She saw that he thirsted for significant connections to occur, and that he didn't care where he found them or what form they took. As she spent more and more time with him, she consciously chose to allow this quality to rub off on her. As a result, daily life became more of an optimistic adventure for her too; knowing that others were craving the same kind of genuine connection.

Being with her was like finding the thing he had always wanted to believe existed but had never completely allowed himself to. Peter was a junky for speed, and ever since he was a boy, he felt most comfortable moving at a fast pace. Perhaps that was why he enjoyed being a bartender and playing sports so much—moving fast was a kind of meditation to him. Sometimes he would have glimpses of the beauty in slowing down and being still, but he could never hold on to those moments for very long. He was always drawn back into his desire for continuous and focused motion. The new lady in his life changed that. Right from the start, time itself seemed to move by slower with Maya around. And it wasn't only slower, he seemed better able to shift to varying speeds at will—at play. Overall, there was a sharpness that wasn't present before—a vitality that comes to life when you're connected to the feeling of relaxed existence because of how content you feel.

They walked together for hours, talking both freely and passionately. Or, they'd appreciate silence in company—individually taking in passing observations and sharing when it felt worthy. They would explore varying areas of land in and outside of the city. They'd take the trains to random stops, and then spend their days roaming about in whatever direction intuition drew them. With knowledge as to the effect, Maya chose to confess much of the spontaneous beauty she saw (which was often moving at slow speeds). Her perception told her that he could appreciate what her mind picked up, and he was the first person she chose to share her intimate stream of consciousness with.

"Have you ever played the 'I am aware of' game?" She asked as they were pressed up against each other on the train one day.

"Nope—can't say that I have."

"Alright, here it goes. All I do is share with you what I'm aware of." She looked at him quickly before closing her eyes and feeling.

"I am aware of the vibration of this moving container. I am aware of the sound of the wheels moving on the tracks as well as the sound of the engine rumbling. I am aware of skin on our hands touching. I am aware that I feel light. I am aware of other conversations happening around us. I am aware of how nice it feels to simply hear noise. I am aware of the air passing in and out of my nose. I am aware of my belly. I am aware of looking forward to when we'll eat next. I am aware of being 'tuned in.' I am aware of my happiness at considering what I am aware of. I am aware of feeling safe while I'm with you. I am aware that you probably like hearing that."

Most women he'd been with were too deep into their own games of getting what they wanted, to see the kind of partnership Peter offered. Not the case with her. Constant acknowledgment of the specialness of each other's value was vital to their success as a couple. They fell into progression like a pair of expert dancers—they knew the direction they each desired to travel on the road of partnership and went there fluidly a step at a time. They found what they were looking for, and then gave their best to ensure the relationship flourished. A big part of that was not playing games derived from self-conscious suspicions. People were right to say that relationships took work, but the second part often unseen, was that the work could actually be enjoyable. From the very beginning, they were aware that faith would be essential.

"This might not work out for us," she said to him one day. "I'm well aware of that possibility. But maybe we can try keeping faith in our success—then see what happens after that?"

Peter had always thought himself happy and secure, but now he seemed to reach a new level where the joy of life was bursting. He realized how much he had wanted this intimate connection of commitment, of brutal honesty, and of teamwork ever since, and especially, since he had been a young boy. That awareness served to motivate his state of being and combine both a playfulness and wisdom to his actions. Holding back the drive for reaching his potential was no longer an option. As he intentionally chose to see it, life experience was too generous for him to be timid. He had always felt blessed, but this new blessing was thankfulness on his knees and honor to the force of existence that gave him such a gift. He was always aware of the possibility of having it leave…*it's important to remember that.* But it never did. He found that the truly grateful heart had no choice but to preserve its' permanency.

He began altering his method of writing from a compulsion he didn't quite understand. He was no longer merely journaling for the activity of it; he was writing to do something of greater purpose. He attempted to use words as a platform to help infuse the kind of change he believed in. Its objective was to heal, and as a result—it took on a whole new level of intrigue.

The words flowed out of him like the tap of a rusted faucet discovering that it was still fully operational once appropriately motivated. He now felt he had so much to say and no reason not to say it. A quality emerged that was due to the trust in his own taste, the love in his life, and the importance of what he was doing.

About four months after their initial meeting, he asked Maya to take a look at one of his latest creations. He had shown it to no one else. She called him the next day, "Peter, how will you make sure that people read this?"

Her reaction was incredibly satisfying to him, and better than he hoped. "I don't know. I've been thinking about that. I feel like that part might be harder than the creation itself."

"You're an idiot, and the smartest man I've ever met. Email me everything you have. You said you have notebooks? I want to see those too."

She stilled his deeper self-consciousness regarding how others might criticize his work:

"Anyone who can't see the honest intent behind your words has become too consumed with the practice of finding fault in everything they come across—in the value of their own opinions. The fact that most of us fall into this tendency should take nothing away from the confidence you have in the quality of your product. End of story! Don't worry about it."

Without her, nothing would have ever happened. Finally, her academic success seemed able to transmit itself into the real world. Somehow, she seemed to know exactly how to take continuous steps of progression. Aside from her brilliance in marketing, she taught him that the most important part of editing was believing in your ability to improve upon the work every time you revisited.

"You don't have to achieve perfection all at once. Allow the pieces to come together with time."

What she loved most about his writing was that it was a completely different style from anything she'd ever come across before. The uniqueness was what gave her the most assurance in its potential public appeal.

It's not shallow, but it also doesn't fly over the reader's head, she thought. *It's clear and powerful at the same time.* If she had to describe it more directly, she'd say that it fell somewhere between poetry and philosophical preaching.

Maya felt that the word 'preacher' tended to carry an unfair stigma attached to it. *They're just leaders that may or may not have anything to say.* But she also saw how badly the right ones were needed—the ones who were focused on improvement, not simply personal success. *Why? Because truly honest leaders have the ability to whip people into shape. That's exactly what we the public need right now. People who actually speak to the higher intelligences within us—the parts of us that crave truth and challenge—doing the right thing, and trusting in our own individual deciphers.*

Together they came to agreement on the title of their first piece of published literature:

The Battle

It's not too much because I understand it. I understand how insane all this is, and I am just one simple human being. The craziest thing of all is that we tend to deny our own insanity.

Can you see that we deny the amount that we're controlled? To such a degree that it is indeed frightening. I understand why you choose not to look. It's amazing how much can be accomplished as a result of determination—most especially denial. We choose to ignore the reality we are living with—that our sanity has been supplanted with an out of control ego. In our constant game of assessing ourselves, we fail to see that that is precisely the issue.

Our days consist of our attention going from one thing to the next—on a track until we say good night. Can you see that the future generation will laugh at us for taking our to-do lists so absurdly seriously? They'll have their lists too, but they'll check them off with ease instead of anxiety. To add to the distinction, be sure to know that they'll also accomplish their tasks more successfully in virtually every situation.

What does all the material wealth in the world matter if you cannot stop to give thanks and let yourself go with the flows of existence? This is the battle. So what if no one else is doing it? Don't follow just to follow. Our future hangs on this very precarious edge. Giving up our sensible calls for actions, is a great sadness that we are never meant to grow into. It's a waste of life—a fear-based existence that's insulting to the freedom we've been granted. All the stuff you are worrying about—don't you see that nobody cares? Ah, they might say that they do—but they're just convincing themselves too. Get out of your own ego—your own small, little life. Then it becomes impressively more expansive.

In my opinion, there are only two things to take seriously. One, take the time to give thanks for your existence. Not to think about it—to really do it. Never mind those who have less or all those that don't do it. You must do them all honor by being thankful for your own circumstances and seeing the best within it. Never mind those who have more. They're probably not as free of anxiety as you think that they are. Not even close. More to the point—what is more or less anyway? What a silly ranking system we attempt to create! How laughable. How can we know what any other reality is like but our own?

The second thing to take seriously, is trying to create positive change in the world. Without purpose, we limit our potential experience. Find purpose—it isn't as hard as you might think.

Destructive and illogical behaviors should never wear the mask of purpose. Those who do this usually regard the opinions of others above their own; which is the most heinous sin of all time.

These two focuses can be combined to form the battle to achieve a life of 'gentle determination.'

Gratitude and positive purpose are mindsets that must both be loved passionately. They should become the pillars of our lives. Again, simply my opinion—take it or leave it. Regardless, I believe in my heart that we must remind ourselves of their importance all the time. Feel gratitude flowing through your body, and take the time to remember that deeply improving yourself is creating all the change the world needs. Improve yourself in the ways that you choose. But choose. Think about it and really choose. Do it. Stop being such a baby and accept that your improvement possibilities are vast. It'll be awesome when you do. You have nothing to be scared of. Conscious leaping is what we desire most. Everything is the same level of danger—too high for us to assess. When you're truly thankful, that fear snaps away. Watch it.

I think it's very important to remember that our mind is the place where this battle is won. It's won by realizing that there is in fact no battle at all. Yes, it would be good if we all committed ourselves to moving slower and being friendly—if we tried to intervene and break the cycle of greed. But everything is also okay. Why? Because this is the way it's happening—that's why. We must remember to accept things for how they are, and that fighting the unchangeable is a core part of the problem. We are taught that anger is the best method for creating change—it is a lie. Only by accepting, can we take soft action to improve most rapidly. Only an underdeveloped person refuses to deal with what is real. Our existence is a miracle, and even death is not meant to be feared. Remind yourself of it as often as you can, and take the time to *believe it*—as you watch the fear subside. Fear is the barrier, and we must practice letting go.

The world does not need you to be angry for all the ways it isn't, although a small bit of anger can be used productively. What it needs is for you to start believing in your own potential for growth. We're here to simply watch—to take the doing as it comes. I give you permission to release yourself from all the ridiculous weight you've been carrying around. Who am I? Doesn't matter. But I'm still going to release you anyway. It counts for as much as you decide that it does.

HITTING A STRIDE

Publishing his writing gave Peter great purpose, and although she had never known him before, Maya knew that an artist discovering their passion brought about monumental change. He was so relaxed—as if all the work he had done to achieve a healthy independence was now being rewarded with a clearness of dharma.

Maya's perspective of his character was that he was a combination of a child and the most mature man she'd ever met. No matter how relaxed he allowed himself to be, there was still always a layer of fire burning—a switch that could be turned on immediately—the one that knew how to put away all the bullshit and utilize common sense in the present. That was perhaps what she loved about him most.

Although he sometimes questioned his own levels of ambition, she helped him realize that his ambition was in fact not lacking in the least. It ran so deep that he wanted to help relax the entire planet. She understood the dilemma that came along with having such a lofty goal.

Taking on something like that automatically makes you an outsider. It feels both laughable and pretentious. But can you move past that and get to the part that matters…the questions of substance. The ones that lead to positive ripple effects. We need people to believe they have answers while staying humble. That's the only way they'll take the next, more challenging step—to share.

As is the case with many successful partnerships, their differences strengthened them. He believed more in letting things come, and she in going out and taking hold. Regardless, they each saw the value and respected the other's intention. They were two differently designed puzzle pieces that somehow fit together to make something more beautiful than either could be on its own. It was as simple as that. Of course, there were sometimes disagreements between them—things that one of them did that bothered the other. Remarking, "I'll only be a second" when clearly it was going to be more like five or ten minutes. But a policy of brutal honesty and a willingness to be vulnerable pushed them forward without any major doubts. There was never a question of the character or integrity of the other person. They both had the ability to let go of arguments—knew how to recognize pettiness and understood the benefit of practicing to be the bigger person.

That last one was key. They both were aware that stubbornness was a whirlwind of disaster—each person taking his or her own 'rightness' far too seriously. On top of that, there was a certain acknowledgment of what it meant to be human. Each had matured enough to know that no one really knows what they're doing all the time. They were both searching for growth and open to being challenged for the sake of improvement. They were also secure enough to stand their ground and respectfully disagree. Years of independence in both of their lives, lent itself to a healthy confidence in their own interpretations of objective reality. It was not about being right; it was about giving "rightness" it's due.

Superseding all other factors, however, was a certainty that each of their lives was far better with the other one in it. The stable presence of that truth bestowed a great deal of latitude. He spoke to her about his sister often. It was important for him to keep Jo's memory alive by describing to others the nature of her powerful being. He had made a promise to her that he'd appreciate the variety of experiences he was able to have and use them to do something good. Part of that was spreading her truth. Part of that was allowing Jo to teach him the tools to make his relationship that much more successful.

Maybe it's because of her that his focus is so monumental? Maya realized one day. *Most importantly, it seems she has taught him not to betray his feelings. That's what makes me love him so much.*

In time Maya quit the law firm and committed herself fully toward—finding their audience. She had had enough of bending herself to the rules of the corporate world. It hadn't been a negative experience for her, but she was ready for a shift. She saw two paths before her and took the one less traveled. She'd been saving more than enough money and figured that she might as well use her accumulated freedom to go after something on a grander scale. When she considered, it was obvious which way of spending time was more important. She also had enough self-value not to question her ability to find another job if necessary. *That's not a concern…as it should never be for anyone. If you don't believe you hold value, you are wasting space.*

The most pressing qualities that Peter lacked and Maya brought to the team were twofold: self-advocacy and organization. *The first one is easier,* she knew. *I just have to help him believe enough in his work to be alright with self-promotion. The second part is trickier.*

His writing was scattered about in broken segments. The pieces were brilliant, but they needed to be sharpened and more strategically placed. It was almost as if he felt it were his role to simply create, and someone else's to figure out what was particularly entertaining for the reader. He didn't want to mess with the natural joy of the activity by considering anything else but allowing creation to flow out abundently.

Maya thought, *organization is usually a tough one, but it should be forgiven when the art itself is this powerful. Anyway, there's an art to organizing as well. I see that. I'm happy to take it on and make it my own.* She pulled out what he had reflected upon in one of his journals to promote this attitude within:

Our attention on the aspects of life we enjoy must easily outweigh those which we do not. Attention is chosen and can be largely controlled. For the majority of my life, writing was generally associated with negative feelings. It was schoolwork—mandatory assignments. But I have been able to reassess it now and see it in the light of enjoyment instead. Doing so has been one of the great successes of my life. I have found my outlet—it is my purpose and my love. Each time we're able to alter our previous assessment and see further toward the truth of our honest desires, a victory is won. I was going to say "small victory," but it is usually not. It's a big deal when our eyes pierce further, and our taste for worthwhile activity improves.

She printed out everything and laid out piles of paper all over the room. The more she read, the more she was convinced that Peter had a message worthy of spreading. He sometimes repeated himself, but that was to be expected when dealing with such passionate and deep subject matter. *The higher ground is never perfect. So what if they hear something twice? If they can't dismiss the flaws of being human, they're most likely not very well cooked themselves.*

She decided to gather as many e-mail addresses as she possibly could. Between her network and Peter's, they began with about nine hundred. They started by sending out one piece of writing within the body of an e-mail. They gave the opportunity not only to subscribe to their listserve, but also to receive a hard copy delivered in sleek paper form (costing one single US dollar). A lot of people liked the effect of reading something twice—once on a screen and once on a piece of paper in their hand.

At the bottom of every e-mail was also a link to select any other friends or people to receive an invitation to their newly christened network: 'Responsible Minds.'

"That's all it'll be—an invitation, Peter," she said in response to his dislike for pushing people to do much of anything. "The process is simple. It focuses on offering without being obnoxious. We offer once; that's it. If they change their mind later, they can find us."

Readership grew steadily in the first year. Maya put together all of what she felt were his best pieces and began sending out one per month. During those four weeks, that given piece of writing would be shared and promoted all over social media. Like most things of quality, there were a few pops of explosion to increase their numbers. Perhaps it had something to do with the coverage of the upcoming presidential election and the pathetic options the country was being presented with—but 'Responsible Minds,' was instantly intriguing to a great many. By the end of the year, they were sending e-mails to thirty-five thousand people on a monthly basis. Numbers doubled and tripled in the following two years. It seemed to be causing the sane portion of the population to finally understand that the only way things could improve, would be to focus more on the self.

A blog and website were also created—with all their published pieces and space for open discussion. The eyes and ears that found them were most importantly the right kind—the ones that were fed up, and also secure.

Peter wrote about his belief that change must first start with philosophy:

> For whatever reason, the most practical and most needed subject in the world has been dismissed as unnecessary and purely academic. This is as big of a mistake as our race has ever made. Thinking deeply is absolutely the only path toward greater freedom and growth. Otherwise there is nothing to hold us at anchor as we pass through a variety of life's' challenges and emotions. You must believe in the power that comes from disciplining your own mind, or you are a lost creature incapable of successfully harnessing the opportunities of freedom.

The current generation that called themselves 'millennials,' were experiencing a surge of stimulation unlike anything before. It was an issue that led to a life comprising of rapid and constant distraction. The only way Peter saw this problem being solved was through awareness of the tendencies occurring.

People have to be interested in what's happening to them, don't they? At least some of them do. Otherwise…God help us.

Luckily his first few steps into a world of greater exposure gave him hope. He saw the desire that many humans had to leap to a higher plane of thinking. Although things could feel hopeless, Peter felt deeply that the human race was evolving much more quickly than it realized. *We're just becoming aware of problems that have existed for such a long time. It's fresh and new still.* As Daniel had said to him many times: *"Patience is key."*

His conclusion was that an outlet was needed for safe discussion. He felt people were so afraid to think deeply because they were unsure where it would lead them—afraid of dropping their personal stories enough to admit that they had so much more room to grow. Perhaps most powerfully—afraid of what it might do to them socially.

They keep themselves moving and "productive" in order to avoid seeing the overwhelming nature of life. Most pointedly, the truth of their own behavior is being ignored. Overstimulation is a tremendous barrier. Distraction, in fact, will almost always lead to breaking down. People need to realize that either they will continually experience despair, or their lives will end not knowing what they really did or for what reasons. That's the choice. It's inescapable.

He knew for a certainty that the practice of reflecting on the truth was the only thing capable of setting humans free and preventing the disaster that is depression. *What would happen if more of us started seeing that? Incredible change, that's what.*

CONNECTION

S lowly but steadily their network grew, the community growing internationally. Words began to be analyzed and debated all over the internet. They were a dividing force, both supported and criticized. In many ways—it was all Maya and Peter could ask for; simply to be considered.

They saw each other as a team, and Peter insisted that everything would be published under both of their names. Most people liked that—a couple using their love as a force for greater impact. As their notoriety grew, they often wondered why so many others who attained fame didn't use it to try infusing positive change with their own honest beliefs.

"After all, they already have the audience," Peter said to her one day. Organizing a community, they knew, was the hardest part.

"Some do," Maya replied as she was pouring over some notes, "but few, and not as fervently as perhaps they should—you're right. Most importantly you have to first be the example; otherwise your opinions don't have legs. The weight of that truth is too much, so most people creep back into their personal caves of obsession. There's so much confusion Peter."

For the two of them, expanding the network of 'Responsible Minds' became their primary focus. Money and fame were only tools for allowing progress in their greater work to take shape. They held steady and didn't allow retreat to be a possibility.

In private, they talked about the dangers of their personal connection to each other. They knew it was strong enough to forget about everything else they were doing and contently enjoy carving out a little spot of earth, getting regular jobs, and passing away time. In a real way, it was their greatest obstacle to overcome. The completeness of their love could be used to influence change, or it could be used to create an igloo of isolation. That was their choice, and they saw the challenge of it early on.

They decided to move out west and bought a house along the central coast of California. It was an old light-blue Victorian home two blocks from the ocean. Before long, they took on a third family member. A mix of unknown kind with shaggy grey hair and deep-brown eyes. Izzy was the first dog Maya had ever owned. Having him was a blessing for them both. Considering their desire for continuing to influence change, they weren't sure if having a child would be strategically wise. *That distraction would be too great,* Maya realized. *Sometimes you focus on getting everything and instead get nothing.* Presently, a dog seemed to be enough.

Izzy was able to show them the world from another perspective. His only desires in life seemed to be to keep them company and to sniff, rest, and eat. He was a reason for them to venture outside on walks daily and was the best icebreaker imaginable for interacting with strangers. He quickly added a new kind of joy and lightness to their lives...*and energy!* Maya read books on dogs and was determined to train him as best she could. It was fun and fulfilling for her to witness the effects of intentional nurturing.

Their little family felt at ease by the ocean and drew on the energy from it. At night they'd sit out on the front porch listening to the sounds of the waves and the seals making their odd grunting barks. On occasion they'd be lucky enough to hear whales chiming in with their thunderous explosions of noise. Izzy would get all worked up. It was a very happy time, and they were proud to have it.

They'd often take up projects to improve the physical space but tried not to be judgmental about how much each of them did in comparison with the other. Work, they felt, had to be done without pressure. *Many people think this impossible only because they haven't yet experienced the truth of the way,* Maya thought. *In pressure and stress, activities lose the inherent beauty that always exists.* Having this mind-set, they knew, led to far greater accomplishment.

At times, it's necessary to judge—it's a way to weigh our own beliefs. But also, judgment is a very tricky path. The trap is when it leads us to placing ourselves above or below other humans. That aspect of it they tried to avoid. *It's not for us to decide.* If judgment was used, it was in the direction of something constructive. *The hard part is when others don't see that and they fire back at us with personal attacks. Oh how sensitive people tend to be.*

The time came when Maya decided she needed a bit of travel in her life. Something Juliet had instilled in her when she was younger was, "No matter how well a relationship is going, it's never a bad time to take a little break."

So she took a week and drove northward. The destination was an old friend from elementary school living up in Vancouver, Canada. Being a city girl, the simplicity of driving delighted her. She sometimes would catch herself feeling overburdened by the variety of daily tasks in her life and was at ease only to be concerned with getting from point A to point B. *Keeping it simple is fantastic.* She drove along the coast marveling at the beauty of nature she hadn't yet been exposed to in her life. Izzy sat in the passenger's seat doing similarly.

Her second day of travel brought a visit to the place in which her father-in-law grew up. The winery of his youth wasn't far off course, and she seized the opportunity to connect more intimately with Peter's family. As a result of both of their skepticism regarding marriage, Maya had yet to meet her partners family in person. *Perhaps that's enough of a reason for marriage—an excuse to bring people together.*

Brian, Peter's uncle, still owned and worked the winery. He had never stopped. Maya strolled around the grounds with him inspecting grapes, vines, and soil. She opened herself up to listening—learning about the business and his life. *The one word that must come to people when they meet this man,* she thought...*tough.* He was average height but carried with him tremendous arms and shoulders, along with a jawline of steel. Years of work in the field tanned his skin and gave it the look of brown paper. He was completely bald, and sweat glistened lightly off the top of his head. *He's hard, but there's also a kindness to this man beneath that intimidating surface.*

They spoke as he led her around the property, Izzy hopping around them with vigor—playing with his two kids. Although he was the older of the two, he had waited much longer than Daniel before having children of his own. He spoke to her about what happened to Jo. She wasn't sure if he was angrier about the incident or the fact that he didn't really have anyone to talk with about it. He let out a lot of his feelings of frustration, which were directed both generally out toward the world and to no one at all. He looked at her as though he was surprised he was sharing as much as he was.

"I prefer to stay away from all that garbage," he said. "I know what's out there, and I don't want any part of it. I don't have a television and I don't even read the newspaper. I have a computer that I use for work, and that's about it. The world is going to hell. How much evidence do I need to see before I'll admit that it's only going to continue getting worse!"

He had met Jo only once when she was a baby and clearly felt guilty at having let the gap in distance between him and his brother get the best of them. "I wish I could just—I thought there'd be more time." She watched him struggling with it. *To this man, it seems that determination should make anything possible, even the replaying of time.*

They sat on a small bench on the far side of the vineyard. She listened to the sounds of birds and a far-off plow working steadily. In front of them lay rows of neatly toiled vines of pinot noir and chardonnay. His large house sat quietly, firmly set in the distance— built with a quality from the past. There was also a massive silo and workhouse to either side. None of the structures were decrepit.

They had been maintained with impeccable care. The scene made her impressed with the Sol family as a whole. Although Peter had never lived here, it somehow gave her deeper insight into the quality of his stock.

"How's he doing?" Brian asked her abruptly. "The last time I met him, he was a teenager. I remember even more vividly when he was a boy though. He didn't say much, but I could tell that he had a sharp ability to take in the world. You watch a child playing with his toys, and you can see a lot. Don't tell me you can't. And now all of this commotion the two of you have created. Even out here, I've heard some of my friends rumbling on about 'Responsible Minds.' But how is he holding up? It can't be easy dealing with all this scrutiny. You too for that matter. I wouldn't know what to do with it all."

She thought for a moment before answering. No one had asked her that yet.

"It's interesting—I'm not sure. Both of us are starting to feel more and more pressure, but we try to turn it into our fuel. More important than our situation, we feel the suffering. We feel how hard it is for people trying to find direction and answers all on their own." She looked at him quickly and saw that something had hit him and resonated. "There's so much to take in with the position we've brought ourselves to. If we look too hard, it might get cloudy. But we give each other the support we need and try to enjoy the process of the work. It feels right."

He smiled at her, and then Brian had a flash of insight. He prided himself on seeing people; and just then he saw her. He understood better. *Together, she and my nephew are one incredibly powerful force. The world had better watch out because there isn't much that can stop them. They've seen it, and they don't care.*

It had been a long time since he'd felt a thread of hope coming from another person. *The only other one who makes me feel that way is... well, Daniel.*

"It makes me happy to be spending this time with you," she said. "We live in a world where it's extremely comfortable to sit back and play the role of spectator. Perhaps the most important thing Peter and I have learned together is that there's no better way to spend time than trying to make change. It gives purpose, and I have to say that it's also kinda fun." She took a moment—nodding her head and gathering thoughts. "I've learned that change doesn't happen by being frantic but rather with a calmness—a feeling that there's nothing to be lost and everything to gain. I didn't realize our need for maintaining that mind-set before. In a way I think it's the most important thing we've done for ourselves."

He looked at her in amazement. Her words spoke directly to his truest desires. He surprised her by asking; "Can I give you a hug?"

She laughed. "You don't seem like the kind of guy who asks for a hug very often. Absolutely."

As they both stood up, he said, "I haven't heard anyone speak like that my whole life. Even my genius little brother."

He tried for a quick embrace, but Maya squeezed a little harder and held on for another moment of time. She felt his body soften and accept the awkwardness as being okay—then she noticed as it moved into a space beyond. *Men of his generation have to be so hard. What a pity. They have so much love to give, and so much strength to back it up with.*

ADVERSITY

She woke up early the next morning and had a nice breakfast with Brian and his family before hitting the road again. After about six more hours of breathtaking scenery and stress-free driving, Maya arrived at the Canadian border in the late afternoon. She pulled up through one of the border lanes and stopped at the booth to answer questions. Perhaps the answers she gave weren't adequate, or perhaps it was random bad luck.

"Pull over to the side. Wait for an officer to tell you what to do."

Eventually two men in stiff uniforms approached her, giving instructions to turn off the ignition and step out of the car. While the one officer went through her belongings, the other stood facing her asking about where she was going and what she did for a living. As she answered, she saw the other officer pull out a small container of marijuana she had in a pocket of one of her bags.

In that one still moment of time, the man held up a pouch of herbed greenery in the air to examine, and a burst of fear stabbed at her guts. *How could I forget that I had that with me? Stupid, idiot, Maya!* Berating herself wasn't something she did often, but it seemed appropriate for the circumstance.

As soon as the officer standing in front of her realized what it was, he pulled out his handcuffs and told her to put her hands behind her back. "You're under arrest." He proceeded to give her the usual legal spiel about rights. They roughly searched her whole body—feeling everywhere and forcibly hustling her inside. *What the hell just happened to me?*

In California she had a medical card, and the use of cannabis was not a very big deal at all. She had forgotten that was not the case elsewhere. She hated believing that she ever did things that were intentionally wrong. She didn't want to live having to hide her possessions or not bring along something she wanted to have.

They emptied out all her pockets, hustled her body inside, and locked it up in a small cell. They took Izzy from the car and did the same (although his cell was much smaller).

She was totally in shock as she realized where she was. Locked in this room with nothing but the four pieces of clothing on her and a pair of sandals. *Big trouble.* She sat on the single bench and tried focusing on her breath. There was a camera pointing at her which made her uncomfortably conscious of her actions. There was a small window, but the glass was so thick she couldn't make out anything outside.

She paced the four corners of the room—getting to know each one intimately and quickly seeing how easy it would be for someone to go insane in here. She stared at her feet, the floor, the ceiling—investigating cracks, colors, and markings. Finally, she found some peace in her meditation. Although the terror kept returning, she was able to slow her heart rate and focus her mind.

Maya was a practiced lawyer but had absolutely zero experience in the criminal sector. However, she knew enough to know that she had very few rights on the wrong side of border control. She tried telling herself that this was just another experience of life—that it would end. She was well aware that everything could be taken away in an instant, but what was being proven to her in this moment was the difference between knowing something and experiencing it. The harsh reality of her situation caused her to feel hopelessly distraught. *How much longer will I be in here?* There was no way of knowing. *This lack of control is terrifying.*

The only object in the room besides the bench and the camera was a single button on the wall. *A buzzer to call them if need be…regulations, I guess. Am I weak if I press it?* She saw the laughable story of desiring to be tough rising to the surface in her current predicament. It felt like hours went by, but she couldn't be sure. They took away her phone too of course. She finally pressed it. *This is all so ridiculous. I'm not a bad person.* She saw how this experience could drastically impact her self-value if she allowed it. *Don't go down that road dear girl.*

The officer came to the door and slid open the miniature window. When his ovular beady eyes cast their gaze on her from a soft pudgy face, she yearned for a turn of luck. *Why couldn't it have been the other one? This is a dangerous man,* she knew, *power hungry to the core and a sloppy, sloppy confused mess.*

"Yes?" he remarked as though nothing at all were the matter.

"How long will I be in here?"

"Well, it's a national holiday today, so we're trying to contact our supervisor to see if he wants to press charges. Just try to relax lady."

"I don't understand why you're treating me like I'm a violent criminal. I'm coming from California, and that's legal for me to have there. You saw my card."

"Excuse me, but you've just brought an illegal substance across a national border, OK? It really doesn't matter where you're coming from or what the situation is somewhere else."

"Can I at least have my dog with me in here? I can hear him barking down the hall."

"Your dog is fine. No, you can't have him."

"I'm a lawyer."

"I don't care what you are."

He slammed the window shut and left.

As she stood up from her single piece of furniture, Maya realized something that finally gave her a bit of calmness. *No matter how terrible of an experience I'm having in this moment…I can't imagine how much worse it is for so many others. Isn't that always the thought that should calm us down when we're all worked up and pitying ourselves? It can always be worse. I know that for sure.* She used her maturity practically.

She thought of all the people in prison for years. She knew that many of them were there for reasons that did not come close to justifying the penalty. *That's a terrible testament to the sensibility of our culture. Perhaps punishment can be successful to someone who has truly done wrong... perhaps. But punishing the innocent; that creates horrifying confusion for everyone. That turns decent people into criminals.*

She continued thinking. What else was there to do? She thought about the ego of the law and how sensitive it was. *It pretends like it's infallible when in fact it's packed full of drastically gaping holes.* She thought of torture and suffering and how hard and helpless life could truly be. She prided herself on trying to learn from any and all experiences, but in this moment she saw how deeply challenging it was to have that perspective in the midst of turmoil. *It almost, almost can make the good parts of life not worth living—knowing that your heart is sitting there waiting to be ripped out one day by the force of a confused man working an even more confusing system. Being locked in a cell might not be that big of a deal, but it isn't every day that my physical freedom of space is taken away. In a way, limiting the movement of the body is the definition of torture.*

She fully realized that she had broken a law, but when she thought about it, she had never agreed to obey that law either. She had never signed a contract. There really wasn't much of a choice whether or not to obey. *I can try to move to another piece of land on the planet, but there will be another set of rules waiting for me. I understand the necessity, but can't the rules at least exist on a higher plane of logic? Is that asking too much? This experience is teaching me that we don't have nearly as much choice or as much freedom as we're led to believe. I don't care how loudly we sing about it before every sporting event, and I don't care how much worse it is in other places. That concept only pacifies the masses and stagnates our natural tendency to improve.*

They kept her for about five hours before charging her $1,000 to buy back her freedom of space. *What if I didn't have the money?* she wondered. *I guess governments are as greedy as anyone—perhaps more so. I've known that, but still...what a racket! If I were poor, I'd still be sitting in there...*

that's for sure. Justice, they call it. How can a system claim to be just when the wealthy have direct access to more of it? Don't they already have enough advantages? We shrug our shoulders and say, 'well that's just the way it is.' Why? Does it really have to be? What else is there to fight for? Maybe it is that way because we're not surprised—because we don't see how necessary it is to our own health…to stand up—to look feelings of helplessness in the face and call 'bullshit.'

They allowed her to enter Canada, and she decided to continue on with her trip. The experience that day proved to be used as extreme motivation for Maya Sol. She was right about it giving back to her. Not in the moment; but afterward. If there was any doubt before that her work was important, there was none that existed any longer. She was resolved—in her life she would be a force for change. In fact, it now became more than a desire. The new word was *compulsion. Sitting back, occupying our thoughts with trying to improve our own small lives all the time… it's a luxury none of us can afford. It's the whole trap itself if you can break through and see it. Being a truly good citizen means thinking beyond yourself. The future depends on us getting past the falsehood of separation. Getting past caring about change until you're the one who needed it to have happened.*

Being detained had given her a newfound appreciation for the freedom of movement itself. She wanted to hold on to that appreciation. It was almost as if releasing her from a cell gifted her with a new kind of spark. *I can go anywhere I want. I'm not confined in that damn little box.* It was awesome.

Spending a couple days in Vancouver with her friend, discussing what happened along with a slew of other things—she realized how beautiful it was to have trusting relationships. Since she was a child, she had vowed to be strong and independent. In a moment of deep reflection, she realized that by taking on this mindset she had in a sense prevented herself from fully trusting in the value of her connections. She saw that many thoughts and ideas were brought about from this seemingly simple journey northward. The desire to be more vulnerable was at the forefront.

PRACTICALITY

When she returned home and saw Peter sitting in his favorite chair on the back patio, she felt more deeply thankful for him than ever before. With awareness of the inexplicable nature of life, she turned to him and said, "I don't know if I could deal with it if something happened to you. I don't know if I could still have love in my life."

He stood up from his chair slowly, held her hands in his, and spoke softly. "Yes, you could. Listen to me Maya. Our connection to love can never be dependent on just one other person. That cannot be our only path to its source. We have to remind ourselves that the idea of love is larger than my love for you or yours for me. We can depend on each other, but it can't be fragile. Do you understand? It's the hardest thing."

She thought for a moment, working through her stubbornness and then finding agreement. *He knows. He lost his sister and still found a way to go on.* She nodded her head. "Okay, I think you're right. Still, I don't want to lose you."

He smiled seriously before lifting his hands and parting back the hair from her face. "Neither do I."

Fantastically, it was their piece on addiction, law, and drug use that sparked something in the cultural thirst for reading material, and propelled 'Responsible Minds,' even further into the hemisphere of massive public appeal.

It seemed just and appropriate that this occurred; in cohesion with the motivation Maya had drawn on from the obtrusive invasion into her life by the authorities. Soon after it was written, their e-mail network spanned over a million people, and their website received over a hundred thousand views a day. It was one of those blasts of intrigue that somehow finds its way into the culture. The words were debated on talk shows, posted on social networks, and popular pieces of dinner conversation. It had been a long while since written words standing alone had such a deep effect on popular culture.

Choice

Please heed! When you take a drug or ingest any substance, remember that you can never escape from being yourself. That might seem obvious, but it's something that we must become more consciously aware of; in caution of our desire to clean our hands of devious kinds of behavior. No excuses—none at all. Every action we take or thing we say remains our responsibility—whether we're drunk, high, sober, or hungry. You might feel differently and enjoy blaming some external force, but as long as you remain in your body—it's your responsibility to operate it. There can be no other way.

Probing onward. News alert (and this is something that will make many people feel quite uncomfortable), addiction itself is not a real thing. Try it on before you disagree. Consider before you find safety in continuing to stand where you've already stood. The conceptual notion of addiction is a weakness of the spirit—an excuse for inappropriate behavior, and a failure to acknowledge human strength and possibility to change. It is the source of the problem.

The fact that we pretend substances have the ability to take hold of us, is the most significant element which allows them to do so. There is no substance that is as powerful as a determined mind. Yes. Each and every one of us has far more self-control than we are led to believe by our culture. In fact, it is within this choice of perspective that our battles are won and lost. Believing that you cannot control yourself is the fastest path toward a life of dependency and despair. If that is what you believe, then in a very real way—you have already turned your back on your capacity to live fully. Why? Because you do not believe in your own ability to hold focus; to discipline and direct your behavior in the ways that you have consciously come to decide—to use the tools at your disposal. Discipline itself is a muscle of the mind. Like any other muscle, if we do not flex it, it grows soft. If you believe that you are a slave to your addictions—you are one. Psychology flies above all else.

We have established a culture of all or nothing—of extremes. What's needed instead, is a culture of balance; balance the most. We're never able to find the exact center point, yet we find ourselves somewhere in the middle—and feel for a 'rightness.' We need not deprive ourselves of the benefit that can come from altering our states of mind if we consciously decide it to be wise. There are so many documented examples of geniuses who have used substances to further the development for all of mankind. Many others have done so and told no one. I think we'd be surprised to know how many there have been. In a sense, it is the duty of our artistic leaders to share the honesty of their practices. Instead, many have allowed their own guilt to lead them down the path of secret keeping.

However, types of drug use are of course deplorable—there should be no dispute of that—mainly when they are used to enhance feelings of depression, instead of the other way around. The only question: What is the most effective method of engaging the troubling situations?

We get sidetracked, when this is really the only question of worth. Is outlawing the most rational game-plan for our society in order to best deal with this problem? Instead, would it not be smarter to work with people to develop a better relationship to making choice itself? Giving choice is the most effective method of teaching. It's time we learned that. Force is a laughable method—that is; if you ever plan on allowing those you are holding down to roam free healthily. If you truly care, if this isn't about continuing to stand in a place where you feel comfortable—then ask the question honestly; what would help the situation? Perhaps you will come to similar conclusions as we have.

Regardless of our own internal ranking of ourselves, as long as we do not physically harm another, the choice of how to best foster the growth of our body is a freedom every individual *needs* to be entitled to. Why? Because no matter how badly you might want it to, our society cannot sustain any other way. We need to teach people to use their freedom, not force them to walk a straight line that inevitably leads to zig-zagging into the same danger zones that we ourselves have tragically been herded into.

If you have reached the point where you prefer yourself under the influence of a substance and feel an inability to let go when you are sober (although it is your right to feel that way), you have missed something about the basic experience of life. Without acceptance of our own variety of demeanor—we lose. We have a tendency to obsess over what we see as "our best selves," instead of accepting our entire beings in all of their complexity. This has everything to do with unnecessary insecurity. Moods fluctuate more quickly than we like to admit, and the truly secure person realizes that all of them are OK. If people don't like you when you're real, you do not need to bend yourself to accommodate them. The only thing we have to worry about is being authentic to our feelings and striving toward what serves. Being phony isn't ever a successful strategy—except on a very superficial level which is akin to a freezing man finding shelter in a doorway as opposed to turning the knob and entering a heated house filled with comfort and entertainment. Others aren't interested in finding connection with us when we're being fraudulent; except those that use you to inflate the standing of themselves within their hazy minds. And in that case, often without realizing it—they've already made you their enemy. No space is left for another kind of relationship. Make no mistake, they are in a great deal of pain as well. Still, you could do well with alternative influences.

If we want to have a real and honest conversation about illegal drugs, we must admit to their potential worth as well as their potential harm. We must also admit that many of the foods we eat and drugs that are legal, are easily as harmful as the ones which are not. Doctors are often the biggest drug pushers. This mind blowing reality is a major problem of contradiction—one that is too severe to warrant distraction any longer.

The benefit of altering our states of mind when using substances appropriately (key word) is that they can help us gain wider perspective; and most importantly—the spark we need to *slow down*. They can help show us that there isn't a need to take ourselves or our life decisions as seriously as most of us are pushed to. They can shed true light on the wormhole of suffering that we have been taught to immerse ourselves in. Certain substances can aid in our search for beauty and give us the tools for seeing more of it—*all the time*. The same goes in reverse. The quality of our sober realities is harnessed while we explore the experiences of being chemically altered. Work at both ends feed off of each other. Yes meditation can do this too—but tools, like people—are each unique.

The major dilemma concerning drug use is that most of us take drugs with feelings of guilt and shame. It's impossible to analyze their present effect and consequences without taking into account the fact that they are outlawed. Any half-way decent psychologist could tell you this. We think that they are bad, yet we imbibe anyway; and this changes everything. It creates a stigma of self-doubt and therefore detracts from the value of the potential experience—especially when we reflect back afterward and often berate ourselves for breaking the law and doing something wrong. Often, we take it to mean that we must be bad overall, which consequently leads to destructive behaviors of mankind. If we dislike ourselves, all our action that pours forth will be poisonous.

This is a crucial point; if you think that what you're doing is bad for you—you've lost before you've started. Every time we take action we believe to be wrong, more inner self-destruction occurs. Everything we put into our body should be viewed in one way only; as medicine. Food, drink, pills—all as medicine to assist in the functioning of the body and the experience of life. Even ice cream that makes us bloated can give us happiness that has the ability to supersede the negative effect of the heaviness. Again, it's for each of us to decide—we individually search for a healthy balance. The mature person weighs their circumstances and makes a decision; then they reflect upon the wisdom during and after the experience in order to improve.

You of course do not have to try anything you don't presently want to; but you should also be careful of the judgment you hold over things that you have not experienced for yourself—it's fundamentally and morally unfair. Especially concerning drugs, because the journey is often so far beyond the expression of words. The more drugs are kept secret and out of reach of our youth, the more they will be put atop a pedestal and used in the wrong ways—abusively with guilt. Can you not see proof of this everywhere? If a substance is truly evil, we should eliminate it from the planet. If that's not possible, we must learn to deal with its presence through the wisdom of accepting the danger of free choice, in order to prevent catastrophe.

Most importantly, we need to stop believing that other people know what's right for our bodies better than we do. And we must stop obsessing over what we think is best for others—which serves as a distraction from the responsibility of making our own decisions. Freedom is the only way. It isn't easy; but it's all we've got.

DEBATE

fter a long while of observing the playing field from the co-
coon of 'Responsible Minds,' Maya decided to go on television and be interviewed by what she believed to be one of
the safest and most naive talk-show hosts in the media. *Safe because
she follows all the rules, and naive because she actually believes that it's a
strategy for success*, she thought to herself. *What kind of success is the
question?*

Regardless of what being successful actually means, Lorie Snyder
did have large viewership. She was a tall attractive blonde who thought
that being a female member of the conservative media entitled her to
the title of 'rebel.'

The two of them sat opposite each other, sipping tea in lush chairs
with high backs on a small studio set. There was a circular glass table
between them and an electric fireplace in the background. The appearance of the setting perhaps softened the battle of words that was
about to take place.

Lorie had been ripping away at the words of 'Choice' for the past
few weeks—using her nightly talk show to dispel its credibility. She
had been calling for the authors to defend their claims, and Maya
finally decided to oblige.

The excitement of debate and the precision of words was more
than enough to get the fire in Maya lit. She had always enjoyed rising

to challenges of the moment and testing her own capabilities. This was another opportunity.

"Hello, Maya, thanks for coming on our show. I've found it interesting the excitement that you and your partner have been stirring up recently. Although you've had some insightful comments, I can't say that I agree with the majority of your platform. I hope you don't mind if I jump right in here and tell you why?"

"No, please, go ahead. Thanks for having me on."

"Well, I'll start out with the biggest one—drug use. You seem to think it has benefits—that it can be productive in some way. I'd like to hear from the horse's mouth why? How are they good? Have you not been witness to the despair and destruction that they cause? Do you see how it ruins people's lives? How can you possibly think that all drugs should be made legal?"

"Okay, I understand your point. Let me ask you first—have you ever ingested any illegal substances in your life?"

Lorie's face immediately turned red from the shock of the question. She stifled at having been asked something no one had dared to before on air. Apparently Maya hadn't read the rulebook which clearly stated that it was only acceptable to chat about subjects peripherally and never dare to step into the circle personally.

"Haha," Lorie chuckled nervously as she leaned back in her chair and attempted to maintain her composure. "I don't really see what relevance that has. My personal affairs are my own business—don't you think?"

"No, not really. Not considering the stances you've taken, and the influence that your words have. You sit in judgment of something that perhaps you haven't even experienced yourself. Or you are willing to hold strong opinions and tell other people what's right without fully exposing your own truth. How is that responsible? How can we have an open and honest conversation if you're willing to be neither?"

Lorie rebounded quickly, allowing herself to blow her lid and believing that it made for good television. "Well, I don't think I have to have been a junky in order to see how it destroys lives—everyone knows that it makes people lazy and unproductive citizens. But to answer your question—sure, I have. I smoked pot a few times when I was back in college. I don't really know what all the fuss is about. I don't see the appeal in losing control. When I did it, I knew I was doing something wrong."

She thinks she's won something by saying that, Maya thought to herself. *So personal. So unaccustomed to honesty.* "Only in college?"

"Well, OK, maybe a few other times since. But not in years. Anyway, pot is very different from heroin or LSD. That stuff I've never touched, and you've grouped them all together."

"How do you know how different they are if you've never experienced them?" Maya continued on quickly before Lorie had a chance to answer. "I can't really comment on heroin because I haven't ever used it—it appears to be very destructive and all consuming; but I admit that's only what it appears standing from a place of ignorance. I haven't done much research and have no personal experience. LSD, on the other hand—I have experienced, and I must say that it blew away many of my old neurosis and slapped me in the face with tremendous amounts of life beauty. Although it also made me nervous and showed me parts of reality I had been avoiding—I worked through it and saw that the darkness really wasn't as scary as I thought. I thank it for that, because it has dramatically transformed my life to a place of greater maturity. What was scarier was the thought of how much I had been avoiding bathing in the uncomfortable. I'm not sure if I'd want to take it every week, or even every year—but I absolutely wouldn't put a ban on it. Who am I to say what's right for someone else? And who are you? Can you see that that this is a battle of the ego at the core? A battle over whose opinions are right? However, the fact that you grouped LSD and heroin together sheds light to me on yet another major issue. Each substance must be analyzed separately as they are all most definitely not the same. Grouping all the ones you haven't done into a box of 'bad,' kind of disturbs the credibility of your opinion—don't you think?"

Lorie decided to side-step Maya's aggressive question. "What about kids? You want to give them that freedom too?"

"Well, all right. I think you have a point there. But even that is tricky. Personally I'd rather give my child choices and allow him or her to practice making good ones. Parents trying to force their children to their ways scares me as much as any substance in the world. But maybe some parents don't have the tools to teach decision-making. Those people probably shouldn't have kids at all which puts us in a whole other predicament. For that reason, I'll agree that laws might be necessary for brains with less years of development. Still, I'd rather see a law which required parents to pass an exam on how to effectively raise children. That's a battle worthy of engaging. Bad parenting is a thousand times more harmful to our culture than any drug."

Lorie seemed to gain confidence from this small victory—leading to the continuation of her attack. "You say that alcohol and sobriety can be as harmful as drugs? You say that there is benefit in not being sober? How so?"

"OK, let's get into it then. I like to compare the mind to a rubber band—if it's not stretched and expanded, it sits stagnant, and the same tendencies and fears often repeat themselves. These are my personal beliefs. Please don't take them as anything more than that. There are many ways to expand your mind—mainly with mature, creative thinking. Also exercise and meditation can do wonders. But drugs—when used appropriately—can be extremely successful tools in the exploration of the mind, and our relationship to nature."

"How can you say that you don't think there should be any bans? *That*, I think, is crazy. Of course the government should make these things illegal and help prevent people from going down such a dark path. How can you even compare food and alcohol with LSD?!"

"You can disagree and think that what I'm saying is insane, but my opinion is that it's simply proof of how afraid you are to burst out of your own shallow box of containment—which has no desire to take on new perspectives honestly." *That hit her hard. I would never have been able to say that a few years ago,* Maya thought. *Thank you Peter.* The reminder gave her strength to press forward even more aggressively. "You can't get past these labels you have firmly placed as facts in your own mind. The truth is that you are in no place to sit in judgment of other people and what they do with their bodies; end of story. You can tell them that what you think they're doing is suspect and give them advice, but you can't force them to do what you want, and you should never try. That's basic. The hypocrisy of outlawing drugs is so obvious, it's hardly worthy of a conversation to me. We claim to protect people and help them take care of themselves with these rules, yet we promote destruction for them through plenty of other means. Have you seen commercials? Do you see what we advocate as being necessary? You don't want to look, but see! Especially look if you think your opinion should hold value enough to be shared on television. We throw in the public's faces constant appealing images of foods that are toxic for their bodies, materials they can't afford and only bring a glimmer of contentment, and ideas of winning the lottery that are barely mathematically possible. How come we don't monitor all of that? If we truly cared about the health of the population—well?"

"People need to be accountable for making their own decisions."

Snyder blurted the words out before she realized what she had said, and how quickly she had lost track of what Maya had been talking about three or four sentences back. The words hung in the air like a giant matzah ball of palpable falseness."

"Well there you go," Maya responded calmly, "you've made my case." It was akin to the pivotal moment in a court room. She squeezed the moment for all the juice it was worth. Maya glanced and locked eyes with the camera for a brief moment. She was looking at her unseen audience. She knew Lorie was not really the person she was talking to here, or why she had come. A quick flashback invaded her—being locked in that cell on the Canadian border and feeling so helpless. It motivated her to take a step that she might not have before. *No holding back*, she thought.

"I'll tell you something else Lorie. Don't for one second believe that our leaders have proven to us that they truly have our best interest at heart. Maybe if they did, things would change—but for now they've only proven that our institution of government can be used as a profit and power making machine; without a moral compass. I'm tired of the media pushing down true peaceful revolutionaries with labels of being lofty and unrealistic. You want to talk about problems? This is the most serious one. Capitalism can only be successful alongside morality. Our leaders are still not wise enough to see the virus that can spread from thinking that it's OK to do one bad thing in order to prevent another. That's trying to play God; it never works. The smallest good is capable of blowing up into some monumental powerful force—the same is true with the smallest bad. There are no contradictions in life—one negative action stands alone by itself. If it's wrong to take away freedoms that don't intentionally cause harm to others—it's wrong in all areas."

Again Maya looked at the camera before slamming forward with her fire. "Do you think obese people could possibly feel better if they had a more appropriate weight? I'm sure of one thing—having a body that's difficult to move around doesn't make a confusing world any easier to navigate. I think it's harmful for them, and I think it's a bad influence on others; I think if we saw an animal that was as overweight as many humans are, we would clearly label them as being sick. But we wouldn't judge them as good or bad—and I don't—we would simply try to help them get better. What does it mean to live so many years of life eating three meals every day and hardly experiencing the feelings of an empty stomach? What does it do to us when we're full? Our addiction to doing, has everything to do with our relationship to eating. When we're really full, we're less able to take on the kind of doing that we're really proud of—the doing that is focused on our truest desires. Instead, it's the doing of distraction. It's the escapism that seeks merely to burn off our lethargy. If we do not become more advanced masters of our eating habits, we will never evolve into the most progressed incarnation of human. And it isn't hard work to discipline ourselves; it's awesome! The purpose of our self-imposed discipline is not to confine us in a box. No! It's meant to serve the opposite. The purpose of our discipline is to help set us free. Yet, I still believe everyone should have the freedom to do as they will with their own bodies. I don't think I should be able to force others to exercise, or eat less every day; but rather I choose to freely share my own beliefs and manifest a better example. I don't see why drug use should be any different, yet we make it so. That is my only point. You seem to want it both ways, Lorie. On the one hand, you say that people have to monitor themselves; on the other, you want to decide for them. Which one is it? The time for being so morally confused has ended."

Lorie gaped at her with an intense stare. She wasn't used to people speaking to her this way. In fact, she was used to minions bowing down to her fame, getting her drinks, and agreeing with all of her opinions. But she was also so entrenched in this powerful image of herself that she barely acknowledged how much the dialogue had deviated from her expectations. Over the years, she had inflated her own standing to such an astronomical level, that she failed to realize when she was backed into a corner.

"We can't just let people do whatever they want," she spurted out frustrated. "People can't control themselves from falling prey to these addictions."

Struggling, Maya thought.

"Peter and I don't mean to belittle addiction," she responded softly as she extended her arm out with the palm of her hand facing down in signal of appeasement. "The body experiences the same stimulation so often that our mind develops the perspective that we *need* to have certain things. I know. There are also chemical imbalances going on that we often aren't aware of. Getting our bodies straight can actually help us move away from addiction as we're reminded of the power of our will. However, we fail to objectively assess and break these cycles of cravings because our body training is so poor and our will power so drastically underutilized.

Maya took a moment and saw that Lorie had no quick response this time. "I think I've said enough. Thank you for your time, Ms. Snyder."

The studio audience clapped appropriately, and Lorie flew comfortably back into her role as host. "Thank you, Ms. Frankel, that was interesting. Next up, chef Chandler joins us to share a few recipes for some tantalizing holiday treats. My favorite—in studio baking time!"

When she got back home, Maya and Peter sat outside on the peaceful chairs on their porch, and talked about how it went. They considered their current position and how to move next. The attention they were getting was useful, but the momentum had to be maneuvered appropriately.

"Did I push that woman too far?" Maya asked.

He laughed. "Probably not, but who knows?"

"Do you think I said too much?" Being around him allowed her to comfortably root out her self-consciousness.

Peter considered it. "For some, maybe. For others, not enough. Anyway, this whole thing we have going here is all about letting out our truths and not holding back. I don't think you have anything to apologize for. I think you were incredible actually. I'm sure that honesty is the only method that can sustain the kind of success we're looking for; and you were brilliantly honest."

"Thank you," she said in a sincere whisper. She shifted her body forward over the arm of the chair to press her lips to his.

"One other thing though," Maya said as she leaned back into her seat. "I don't really think we should ever get married, and I don't care if it makes its way onto any of the official forms—I just want to start using your last name everywhere. I want to be Maya Sol."

He smiled wide, and the glimmer in his eye took on a new form. "Fine by me—your choice." However, he strangely experienced the feeling of having just been given a gift.

NEW PLANS

I n the weeks that passed, they continued publishing more writing. Although they kept gaining more support, they were aware of the possibility of their momentum ending as quickly as it had begun. People were reading, but something greater seemed to be needed—a more permanent type of project. *A crack has been split, and we have to open it even wider now*, Peter thought.

He found himself continuing to think more and more about education. He reflected on his experiences as a teacher and how the natural perfection of children was slowly being eroded away through years of exposure to the current system of learning. The senselessness in it motivated him with boiling determination. It created a clock in his mind that required immediate action.

Helping to positively influence the development of a child should be the most sought-after activity for any adult. To be a role model for how other humans exist should be the highest-prized job in our society—there is no more meaningful way to spend time. It's all of our responsibility to best develop the continuing generations of our species. If we are serious about turning our culture in a direction of success, then "teacher" has to be the highest-paying, and the hardest job to get. It also has to be a word of deep respect. I don't care if they have their summers off! The act is simply too important to any sensible mind that hopes to travel on a path of societal progression. Until we completely recreate our system of education, we'll continue to be a planet with needless and overwhelming mental despair. Scary. Yes. Now.

"Maya!" Peter exclaimed one day, as if the pieces of some complicated puzzle he didn't even know he was trying to put together had fallen into place. "It's a school."

"What?"

"It might sound a bit desensitizing to put it this way, but what we need to do is start helping to create better humans. From the ground up. The only way things will really change is if we start doing a better job cultivating the health of our species."

Other people often didn't like it, but Maya was in love with the way he spoke so grandly when he got all worked up.

"What if, instead of having to 'reprogram' ourselves, we got the programing right from the beginning? All the change we're hoping for would be possible. I think maybe this is what my dad has been trying to get at for so long, but no one is listening."

"So what exactly are you suggesting—that we build our own school?"

"That's exactly what I'm suggesting. It's the next step and where we must direct the energy and support we have building up with our following. It won't be perfect at first, but we have to start already."

It was fairly easy for her to get on board, although she knew what a monumental undertaking it would be.

They created a not-for-profit organization and saw right away that they needed a lot more money than they had. Profits for their service as well as donations were coming in, but nothing that could allow them to build something on the scale of what they had in mind.

So they split the work between them and went after each of their self-assigned duties with vigor. Peter imagined money not to be an issue as he mustered up all his creative capacity in forming his ideal environment and curriculum for children. Maya on the other hand, worked on the specific location, legality, and finances that would be needed. She started reaching out to all her contacts. At the top of her list was an old college friend—Marty Linden.

PART III

THE SCHOOL

MARTY

"Anything I say that I know I probably do—just going based on my reflection of previous history. It's not always the case, but my filter for uncertainty is pretty secure. If I'm eighty percent sure, I'll let you know; if I'm fifty or even twenty percent sure, I'll tell you that too. I don't give a shit about knowing everything. Can you see that? It's an impossibility I gave up on a long time ago. You still don't seem to grasp or believe that being right doesn't matter very much to me at all. I've worked hard to eliminate that desire from my system. The only thing that matters is getting the best answer, no matter who's the one coming up with it. That's how we run our business."

This bluntness was fairly typical of the way Marty Linden spoke to others; especially those who worked for him. Perhaps it could be taken as condescending, but that perception failed to see that he was simply being productive. He was now thirty-seven. Short in stature, but not so small. He had a full light-brown head of hair, wide shoulders, and a slim waist. By most estimates he wouldn't be considered handsome, but there was a certain uniqueness to his face that did have an attractive quality to it. Most people were drawn to his high cheekbones, his strong nose, and long eye lashes which surrounded hazel green eyes.

Marty had been financially independent and successful since the age of nineteen, when he created his first hit reality TV show, except that it was not on TV, but the Internet. The premise of the show was to reconnect old friends from childhood that hadn't seen each other in at least twenty years. They were paired up to engage in a variety of competitions with other pairs of long-lost friends. Fourteen years later, *Past People* was still bringing him about thirty million dollars a year.

Soon after, he had another hit show called *Neighborhood Race*. It was a timed race where contestants ran from one backyard to another—jumping over fences, climbing trees, doing whatever they had to do to overcome obstacles and make it to the finishing point in some area of land behind a house far away. The only rules were that they had to always be in a backyard and they would be penalized if they broke something. Entire neighborhoods would come out to watch these nutty athletes race through the obstacles on their properties. It was a reason to have a party and also to see what was going on behind all the houses in your neighborhood. What people found was that often what was hidden behind fences was quite a different variety of appearance from what was being exposed out front. Helicopters would shoot footage from up above and catch contestants taking on unknown obstacles like a live game of "Frogger." It brilliantly used what was commonplace to create entertainment.

But Marty kept going. His creative mind never seemed to stop for very long. With some of the money he accumulated from *Past People* and *Neighborhood race*, he launched a phone app called *Memory Recirculator*. The function was for people to input as many random life memories into the program as possible—things considered and current happenings. Then, once you input a certain amount of memories, the program would grab one (often forgotten about) and spit it back out at the user unexpectedly. The idea was that being reminded of memories from the past (especially in a random and unpredictable way) served to increase maturity and gain some perspective. Often old obsessions which had felt so permanent, had now been free from the mind and forgotten about for so long that it didn't take a great genius to take one more step and connect the same perspective to current stressors and obsessive thoughts. It served to help many find ease and perhaps engage the challenges of a given day with more calmness and less anxiety. *Memory Recirculator* soon became the project he was most proud of, as it substantially effected greater culture.

About six major investments later, Marty found himself in the billionaire club. *Once you start making money, and also get over the hump of jumping into new things, it becomes incredibly easier. Those first few steps are the hardest.*

Expansion and decision-making became fun games for him. Marty became masterful at cutting through to the most important pieces of information within any type of business. Most of the challenges came down to personal relationships between humans. Once he created an effective team where people clearly understood their specific role— problems took care of themselves.

One of the major secrets to his success was that he made a practice of clearing his mind and refreshing himself daily. Sometimes it would be structured meditation sessions where he'd sit or lie down to do that exact thing; but often it was simply a moment that grasped him unexpectedly. He'd allow himself to stare outside at some trees or take in the image of his pen lying on his desk when he had the time. When he focused on holding one image or thought, all else would become blank and clear. He would watch thoughts come in and out of his mind, and then he would hold on to the relaxed peacefulness of stillness when he found it. His constant creativity, he knew, came from his love affair with letting go and believing in his ability to hold onto that space of emptiness. Although more and more people were using meditation techniques, he found that for a great many, twenty minutes in the morning seemed to give them permission to be assholes the rest of the time they weren't in meditation. *It's a lifestyle.*

Another secret he kept close to the heart, was knowing that money rarely coincided with actual value...*people just think that it does.* He saw that a person's favorite album of music or novel usually cost less than what they'd spend on a dinner. Life-changing words and sounds were cheaper than immediate, short-lived and repetitive gratifications. *How does that make any sense at all?* It was actually what he found to be the most difficult aspect of business. *Humans cannot always be counted on to act logically.* In a world where consumers should have demanded higher value placed on elements of support most dear to them, and cheaper prices on the frivolous—it did not seem to be the case. *They accept the prices and don't give much thought to assessing where any given gratification should rank in value. The only thing they're aware of is that gratification and desire exists. Once they're hooked, something small grows larger until it has been driven out of proportion and must be satiated before the next gratification can take its place. Repeat.*

His conclusion—*overall most people are extremely sloppy with their money; either too frugal or too flamboyant. This is an extremely valid argument against capitalism itself. It doesn't work if consumers aren't intelligent enough to assess what's truly valuable. A great example; those damn prices that use high flying cents to play psychological games with the consumer. And we allow them to do it by accepting their trickery so meekly…as if it's OK for them to try and fool us! I'd like to start a protest against buying anything listed with a .99, or .95. Call it $10 damn you!*

As a boy, Marty tried hard to convince people of his points of view. He would get extremely worked up in debate and then consider for hours and even days afterward things he could have said to make a better stance. As he had seen it—*if I keep improving on my enthusiasm, my directness, and my logic—shouldn't that yield better results?* He found out quickly that it wasn't the case. No matter how much reason came out of his mouth, he still found little success in trying to sway the opinions of others. Perhaps he got through to some, but they definitely didn't show any evidence that a piece of the hard exterior they had brought into the conversation had been realigned. Backed into a corner he chose to free himself by simply listening to his own reason concerning obstacles. *Do something different.*

He abruptly put a halt on trying to sway. He realized that most often there was nothing he could say to change the mind of another person. *Especially when it is a mind wrought with conflict.* There was a period of a few years where he held his tongue—even when it came to conversations with those he cared about. He would hold off on trying to convince them of truths he had figured out long ago. Even though he knew he had logic that could help—he said nothing and saved his energy. It was a very successful practice for him. It transformed him into as good of a listener as he was a speaker. He discovered that, often, all that people wanted was an ear—not answers. Silence often worked better than words, and he simply tried to be a platform for allowing others to form conclusions on their own. When he did speak, he asked questions and let them do the work for him. Often they saw nothing, and it crushed his soul.

As an adult, he now found himself to be a mold of both of these strategies. He didn't mind being silent, but he also didn't mind letting his opinion loose either. *Perhaps that's one of the aspects that a position of success affords? People see what I've done and are more willing to believe that my perspective holds value to them. Where they go wrong is in not allowing words to speak above the person...not allowing the stranger to teach lessons.*

He found this reality to be quite troubling. *It shows me how poorly we do two things: one, listen, and two, believe in our own ability to assess what is sensible. We need to see a track record of results first in order to have resolve. It's just another way of shirking responsibility to accept your own individual interpretations. It reminds me how our culture tends to make such a big deal about interacting with famous people. We get so excited we can't even be ourselves, and we tell everyone we know about it later. The later takes the place of the now.* In made him feel sympathy for celebrities. *People might know who I am in certain circles, but at least I don't have strangers gawking at me when I go out in public...treating me like I'm something other than a regularly constructed human being. What have we done to ourselves by placing so much importance on the attention we get from other sapiens?*

Considering this caused Marty to take on the practice of utilizing a new saying: "So what?" He was aware of it every time he heard people trying to use their experiences to make themselves into some kind of a big deal.

"I saw a superstar baseball player walking in the park."
So what?

"I bought a new piece of property on the coast—don't even ask how much." *Good, I don't care. So what?*

"When I was at Harvard…"

So what, so what, so what?!!

What are we doing? We're just going to openly use each other as platforms for bumping ourselves up out of our repetitive self-consciousness? How obnoxious. Don't say what you think is impressive…say what you think is helpful. If it happens to be impressive…super great then. Whatever.

Marty believed in trusting his own mind and it was leading him to great change—becoming more and more aware of his own personal role to help infuse a shift in patterns. He reveled in the ability to walk away from a heated conversation and in a matter of moments turn his attention completely onto something else. The only way he was able to do so authentically was from a deep knowledge that not of any of it—none of it—was a big deal. He liked playing the game…*how quickly can I put the past away where it belongs…in the past?*

Presently he found himself in his own office talking to his team of lawyers. He wore a sharp suit without a tie and stood with his hands in his front pockets.

"Using my money to finance a school that Maya and Peter Sol want to build is just about as good a use as I could imagine for the stuff."

His lawyers sat lounging on comfortable sofas sipping their selected beverages and wondering how anyone could ever treat money so loosely. They would not try dissuading him for long, but it was in their lawyer nature to be skeptical at first. Overall Marty agreed with that approach and valued it. *Skeptical yes, but stay away from cynicism like it's the plague.*

"What you don't understand is that some things are about more than money to me," he told them—reading their thoughts. "Money is a tool with limits just like anything else. And anyway, how many times have we decided to do the right thing not for financial reasons and seen money spring up magically later on down the road? It comes and goes and is often hidden in places we can't yet see. Knowing the limitations of foresight is an investor's best weapon."

They can't argue with that…they've seen the truth of it too many times now. Either way, according to their rules, it's my own. "Allocate fifty million to start, and I don't want to hear another word about it. Watch—watch what happens with this. We are in uncharted and very exciting waters boys. The power of words, eh? Still haven't lost their value after all these years! Simplicity is where it's at."

When they left, he called Maya immediately. Going over large financial decisions with his team before they were made was a fail-safe method he had developed for his own peace of mind. Sometimes they'd bring up points he hadn't considered and he would allow them to influence him. It was a filtering process he believed in—fully engaging opposition before moving forward.

Marty had met Maya back when they were friendly rivals at college. She was still one of his favorite people in the world because she had consistently challenged the hell out of him. "Haylo," she answered with a vibrational sound exuding self-confidence.

"You got it, champ. Twenty for starters and thirty more on hold until you need it."

Silence gripped Maya on the other end of the line. She had hoped that maybe he'd go for her request of an investment of $500,000. Now she thought that it might only be $50,000. *Not what I had secretly hoped for, but that's OK. Still extremely generous.*

"Fifty thousand, Marty? Wow, thank you."

How far does she think I've gone, or how cheap has she experienced other people to be?

"Fifty thousand! Thousand!" He sounded like Han Solo in Star Wars telling Chewbacca about the deal he had just made with Obi-Wan Kenobi.

"Million, Maya. That's with a big fat 'M.' I know you asked for a half, but I'm going to give you a lot more than that. I don't want you holding back because of finances—clawing by the whole way like some poor Montessori school. I'm also going to want to be included though.

I rarely invest so much without being extremely involved in the steps of creation. I don't give money away like it's nothing. It's useful stuff. So I'm expecting to be with you every step of the way on this. Part of my decision is because I want to. It's only because of how much respect I have for you and Peter that I'm OK with letting you both take the reins and lead. I'm going to be one hell of a sidekick for you though."

Her mind fluttered in amazement. *This will change everything. Life can be very real.* They were already in well over their heads with all of Peter's monumental ideas. She'd like to say some of them were lavish—but they weren't; they were good. *Now we can build them all—now we can really make something.* She felt giddy.

Only in that moment of great hope could she see how she had been holding on to doubt. *Money is freedom to explore the limits of our creativity. This ride is about to take another sharp turn.*

The next call Marty made was to his wife, Stacey. He couldn't believe he had now been partnered with this other human for over a third of his life. "Hey, weirdo," she answered. The woman that had given him four amazing children took pride in having an odd relationship with language.

"Are you having a pretty fun day so far, babe?" he responded. He put down the papers he was holding. Marty didn't like to multitask. He didn't believe in it. He tried to fully do whatever it was that he was doing. In the back of his mind, he knew it was a big factor of his success.

"Yeah, it's been pretty smart. *Brendan!*" she called out into the next room. "Teach Sherman how to tie his shoes please. Yeah, you can! Think about what you do." She brought her mouth back to the phone. "So you're crushin' it today? You did it, yeah?" she asked excitedly.

"Yup, just got off the phone with her now."

"OK, excellent. Keep doing your thang. Taking the kids on a hike. Love ya like a smack truck!"

Marty shook his head. He almost asked her what the hell that even meant, but then realized that he didn't really care. He hit the red button to end the call. *Words are all intuitive with her and that's perhaps one of the things I love most. It's the sound of them for her...over meaning.*

Years ago they had figured out that it was their job as partners to help each other figure out their deeper desires and then support the other one in bringing them to be. Marty saw that, more than anything, she wanted to put all her energy into being a mother. It was a hard thing for her to accept in the futuristic age they were living in, but together they leapt over that story. With all of her years invested in schooling, it was easy to feel that being a stay-at-home mom was somehow lacking in weight. However, she thought she could develop children in a creatively intelligent way, and was most determined to do just that. He saw nothing wrong with it and supported her dream.

However, being a father meant the world to him as well. He had changed a great deal since having the responsibility of taking care of other life. *My children help me relax,* he often thought. *When I get excited, it causes them to do the same. I allow them their wildness for a bit, and then I remember the importance of being calm. I watch as the change in my mindset settles us all back down. Being a dad demands my higher self.*

Since they had found no worthy educational options, they decided that Stacey would take on the task of homeschooling. Watching how talented she was at it was incredibly attractive to him. She took serious pride in making sure the children developed in a well-rounded fashion. She had a few other quality teachers that came by daily to help balance things out, but overall she was the one who decided curriculum. Part of his decision to invest, was knowing that his wife would make a great teacher at this new school.

Similar to the way he supported this dream of hers, she helped him to clearly view his own motivations. What Marty wanted most was to build a team and to handle his money as productively as possible. He wanted the freedom to do good, and building a team and making money were the best ways he could imagine doing it.

Both of them we're thrilled when they got the news that Maya and Peter would soon be opening up a different kind of school. Homeschooling was successful, but not ideal. They would have loved for their kids to be in community, but refused to have them sit at small desks for hours and be infused with unrealistic and unrelenting pressure as their bodies lost confidence.

As he hung up the phone, he thought to himself, *this woman loves me—that has given me great freedom to explore. This last decision was a huge leap in doing more of what both of us really want. I'm glad she's on board with it. The worst thing that can happen is that I'll fail, but I can't really fail because there's always something to learn. That and this ridiculously joyful woman to come home to.*

Marty then picked up the papers he had just dropped, fell into his next task, and prodded himself to see how quickly he could put away the past.

MILES

Most people looked at Miles Carson and saw a shy, regular boy. He was the kid who blended in so well that you often forgot he was there at all. During recess, he would sometimes play games with his classmates but more often simply wander around the playground observing the surroundings—or sitting quietly immersed in the world of his book off to the side.

He was a ferocious reader, and he had to admit that it gave him more joy than just about any other activity in his young life. He wasn't terrible at sports or schoolwork but preferred entering himself into the fantasy of other adventurous worlds that came to him through the minds of authors. The characters in the stories were his strength—they were his role models, his heroes, and his friends as well. He kept them present often, and when he was unsure of a decision, he'd think to himself something like...*what would Hermione Granger do here?*

Miles had his first interaction with the words of Peter and Maya shortly after his eleventh birthday. It came one night as he was brushing his teeth before bed. He had an unusual practice of wandering round the house while he brushed, and therefore found himself standing in the living room with a mouthful of toothpaste, watching the television over the backs of his parents' shoulders. It was a position of excitement, as he liked nothing better than to view life from the vantage point of 'sneaky observer.'

He only caught the last few minutes of the talk show they were watching, but a minute was all that was needed to influence his dreams an hour later. There was something about this person's voice on the screen and the image of her face that caused her to flutter into his sleep consciousness.

The following day, he couldn't quite remember what the dream was about aside from the feeling that he had received some sort of crucial message. Most people ignored these sorts of feelings that came from their dreams, but Miles was a boy who liked adventure stories for a reason. He reveled in the unknowing, and craved the idea of finding clues that led him down trails of meaning.

After quickly eating his lunch that day at school, he went to the computer in the library and looked up the name "maya sol." Immediately, he found her and Peter's blog and found himself quickly engaged in their most recent posting. It was titled 'Practice.'

Practice

The reality is that most of us are afraid to move out of the comfort of our distraction. These issues that occupy our minds don't really matter as much as we tend to decide moment by moment. Incredibly, they are often things that have already happened in the past. What truly does matter is what we feel— if we are existing on the plane of our higher and more secure selves—if we have confidence in our flow.

As humans, we should feel compelled to do one job: be thankful. We need to start seeing that as our duty. Only then we can trust in whatever springs forth from being on a plain of higher humbleness. Gratitude must be taught as our first priority—before anything else.

Not just thinking about being thankful but allowing our bodies to feel its energy and heal from it. Reality bomb—it takes practice like anything else. The first step of experiencing a new feeling is usually the hardest. Once you're there, however—everything is simple, and fear is swept aside as perspective falls into a more appropriate place. Perhaps our biggest issue is not fessing up to how much better it can be.

It's deep, but deep is actually a place where we crave to be. Going there sets us free. Can you believe that? We yearn to be spiritual. Even you. Everyone. I'm sure.

The key to unlocking this door, is to put an end to concerning ourselves with what we are without. Instead, we must turn our attention to loving our lives with passion and appreciation—to seeing them as gifts and allowing that knowledge to crush away fear when it rises up. Doing so does not deflate our ambition but rather allows us to focus on what we want with the calmness of the 'middle way.'

We're at a place in our evolution where it's easier than ever to have perspective and go to this next level of thinking. Perhaps not all the time but more of the time. This ability to zoom out and see the larger picture is still relatively new to us. What clouds its truth are ingrained habits of survival, as well as our culture's push for us to take on a tremendous amount of unnecessary pressure.

Are we too childish to notice what we already have? Earlier in history, people did not have much exposure to life outside of their small communities—but now, all we have to do is look, think deeper, and ask questions to gain the almighty currency of honesty. For instance, have you ever really asked yourself where you currently are—in space, physically? You probably have, but allow me to remind you.

You're currently residing—moving your body about—on a ball spinning in the Milky Way Galaxy somewhere in the universe, which is so large it's beyond our abilities to comprehend. This ball of energy that is our tiny home within that endless mass, is the third from our sun—which is a source of power and energy allowing for the creation of magic. Contrary to popular belief, these are not thoughts too deep for the common person to consider. In fact, we should think about them all the time—every day—practice it. We can ingrain the habit of thinking about them in our classrooms.

Instead of practicing to see the awesomeness of life, most of us show more interest in lines on the land that our ancestors created out of fear of exposure. What does that say about where we currently are in our evolution and where can potentially go?

We've searched pretty far now and haven't found anything as wonderful or as conducive to life as our reality on Earth. But what is even more the truth is that we will not live forever. We have only a certain amount of time before our hearts in these bodies will experience the extent of their longevity. Whatever death means, it is an end of sorts and not meant to be underestimated while we are alive. We need to use the truth of time as motivation to appreciate all variety of experience.

We are just beginning to understand what it means to be in a state of love—of lifting others up instead of trying to knock them down—of sharing. Whether you believe it or not, if we do not destroy ourselves, we will eventually go to this place. Why? Only for one reason—because it makes sense. Eventually humans do what is rational. That's our most special quality of all. That's the quality of life that all of nature abides by. But first we have to see it. It might take a while, but slowly we will begin throwing away this mental nonsense of competition that we have been accumulating into our habit of being. Perhaps it was sensible before; no longer.

The way I see it, we might as well get ahead of the curve—take a leap forward now voluntarily and set our sights on where we are going. Can we travel there out of free will, can we redeem ourselves for lacking gratitude—before a catastrophe forces us to realize how spoiled we've been behaving? It is indeed possible to have that much resolve. Remember your capacity for leadership. Don't believe the rules you've been told which you know in your heart to be shallow. Become a leader; it's what we need the most.

What we have learned is that thoughts and feelings are usually more fleeting than we give them credit. Just because you realize something one day (or right now in this moment) does not mean you will be back in the same state of mind tomorrow. You have only taken the first step. Know this, and decide whether you want to take the next one—practice. Quite often, each day is an extremely different place. Even within a day, our emotions jump from one state to the next fluidly. One of the lies of our culture is that we are much more consistent than we in fact are. Like anything else, being in a state of love, of strength, of your higher self—it takes repetition. Before the discipline, we have to decide if we want to go there. And yes, you do. Still, always, it will never be a permanent thing. The more often we go, the easier it is to return. The more we return, the more our bodies will become a permanently improved vessel. Success is only a matter of setting our vision firmly and believing in the trainings we choose.

We can never be sure of our change. Instead, we try at it. We have to respect the powerful force of reverse motion—of that which is known comfort. It is gravity; forever pressing down with the energy of fear. The mountain that we must climb must also humble us. Why? Because there is no peak. It rises into the unseen clouds which tower above the blue sky. Regardless, we must love the journey of traveling up and down—but always up.

Miles sat back in his chair, staring at the words on the screen but no longer reading them. His young mind had never encountered anything like it. His body automatically pulsed with the energy of motivation. He was overwhelmed because so many thoughts and feelings he had previously had were now reinforced and stated clearly in a single piece of symbols. *What to do with this? Where do I go from here?*

FRIENDSHIP

H e allowed the information to settle in over the next few days—going back and reading 'Practice' again and again. He was certain he had to take action, but what kind?

An idea came to him one day as he was watching his friends play capture the flag during recess. *Maybe I can start a club? For what? For just thinking and talking. Would it be fun?*

Like so many budding leaders before him, doubt crept in. *What will others think? What if I fail?* But the words he had come to know so intimately gave him strength. *I think maybe that's what this is all about. Moving past the fear of what other people may or may not think of me.*

Even at his young age, he had seen enough to know the power of a thought. *I can control my mind,* he realized. *Those negative thoughts only hold me back from taking the kind of action I want. When the action is important enough, there's no time for considering failure—only doing.* Again the heroes from his stories gave him courage. It wasn't that they were immune to the pressures of fitting in—it was that they were drawn by something even stronger. He knew that following that instinct was what made them heroic.

Miles made an announcement at the end of study hall and put out fliers around the school advertising his 'thinking club.' When the day arrived, only three people showed up. Two of them were his best friends, Patrick and Duncan.

Patrick, Duncan, and Miles had been friends since they were toddlers. Their parents had sent them all to the same preschool, and they had experienced every grade together since.

Duncan was about as different from the other two as possible. He was thin, good-looking, boisterous, and also people smart. He didn't care much for school and seemed to be occupied with only one thing—girls. That being said, Duncan could have hung out with almost anyone at their school, and chose two of the least popular kids. They didn't understand exactly why, but their friendship made it so that it didn't matter. Duncan was loyal, and his friends were his friends. The three of them always had a good time—similar to how peanut butter, jelly, and bananas always crave to be included in the same sandwich.

Patrick was the big boy of the group. He had always been particularly large for his age, and currently most people thought he was already in high school. He was broad shouldered and had a belly that would be largely adorable if it were not for the serious health implications. In fact, having a deep love for sugar was something that Miles and Patrick shared. The difference for them rested in the hands of their mothers. While Patrick's mom wanted to make him happy and therefore packed his school lunches with all his favorite treats, Miles' mother made him drink carrot and beet juice before he left in the morning. He hated it. For Miles, going over to his friend's house and opening up the cabinet or refrigerator was one of the great pleasures of life. It wasn't until years later that he could appreciate the fact that those items had no place in his house of upbringing.

From Patrick, however, Miles learned a very important lesson; the complications of being a good listener. His large cuddly friend truly paid attention to what was going on in his surroundings. He opened himself to others with a heartfelt devotion. Miles saw two sides to this character trait. He saw that it allowed Patrick to have great compassion and understanding, but he also saw the deep pressure it put on his friend to please and bend. *It's as if the desire to gain respect is so important that it disintegrates his own innermost individual opinions. It seems unfair that anyone should have to spend so much time not being in charge. Teachers, parents, friends, TV, the radio, conversations. Wouldn't it be good if there was time without any of that? Especially time with each other where we didn't have to always be filling the space.*

Playing! It hit Miles suddenly one day. *Playing is our time without pressure!* When he understood this, he instantly knew that he had discovered something valuable. What that exactly was, was unclear; but somehow it seemed as if the idea of playing itself was a huge answer to a puzzle he'd been unknowingly trying to solve. *It's the greatest thing in the world to play. Within a given boundary, I can do whatever I want.* Realizing this had a profound influence on his outlook. The discovery, however, was almost outdone by the discovery of something else even deeper. It instantly sent shivers down his spine and even some terror when he had a second realization. *Adults don't have it. Yes, they have other things they enjoy doing...but I don't see them play—smiling so hard that one instant flows into the next. I only see that in other kids.*

"Guys!" Duncan said as he pulled open the door of the library. "Did you hear that Jennifer and Kyle held hands yesterday during..." He trailed off as he turned open jawed to stare at the fourth person in the room. He was looking at the most intimidating individual and unannounced, accepted leader of their sixth-grade class; Amanda Keegan.

Amanda's motor ran from the time she got up in the morning until the time she went to bed. Her body seemed to have only one setting—lightening mode. This was how she thought:

There are questions, I need answers. Can you give them to me? Yes, thank you very much. No, OK, moving along until I find them elsewhere.

She had a face that was more handsome than pretty, but most of the boys still found her attractive. She had hair that was closer to orange than red, framing a regular sized head with a very small nose. Her body was well developed for her age, but her maturity of spirit was even more so. She did things well because she wanted to, and had five hobbies she considered to be "very serious." Her reputation was so profound, that the letter 'A' usually found its' way into her teachers minds before the first day of class.

Miles was extremely surprised that Amanda would give up her recess for this. Nonetheless, aside from his two buddies, she was the only one who came.

Scowling at Duncan, she quickly broke the silence. "Are we going to get started with whatever this is already, or are you just planning to gossip the whole time? If that's the case, I'll see you later, and no thanks at all for wasting my time." She started to lift herself out of her seat.

"No, please, stay," were the words that instantly came out of Miles' throat. "That's not what this is about at all. I'm not sure exactly what it is or what I hope for it to be, but definitely not that."

He felt this to be an important moment for him personally. Just like with the characters in his stories, now was the time for him to step up and see what he was made of. Honesty always seemed to be their last hope when backed into a corner, so he tried using it now. He focused and allowed the words to flow from his true heart.

"I read something recently that got me thinking. I don't know if I really understood all of it, but it seems very important. Sometimes I feel like people don't really want us to be thinking for ourselves, or doing what we actually want. That bothers me. Do you know what I mean?" Patrick nodded his head but the other two just stared back at him. Miles took a deep breath. "I'll try to explain it like this. I have all these thoughts and not really a safe place to share them, to work on them, to hear other people's and see what they have to say. Don't our deeper thoughts and feelings need to get out? I know mine want to escape. School doesn't really allow for that. That's what I want this club to be for." He chose to go deeper—attempting to provide them with an example of what he was talking about. "We're told that we have to do well in all these different activities—get good grades and find activities to occupy our time. But, I've been thinking that maybe all of that is just to distract us. I mean, I feel like life should be taken somehow more seriously than that. People don't like to talk about it, but I think it's true. There will probably be a whole other group of humans on Earth once we're gone, and I don't know if it makes sense for us to keep distracting ourselves until our time's up." *I know I just took that right from the passage, but dammit…I believe it too!*

He looked at them with heat in his eyes and felt that something electric might have occurred. Not one of them had ever heard him speak like that, and they looked at him with something close to awe. The shy boy exploding with passion had a stunning effect. After a few moments of silence, Duncan cleared his throat. "Yeah, I've gotta say that I agree with you Miles."

In a way, he wasn't surprised that Duncan was first to respond. He and Duncan had sleepovers where they'd stay up half the night talking about cooler topics of life. Here in this moment, his friend continued with his support. "Do you ever feel like adults don't really know any better than us what they're doing—that they just pretend like they do?" The comment brought about some nods and smiles. Duncan was the type of kid that was so outgoing that he had a natural ability to make people feel at ease. There was something about the pitch of his voice that was simply inviting. "But for real, I think back on what I was like last year in fifth grade, and it feels like I'm almost a completely different person now. I've learned so much and definitely grown a lot. Then I look at my parents who are forty something, and I think to myself—shouldn't they be masters of everything by now? Shouldn't they have complete control over themselves and endless amounts of wisdom? I see them make mistakes that I've already figured out. How can that be? It scares me because I wonder if there will be a day when I'll stop figuring stuff out too. As if there's a time when growing might stop or even start moving in the opposite direction."

Miles smiled fully inside. This was exactly what he wanted. A chance for him and his friends to be open to sharing what they really believed. He couldn't explain exactly why, but it felt right to him…*and definitely necessary*. It was the momentous moment of satisfaction that comes about when evidence backs up an idea.

Miles watched Amanda sitting quietly and listening while the three boys piggybacked off each other. He had no idea what she was thinking until the end of the meeting when she finally spoke up. "Listen boys, if you're serious about this, we need to get organized." Although her tone was instructional, Miles could sense a genuine excitement behind it. "First of all, this can never be during recess again. No one will come. No matter how interesting it is, you can't get kids to give up running around for it. Hmmm, after school won't work either." This was what Amanda did. She would talk out loud about things most people would work out in the silence of their own minds. But she didn't seem to care who was listening when she had purpose to direct her.

"I got it," she said calmly as she held up a finger. "School has to give it to us as a class! Yes, principal Terrence keeps giving speeches about us becoming better leaders. What better way than to run our own class, right?" They looked at her skeptically. "Why shouldn't they let us?" She asked in response. "We'll make it a true democratic system. We'll show them what it means to learn and grow for real. You'll see."

Miles took a deep breath. He had witnessed too much of her success over the years to doubt her now. She was smart and more importantly; ferociously determined. It was a blessing for anyone to have her on their side and it gave him great hope. Although today was just a beginning, for whatever reason, Miles couldn't help but feel greatly satisfied with how his first meeting had played out.

THE CLUB

These four young rebels on a mission drafted up a letter and followed it up by scheduling a meeting with their principal. They tried to consider their intentions from as many angles as possible—practiced what they would say at the upcoming meeting obsessively. After weeks of preparation, they felt as ready as they ever would. They handed their principal an expertly drawn-up PowerPoint presentation with a mission statement that read, "We create this class in the hope that thinking more deeply about life and using each other as resources will allow us to grow and therefore become better people. We propose that there is no part of the current curriculum that is as important to achieving higher levels of consciousness than deep personal thought. We need a class for it."

Principal Terrence was in shock. He had been making speeches encouraging his students to be more proactive in their lives for the past few years of his tenure. They held his own words over his head now, and it backed him into a corner. But it wasn't really a corner at all. He knew he could still easily dismiss them if that was what he wanted to do. *After all, they're kids.* The truth, however, was that Philip had been getting fed up with the system he was currently shoulder deep in for all too long. What they brought him, was exactly what he was looking for. The high school Terrence sent most of his kids off to, was posting record high numbers of suicides. He knew that some kind of new approach had to be attempted in order to stop this madness, this failure. *Perhaps an outlet like this in their developmental stage is just the thing. It will be incredibly difficult to make way for it in the schedule—but is it possible, is it important enough?* He knew he might be in for a battle with most of his faculty, as well as the board—but in truth, it kind of excited him. He was in his twenty-third year and hadn't been a poor strategist along the way. He now held an accumulated wealth of political cards of influence and was waiting for the right purpose to use them. *There are a few adjustments that need to be made to their outline...but I'm going to turn this into a reality,* he immediately concluded.

Miles, Patrick, Amanda, and Duncan, were all ecstatic and prideful when they got the news. One of the concessions they had to make was allowing a teacher to monitor the class. But it wasn't really a concession, as Mr. Norris, last year's math teacher, was about as cool and smart of a teacher as they could hope to be given. In fact, they were happy for him to be included. His point of view would be honest and most likely add to the level of conversation. He was a strong proponent of class participation, and that was what this was going to be all about.

Another concession was that the class would have to be graded like any other. However, the criteria for the grading was up to them. So they developed a system based on the average score that all classmates and Mr. Norris gave to each other.

Scores were given based on one question: how much value did this person add to the class? It was simple and to the point. Everyone could decide for themselves what was of value, and then the scores would be averaged.

The rubric went as follows: If you were invaluable to the class, you got an A. If you were a key influence, it was a B. If you needed to push yourself a little more, it was C. If you detracted from the experience of the class, it was D. If you were a follower of negativity it was F. If you got an F, you could petition again to return in a year but were not allowed back for the following semester. It was in this way that they bent themselves to the need for grading.

However, no one ever got an F. No one even got a D. There were some C's, but almost always those were improved to B's and A's the following semester. Philosophy club was a resounding success and a place absent of nonsense. The children made it so.

To start and end every session, they sat silently listening to music that the student of the day got to choose. The music set them at ease and put them in a higher place of mental focus. No matter how passionate the conversation was, when the last five minutes of their time was reached, the music would start, and they would all stop to listen. In fact, they set it to a timer, and when the music ended, philosophy club was over (or just beginning). This was a firm rule.

The first real class had thirty-one sixth graders, and when the beginning music concluded, Amanda stood up and explained the rules. The first rule was that when you had something to say, you stood up and said it—addressing everyone. There was no time limit, and if two people stood up at the same time, one of them waited for the other to finish. The person that waited was next in line. She explained that every day would have a different theme to guide them. It was OK if the conversation steered away from the theme, but the theme was supposed to be kept in mind in order to help with directing the dialogue.

The themed days went as follows: Mondays were designated for "letting it out." Basically it was a free-for-all, where people were encouraged to let go of whatever feelings might be putting pressure on them and holding them back. Tuesdays were "life amazement" days, where they spoke about what each person thought to be the most amazing parts of life. Wednesdays were for discussions on "personal passions and interests." Thursdays were "morality" days, where scenarios were presented and right and wrong debated. Fridays were devoted to "our relationship to fear," where students tried to identify how fear drove people in life and whether or not it was beneficial.

It was on a seemingly ordinary Thursday that Mikey Clark stood up, and everything changed. Philosophy class met in the small assembly room. They all sat on the floor lining the outer walls. There was comfortable carpeting blanketing the space, and many students lounged on their hands or elbows to listen. Others sat up straight with their backs against the walls. A feeling of ease seemed to cling in the air as focus was kept on the new speaker. Tall, wide windows brought in light from the sky above and the outside play yard behind. "Comfortably Numb" by Pink Floyd had just been cut off at the end of the second chorus when Mikey rose to his feet and started speaking in his own passionate style.

He was a small boy with dirty-blond hair and the only fifth grader in the class. He had been granted permission to join, by writing a letter to the group and also getting both his parents and teachers to sign off. He hadn't yet reached puberty, but his voice was on the verge of change. Regardless of his youth, his intelligence could be hidden from no one. The class listened attentively to his well-crafted sentences. He articulated himself while using his arms to reinforce his points.

"I don't think any of this makes sense." He began. "I want to talk about school for a minute here. I mean let's really talk about it. We all have to be here, right? Why? Why do we have to? Why can't I sit at home and read all day, exercise, and study what interests me on my own? Why do they want us to be here, and what is the real purpose behind it?" He stopped to take a breath. "I've thought about it, and the only conclusion I've been able to come up with is that they're trying to implant worry and fear into us. Perhaps not on purpose—but they're still doing it. 'You have to do this, you have to do that, you have to be better than everyone else.' He pointed with his hands in all different directions. 'Math, science, english, and history are to be taken more seriously than health, gym, or this class.' Why? Let me ask you this— for what reason am I supposed to compete against all of you? Why should I care about being better than anyone else here?" The maturity of his words was lost on no one. "I've been listening to what Amanda,

Miles and others have been saying, and I'm starting to put some pieces together. I try to understand the reason behind school being the way it is. The answer I've come to is that maybe there isn't a good reason at all! Maybe they don't know what or why they're doing what they are? Maybe they're just doing it because it's what's been done before? I understand that there should be consequences if I do harm to someone else, but why can't I choose to do whatever I want with my time as long as I don't hurt anyone? I don't get it. Isn't this my own life?" His youth caused him to ask questions most adults had lost sight of. "Shouldn't I be in charge of deciding how to spend it? They get to decide for me because I'm young and stupid and don't know what's going on, right? I don't buy it. I can tell you one thing for sure; I'm not so impressed with this whole system we've been born into here. I look around while I'm out in public, and I don't see many people letting loose, celebrating life—why not? Most people seem scared to me. Maybe that has something to do with the way school works; everyone has to go right?" He finished with a gasp of breath before abruptly taking a hard seat back against the wall.

The class was frozen with deep, thoughtful expressions on their faces. After a few minutes, Miles gave Amanda a nod and she stood. She spoke with a fraction of the volume at her disposal. "I have to admit that I've been thinking a lot about exactly what Mikey just said. Putting aside for a second the prejudice that people have toward kids, I think what this all really comes down to is *choice*. Isn't the ability to choose what you want to do with your time the ultimate freedom? I'm starting to get that. It has to be a mistake not to allow children to get in the habit of making choices for themselves—instead telling them what to do all the time. As Mike said, if you're not hurting anyone, why shouldn't you be allowed to do what you want with your time? Why do I have to set my alarm and wake up tired at five thirty every morning? Because life is supposed to be hard? I might choose to do it, and that's fine; but for most of us it isn't a choice. We have to! I understand that adults have to take care of children when we're helpless, but shouldn't they be backing away from us much more quickly as we grow up? I keep getting the feeling like they don't realize how smart we are, or how much we see. I'm valuable and I think each of you are too. They think we don't know how to make choices, but maybe we know better than they do? From my experience, to get good at anything, you need to practice doing it! The way adults treat children, they're not letting us practice deciding what to do with our time. When you become an adult, you have to choose what you want to do with your life, right? But how are we supposed to be good at that if we're being told what to do for the first eighteen years of our life? Maybe that's what's wrong with adults now? Maybe that's why they fight all the time and seem to hate each other. Our parents were never given a chance to practice; until it was too late."

Mr. Norris wasn't sure how to take all of this. For over a year, the group had only been seen as a success throughout the community. Certainly there were subjects that had come up that he found to be borderline inappropriate for eleven-year-olds to discuss; but they had stayed away from the dreaded topic of sex, and overall he thought this class to be harmless and productive. For the first time, he was questioning whether this was getting out of hand. He wasn't sure he felt comfortable with the way the conversation was attacking the very institution they found themselves in. It was certainly interesting, but he was frightful of where it could potentially lead.

Sarah Potter, who wore black makeup and only T-shirts with her favorite bands on them, stood next and said, "Well, what should we do about it then—just talk more? I'm sick of talk."

At that moment the music started, and everyone took a much needed break. Class was over, and they all knew it. Most went about the rest of their days considering what was said and wondering where the discussion might lead tomorrow.

Friday, the next day, Jack O'Neil immediately began and decided to pick things up where they had left off. "So a couple days ago, my dad was telling me about an e-mail he got from 'Responsible Minds.' They're offering to build a school for a community that writes in with the best plans and curriculum. It seems like this has come at just the right time. Apparently you guys aren't the only ones complaining about this here system we're in. Perhaps it really is time for a change? Here's the letter. I'm going to read it."

Jack unfolded a piece of paper taken from his back pocket and began:

Dear Youth,

It is our belief that you will be the ones to make this project successful. It is you who can still see and sense the changes that need to be made.

Our goal is to create a new school. We have been blessed at this point in our lives to have acquired notoriety and resources. The future is you, and we'd like to create a school unlike any that our species has seen before. But we need partners and want your help. We call for you to create your ideal school. Use the full extent of your imaginations please—combined with a decent amount of practicality. We have our own thoughts and ideas, but we will unite our minds to form the ultimate place of study and growth. Make sure to leave room for changes and new ideas, as the creative spark is an ongoing and never-ending process.

E-mail us your results.

Think deeply and always for yourself, my friends.

With love,
Peter and Maya Sol

"OK, that's enough of that." Mr. Norris stood up. "Change the subject now, or class is over. You shouldn't be talking this way about your school."

He had had time to think over the past day and had begun panicking over his role in making sure everything was being kept appropriate. 'Responsible Minds' was a divisive entity these days in the adult world, and he didn't want his students getting swept into whatever was happening with the movement.

"But it's not just about *our* school, Mr. Norris," Amanda said, rising. "This is about all schools. Wasn't the basic system of learning that we still use developed in like the Middle Ages? Maybe there have been small improvements and technological shifts, but the basic premise is still the same. Do you really think it makes sense anymore to take away freedom, listening to someone else blabber on about what they have been told that we *need* to know? Often, I can't hold my attention through half of it, and I get the best grades out of everyone here! The truth is, that I can most likely understand virtually any subject matter by going online and figuring it out for myself much better than listening to my teachers. That's real. They're teaching us to behave, not to learn. This philosophy class that we developed has become the most beneficial part of our days. There's no question about it. How can that not give us courage to make greater change? Most of our studies are filled with memorization. Shouldn't I be able to decide for myself the things that interest me enough to memorize? Who said taking away freedom of movement is a good way to learn anyway? Who said that I should compete against all these friends of mine? This is nonsense, and I think you know deep down that it's true. Isn't life supposed to be an adventure? School doesn't really feel much like that to me or any of us, I think. It feels more like slavery to be honest, and it's about time we started honoring life by enjoying the time we have. We're writing a letter in response, and we're going to help them build a better school. Thanks, Jack!" She sat down with one last nod of her head, and certainty in her position.

Mr. Norris considered for a moment and decided to let it go; he resigned himself to sitting back down as well. *I guess I'll let it ride. What's the worst that can happen? I have my tenure.*

AMANDA

S he would have mentioned what she was doing, but she didn't think they'd care too much. Her parents were going through a divorce, and their main concern at the moment seemed only to be how to beat the other into some kind of unrealistic submission hold through rage. It amazed her that two people who spent so much time supporting each other could one day decide to be at war. In her opinion, it was about time they made an end of it. *But can't they be better at parting ways?* She wondered. They had been fighting for years, and she was done feeling dread every time she walked into the place she called her home. *Perhaps that's one of the reasons why I do well at school—in many ways it's much better.*

It was an odd coincidence that the day Miles Carson started his philosophy club was also the day Amanda Keegan decided that she'd had just about enough of obsessing over her studies.

Her father had gotten home past her bedtime the previous night, and she could hardly sleep from anticipation to show him that she'd been awarded first place in her school's science fair. In fact, it was the first time anyone so young had ever won the first prize. This was the kind of thing that would make him happy, she knew. It usually caused him to ask smart questions that she was all too excited to answer. But when she found him outside the next morning sitting in his favorite chair looking like he hadn't slept; he had virtually no reaction when his record-breaking daughter presented him with her first-place ribbon. He continued to stare off into space with his own thoughts.

"That's wonderful, Amanda," he mumbled blandly. She was smart enough to know that there was no meaning behind those words. *I guess my success at school has become boring even to him.*

"Dad, this wasn't even just a competition within my grade—it was with the entire school!"

"Honey, can you go check on your mom and brother please? It's getting late."

Her mom was still in bed. Amanda decided to let her be and made a lunch for both herself and Richard.

On the bus ride to school and throughout that day, she thought about what was going on at home and everywhere else as well. She was feeling more confused than ever before. Somehow things weren't adding up like her clean sheets of math homework did. She was a natural detective, but couldn't seem to find any major clues to help alleviate the feeling of dread in her stomach.

When she got to class, her teacher quickly congratulated them on their science projects, even identifying Amanda specifically, before launching into the next writing assignment they'd be working on.

Amanda had become a star student by being focused and ready for whatever her teachers presented. *You have to have a good start;* she had always told herself. But on this day, in that moment, she realized something that would never allow her to go back to being the same kind of perfect student again. *This doesn't end. There will always be more projects and more tests. No matter how well I do on one, there will always be another. Why is this so important anyway?? My parents don't even really care anymore. They were proud for a while, but like most things, my success has gotten old. Maybe it's gotten old for me too. Maybe trying to impress makes you depressed?*

Needless to say, when Miles announced he would be starting a new club that same morning, the connection intrigued her. She also found it curious that a boy like Miles had decided to take on a leadership role he had never seemed motivated for before *Most of the time he's barely able to pull himself away from his books to acknowledge that other people are even in his orbit.* She was very curious what had changed for him. It led her to the library later that day.

When she had first seen the other two boys, especially Duncan—she doubted the venture. She couldn't imagine that the three of them could actually do something productive. But when she heard what they were saying, she realized that they were actually thinking about some of the same things as she was. She looked at their unit of friendship and saw how they made progress; feeding off of each other's energy. For a brief moment, she longed to have similar friends. *So natural, so honest.* Especially in Miles, she saw bravery and an undeniable spark of intelligence. From that moment of the first meeting, she was in—and with them in full force.

After their presentation to Principal Terrence and their first month of classes—when it had become clear philosophy club was sticking around, Miles brought Amanda aside and asked her very confidentially, "Should you be the leader of this instead of me?"

She considered for a moment and found herself responding somewhat surprisingly, "No, I think it should be you."

"OK," he said, and that was it. They never discussed it again, but that short exchange of words had a profound effect on both of their lives.

Once Mr. Norris challenged them in their critique of school, "but don't you have to accept the situation you're in and make the most of it?"

They knew he made a good point, and it changed many of their perspectives concerning school work. Overall their grades started going up, their calmness in class improved. That was the reason why they were given support for their club, and their experiment seen by the adults in their lives as being a success. Little did they know; everything was about to change.

"Yes Mr. Norris," Miles had responded, "but we can accept our situation while at the same time trying to improve it. Can we not?" That received many nods from all the kids lining the walls. The teacher looked at this young man and actually experienced himself feeling envy toward his wisdom. "Good point."

The letter they wrote the Sols was pored over and worked on for a long while. Amanda wanted it to be perfect. Her obsession came from the deep desire to have a new school, a new way of doing things...*even a new kind of life.* This was her chance, and she had no plans of missing the boat.

Taking the time to create the school they wanted within their minds was the perfect first step in making it closer to becoming a reality. They tried to think of everything. They didn't use time during philosophy club to work on writing the letter itself, but did use it to bounce ideas around. The writing happened in a smaller group. It was mainly Amanda, Mikey, and Miles that really had a knack with taking ideas and forming a sophisticated flow of words. They did use a thesaurus often, but could sense when words fit well and when they were simply pretentious.

Regardless, most adults did not have the ability to write on the level of these three younglings. Perhaps the only flaw was their excessive use of exclamation marks. Their excitement needed expression, however, and they used them too with purpose.

Amanda and Miles were thirteen at the time it was sent. Two years of philosophy club had advanced their development greatly. They had a goal, and quality was produced as a result of their focus.

Dear Maya and Peter,

Thank you for giving us this opportunity. Here is a brief description of our dream school:

First, and most importantly, we would like to have more personal choice! We want to be passionate about how we spend our time of life. For that to happen—we need to choose. We don't claim to know everything that is best for us, but we'd like to be exposed to new areas of interest with a feeling of equality. We demand the freedom to use our own creativity to understand and make progress.

We don't like the attitude school takes in believing that most knowledge has already been found. Anything new hasn't been discovered before, right? We'd like adults and children to be seen in a similar way—that we are all explorers in life and that we all only know so much about so many things.

Why can't anyone have a chance to become a teacher of a subject that he or she believes himself or herself to be an expert in? We want the opportunity to teach! That is what we know.

Depending on the number of students, we think there should be a certain amount of classes offered during each period of the schedule that we can pick.

Here are our ideas:

In order for a new class to become a reality, there must be at least four students who want it to be in their schedule. Regular classes will run every day at the same time for one month. At the end of the month, a poll will be taken, and based on the response from both existing and potential students, a decision will be made as to whether or not to extend the class into the following month.

Next, we feel that individual studies should be a larger part of school. We'd like time in the daily schedule to investigate subjects that interest us on our own.

Preparing for life after school—we'd also like to have time to research different professions. We feel that regular schools give little time to investigate or form true opinions regarding the options that exist for us in the outside world. We need to be prepared! How can we make decisions for our future if we don't have a good understanding of what opportunities might be out there?! Our philosophy club has talked about how many possible jobs a person can have, and we believe significant time should be spent investigating and talking about what those are.

If there will be testing, we'd like it to be for different sorts of things. Such as, how quickly can you rebound from failure, or how fast can you make agreements with others? Those are traits we believe to be vital for success in any of life's situations!

We want to enjoy all aspects of our lives; even school. The name we came up with for our place of learning is Gratitude. Your words have inspired us to see life that way—and to keep working on doing a better and better job of it all the time. Then on top of that—to find purpose. Thank you for making our direction so clear.

Rules and mandatory classes are as limited as possible, but we do still think they should exist. Structure should be managed carefully, but we do not believe in having no structure at all. We believe in democratic structure!

Many students are not yet capable of having complete free reign over their time. We get that. This will especially be the case for many that don't know any other way aside from being told what to do all the time. There will be a transition period for coming to our school. In most cases it will be extremely dramatic and even confusing. It will take time to adjust to this new way, but it is possible. Every student needs different amounts of structure, and we'd like our teachers to be masters at figuring out how much is needed for each of us. If a student is focused and has direction, he or she might not need any at all—that is for the teachers to decide.

Before a student begins his or her study, he or she must sign a contract agreeing to accept the terms of Gratitude. We feel that a big mistake with the current system is that none of us ever make the choice to be here! Instead, we are led to believe that there is no choice but to obey. We realize, now, that there is always a choice!

After every six months at Gratitude, students will either sign an extension to their contract or choose to leave the school. As we see it, if you do not take the step to accept the policies of an environment, the feeling of being forced to adhere to rules you did not accept will prevent you from making the most of where you find yourself. This is important. This is the main problem with schools now. We want everything to be up front; and honest! No more secrets. We do not believe there is much benefit in making decisions for people when they aren't involved—people who do have a voice, and a mind capable of deciding what they feel is best.

We have listed three rules to be accepted, and five classes that we think should be mandatory at Gratitude.

Rules:

1. I will contribute my talents and attempt to improve my personal self as much as possible.
2. I do not allow myself to be in anything more than friendly competition with other students. My goal is not to bring down others but rather to help each person believe more in themselves—to help them accept who they are so that we can all live in a better community.
3. I accept the disciplinary procedures of Gratitude.

Mandatory classes:

1. How to Be a Good Consumer: Handling finances and making proper decisions regarding money and time.
2. Morality/Justice: What are the proper relationships humans should have with each other, animals, and nature?
3. Preventative Health: How to best take care of mind and body through daily practices of cooking, physical exercise, and meditation.
4. Emergency Health: Basic life-saving emergency practices.
5. Home and Transportation: Plumbing, carpentry, auto mechanics, gardening, and electrical.

These are the things that philosophy club has collectively decided are the most important topics of study. We feel they will lead to better definitions of the word 'success.' Of course they can adapt.

Reading, math, science, history, and language can be wonderfully interesting studies but are so obviously secondary in importance to being a positive, healthy, freethinking, helpful, and secure member of society. Don't you think? It doesn't make sense for us to rely on only a few people to acquire basic strategies for body recovery. If we get hurt on the playground, we don't want the nurse to simply mend our wound. We want to be taught how to do it ourselves—before the injury happens! It isn't practical to depend on ambulances arriving soon enough to save us or our friends throughout our lives. We think we can spend more time at school learning to understand the body!

Motivation based on fear of falling behind children at other schools—is a competitive joke we want no part of. The current system is not preparation for life but preparation for more school, and more battle between humans! What happens after school is finished and we need to be good members of society? Have we learned how? No. We feel school is more like studying to win at a game—not really learning to grow securely. We want to be the ones to help change this.

We do not wish to be held in slavery any longer. It is not an exaggeration that children of the world are indeed slaves to the decisions of adults. We have decided this. Perhaps it is difficult to see, as the decisions do not seem to benefit anyone else aside from the children themselves—however, we would argue that even if the intentions are seemingly good—it does not necessarily imply that the action is sensible. You want to keep us safe in what you know, but what you know is flawed and limited!

We have chosen not to give in to the feeling that change is overwhelming and impossible to overcome. We know that at first most people will disagree. We embrace the process of making things better one step at a time. We see no better way than to spend our time trying! If we are the ones who have to do the work—so be it. We can change the cycle. We are capable of being the best students in the world. Just give us choice and let us speak our minds.

With Complete Sincerity,
The Children of Philosophy

GRATITUDE

Peter was so impressed it was challenging to contain himself enough not to shake. He'd never met children who could express themselves so profoundly, and it instantly gave him an incredible infusion of optimism. Still, he wasn't surprised. This was exactly what he had hoped for and more. The wheels of progress were starting to pick up even more speed. Just the name itself, "The Children of Philosophy," made him grin widely.

In a world where thinking deeply is often looked down upon, this group has chosen to dive directly into that arena and use it as their flag. Perhaps they understand that, or perhaps they don't. It doesn't really matter.

Not that he was in need of more reassurance, but it was further proof to him that it was natural for humans to enjoy the process of meditating on what made sense. *Here are these young humans with very little experience, and all they want to do is think. That's what they asked to do...to be themselves! Natural.*

With the abundance of currency which came their way from the Lindens, Peter became certain of one thing: *the school will become a reality. Gratitude...the name alone is enough to decide the winner of our little competition.*

Peter brought together a team of the people he respected most, and they set to work. He knew he had much to offer and had given a great deal of consideration to how he believed a school should exist, but the best thing about his style of thought, was that he was under no illusion that he had all the answers. *This letter is proof enough of that.*

Part of his petition for the help of children themselves was because he knew that many of the most important ideas would end up coming from them—that they must be willing partners in the entire process. *When you're an adult, it's so easy to lose perspective of what it's like to see the world fresh.* The brilliancy of how this letter was written, their suggestions themselves, and what it implied about this group reinforced his decision. *One right group. Sometimes one is all you need.* He immediately incorporated these ideas into their growing system. Then he began contacting their families.

He allowed the kids themselves, however, to do the brunt of the work in getting their parents to sign off on this experiment. He also not only made tuition free, but also offered the families a stipend for being the first trial class. It made a big difference of course to those who spend a large portion of thinking on finances.

More to the point, the desire to change the method of education had to come from the students—and they had to be the ones to convince their parents. From the quality of the letter, Peter knew that this group had enough accumulated organization not to be denied by the adults in their lives. Peter was there to help, give information, and make it a financially worthwhile endeavor—that was all. He communicated with parents openly, asked them to become a part of the team, and made it clear that this school would be more than a school; it would be a community. In fact, he felt that parental participation was essential to their chances of success. "Need a day off, come to school. Our door will be open to you anytime. Participate, teach a class, be a student—great, not a problem."

No matter how much talent was brought together, he knew that, in order to be successful, there had to be someone steering the ship—keeping it all in perspective—zooming out again and again. The need for leadership often led to uncomfortable situations. He felt it best to be grabbed onto and established clearly from the start. He realized that perhaps his greatest challenge would be in accepting this role. *You made that decision back when you set this in motion Peter,* he told himself. *It's not a big deal. Go with it now in strength.*

He chose himself because when it came down to it, there was no one he could trust more. This was too important to put in someone else's hands. If he was being honest, he had confidence in his ability to judge reality and to stand firm when he was sure. The variety of his experiences gave him faith in his skill to assess himself more objectively than most. Time after time he had sat back and allowed others to take the reins—trying to be a supportive follower. It had taken Peter a while to realize that being too humble could be as much of a flaw as any other character trait. Humbleness came naturally to him as he had a tendency to be uncomfortable when he was the focus of attention. The fortitude to enter a space of leadership was itself the work for him. Followers often failed to see the depth to the burden of leadership. Without Maya, perhaps it would have been impossible for him to acknowledge that the problems were too serious for him not to take command. Regardless, he brought himself to that place now. With a clear mind, he accepted the position.

Make better people…make a better world. That was the whole idea behind this battle of education for him; and he kept it close to the heart. One of the greatest obstacles, he knew, would be the stubbornness of the older generations to see and to believe. *It will take time. The threat they're going to feel in the creation of a more evolved sort of person will be real and challenging for a while. After all, people are very bad at allowing others to pass by with less suffering than they had to go through. Parents usually want their children to have a similar experience of childhood as they themselves had. They don't realize how impossible that is anyway. They have not grasped the purpose which comes from being the one to break the cycle.*

Gratitude was built on a magnificent piece of land in an area that humans chose to claim ownership over and call Northern California. There was a large pond, a flowing creek, and a beautiful forest of trees. It sat atop rolling hills that allowed for a magnificent view of the ocean a few miles off in the distance. The estate was twenty acres, and Maya named the entirety of it Revolution.

"True rebels aren't interested in violence; they're interested in making things better," she told him on that day. Soon after purchasing the property, they moved to a small house on the outskirts of the land. They knew they had to live the change.

The school itself was a masterpiece of architectural design. About half of their money went into the main building itself, and Marty brought on the best builders and designers to complete the task. A few of the outer buildings were steps away from the forest of trees. The structures of man were surrounded by the security of immense greenery.

Peter had great ideas for what the campus would look like, and fed the professionals his visions. He knew this would be the first of many to come, and stand for something of enormous significance. He did not like to use money frivolously, but this was important, and even aesthetics had to be strongly considered.

There were spires, winding walkways, large arches, sprawling yards, and beautiful gardens. It had the atmosphere of an old university mixed with the modernism of a fun Silicon Valley start-up. *Embracing the new but paying homage to the old.*

Perhaps even more important to him than the outer design, was the creativity of the interior. He wanted it to be crystal clear that this was a place for explorative, relaxed behavior and growth. Half of the rooms were dedicated to simply lounging—doing independent or group work on sofas or comfortable seats. In almost every room, there were games to be played—table games like Ping-Pong and pool, board games, yard games, and even balance beams, pull-up bars, and dartboards—anything that helped spark the senses and give students a needed break. Yoga mats, rugs, and pillows took up many corners, and soft padding lined the walls. The floors and ceilings were all of funky and unique design. There were little nooks and crannies that allowed students to curl up and find seclusion within the immensity of the building.

Peter and Maya both loved doing puzzles. It was important for them to share this passion inside of Gratitude. *Puzzling is a never ending inquiry into the realm of common sense,* Peter had discovered. *The varying types of strategy are amazingly overwhelming. Every time you put a piece to-gether, you have to start the process all over again. Search and find, search and find. How do I search? So many ways. It's easily as healthy for the mind as any other activity I've ever come across.* Throughout many of the rooms were tables set up for puzzling. There were double sided cards that either said "leave as is please," or "help yourself to fit some pieces."

Each room was different, but most had one thing in common: they were all colorful. Peter remembered being a boy and asked repeatedly, "What's your favorite color?" Now he saw how picking a singular favor-ite could directly cause a child to not harness the beauty and unique-ness that each shade had to offer. *That's just how it works. Why would it even be necessary to ask such a question?* he wondered. *Picking favorites is the whole problem—it becomes an obsession. It stimulates a culture of seeing everything as for or against and taking our opinions far too seriously. Favorite teams, favorite games, favorite people. Can't we like, really like, or have no opinion at all? Ah! It's exhausting.*

Another unique and extremely creative aspect of the entire cam-pus was the 'speed track.' The track not only wove its' way from build-ing to building, but also through the wide hallways of the interior as well. The speed limit sign didn't have a number—it simply read, "care-ful." Students could ride their skateboards, roller skates, or any other form of the latest transportation that could appropriately be used on the track. It wove around in all sorts of funky ways—even through outer glass enclosures on upper levels. These were especially beautiful spots to stop during the winter months and enjoy a peaceful moment. A student could hop off his or her board, lie down on some soft cush-ions off to the side, and take in the falling rain or snow from up above, to the sides, or even beneath them.

Aside from the physical layout, there was one idea Peter had that he knew was perhaps most important to the success of Gratitude. He had built and placed all around the interior what were called GPs (Growth Pods). These were places where any student could choose to spend time in countless ways—by themselves. One of the major differences he hoped to facilitate at Gratitude was eliminating the fear of having children be without supervision. In order to combat the problem, he had video cameras placed everywhere in the school (even inside of the GPs). It was not a secret—all students and parents were well aware of the monitoring. They were not constantly watched, but if an incident did occur, it provided a way to handle the issue by going back into the bank of recordings and viewing objective reality. *It isn't ideal, but sometimes difficult choices have to be made. The ability to see what actually occurred is too valuable an asset for providing safety.* Peter had witnessed this while teaching abroad. The schools he worked at had cameras in the classrooms and all of the parents accepted it as necessary. Americans just seemed to be all messed up with their conceptions of freedom. *Great power simply requires trust. If you don't trust the people holding the container for your children...who can you trust? Questions—no problem...ask away. Jumping to negative conclusions based on fear—no way.*

Peter understood the desire humans had to interact with one another, and the benefits of doing so; but also felt that a major problem was that most people (especially children) were not spending very much time experiencing the flavors of life on their own. *Those kids are certainly right about that,* he thought—reflecting on the letter. *Kids aren't usually being guided to spend alone time productively...or it's even insanely used as a form of punishment!*

He felt a balance was needed and that the scales needed tipping more in the direction of exploring alone time. *Being alone and feeling good about it creates a great opportunity for actually figuring out what you believe—for developing the self. If you don't take the time, you can't decide what you want to do. Social interaction can overwhelm us with stimulation, and taking the time away, generally will allow for more conscious and well-thought-out behavior when we re-engage others.*

In the traditional system, virtually no time had been given for this purpose. Peter was resolved to change that with his GP's.

Each Growth Pod was a small enclosed chamber that cut off outside light and sound. There was a viewing screen within, where you could access the internal network of Gratitude, do research, or watch all sorts of varying videos.

People watching, or anthropology, became one of the most popular activities for students to engage within the GPs. All sorts of human activities were observed, as the internet provided an incredible resource to watch almost anything. Students did not have free reign over the internet, but rather Gratitude assembled an enormous bank of appropriate material that was viewable. Ordinary activities like buying groceries, performing tasks at work, training pets, interacting with others at a party, or traveling through an airport could be comfortably observed within a GP. More complex situations were also available; such as— experiencing loss, dealing with conflict, or the first moments of becoming a parent. Students could comfortably observe these events and form essential conclusions.

Anthropology was considered extremely important at Gratitude and many classes were based on the observations of human interaction. Peter felt that it allowed for his students to see how similar most people were, and therefore dispose of much of their own personal egos. The result was less obstruction to focusing on improvement within oneself. Students began to understand the implications of trends and 'social norms,' and the difficulty of not falling helplessly to them. His students became great little human analyzers, and that made them great at analyzing themselves too.

However, there was perhaps an even more important purpose to the GPs: the ability to listen to music in an optimal setting. Students would close the door of a GP—basking in the glory of isolated sound in the darkness.

Taking the time to sit by yourself and be infused with the power of noise was promoted so heavily that it could almost be considered a mandatory class at Gratitude. It was not the same as sitting somewhere with earphones in, listening to music while completing another task. Music at Gratitude was considered to be a treasure to be appreciated almost as much as breathing itself. It was regarded as falling into a container of love and spirit. Music, it was felt, was one of the greatest gifts on the planet and deserved enough respect to hold a person's entire focus. Concentration on music, it was trusted, healed and improved the mind. It permeated the soul and allowed for deeply gratifying and growth-inducing moments. It was common practice for a student to stop within their day, hop for a few minutes into a nearby GP, play something like "Subdivisions" by Rush—pump themselves up with motivation; and then continue on with their other studies.

These chambers were incredibly expensive but Peter and Marty both felt they were worth every cent and more.

Aside from the few mandatory classes, at Gratitude, each student was encouraged to spend time in whatever way felt to be most beneficial. Peter followed practically all of the requests from "The Children of Philosophy."

Out of the mandatory classes, only half of them were spent with other students the same age. The mixing of ages was something deeply considered. It was thought to allow for added perspective, and conducive to forming a community. The traditional school model mostly kept students of the same age together. At Gratitude, they decided this to be obviously limiting as it cut students off from gaining the benefit of interacting with those in different stages of development. The mixing of ages created dynamics of responsibility and respect. There were certain times when it was nice to be in the comfortable presence of those with the same amount of years of life, but there were other times when a person could feel both empowered and humbled by being around those who were older and younger. For those who didn't have siblings, this was an even more vital and necessary experience to have.

It was Maya who saw the need for the interaction of different ages and pushed for it. She also saw that much of the reason why this wasn't being promoted in schools had to do with fear of sexual development and experience.

"Much of our current structure is a result of our history of sexual repression and confusion," she said one day at the leadership meeting. "However, there is no success in trying to force people to do or not to do. Many of our problems are a direct result of that attempted force. All of this misguided logic is mixed up in archaic religious principles. People are shortsighted and miss the consequences of the rebound that comes as a result of repression. Most people are more afraid of their children having sex than just about anything else they can do. It baffles me. Don't they see that if you don't have the freedom to trust your child, you have lost everything already? Anyway, it's not their children's sexual development that they're really scared of—it's that they have never truly come to grips with their own.

"If you need proof of the depth of the problem, take a look at the qualifications for movie ratings. A movie is allowed to show extreme gore and violence—a person getting shot in the head or tortured—but it is not allowed to show the natural nakedness of the human body? How absurd is that! Just please consider the depth of that insanity for a moment. Consider what we have done to the concept of making love. It might be a complicated issue for children, but avoidance certainly is not the answer. Look at all the unhinged males out there who have become the way they are because they are so horribly sexually confused! Their opinions of what makes sense were never asked, and the conversations were hardly had. Through avoidance we've taught them shameful desire. I don't care if you're watching sports, shopping, smoking, playing with Legos or masturbating. If you decide to do it, and you aren't hurting anyone else—don't be ashamed! Furthermore, we can enjoy doing things while simultaneously deciding not to have as much of it in our lives anymore; or not at all. Making these decisions within the moment is how we grow—as well as how we move away from addiction."

Their enrollment was small at first but increased every year. All that could be done was to take whatever action made the most sense, and continue moving forward toward improving their environment. They knew that being in uncharted territory would be the hardest part of all, but they also enjoyed playing the role of transformers. *Decide what's moral and go forward. Analyze what you see and allow that to influence better judgment.*

However, there were some striking effects clear from the start. The system of mixing ages exceeded their expectations toward forming a sense of community. Often students took on the role to look after those who were younger. It lent itself to feelings of both responsibility and security. Within these relationships, good manners and kindness were advocated. Sheltering at Gratitude was generally thought of as not the best practice. Peter felt that you didn't need to go out of your way to expose children to some of the harsher aspects of life, but when those issues did crop up, they should be dealt with—*honestly, bravely, and with acknowledgment of the opportunities that they can be.* He also felt strongly that dealing with harsher reality at a younger age invigorated his students with a stronger moral foundation. This was imperative for the development of their confidence. Children, it was soon proven, had a greater ability than once believed to grasp difficult concepts. Years later, students at Gratitude far out-performed average adults in moral testing when presented with complicated sceneries of choice.

Peter set a different precedent in place. Teachers at Gratitude were master guiders; not teachers. After the first year, they got rid of the word 'teacher' altogether and replaced it with the word 'guider.' *Difficult situations are the best opportunities to teach if you have confidence in your own ability to improvise. Professional teachers do.* Guiders asked questioned—pressed gently. They shared their own opinions, stating clearly that that was exactly what they were. They were simply a part of the community like anyone else (also trying to grow through life, also trying to have opinions). He did not try to force them out of their own humanness. In fact, he did the opposite—encouraging them to draw it out while simultaneously maintaining a level of maturity. Guiders respected their own limits and knew that they didn't have all the answers. They were impressed as easily as they impressed. And so it went.

M AND J

O ne-day Peter stood observing M and J (morality and justice) at the back of the class. Marty Linden had wanted to be a guider as soon as they decided on the definition of it. "Yes," Peter and Maya had both declared simultaneously upon his request. Marty's intellectual brilliance and individual perspective were seen as just as valuable as his financial resources.

The class met three days a week, and Marty committed himself to being there. His own children were all now enrolled at Gratitude and his wife Stacey was a guider of 'preventative health.' *Schools can be the rock of community. Ideally all parents should be guiders here*, Peter decided.

Today's class was taking place inside of a gazebo out by the gardens. Peter stood nearby eavesdropping beside one of the avocado trees. Sometimes he would participate, and sometimes he would just listen. Today he chose the latter.

The class was comprised of nineteen students—their ages ranged from eight to twelve. Before the actual class started, Marty had a practice of bringing in his guitar and singing a song. He didn't play silly songs; he played stuff that he loved and felt passionate about. It wasn't only a way for him to use the effects of sound but also a way to build trust. As a leader, Marty had learned the importance of openly exposing both character and vulnerability. They could look at him and say,

"OK, this guy's all right. He's trying to open his heart just like the rest of us. I trust him; now let's learn."

"Who wants to start us off today?" Marty offered while placing his instrument carefully back into its case.

Steven Gross raised his hand. After a nod from Marty, he began. "We spoke last class about not trying to feel that you're bad. But I've been thinking about the people who do really bad things—shouldn't they feel that they're bad? That's where I'd like to take us today."

There was silence for a few moments. Although he often allowed the students to try answering each other's questions, Marty also wasn't afraid to gently push in the directions he believed to be right. *That's what discretion is all about,* Peter said to himself. *Try to take your subjectivity out of the equation and everything goes to shit. What's the point of having beliefs if we can't be strong enough to share them?* Peter leaned against the tree and tuned back in to what Marty was saying.

"I'm glad you brought that up, Steven. Yes, of course you should feel bad if you do bad things. But perhaps a greater question is—what makes someone do something that's bad? Especially someone who is an adult and should know better. Why are people doing bad things at all? That's what I'm interested in."

Peter loved the way these students considered before answering—setting the words in their mind before speaking them.

A cute light voice broke the silence. "Well, maybe they just want something so badly that they don't care about anything else," Courtney offered.

"Yes! That's a great answer," their guider replied instantly. You can all remember when you've wanted something really, really badly, yes?" Many nods responded. "Have you ever done something that wasn't super friendly in order to get that thing you wanted?" Again nods. "Does anyone want to share an example?"

Bold Steven spoke again. "Yes, a couple weeks ago it was my sister's birthday. My dad bought her an ice-cream cake. They were saving it until dinner, but my dad brought it home in the morning. I love ice-cream cake so much. I thought I could sneak a small piece and that it would be fine. It was stupid, I know. As I was taking it out of the freezer, I heard someone coming down the stairs. Before I could cut myself a little bit off the end, I reached in and quickly grabbed a chunk with my fist, stuffed my face with as much cake as I could, and then put it away again real fast."

The whole class started laughing hysterically and couldn't stop for an entire minute. Steven allowed them their moments of indulgence with his arms crossed over his chest, face red, before continuing on with the story—smiling.

"After dinner, when the time came to present the cake, everyone was pissed at me. I mean really mad. My sister cried, and my dad sent me up to my room. I felt terrible and couldn't really understand why I'd been so stupid to do it to begin with. Considering it now, part of me did think that I must be bad. Why else would I have done that?"

Steven's sister Tina was also in the class and sat there glaring at him. She was the only one that didn't seem to think it was so funny.

The class went back and forth discussing what Steven did—Tina included a personal account of her frustration. Finally, Marty worked them toward a conclusion. "OK, so do we agree that what Steven did was wrong? Do we also agree that it doesn't make him a bad person? Good. Now let's get to this next question—what *does* it mean about him?"

"That he still has something to learn."

"Nice! Yes, exactly, Miles. That's my opinion too." Marty gave him a nod of approval. "That's all it means people. We're humans. We can always learn more. And what's the lesson for him to learn?" Miles Carson was the oldest grat in the class and getting sharper by the day—holding his tongue when he was unsure of what he wanted to say and plunging forward when he was certain. "That Steven needs to have more discipline," Miles decided. "If we want to have relationships and interact with other people, we have to be considerate. The golden rule, really. But sometimes it is hard to know how a person might react. Sometimes we try to do good and end up hurting people instead. I guess it's impossible to stop that from happening, but trying to do the most good is still what makes sense to me. What other option is there? Sometimes it's hard, but the more we can think about our actions before doing them, the better we become at making wiser ones. Sometimes decisions have to be made quickly, but we deal with each particular situation as it happens. That's what I think at least."

Peter enjoyed Marty's style. He was adept at seeing which students needed to be complimented and which needed to be encouraged. They had discussed Miles before and agreed that his potential was over the moon. They felt that maybe he was the type that could be sidetracked if he received too many compliments. Every student was different, and trying to decide what was best for each of them was what made a guider brilliant—was what made Gratitude unique in itself. With Miles, they decided they wanted to see what would happen if they gave him a wide berth of freedom. His mind was coming up with so many positive conclusions on its own that they felt it best not to interfere very much. Already he had become vital to the success of their entire community. He set the example for the other grats.

"But what should we do with the people that do really terrible things? Should we kill them? How do we punish them?" The prodigy continued. "It's the question that we as a community have to decide."

"That's a pretty hard one to answer," Marty replied, "but you're right. You have to really think about what you believe. When we hear about people taking such horrible actions, it upsets us. It's hard to understand, so we feel that it's safest to not have them around—to put them in prisons. But I can tell you that I really believe that anyone can be taught differently and be turned around if the treatment is intelligent enough. Currently it is not. It would be a great honor and testament of our society if we could help those who need it most. Maybe it starts with getting them to stop thinking that they're bad, right? They can accept what they've done as horrible and be willing to pay the consequences; but it's never too late to improve and start providing something of value. Maybe if they do get better, they'd be the best ones to relate to others who are struggling as well? Anyway, that's what I think. Each of us needs to decide for ourselves. Part of morality is just that—believing in your own ability to decide what makes sense and being OK with others disagreeing. Don't just take my words as truth—you're the one who decides." He stopped for a moment, giving his students space to consider.

"Now we'll take a moment to close our eyes, be still, and focus on our breath. Take in as much as you can of what was said here today and promise yourself to work on thinking about it at some point later on."

Students were used to ending classes this way at Gratitude. "Such an excellent job today. Notice how you performed, even if you chose not to speak at all. Only you know how open your own ears were, or what your potential is. See you next time. Have a good rest of your day."

"Can we talk about one other thing before we leave?" a familiar voice quickly spurted out.

"All right, we still have a bit of time. Go ahead, Steve."

"We've spoken a little, but not too much, about God. I want to believe, but if there is a God, how could he or she or it let all these bad things happen? Why would God allow people to take such horrible actions in the first place?"

Whoosh. They want to go even deeper. Unbelievable, Peter thought. *And here I was thinking that we had been pushing them too far.*

There was a part of him that considered whether or not these conversations were best had among a family at home. Then he remembered how many parents lived in confusion themselves and had no ability to answer these kinds of questions. One thing was for certain—this dialogue was too important not to be had. Not only that, but having the ability to hear what your peers' thought was invaluable. *School,* he thought, *is exactly where this conversation needs to take place.*

Miles chimed right in as if they had just entered into his favorite topic of thought. "Well, I think before we can answer that question, we need to define what God even is, don't you?"

So they began discussing what they believed to be God. They settled on two different conclusions. The first was that God was energy—all matter of things. It made up everything in the universe, including people of course. *That's a mind-blowing concept to many—thinking that they're God. Good for them.*

The second was that God itself was simply an answer—an outlet for all the things beyond what people were capable of knowing: How did we get here? Why do bad things happen to good people? Why do some only get to live a few years while others for more than a hundred? Why is it so hard to make decisions? Does anything happen after we die?

What they concluded was that it was all right not to know everything—that that was part of the experience of being a human being. That certain things were beyond us and that those things were the reason for the creation of God. Basically, that people should be smart enough to know what they can't know.

Peter waved to the students as he entered the gazebo. The conversation had gotten too juicy for him to keep standing on the periphery. "I love the conclusions that I'm hearing you make, and couldn't agree more. Humans are amazing, but we do have our limitations. For our limitations, it makes sense to turn to God—to something higher. I think it's really cool that you figured something out that can help you navigate life with much greater ease. It's something many live their whole lives and never admit."

They continued together, moving on past the time for the class to be finished. *This is too important for us to stop. I might have to ask them all permission to show the recording to the rest of the school at some point.*

That was another reason why he loved having cameras everywhere. Moments of exceptional brilliance could be captured through a technological marvel of mankind and shared for the benefit of many more.

Marty wrapped up the points his students had made and packaged them together for them. "We need to be OK with not knowing and embrace the feeling of letting go. Often it is in letting go that we receive back our best answers. It takes a humble person to admit what they don't know. Life is too wild and unpredictable to try to control everything, don't you think? Maybe part of what we should be doing—is learning how to better let go?"

They seemed to agree with that.

"Can we come up with a symbol for God?" Melissa asked, speaking her first words of the class. "Something to help us when we're confused or feeling a need to figure everything out?" *She might not be participating with her words,* Peter realized, *but a question like that shows the complete depth of how sharply she's been listening.*

They all considered for a few moments. Miles offered. "How about the question mark itself?"

"Perfect!" Steven shouted with vigor."

"I love it," Melissa added.

"So do I," said Marty. "If you want, you can all write a big question mark on your notebooks to help remember. On that conclusion, get out of here already beautiful humans!"

They left with invigorated looks on their faces—as if going so deep had given them something they had unknowingly been yearning for. Peter took a seat next to Marty in the gazebo. They sat together for a moment considering everything they had just witnessed in the now empty space before them. They both experienced feelings of deep accomplishment. They knew that none of those kids would have spoken together this way virtually anywhere else in the world. It was a great moment for them; and they chose to soak it in for a while.

IDEAS THAT POP

The details of Gratitude's inner working technological flavor are essential to understanding the kind of atmosphere that was created. The internal system, along with the GPs, created a different sort of relationship with technology. No expense was spared in producing a well-developed network of communication.

Anyone of any age could attempt to create a class and guide it. All someone had to do was enter it into the network. It amazed Peter that more schools didn't use the increasingly ingenious and easily accessible resources of technology to better communicate and develop efficient organization. At Gratitude, that's exactly what occurred. As soon as an option was posted, the class would be classified as 'tentative.' Once four students signed up, the location chosen for the class (if still available) was reserved. Every student was in the system and was sent a notification to their profile when a new class was created.

At Gratitude, there was truly no compulsion to study a certain curriculum. If you wanted to read a fantasy book, that was seen as worthy as taking a class on economics or learning to play an instrument. Peter believed that knowledge and truth could be found anywhere and that choosing how to spend your time led to far greater productivity during the space within.

Inscribed in large letters on the wall of the main hall were the words:

It is uncertain when a person will be overcome with a spark of insight that might alter the course of their life; as well as the lives of many others. Therefore, we guide each other gently.

This belief sunk deep into what Gratitude was at its core. Even if a student wanted to sleep during the day, that was all right too. How could someone else say that it wasn't what the body needed most at that particular time? After all, it hurt no one else.

But the opposite expressions of behavior were far more common. Most grats had to be encouraged to remove themselves from their studies every once in a while. They were discovering free learning itself to be the most intoxicating activity of their lives. They had no idea that acquiring new information could be so entertaining.

Everyone used their phones to check Gratitude's app—to see new classes, announcements, events, discussions, and locations. It was on the individual level of discretion to independently monitor phone usage and silence them when complete focus was appropriate. That discipline itself was seen as preparation for an independent adulthood in the current age in which they were all living. It was only hard to imagine children being able to monitor themselves this way until you witnessed a system that promoted maturity and discipline as much as Gratitude did. These personal devices, Peter felt, were something humans were going to have to get used to balancing their time with. *They're too useful not to have available...even in school. The older generation doesn't like it because it's not what they had. Too bad. Cell phones are a magical technology*—they even allow you to *turn them off or silence them. If you can't bring yourself to take that simple action...that's on you.*

There were rules as per requested by the Children of Philosophy. It was not a complete free for all. Peter liked the balance created between pushing for generally greater freedom, while also acknowledging benefit to be drawn from conformity. As the Buddha taught—the middle way. They had rules, but they were adaptable and every person had an opportunity to accept them. For any behavior that negatively affected others, an infraction could be filed and potentially lead to appearing before a council of peers to plead your case and be accountable to their judgment.

Miles was consistently and satisfyingly overwhelmed as he became used to his life at Gratitude. He found himself quickly accepting his new environment and allowing his voice to be heard more boisterously than ever before. He held on to the leadership he had found, and built off of it. Perhaps his favorite part of Gratitude's philosophy was the view it took of living your life as if you were creating a piece of art. *All life is art.* What a concept he marveled. *Can that not be true?*

The acquisition of knowledge was done by traveling down a certain path for as long as you wished. Learning was not done to show off but rather simply for its own sake alone. It was accepted that people only know so much about so many things and that we do not learn in order to better engage discourse, to prove points, or to appear more intelligent than others. He loved this mentality and knew in his heart that it was intuitively the way. Everyone's opinions were their own, and a title was not necessary in order to have conviction in an assessment. It was easy for Miles to see how titles and degrees constricted the path of development and prevented an attitude of humbleness. *Either you consider someone an expert—feel that you have something to learn from him or her—or you do not. It's merely an opinion and choice for each person to make.*

He thought to himself, *qualifications do serve a purpose, but they have to be seen as secondary to the act of gaining knowledge itself...not the other way around. Otherwise, there is little wiggle room to explore areas outside the box of one's qualifications. Otherwise, people think that titles themselves make them experts (which has been proven all too often not to be the case).*

I've seen too many adults who don't seem worthy of their titles. I've also seen plenty of disasters and scandals in the news from those who have been utterly "qualified" for their positions.

It's a part of the same beast that leads people to place their own lives into the hands of others. It's a form of laziness…not having to assess. Instead, we have to get better at seeing the 'X' factors and trusting in our own intuitive judgement concerning any individual who stands before us. Not because we dislike them, but because we need to understand.

Amanda Keegan had fallen in love with the concept that school should be most importantly; a housing for enjoyable progression and activity. *The only pressure students should experience is what they choose to place upon themselves…for fun.*

All the time the phrase "To know one thing is to know a thousand things" rang about with loud emphasis at Gratitude, along with "How you do one thing is how you do everything." Amanda believed those sayings to be exactly right.

Learning is a state of relaxed determination, she came to believe. Amanda realized very quickly that a relaxed mind-set led to discovery that could far exceed what was possible for a person who was anxiously backed into a corner of stressed, compulsive work. *It's not some kind of unrealistic ideal; it's simply how we learn best,* she practiced saying to herself. *Here, philosophy is seen as a path toward growth and freedom. Creativity is prized most of all. I love it,* thought the very person who thrived so profoundly in a very different system.

There was one more function of Gratitude that was of extreme importance and use (it was actually voted on and put into action three months into the first school year). The idea came from Duncan.

It was the creation of teams within the school. The idea was this: Students could form a team with anyone else they wished. Once you formed a team, you decided together on projects to take on. Often team projects sought to make improvements on the institution of

Gratitude itself. It was understood that it was up to the entire community to make the school as grand of a place as possible—that Gratitude was still young and that often what was fresh and new needed sharpening. *In fact,* Duncan thought as he developed his system for teams, *all things need sharpening…forever. Most importantly, we sharpen and improve best if we're united. Using what each person has to offer (for most projects) has a much higher yield than a single person working alone. The challenge is to prevent, or better yet, to productively use conflict…as a means for discovering greater peace.*

Teams of students would bring propositions to be voted on by the entire school. If they got the OK, they put themselves to work implementing their own ideas. The smallest team was of two and the largest about twenty. People were constantly combining their teams after the completion of projects and also combining efforts to take on multiple projects at once. However, each student could only be on one team at a time. They didn't switch teams very often, but when it did happen, it was seen as a basic right. Every potential new member was voted upon, and members could also be voted out of a team. In either case, a strict majority was needed. There was a constant rotation of leadership within these groups, and each member took a turn at being the leader. Their only job was to cast a deciding vote within the team in case of an even majority. That, as well as perhaps taking a stronger role in directing the flow of the work with more aggressive opinions. So, they were important.

It was ideas that flowed constantly and bounced around in a slew of directions at Gratitude. Ideas for making physical improvements, ideas for gaining happiness—even ideas for making money. But mainly just ideas for the sake of them; because it was realized that humans enjoyed filling their minds with them…*we all find purpose in improvement,* Duncan thought. Most challenging, was keeping the wheels turning so that ideas became reality. At Gratitude, they were afforded the container for giving it a shot—taking the embryo of an idea, and incubating it. Still, if ideas arose and fell away—that was no problem at all.

Duncan, Amanda, Miles, Patrick, and Mikey began and expanded their own team—the D.T.'s which was short for 'Dramatic Triangles' (whatever that meant). Their team provided a resource for movement. It was even common to bring personal life struggles if you needed help with relationships or other drama in your life.

Teams were considered almost as a second family, and the team structure became one of the great lasting foundations of the school. It was decidedly insensible to take on all of life's ambitions alone. For some reason, America in particular had gotten itself all caught up in individual ambition and what it meant to succeed alone (an impossibility anywhere except within the delusions of one's mind). The community of Gratitude saw that each human is blessed with a different set of strengths; and that, when combined—greatness of many sorts is possible. The D.T.'s certainty took on the desire to accomplish greatness. "What we started back at public school," Duncan said during a meeting, "is still only just beginning."

As all of this was happening, Peter and Maya continued to expand their global community. Gratitude's initial and fast paced success, inspired the title of one simple idea. It became a lasting piece of writing titled 'Cheating.'

Cheating

Is the type of cheating where you give a friend an answer criminal? Consider; why wouldn't it be a good idea to help a friend?

It wouldn't be fair; you might say in your mind. *It would unravel our system of ranking,* you could argue.

Well allow me to respond with this: Why are we so busy ranking each other to begin with? What true purpose does it really serve? Any? At least contemplate the thought if you're going to take your conservative stance. Does our ranking provide us with anything of value above and beyond the act of lending assistance—above the idea of working together?

The conclusion we've come to at Gratitude is drastic and clear. No—ranking is overall an attempt to coddle an insecure ego that doubts its' own self-worth. We don't see the real-world application for ever stopping someone from helping another if that's what they desire. In fact, we believe it should be every person's right to give as much help as they want, and that preventing our children from doing so is the only facet of the interaction which can be considered 'criminal.'

What kind of a rule demands you not to help? By making cheating 'a thing,' we're preventing our children from developing the habit of combining effort, which is a much-needed skill to foster successful community. We're setting in their mind a destructive mentality of competition and assessment. This, as opposed to cohesion and cooperation.

The only reason we see for emphasizing individual scoring is to try to perpetuate a system of classes that only exists in our minds and can never exist in reality. We can make scoring a fun game, but do we really need to take it any further than that? Do we really need to know who's better? Is that even possible; and does it matter? These are the questions.

When happiness is more valuable than money (as it should be), working together becomes a much more sensible investment of our time. The feeling we receive and the benefits of building trusting relationships become a different type of winning. Don't you think?

This unnatural and heavily cultivated mind-set of competition obviously manifests itself outside of the classrooms as well. As adults, it causes us to be far less open and honest with our thoughts and feelings.

There are many personal tools we use for finding mental health and dealing with challenges in our lives—good ones. Most of us have great secret gifts to maintain higher levels of perspective and cope with reality that can often be stressful. But, through this system of competition, we are taught to be greedy with our best thoughts. We don't share the tools that work for us—the mental habits that allow us to prosper and be steady within the abundance of stimulation that surrounds. Instead, most of us keep our little bits of honest wisdom secret. Why? For one simple reason: because we were taught that cheating is wrong. Because we were taught that we shouldn't trade answers. Because we were taught to compete in some make-believe game of separation that isn't real. It's time to be done with it. Teamwork is too important. Let the sharing flow. It will be to all of our benefit.

MASSIVE SHARING

The notebook room was the largest room at Gratitude. It opened up to high vaulted ceilings and enormous stained-glass windows emitting colorful rays of sunshine. There were open spiral staircases around the square perimeter allowing access to all three levels of what could be considered their version of a library.

Row upon row of shelves lined the gigantic space amid places to sit and read or write on tables or floor. However, only the middle floor held the regular types of published books.

The top floor was a floor of artwork, becoming the home for many student projects over the years. But it was the bottom floor of the space that gave the room its name.

Through the entrance on the bottom level, there was a table to the left with a pile of fresh new notebooks. On a wall hanging above the table read a word—*beginnings*. Lining the shelves on this level, were not regular books but notebooks containing the work of the people within their community. Notebooks were organized by subject matter and then by author's last name. A notebook could be created on any subject at all. It was the clear first act everyone knew to take when starting a new project. Once a student began writing in a notebook (similar to speaking a goal out loud and therefore having a better chance of achieving it), he or she began down a new path of creation.

Grats could spend a month, four years, or even just five minutes doing work on any topic; but when they were done, that notebook went to its place of standing on the shelf. There and forever that notebook would rest with their name attached to it—research to be continued at a later point if they wished, or to be taken up by someone else to feed on. The Internet was invaluable for acquiring new information of course, but the bottom floor of the notebook room functioned as a more intimate and connected resource for organizing the work of their internal community. It was a project they all took great collective pride in.

An online system of note-taking also existed and was used more frequently as it provided a convenience that couldn't be matched. But there was still something significant about physically having the space to write thoughts and ideas down on paper, and it seemed that for many, no method of technology could provide an adequate substitute.

Some students never started a physical notebook, but rather only used the online system. Regardless of which system suited each particular student, the most important factor was that they learned to organize their thinking and their work—that their projects were kept track of and that they acquired the satisfying feelings of progress.

One day in her third year, Amanda found Peter sitting in the back corner of the top floor of the notebook room. He was scribbling away furiously in one of the plain brown notebooks available at the table downstairs. She glanced at the title, and it read 'Honoring Water' (it was more than halfway full).

To Amanda, Peter Sol was in a very real sense her personal hero. The security and support she felt at Gratitude were unlike any she'd experienced before in her life. Her peers were not jealous of her but rather welcomed her to try her hardest in all the ways she desired. They saw the depth of her skills, her spirit, but also respected her enough to spot when she was feeling insecure and help her back to her higher ways of being. It was that aspect that she cherished most.

She was not prone to nervousness, but she was in this moment.

Peter looked up from his work and smiled. "Amanda Keegan," he said lightly.

"Peter Sol."

They stared at each other silently for a quick moment—meeting eyes.

"How's your day going?" He asked.

"Are you busy?"

"That depends on your definition of busy," he chucked to himself. "Take a seat."

She sat down across from him cross-legged. "I have this idea I want to ask you about."

"Oh?" Peter closed the notebook, sat up straighter, and gave her his full attention. He knew more about this girl than she realized. He was well aware of the role she had played at her old school—in forming philosophy club, drafting the letter he now had posted in his office, and working to open up the minds of so many stubborn parents. She had as much natural leadership as anyone he'd ever met before. *If she has an idea, I'm listening*, he thought. "Please, share."

"Well, I was just thinking about 'opinion' and 'voice.' Through this whole experience, I've realized how important it is to speak up and share what you're really thinking. In most schools, sure, you might have a presentation every once in a while—and if you're a loudmouth like me, you make yourself heard. But I think most people tend to sit comfortably in the background never really sharing many of their thoughts. I can't explain it completely, but somehow I think this isn't such a terrific thing at all. I feel everyone should have a chance to share what he or she is thinking, and we should have an opportunity to listen. Not on a particular subject or topic even but on anything at all that might be on this person's mind."

"Hmm, I love this, Amanda. We need to help people practice speaking up and getting comfortable sharing their opinions—there's no doubt about that. You may or may not have had enough life experience to know this yet, but people playing it safe and sitting off on the sidelines is as much a reason for the tremendous problems in this world as anything else. That's probably what you're getting at. It creates problems for all of us. OK—what's your idea?"

They began working on it together right there and then. They drafted up another agreement needing to be signed by every member of Gratitude. They called it 'The Cycle of Speech.'

The Cycle of Speech was to be held every day at two thirty in the main auditorium. It was fifteen minutes where one person (it could be an adult or a student) got up before the entire school. During this person's fifteen minutes, he or she was free to say or not say anything. The person did not have to speak, but it was agreed that they would at least stand before their peers in a position of leadership for the short amount of time.

Some cracked jokes, which was entertaining, but most used the platform to discuss a subject they were studying or a change they wanted implemented. This single activity bred strength and united their community more dramatically than any other element. Often a person who many might not have expected to think so far outside of the box would bring forth an issue or have an idea that was absolutely brilliant. It was exciting and motivating to watch speakers gain strength and confidence every time their names came around in the cycle. Like with anything else, expressing your thoughts to a large group took practice. At Gratitude they were given the platform to sculpt their speeches and become proficient at staying calm and focused even as the spotlight was on them.

"One more thing," Amanda had said as she got up to leave her and Peter's formative interaction that day. "After each person finishes, I think we should all have a giant dance party for ten minutes."

Peter smiled at her broadly. *These kids are unbelievable,* he thought for the zillionth time. "For sure we should. I see no reason why we can't. Dancing is as worthwhile of an activity as any other I can think of,"

This was what she loved most about this school. *Anything is possible; you just have to think of it.* She let the thought bounce around her mind as she contently made her way to her next class.

THE COUNCIL OF LEADERSHIP

T he decision of whether or not to even have a grading system was one the school pored over for some time. Eventually they decided it was necessary. The main reason being completely different from why traditional schools used grades. It wasn't for measuring specific knowledge—it was a way for Gratitude to appropriately choose its own leadership.

From the onset of creation, Peter realized that constructing a new honest system of education would be overwhelmingly difficult. Therefore, he figured that he could combat the challenge by setting up Gratitude's system to adapt and evolve. *That's the only way to sustain it,* he realized. *Similar to the construction of an adequate and intelligent government. A container for constant evolution.*

Amanda's suggestion reignited this concept and opened him up to creating even stronger walls. It made him realize how necessary it was to include everyone's voice. He wanted the best ideas, regarding the most pressing of issues, to democratically reign free and inforce themselves. The grading system would be his method for accomplishing this. It was a pretty simple mathematical arrangement, but it broke down as follows:

Each student was locked into the network and had the ability to accrue points to their personal profile. Everyone received the same amount of new points daily (one). This point was not theirs to keep however, but rather to be given away. They didn't have to give it out that day but could simply store it for later use. It was possible to give zero points one day and five (if you had them) the next.

Points could be given for anything that a grat deemed worthy: for a smile, for a pat on the back, for a cool presentation, for doing a favor, or after reading someone else's notebook. It could be given for something as abstract as spreading the energy of love or for words expounded during the Cycle of Speech. The more points you earned, the more weight your vote held when it came time for school wide decisions to be made.

There was no arguing whether or not you ever deserved to receive points for what you did—everyone was entitled to give out points however he or she chose. They were usually given silently and unknown to the receiver until the end of the day. To give a point, students simply went onto the network, entered that person's name, and transferred it over. It was a testament to the culture of the school that conflict regarding points was almost non-existent. The system was fair, and it was usually obvious that the character of the person made way for his or her leadership role. It was seen as important not to get too caught up in the system of acquiring points. Someone might have been a good leader, but others skilled at plenty of other quiet talents. This was simply a method to stabilize the process for making decisions.

The Council of Leadership was made up of the top ten people with the most accumulated points. At the end of each semester, the ten people with the highest amounts would sit on the council for the following six months and therefore make many decisions that, as a need for efficiency, could not be brought to the entire school.

Exactly like government, Peter thought, *except that the path toward leadership is much more logical and fair.*

With every year enrollment grew. The application process was seventy-six words on "what I have to offer most as a person."

Part of every grats duty was to spend two days a month in the acceptance office. Six people reviewed ten application essays a day. After they read each essay, they voted a yes or a no for admittance. Out of the six people who read over the application essay, five had to give a yes in order for that potential student to gain acceptance.

The other way to apply was to send in a video of yourself, speaking the same allotted amount of seventy-six words to the camera, answering the same question regarding your personal value and uniqueness. Most applicants preferred this method as they felt it gave them a better chance to showcase their true character. Word usage was key, but tone of voice, or a look of the eyes had a lot to say as well.

Gratitude was set up to hold many more people than an ordinary private school. The maximum capacity was around fifteen hundred students. It reached that amount after the fourth year. More than half came from a distance and boarded at the dormitories on the grounds. Most came from families who supported Peter and Maya's ideology, but others were orphans with access to the internet, or had parents with limited awareness or care of their children's happenings. These students were usually pulled along by a friend who had bright, ambitious plans for a better future. It didn't matter—once they were at Gratitude, they were all simply a part of it. History mattered only to the extent it could be utilized for learning.

A news team once came to do a story on Gratitude. The reporter asked a nine-year-old girl how she was spending her days. The question was asked with a tone or underlying belief that what was happening at this school was a joke—a sort of short-term experiment that was bound to fail.

After explaining in detail three subjects she was most passionate about—game making, gardening, and animal study (the girl had already filled half a notebook on each)—she said, "But you have to understand that none of what I study is a big deal. My most important job is to enjoy my life. I've been told that I don't *have* to think about anything, and it allows me to think about whatever I want! Those notebooks I make are just fun ways to spend my time learning about what I find interesting."

Then the girl was asked, "What do you think of this place overall?"

She placed two fingers under her tiny chin before answering. "If a mother could be a place—this would be it."

That girl was Elizabeth Grove, currently having accumulated the eighth amount of points, and holding a seat on the council for the second semester in a row.

REFRESHING

To say the very least, it had been quite entertaining for Daniel to watch the activities of his son and daughter-in-law during the past quarter of his life. It could never be said that he had been a naysayer—but he had been known to encourage caution more often than he found himself doing now. Now, he considered himself to be a full-fledged support.

The great thing about being a student of philosophy, was that it quickly allowed outlooks of reason to effect habits and patterns of thought. When he decided, he changed.

He remembered back to those first years of Gratitude's infancy. In his mind, Peter and Maya simply had had to prove they could rise above the challenges that come from shaking systems which tend to pound their feet and scream as loud as they can when you simply reach out to touch them. *They attack you, complain, and change the subject. They run you around in circles of threat—making you fear what will happen if you take something away from them.* Daniel wanted to see that they could stomach these blows before he'd dismiss his concern. He had watched the world destroy too many of his friends, and also one of his own children. He was a brave creative thinker—but there were limitations.

Now that I've seen the power of their resolve, and the rock-solid movement developed as a result—I've been swayed. Of our movement, he corrected himself. *Dangers exist, perhaps as much, if not more in these boxes of controlled safety that we try to carve out. In the midst of some kind of sick game—we turn away from the realness of our limitation. We lie to ourselves about what we're owed and about how safe we think we can be. They claim school is supposed to be a pretty safe one of these boxes, yet it too has been the scene of murder and destruction. I know. The lesson; unreasonable shelter is pointless. Chances—the rising and falling of happiness, the death of loved ones…inevitable. We think that our worry can save our children from poverty and violence; but too much worry pushes them into realms of wasteful, spoiled, and immature insanity. As harmful as anything else to be sure. More so. Yes,* he concluded. *The major problems we have in our society stem from the place of trying too hard to control.*

Daniel would listen to his friends discuss the differences between generations. "Young people these days aren't capable of paying their dues," they'd often sputter. "These kids want everything now, and they think that they're entitled to it. They don't understand the value of loving to work. They've never even read 'Zen and the Art of Motorcycle Maintenance,' for crying out loud Dan!"

Perhaps there's some truth to that, he thought. As he saw it, there was nothing wrong with 'paying dues.' But then he'd probe to an even deeper place of truth that complicated matters.

"As long as you want to pay them," he said as they sat together on sofas within a basic living room set; sipping on coffee and tea. "As long as you are fairly certain there is something waiting for you at the end. But to pay them just for the sake of paying them? I don't think we're there yet. Perhaps some of us. Maybe that's the kind of psychology that this generation does need. Then again, maybe not. How many people pay their dues knowing exactly what position or bonus they're trying to get—only to find after many years of hard work that they hadn't strategized properly. Perhaps it didn't even have anything to do with a bad strategy—maybe it was a result of change in policy, or leadership—all their years of planning torn to shreds by unforeseen circumstance. Now it's too late, oops—better have enjoyed the process of whatever it was I spent doing for years. The point is this: If you want to be whatever it is that you're being—fine, no problem. You're right about that. But if you're doing it as a state of sacrifice in order to get somewhere—you better be sure as hell that whatever you're trying to get is going to make you happier. You better have a realistic belief that you're capable of actually getting it!" He took a sip of his peppermint tea infused with a bit of bourbon maple syrup. "Regardless, we have to start admitting that most of our systems are a mess and can be dramatically improved upon simply by dropping all this ego bullshit. Perhaps that's what the younger generation is catching glimpses of. They laugh at their parents' game plans because they know what jokes of fear they are. "You think college is an answer? You think money is everything? Your eyes are closed ancient one." That's what they're saying, that's what they're seeing. It goes both ways. Yes, our age group probably works harder and believes more in quality for its own sake; but growing up with so much access to information has allowed this new generation to see the depth of our phony conformity as well. With changing times comes alternative results. It's too complicated for us to figure out which one's better. It's enough to acknowledge that the field of play has altered and that they may very well be beyond us in many ways."

They nodded their heads in agreement. They never told him, but his friends loved it when he got all riled up; watering their seedlings of thoughts, and taking them for a ride.

Later that night after they left, Daniel reflected on his own process of letting go of doubt over the past decade or so—of getting to the point where he now stood. *Doubt...is a killer. But it is powerful. No matter what, there are some parts of it that will always get through.* He saw the guilt it brought up over the years, and how it clawed its way in—digging interesting little burrows for itself in the patterns of his mind. *Did I do enough? Should I have tried harder? How did I look? When was my biggest mistake?* He thought it a powerful practice to begin writing down all the insecurities he could bring to mind.

Sometimes the doubt even made its way into his relationship with his son. But then, one day with the help of Maya, a new thought hit him with significant force. He was remembering it now.

It was about a year or so before Gratitude had first opened—before the whole world it seemed knew who his family members were.

He was getting in his car, about to drive away from their house after supper. As he was opening the door, Maya came outside and handed him a folded-up piece of paper. She gave him one more hug and told him to read it later. He drove himself home, walked into the kitchen, and laid out the quickly scribbled note on the countertop. He turned on a lamp standing within arm's reach and peered at the hand written words:

Dad,

This is a mantra I wrote for you. Yours to take and use if you like:

I use myself to do good. I know that. Therefore, I must respect that which has done, and will continue to do—as much good as it can think of. Although I often get sidetracked, my intentions are pure. I remember this as often as I can.

With love, Maya.

He remembered the lesson he learned standing there in his kitchen that night. *It's not my job to judge the choices they make. My only job is to help them. Is being critical helping? Usually not...unless I offer my criticisms in order to give important information which helps those I love see more and improve. Otherwise it's just me trying to knock others down and lift my opinions up.*

Two years after Gratitude had opened, Peter asked his father if he would apply for a guider position. Daniel considered his tenure at Princeton—the comfort of it—the people and system he had spent so much time getting to know. But really, there was very little conflict in his choice. He knew what was right. His heart told him that he wanted both change and the presence of his family.

So Daniel finished up the year in his longtime home on the east coast, and then moved himself across the country to live in a small house built on the estates of Revolution.

In his new environment, he quickly developed desired routines. He biked to Gratitude's campus daily on a winding dirt road (he had always wanted to use a bicycle as his primary mode of transportation). It took him about six minutes. He would stop at the arched entryway to look up at the brilliantly carved sun set in iron and bronze. *The sun gives us life and needs to be honored,* he would say to himself as he passed underneath. *Without the sun we are not here. A little respect please,* he'd chide himself.

Rather instantaneously, he formed a deep appreciation for teaching at Gratitude. It was nothing like Princeton. In fact, he reached a level of happiness he hadn't known was available. *It's so often like that. We have no idea how much better things can be until we experience.*

Long ago he had given up on his quest to find and join a sensible community. At Gratitude he found the unexpected. His students were something different entirely than they had been in his previous teaching atmospheres. Here, together, all of them were a part of a movement. They all intuitively felt the importance of what they created. They were humans traveling through their lives together—supporting each other in the role of intellectual rebellion.

Sometimes Daniel would go to the classes grats taught and participate with a happy grin on his face—reeling with pride at what someone with few years of life was capable of harnessing. During his classes, he pushed his students to try harder and think more deeply for themselves. As a result, they came up with all sorts of interesting creations that those at Princeton never would have been able to originate—*they have simply been prodded through too many years in the traditional system.*

These children were different. Students at Gratitude jumped to meet his expectations, and didn't complain when they were given assignments. After all, they had chosen to take the class; and anyway knew better. Here, students were so thirsty for a challenge once they allowed themselves to fully engage with the psychology that learning was to be enjoyed. It was amazing to watch and an incredible place to be a part of.

Most of all, Daniel was proud of Peter and Maya for creating something that was so desperately needed. *People speak too many words. Those two understand how to take action.*

Yes, indeed—Daniel no longer had much doubt in regard to supporting their revolutionary activities.

One brisk early December morning, Daniel walked into the school—dropped his things off in his office, and made his way down to the lower level for morning assembly. Grats and guiders alike clamored into the main hall, finding a place wherever they could. When the bell of the main clock struck ten, everyone in unison began reciting the school's credo. Their collective voices rang out in confident harmony.

I am a living part of planet Earth. I am lucky to be alive and to speak these words. Throughout my day I look to discover more and more reasons to be thankful.

To be human is a tremendous gift. To be human means that I can have perspective.

Appreciation is a never-ending journey. As days go by, I learn to reach further and more deeply into a life of gratitude.

My goal is to do as much good as I can. I am in competition with no one else. I respect and admire others, but I do not envy. I would not rather be anyone but the person that I was created to be.

To the forces beyond my capacity of understanding—I thank you for experience.

After the last word, everyone immediately began moving in different directions. This was the start of each morning, and it didn't take long for Daniel to become acclimated to it. Sometimes there were a few contemplators who stayed where they were and thought silently for a few moments before heading off down the colorful halls of their school. Assembly, like most everything else, was not mandatory. It was, however, pushed back to a time late enough in the morning where hopefully most would choose to attend.

Mornings were honored at Gratitude; as the way your day began was thought to have a large impact on what would follow. Forcing yourself to get out of bed from a jarring alarm clock was seen as a harsh existence—exemplary of the kind of pressure most of society were placing upon their shoulders, and therefore crippling their ability to thrive daily. It wasn't a fluffy notion; it was simply practical.

After a lifetime of waking up before his body wished, Daniel was very appreciative for the change. He lounged about at the start of his days—taking care of his garden, doing his meditation, and practicing yoga. Then he'd jump on his bike around 9:50 a.m. and head to campus. It was exactly how he wanted to live his mornings—without pressure to rush. *That alone is reason enough for me to have come here*, he thought to himself many times.

Following assembly, Daniel made his way back upstairs to Peter's office. There was an idea that had been digging at him, and today was the day he planned on engaging his son with his creative spark. He had a desire to expand himself—to take on a larger role at the school; and he had decided how.

Peter's office was small and simple but had monstrous windows to the east displaying a large portion of the forest property. Daniel walked in and saw his son standing with his back to him looking out of those large glass panes. Peter turned around just as Daniel stepped through the open doorway. "Dad! Good morning." His voice was deep and steady. The change in it alone spoke of his growth over the past few years. Watching his son's face light up when he saw him caused Daniel to feel a sense of secret gratification and quiet pride. He knew that not all children were happy at the sight of their parents.

"Morning Peter. Can I have a few minutes?"

"Yeah, absolutely, take a seat."

Daniel sat, considering the sensation he felt toward having so much respect for a man so much younger. The admiration was offset by the fact that he had been the one to raise him.

"I'm hoping that you might be open to the idea of starting a new project together. I know that Gratitude is still in its early years, but I'd like for us to think about becoming more serious in a certain area. One that we're both pretty familiar with."

"Oh yeah? What's that—sports?"

"How'd you know?" he asked sarcastically.

Peter smiled as his father continued on. "We have the land and the money. The way I see it, the biggest issue is for someone to create the right system and take on managing such a large project. Especially keeping in mind the philosophy of Gratitude and making sure it transfers into a very aggressive arena. I spoke to team Invention Dragon already. They're finishing up their last project and are interested in taking on something new and grandeur. They've got a lot of athletic kids, so I think they could be a good fit. If you think I might be suitable, I'd like to be the one who spearheads the effort."

Peter turned around to look out the windows once more. Daniel knew that his son had somewhat of a love-hate relationship with sports. He knew that Peter saw how easily they could get out of hand, and possibly contradict that which Gratitude stood for.

Peter turned back and spoke. "It's funny that you're bringing this up. I've been thinking about the same thing. Tell me more what you've got in mind."

THE MIND-BODY

D aniel had seen enough proof that the randomness of life was a very real thing—to be acknowledged and never lost sight of. However, that didn't mean he couldn't make a strategy and reach out to carve a path when he felt like it. *Making a strategy*, he thought, *is pretty much as good a usage of my time and brain power as any I can think of. Pay respect to the force beyond, but also believe in the power of planning.* And anyway, it was fun for him. Ever since working in the vineyard as a boy, he had experienced the satisfactions that come from the worthwhile implementation of planning. He enjoyed developing strategy simply because it felt purposeful. The harder part was deciding what it was that he wanted to direct his energy toward. The mind could jump around to all sorts of possibilities. *The trick is figuring out the deeper substances that the heart is really after obtaining*, he told himself. *Find it, then go after it.*

He created game plans while at the same time making a part of the plan, the certainty—that plans change. He would always be presently weighing the swirling memories that hung around from the past, with fresh insights from the present. *Adaptation there will always be a need...but knowing the limits of a strategy, is often the best part of a strategy itself. Just another piece to play in our intellectual schemes.*

Sometimes Daniel considered whether he had been a general or military strategist in a previous life. He wasn't sure how he felt about reincarnation—his beliefs didn't either exterminate or solidify the pos-sibility. *Who knows? It feels right to contemplate some sort of battle though. I know that. Strategy is a natural tendency of my soul. Although I don't think it has to necessarily be engaging the game of war though.*

This particular incarnation called for a deep interest into strate-gies for success in physical games of competition—in sports. For as far back as he could remember, Daniel had considered trying to make a career for himself in sports. It had always been a little dream to play at—considering whether or not his skills as a philosopher could transfer into a significant advantage for the body. He believed that challenges of the body had extraordinary power to bring out a fantas-tic part of the human spirit. He was absolutely certain that physical exertion and health of the mind were as locked together as any other two entities in the universe. As a spectator, it wasn't who won that in-terested him (rules being fallible and all). It was the art of movement itself—the assessment of character in action and the entertainment that comes from watching someone try as hard as they can to achieve a very specific goal.

Who can assess the value of one performance; one movement of the body that has surpassed anything previously done? No, Daniel told himself, *the highest level of interest is in what we can do with a focused mind-body flowing together in harmony. The fascination is in watching that body try to win, not in whether or not it actually does. Oh how we've gotten ourselves so tangled up in the wrong things…even in sports.*

Observing Jo play soccer had been one of the great experiences of Daniel's life. Watching Peter had been fantastic too, but his inter-est in his daughter's effort was inexplicably something more. It wasn't that she was better, and he didn't think it had to do with the fact that she was a girl either. It was something about her individuality itself—about the connection of similarity between the two of them. When he watched her, he was right there—experiencing each moment of deci-sion alongside.

Then Daniel realized something he hadn't ever considered before. *My respect for Peter had to be developed over the years. But mine for Jo…for as far back as I can remember; it was just there. I always had a feeling that her knowledge demanded my respect, and so I gave it.*

It broke his heart when he thought about how close the two of them had been. How they never fought for real, and almost always seemed to understand what the other one needed. In a strange way, he knew that even at a young age she saw that he craved for a kind of taking care of. *She was more successful than she realized.* I know that.

When he felt the weight of what he had been charged to go through in this life, there was no way of getting around the horrible feeling of loss. When this happened, he embraced it and allowed grief to have its time as well. He knew that sadness must also have its time.

To cope, he would go to his computer and put on old videos of her games. *Oh how thankful I am to the miracles of technology.* He watched, and found himself with her once again. *She had no fear at trying as hard as she wanted, and she used her love of movement to continuously advance. When she was knocked down, when she hit the ball too hard, soft or with the wrong part of her foot...she learned by planting the memory into the circuitry of her mind.* He saw it every time. He took pride remembering that he had been the one to gift her with the never ending desire for improvement. Although her life was short in years, she embraced that philosophy until the very end.

I'm sure that watching an athlete like this is healthy for the mind. That's why sports are great. Results are irrefutable. If we can put away envious comparisons and fall into more admiration...I think spectating is very worthwhile. Similar to watching any master craftsmen make art—not only is it fun to see others performing well...it's even better watching them break down new walls.

Daniel's position at Gratitude invigorated him with possibility. It caused him to open up motivational avenues that had been contemplated for a long time. He didn't simply want to play at thoughts of entering the world of sports anymore, he was ready to make it a new healthy obsession of his life. It was almost as if he was a scientist in desperate need of testing out a hypothesis that was believed so completely. And anyway, he knew—it was also a way to continuously be connected to *her*.

Daniel believed rules for games should be fluid systems constantly adapting. They already were, but he wanted that knowledge to be further embraced by the masses as truth. *We should respect the history of our sports, without obsessing over making comparisons.*

Listening to the same conversations over and over again in the sports media was pretty frustrating for him. *After all, who really cares who's the best? The immaturity of that conversation should be obvious to us by now. Shame that it isn't. It only plays into the ambiguity of the ego and a ranking system that isn't even possible anyway. Can't we find something better to talk about? Mainly how important it is to take care of the body and challenge it. It's as if we create these safe boxes of conversation that are stamped with approval (this one being debating who's the best), and it prevents us from progressing to far more stimulating and productive areas of discourse.*

He often watched games on television wondering why he had to listen to these cookie-cutter announcers giving their opinions. Instead, he would put on some music and press mute on the remote. He was torn, though, because he also enjoyed hearing the sounds of the game—the bounce of a ball and the cheer of the crowd. He didn't feel it was the appropriate time to be overwhelmed with words. *They say the same thing over and over.* He found that he was able to focus much better on the action without the distraction of the commentary. *People tell you what to think, and it takes away from your ability to decipher for yourself. When will the general population learn about the isolation of senses and the myth of multi-tasking? When the attention splits, a portion of perception is lost from either end. That's just how it is. Do one thing, and do it well.*

So Daniel began his project of making sports an emphasis at Gratitude. They poured money into setting up state of the art facilities; but had no illusions that it would instantly equate competitive success.

Teams of grats even took on building some of the structures themselves. A good percentage of the school wanted to be involved in the project. Daniel sought out great coaches, allowed students to coach each other, and created classes for the making of new games. The athletic wing became a jungle gym of sporting activity—and it pleased him very much.

Most serious to Daniel personally was the sport of wrestling. It held a certain amount of purity in his heart. He loved the idea of two people trying to subdue each other physically—while at the same time working together to be fair and safe. Therefore, he created a team and decided to coach it himself.

He had developed many ideas concerning what could possibly make an athlete most formidable. His belief was that mental strength was by far the most vital factor. *Famous athletes sometimes allude to it, but still drastically undervalue the impact of being able to control and effectively utilize the power of the mind. It goes on and on.*

He had five weekdays to host practice, but only chose to use three actually wrestling. The other two days were spent playing other sports and activities with his team. Many questioned the logic of this; as it was two fewer days to be able to work on technique and conditioning specific to their purpose. He disagreed. The philosophy he held, was that change itself would lead to greater strength. Holding off on participating in the main activity brewed more anticipation and focus upon return. *Sometimes when you discipline yourself to hold back, skill becomes intensified as you hop forward in progression that can only be found with a fresh pair of eyes.*

His strategy also had another effect that he liked. Playing a variety of different games with his team leveled the playing field among his athletes. Although there were usually one or two kids who did well in the majority of competitions, it was not always the case. There were often specialists who gained great confidence from having success in games that suited their skill sets particularly well. He observed as the mediocre wrestler who dominated on the basketball court, would come back to the mat the following day with heighted levels of confidence and vigor; and therefore make great strides of progression.

There were days when he would take his team on silent hikes—giving each of his athletes ten minutes to lead. The speed of the group was the leader's choice (whether they stopped for many breaks or chose to jog at a fast pace). The rest of the team followed without speaking a word and knew not to go ahead of whoever was leading. The silence gave them a chance to sharpen their awareness and become comfortable handling the thoughts that swam through their youthful minds. *This,* Daniel would think to himself, *is how you acquire personal information to allow for growth. How am I as a leader? How am I as a follower? What do I tend to think about? What are my fears? What do I notice? What do I want to work on within myself?*

Another big decision was to incorporate yoga into every single practice. He was convinced that once the body was loose and stretched out—the mind purified and the power of breath acknowledged; it would be most suitable for safe exertion toward limit. He was dumbfounded at the men of his generation who were too macho and therefore also too immature to use such a beneficial tool for greater health. *Can we not all agree that taking care of the body is paramount? What practice is more conducive for health than stretching? Nothing. In the future, every human will have their own personal yoga practice. They will wonder how they could have ever lived without it.*

Most of all Daniel Sol believed that both the body and mind, with challenges—thrived at the experience of expansion. *If the body does not test itself, it forgets its own strength. When this happens, it's far more likely to find yourself taking fearful actions.* That was a problem he never wanted to have; never wanted his athletes to have. All the people out there who were not taking care of their own physical beings scared him more than any other single factor of life. *I'm not sure what's more frightening: that some can't see its necessity, or that others see, but don't have the discipline to take action.*

He didn't have a program long-standing in tradition, and he didn't have many wrestlers who were familiar with the sport. What he had was the system he created—a philosophy rooted in the discipline of good spirit and relaxed focus. His popular saying ran: "It's not a matter of how good you can be; it's a matter of how good you'll allow yourself to be."

He told his wrestlers during their most grueling exercises, "Allow yourself to be great. Can you do it? Will you take the time to meditate on how you see yourself improving? Will you visualize your body getting stronger and quickly reacting expertly to any situation that your mind can predict? See it first, then do it. Remind yourself while you're sweating—in this moment of exhaustion; that strength itself is a birth of challenge. Bask in the hardship. Notice the sensations and allow for them to be OK."

As they sat against the walls resting at the end of their practice, he would give them more of his crystalized philosophy. "In the same way that we build a muscle, our minds must also bare weight. How do we do it? We throw out immediately what we know to be thoughts that don't serve us—thoughts that give into weakness and fear. Refuse to be slaves to them! Considering whether or not you're good enough, worrying about the future, stressing out about 'being liked'—there's no time for that stuff; throw it away. 'Being liked' is not the question. The question is whether or not you find yourself to be likeable. If you don't, then work to change. You have the ability if you engage progress softly. Our work, and the beauty of being alive, is too important to be self-conscious. Know that with certainty. Every time you break through a barrier, it will be easier the next time to go back there again. Keep breaking through mental obstacles—for the joy of the act and for the sake of improvement. Contrary to popular belief, it's not about winning at all. Most athletes try not to even consider the idea of losing. They think it might manifest itself if they put the thought into their minds—they don't bear the weight. I'll tell you, not facing the thought of failure is a horrible mistake. It's a disguised kind of weakness. Doing so in fact makes the chances for loss much greater. Why? Because we know it's there, only hidden. It's the hidden mental factors that often influence us the most. Stare losing in the face! Think about it, know that it's a possibility, and one that you're absolutely fine with experiencing. Losing is nothing—points and records meaningless. Try as hard as you want with no attention to outcome. Behave the same way regardless of whether you win or lose. This, is a whole other level of victory."

I'm being a philosophy professor and a coach at the same time, he realized. He knew that it was the most natural work of his life. He loved it.

Sometimes he did drills where everyone lay down on their backs, closed their eyes, and focused on sending positive energy into and through their bodies. He told them, "People think this is crazy, but that's only because they don't actually try it. Completely accept yourself—right now in this moment. Take control of your body and tune into your own healing strength—notice the sensation that is always present. Try—try as hard as you want; to make yourself healthy. Move your focus to every nook and cranny of your physical body, and then allow your own healing energy to burst from the outermost layer of your skin out into the world." Daniel waited. "Send it! Send out your love! This is true mediation. Only possible through belief."

One day his heavyweight coined the exercise *raising up,* and the term stuck. They'd say, "Coach, raise us up!" They knew that it worked; they felt it once they tried, and they tried because they knew their coach was real.

It did take a few years to make progress; but in the grand scheme of things, improvements could be viewed to have happened rather quickly. His wrestlers completely committed themselves to the joy of hard work and the discipline of the mind-body. His hypothesis was proven; to himself, and to them.

After Gratitude's first state champion stood atop the podium, he was interviewed after the match. Austin Freeman bristled with the sharpness of peak physical health.

"You've come from a school most of us have heard of for many other reasons besides athletics. How has a program that's been around less than five years produced a state champion and two runner-ups this year? That's great success for any school. What are you doing that other teams aren't? What's your secret?"

Austin stood relaxed with his arms at his side, answering without hesitation. "Mental ability. We believe that nothing else matters half as much. It's our secret, that isn't so secretive at all."

"What do you mean? Don't all the athletes here have strong mental ability?"

Austin took a moment to look the reporter in the eye, realizing exactly what she was doing out of allegiance to her work—*she's trying to cut my legs out from under me...making me question the sense of my own belief. We think these little interactions don't matter—they do. It's so easy to give in to doubt when those trying to pound you down have such effective tools at their disposal...and we are sympathetic. Try to give an honest answer, and you're attacked for it. They always go after the best part of the ego. The part that acknowledges our uniqueness. She has no idea about what everyone has...most of all herself.*

He responded carefully. "I think we do an especially good job of it. Of course being in shape is extremely important too. If you get winded and worn down, it's easier to let go of your strength. But if you really think about it—that's when your attention is needed the most. If you keep taking it there, if you change the kind of training you do—it gets easier and easier to tap into every ounce of what you've got at your disposal."

The reporter continued without really hearing him. "What allows you to fight harder than anyone else? Because that's what it seemed like out there—you didn't stop moving."

"I think perhaps because I just really do love to wrestle. I don't get nervous because I'm so happy to even be in this situation to begin with. I take the time to remember that, and also that I have nothing to lose. Neither do you—neither does anyone." Daniel overheard him and smiled at the thought he was training little philosophers.

The reporter was taken aback and pretended that she didn't hear anything provocative in his words. After all, this was just her job. She wouldn't have her life effected by some young kid while she was working a gig. She had her next question ready and well lined up. She had noticed the trend for Gratitude wrestlers to do yoga on the sidelines directly before and after they wrestled. "Also, does all the yoga you're doing give you an advantage? All wrestlers stretch, but the members of your team seem to hold postures for long periods of time—as if they're as important as the wrestling itself."

"Yes!" Austin chuckled to himself knowing that he could have given that to her as a much simpler, and perhaps even better answer before. "Most people don't have the self-confidence to allow their bodies to move naturally. I've learned how important it is to get down on the floor and be the ape that I am—as often as possible—moving in fluid motion and stretching out the body into positions that feel good. I never knew how tight and crusty I was until I finally gave myself permission to open up."

STRONGER

I t was the day after he first moved into the dorms at Gratitude. The previous year he had been a commuter and had worked tirelessly to convince his parents to allow him this next step of freedom.

Perhaps it was the loving community that he now found himself existing in (the nature that surrounded his new home), or maybe it was the fact that today was his all-important eighteenth birthday. In all likelihood—it was the combination of many factors.

Regardless, it was a day when Miles Carson found himself rising up to higher levels of being and experiencing a mental clarity that would stay with him for the course of his life. Even when he thought it was gone—it never left. This day changed everything.

Simply, it was time spent being in different places on the land. He stood barefoot in the grass wearing regular, comfortable shorts and a purple shirt (although his shirt was off and slung over his shoulder much of the day). He explored area. He stopped and stood amid a large piece of rock in the middle of a field. He looked up at the sky and marveled at the energy of the planet that he was a part of. He felt at ease—trusting in both his thoughts and actions. He allowed his mind to easily decide where the body should locate itself. Miles had only to decide whether it felt appropriate to stay where he was, or take his chances with movement. However, it wasn't really much of a choice as he found himself blessed with the awareness that no wrong action is possible for a being that accepts the truth of their positive intentions. *That's the hook,* he thought. *I'm flowing with nature and my decision-making itself is a part of that flow. So much planning 'what to do,' instead of being curious to see 'what might happen.'*

With this levity of spirit, he was free to make discoveries and inspections. Apple and peach trees, enormous grapes on the vine, small streams, and fascination with the intricacies of insects; to name a few. He stayed and looked at the depth of beauty for however long he wished—becoming interested and then moving along knowing that there was an endless plethora of magic to see everywhere. Time wasn't pressurized—boredom not possible.

He discovered a hammock, and it reminded him of looking out into the universe from it in the darkness of the previous night. *What a night that was,* he thought and slowly smiled. *Perhaps that has something to do with how great I feel today...everything feeds off everything else. Days build upon days. In this moment, I don't need anything.* He hadn't eaten in quite some time but still wasn't feeling hungry. In fact, he was enjoying the sharpness that can come from having an empty stomach. *That is something many of us have forgotten. I'll eat at some point, and when I do, it'll be another gift that I've been given—the taste that much sharper because I disciplined my body to hold off until hunger is really felt.*

These were his thoughts. Existence was peaceful, and Miles swam in the happiness of knowing what it meant to be fully tuned in. *This is what's waiting for us if we can put away comparisons with others, as well as the habit of analyzing the worthiness of our selves. I am really OK the way that I am. I'm just me, and that's all right.*

He accepted himself even more completely—knowing for sure that he was both regular and special at the same time. That seemed to be more than enough, and perhaps everything he had been searching for amid the mess of competitive behavior throughout most of his childhood.

He went further. He began to see it as his job to fall deeper and deeper into his own body—to be with it—to make it strong so that he could do the most good. *Love ourselves and then offer that peace to others.*

This is something to be related to only by those who experience the truth of connection. To be felt in the depths of our bones. To be aware...you must be relaxed. That's the secret. There's no other way. Appreciation for existence relaxes us more directly and completely than anything. But first we have to decide if that's really what we want.

Miles saw that thoughts flow constantly, but that if you tried, there could also be beautiful breaks of pure nothingness at the end of them. That was the place where his answers came flowing into. It was also in this place of meditation that he felt his body healing itself and growing more secure without the pressure to do or think about much. *The more often you experience these moments, the more often you'll have them. There is still always more work to do. Just when you think it's over...there's more. But the work is great. The proof of our progress is the amount of exceptional moments we are able to have...to be lifted with the energy to react spontaneously.*

I want to create a t-shirt, he thought. *The front will say, "ALWAYS WORKING," and the back will say, "Not talking about my J.O.B."*

Out of another space of emptiness and freedom, he found himself considering other people. On this particular day, there was no subject he was afraid to look at. His bravery allowed him the opportunity to explore areas that he had been unconsciously suppressing. He considered if being around others made him nervous and realized that in fact it did. He glimpsed the depth of how much further he could go at being natural, calm, and happy within any setting, but that it was the most challenging while immersed within the complications and complexities of so much energy.

What do I have to lose? That's the question I have to ask again and again in order to retrain myself.

He continued to objectively analyzing more of his own behavior. *What ways of being am I most proud of? What could I do differently? Am I positively rewarding myself so that I will have the best chance to repeat the actions I respect? This is the work!*

He felt deep down that he had some sort of ranking system for "ways of being." He couldn't really explain it and only barely felt that he understood it for himself—but this ranking system was an opportunity to assess his own happiness at any given moment of time. Then, he would piece together the correlation between as many other factors he could think of. *If I'm not trying to be my better kinds of self more often—then what exactly am I working toward?*

The next place he found his body sitting was on a porch by the dormitory just to the outside of a group of peers.

It was a beautiful sunny day, the beginning of spring semester. Everyone seemed to be out enjoying the weather.

"Oh, who brought this Frisbee and paddleball? Nice!

The words of his friend Duncan took him out of his meditation. It had been him after all. He wanted to answer the question, but also felt awkward in speaking up to say, "Me! I'm that person you're asking about. Shine that light over here please!"

Luckily enough someone else answered and spoke his own name. He felt his body relax again. He glimpsed how quickly tension could rise up. In this moment he wanted to stay on the outskirts—in observation. His need for politeness had almost impeded on that desire. Fortunately, it did not; so deeper he dove.

You cannot be afraid of the dark places—must not be. That just suppresses them and does more subversive damage. The most absolute truth I know is that the world and life are too beautiful to be taken for granted. No darkness can contend with the light. He had never felt it so fully before—but he did now. *This truth allows me to open up any door without fear and to keep looking for more doors to open. It can be that way for anyone. Deep gratitude, plus the knowledge that going down can most definitely be used for rising further up; has the potential to make fear an entity that slips by as we notice the mere sensation of it. Don't people realize that the darkness is not even dark? It's thinking that it is which makes it so. Belief is everything.*

Those were his thoughts of transformation onto the plane of genius. Although it might seem like a nice place to end, the time in this particular day (like in any other) kept moving right along. So he kept writing in the little notebook he had been carrying with him.

He felt there was nothing else to really think about, but the mind still wanted to do work. *It's because I've given it so much time off,* he realized; *ignoring the larger extent of my capacity. So be it...let's keep going.*

On this eighteenth birthday of his, he thought it appropriate to consider what it meant to be a boy. *Boys don't get weighed down by the burdens of responsibility...they seek them out. They choose to take them on. In fact, they yearn for the chance to be responsible. At least that's how I was, am.* For some reason, this was a huge insight to him. *Children embrace getting older because they are in tune with the natural implications for growth. Maturity excites them. I see how adults lose that and therefore exist in a nonreality where they turn their awareness away from the road of development. They think they can go backward—and that very conception causes them to do so. Oh how they fear the responsibility of age, instead of embracing it! I want it to excite me—always. Children look forward to challenges and use them to strengthen themselves. They do not run away. Perhaps the best men and women are still boys and girls,* he considered, *looking for any opportunity to grow.*

All the while, Miles was very aware that this day was not regular for him—that he could not be this lucid or insightful consistently. But he also knew that being here right now in this mind-set was enough. It increased his likelihood of having a larger perspective more of the time. *You have to remember that you are carrying around this body and moving it on the surface of this planet,* the boy discovered. *That is all. Be at ease with that reality—it's a beautiful one. Achieving the experience of bliss is the first step. Maintaining it is the never ending work of our lives. Specific reoccurring thoughts of truth can help us greatly. Forward and back, but always forward.*

Miles had spent the day marveling at the magnificence of many things, but coloring itself stood out in lasting memory. He had practiced closing his eyes for a while and then readying himself to pick out a particular one to focus on and feel. The shades of blue in the sky, the uniqueness of the white clouds, the green of the grass and the trees, the moving energy of the bright yellow sun, the brown in the bricks, and the small orange coloring of a flower. He had never had such a deep ability to stop and perceive before. *This is what being in a place of true learning is doing to me. The mushrooms are indeed magical, but alone would never have allowed me to journey so far. It's me combined with them, and it's this container I've found which has granted me belief in the quality of my own person.*

Sitting there off to the side of the group with his back against the building, eyes closed, and his legs outstretched in front of him, he let out a sighing breath—then he took a much needed nap. He was satisfyingly well spent.

Later that evening, Miles watched a girl he'd decided to fall for—resting comfortably in the arms of another classmate. She was so beautiful to him; kind, delicate and strong. He hated wanting something so badly, but still knowing that there was such a process for making it transform into a reality—another person's decision which he could not control. *Perhaps that's what makes it so enticing and gut retching to the heart,* he thought.

About ten grats were surrounding a blazing fire; listening to the mixture of sound coming from a guitar and harmonica. *When did Chris and Lily fall in love?* he wondered, as the pain of jealously quickly infiltrated his entire being. The effects of his enhanced perception had worn off, but in its place, he now carried with him both conviction and resolve to hold his state of relaxedness. *Tested so soon eh? I can dig it.*

He watched his own reactions as he saw them kissing and snuggling together—so enamored with the sensations of companionship. He observed what their obsessive admiration made him feel. Miles wanted nothing more than to switch places, and have that girl on his arm.

Suddenly, he chose to take a hard right turn away from feelings of envy and sadness that he observed as being so real; feelings that screamed of injustice to him on his birthday. *What can I do with this mind of mine?* He thought in triumph. *How much can I control it?* Amazingly, he saw that he could, instead, choose to wish them well. *I can do it if I really try...can't I?* He was both stunned and unsurprised at his ability to successfully let go on his attempt at controlling acquisitions which he thought could increase his happiness. The courage and truth he had built up from his day was like a torrent of focus he could direct in whatever way he chose. *I use my own love to bless them with happiness... that's what I'll do. And I mean it.*

Miles felt something happening to his body. He felt the power of the heightened thought take hold and bless him back with the deepest kind of knowing, security, and greater strength he had ever experienced in his life. Oh how good it felt to him—perhaps better than company itself. *Is this what it means to become a man?*

When a well-developed boy becomes a man, or a girl a woman...they can do anything, he thought—*anything*. And with that, he enjoyed the fire.

PART IV

RELIGION

THE OTHER SIDE

An old high-school friend asked Daniel Sol to join him at a casino one night. Bobby Harding was currently going through his second divorce, and had reached out to a familiar face for support. It was unlike Daniel to pass up the opportunity to help; so he went.

Before entering the casino, they sat in the car and talked. Daniel sat comfortable at attention with his hands on his lap as his friend poured out the scope of his current situation.

"The love that we have for each other is real. It's the best thing I've ever found in my life—and now she's going to leave. Why? Because I'm a shithead, that's why. Because I haven't been able to let go of my trust issues. I'm so damn jealous.

"But you should have seen me. It was all too much. When she told me she was leaving, I saw that she meant what she said; I saw that she was fed up with my anger. It caused my body to start convulsing. I've never experienced anything like it. I actually thought I was going to die. Now I have no choice but to change—I know that. Things can't be the same. I'm thankful to her most of all. She showed me how far I'd traveled down into this crazy abyss of control."

Daniel allowed his friend to continue talking. His current job, as he saw it, was not to care about his own opinions. If he spoke, it was only because he intuitively felt that his response, or a question, might help. Mostly in these situation, he felt that people needed someone to really hear them; and that small little signs of being with them—stillness, a small nod of the head, a hum, or an exhale—would do the most good.

"She was packing up her things before I left the house to come here. I was crying. I told her; "I want you to be around for the good stuff. I'm changing, can't you see?!""

Daniel finally decided to speak. "Let me ask you—how much of this has to do with not wanting to tell your friends and family that you're getting divorced for a second time? How much has to do with your fear of being perceived as a failure?"

Bobby swiveled his head from looking out the windshield to gaze at his old friend sitting in the driver's seat. He allowed the question to settle in. "I probably wouldn't admit this to anyone else, or even you before; but yes, that's a part of it—a big part, it's true. It doesn't mean the change I'm going through isn't real though."

"Let me say something to you Bobby, and I can because you know a bit about my past. I have achieved so much social acceptance for the majority of my life—I am secure enough to say that. I am so blessed and fortunate. And that is why I can share with you that it isn't much to go after. It isn't anything much at all. The truly admired lives are the ones which live close to the trueness of the heart and the development of beliefs. That has to be the focus."

"I'm not there yet, but I can see what you mean. I've been crying every day for the past week, and I never cry. She knows something's changed for me. I want her to be around for the good stuff too!"

"Perhaps," Daniel responded intuitively. "But maybe she's also waiting to see something that comes after the crying has ended. Maybe she's waiting for that. Put it in your pocket and think about it later. Ready to go in?"

Bobby boasted about this particular casino's buffet and said that the food was worth the trip alone. But Daniel saw his gaze wandering over to the gaming tables with animalistic desire. His instincts told him that there might be some kind of devious relationship to money that had led to Bobby's current hardships.

Walking into a casino was entering a world Daniel knew existed but still found difficult to grapple with. He was flooded with insights drawn from the things he was seeing before him. Bobby went to play some games, and Daniel sat down on a bench and simply observed what his eyes took in.

There is a horrid stank of an overinflated ego here—people behaving as if the amount they obsess over material wealth in their own lives is reasonable. I can almost smell it. It's just like that scene from the original Batman movie, where the Joker throws money off of a parade float, and the people of Gotham fight each other to the death for their share. When are people going to get hip to the idea that doing something because everyone else is doing it is absolutely the most destructive excuse of all time?

Sitting discretely off to the side, Daniel was focused and locked in. It was a philosopher's job to see, and he allowed himself the freedoms of perception.

It's an obvious lack of confidence when you stop for a second to consider it. What you are really saying by taking this stance is, "I have such little trust in my own ability to decipher right from wrong that I'm going to give up my individual interpretations of truth in order to coddle myself in the protection of the masses. Too bad the masses tell us to obsess about filling an endlessly empty hole that was never empty to begin with. I'm also going to pretend the whole time that I haven't given up anything at all—that I am in control and that I am somehow still choosing." That right there is the death of a society—following and not seeing that you are. It's the root of it all—the source of the problem and the target for improvement. How un-American! He thought.

He felt sick to his stomach. Often the depth of problems Daniel probed overwhelmed him. He handled it by focusing on his breath, and also accepting reality—not by stopping to try.

He thought he might find a brief respite when Bobby finally came over and asked if he was ready to eat.

"Sure, let's do it. I'm hungry."

However, what he saw at the buffet was too disturbing to find appreciation for his food. *If the government really had our best interests at heart, they'd either leave us alone or make these kinds of places illegal. All-you-can-eat buffets are as terrifying as any drug on the planet. Maybe it's not as swift of a destruction, but it's destruction just the same.*

First, they had to wait in line in order to get a black square buzzer that would vibrate and light up for them in twenty to thirty minutes when they were ready to be seated. *That's how popular this place is; unreal.* The time was not that bad, and an opportunity to catch up on forgotten stories was an activity Daniel enjoyed. But the fierce energy around the place was strongly felt and distracting him. He constantly found his perception swimming toward those around him.

He saw an elderly obese man with a cane resting on his knees, sitting in a chair next to the restroom sign. The chair barely contained his girth. Daniel thought to himself quickly, *although he's not very old, no more than sixty, this man can't stand for long, or at least has given up on thinking that he can. The same thing really—chicken or the egg.* The mans' wrinkled, collared shirt was not buttoned all the way, and his belly hung out the bottom, exposing his veins and fat as if it weren't unusual at all. He wore a pair of tan shorts that showed off ghost white legs that were the opposite of healthy. In his hand was the same buzzer that Daniel held in his.

What's happening to us? What's going on? There are hordes of people like this man. What kind of existence can that shape allow for...happiness? No way, not possible. Have many of us really lost the foundational discipline of maintaining the upkeep of our bodies?

When the buzzer finally vibrated in his grasp, they showed the hostess proof, and were then led like voluntary cattle into the inner dining room. Awaiting them was the Holy Grail of eating. There might have been row upon row of glittering, towering, shiny substances to ingest, but in this moment Daniel wasn't very much impressed (or at least not in a good way). *Why does there need to be so much of it? They keep everything full, and then what happens to it all at the end? Waste. I can't even imagine how much edible food gets thrown away here. Do they not realize how insulting this process is to not only much of the planet, but to any semblance of logic within a human conscience? The proof surrounds us with examples.*

He had recently heard that his country was throwing away a third of the food it produced. *A third! Meanwhile, there are those with—let's just keep it simple and say less. Not to mention all the animals who are having their lives tortured, taken away, and then not even having the simple purpose of being eaten afterwards! Can we humans not do better—are there not any leaders who will step up and call bullshit loud and clear? Does this not come from following and believing that others know better than we do? How much lunacy do we need to witness before we'll believe in the right things?*

He looked around and saw half-eaten plates being discarded. He even saw full plates! He wondered how something like this could be allowed. He used the creativity of his mind to explore reasons.

Maybe there has become this competition between customers and an unseen force. The restaurant perhaps...the casino...anyone with more money? People they don't know, created out of thin air in order to serve their desire to wage a battle and find meaning in winning. They think that by somehow taking more platefuls of food and shoveling so much expensive crap through that opening in their face means that they're successful. Do they not see the condition of the vessel that they have to carry around with them at all times...the effects? Are they so unaware of their emotions that they can't realize how terrible eating all that makes them feel?

He realized in that moment how many of the world's problems had to do with people maintaining stomachs that were consistently too full. *A sharpness of the mind is lost. How can humans so easily throw away their intelligence? "I don't want prime rib—I don't like eating cows— but it's the most expensive thing on the menu...so I'll take two portions please."*

Not a lack of intelligence...shallow intelligence.

After dinner he walked around the place talking to the strangers he didn't know in his mind—unleashing his justifiable negativity.

No, you don't—you don't deserve that increasing list of desires floating around up there. That's nothing. You are thankful, and that is all you are. You are willing to help and open to giving. No more complaining about the things you don't have. I understand that you primarily only know how to worry about your immediate future, but please...you're slowly killing yourself—be brave enough to see that it isn't what you want.

He wished he could actually say these things. He tried to consider how he could give hope. He was a man sick of waiting around for the things he knew would eventually happen to take place. He realized that although they'd never admit to it, most people yearned for someone to discipline them. *They're craving it...so thirsty to be shown that they're capable of being valuable. But no one helps them. It doesn't matter how terrible of a monster they make themselves into. Our loved ones often watch because they are so afraid to offend.*

He yearned to experience a future society where people knew how to take care of their own minds—where they dropped self-mania and learned to actually enjoy their experiences by first giving thanks and then keeping everything else under that monstrous umbrella of understanding gratitude.

When the ego is put away in the corner with secure confidence, that's when we can finally observe and relax. That's when we actually feed it with everything it wants. The biggest secret the ego keeps, is that it craves to let go of itself. That's the only way, and that's what most of us haven't yet realized.

Daniel was not a doomsayer. He knew that even his own perspective was only achievable due to the changing of times and the exposure to vast amounts of wisdom handed to him by others. He considered all the people who were starting to change their ways and see more of the truth. He brought Peter and Maya to mind. The casino was perhaps not the place to find them, but he was sure positive change was rapidly occurring all over the world. *People putting in the real work needing to be done. There's a whole army—an army of disciplined adults waiting to take over and lead. Soon. We can do our training in any setting. Be patient, have faith.*

It made him sad to consider how lonely many of his teammates already on the path must feel surrounded by such an abundance of loud, self-conscious voices in this current age.

It is very true that often those who know the least are the ones screaming the loudest about how much they know. How I wish that wasn't the case.

When he got home that night, he went straight to the computer. He was emotionally exhausted but pushed himself to allow those emotions to take the shape of something constructive—he needed to let out his thoughts and turn them into something more permanent. *Writing!*

Daniel was aware that within situations of muck and mire were great gems of insight to be found. He utilized them now.

He never would have gotten away with writing something as aggressive as 'The Brutal Reality of Physical Space' if he didn't have the community of 'Responsible Minds' to offer it to. He couldn't be sure if Peter and Maya would accept his piece, but he leaped anyway. His words vibrated with experience.

The Brutal Reality of Physical Space

You don't need to read this if you're rushing—if you're all wound up with other thoughts. Take an assessment of your state of being and see if it's the right activity for you within this moment of time. If it's not; maybe come back later. That's OK!

If we consciously move one degree slower, great satisfaction is to be found in connecting to the physical space that surrounds us. It's as simple as that—move more slowly—with precise, relaxed action.

When we're children, we're better in tune with our senses. As adults, we have to work harder to get to that level of awareness. We have to regulate ourselves to be conscious of the present moment and to flow with our bodies in the spaces we find ourselves in. The key is believing that you don't have to be doing anything at all. In fact, not doing anything is probably the best thing you can be doing. It's not a popular belief, but it's the truth. It's exactly what's needed in this pressurized culture of "keeping up" and "being better than."

Whenever we're struggling, we can find comfort and stability if we return to our sense of physical space—looking, listening, feeling, tasting, smelling, and even observing thought. Each, one at a time, in order to gain sharp bursts of clarity. Not placidly allowing these senses to pass in and out but taking the time to appreciate and engage them. This simplifies things appropriately and puts us in the present—using our senses as little igniters to feel better. The more still we are, the more we let go of needing to do anything—the better we can tap into doing what is natural. Don't be fooled into thinking this is hard work—it's the happiest thing in the world.

Take it further, and we can start appreciating the wonders of the body and what an incredible gift they are. We don't have to go down the path of thinking about the fact that some have it worse. That's a part of the same process, which causes us to slip out of perspective. That reality doesn't give us a right to take for granted what we have. For some reason, it seems that mentioning what other people lack somehow distracts us from doing our own work to appreciate our circumstances which we must not be ashamed of! In truth, it should be the opposite. If I'm in a place of struggle, the last thing I want is for those who have more to not only have it, but also to take it for granted by wasting their time thinking about me. THAT, is the travesty.

If we want to help others, help them. But if we're thoughtful, we become better at creating the example. Then, as we return to the senses, we naturally observe ourselves taking more and more quality kinds of action. This in itself is doing our part to improve the world—sculpting our own personal being into an improved version of itself. The greatest obstacle is realizing how much further we can always go. The ego does not want to admit to it. The ego wants to justify that we are already good enough—so that we can be lazy. The ego controlled mind never stops judging itself with the same circles of repetition. It exhausts.

The way things currently stand in the world, it is likely that you don't see much of this. It is likely that you are in too much of a hurry to take the time you need to lose your need for developing opinion, and therefore finding your true beliefs. Most of us are so caught up in little pockets of doing, and following rules, that our vision is blurred. We're failing at the ability to do just one thing at a time. The chains around you, which are so tight that they seem impossible to break; those chains have been placed upon you by yourself—you and no one else. There is no one to blame. Someone must do the work and become the breaker.

It has been a choice to believe that things couldn't be much better than they are—that they're only getting worse, and that you're owed anything at all. It is a choice to believe that the brainwashing is too powerful for you to overcome.

Do you want to speak of the truth? Are you ready to hear it?

The truth is that the experience of being a human should feel so satisfying that it isn't possible for us to do anything aside from act out in love, and to help our brothers and sisters (that includes everyone). Instead, we have primarily chosen to be a society of spoiled humans, fear addicts, and complainers. In fact, the compulsion to worry, to fight, to complain, is so strong that we can't even be included in most general conversations if we don't learn to embrace the art form of negativity. To be an actual life appreciator, you have to be considered strange; and stand on the fringes of our society. Many are afraid to go there. Be assured—the cool people are going.

Truth: we don't have the positive sense of self-worth we need to be as different as we truly wish. Therefore, in order to be included and accepted socially, we join the party of medi-ocrity by fabricating worries and complaints until they are no longer fabrications, but have instead become our way of life.

Because you wish to only be so different, because you have prioritized social acceptance, and because you play into this continuous game of trying to convince yourself that you are adequate; you have built yourself up with doubt and false pride.

Do you want to turn away? Is this uncomfortable? Why? If you are truly as strong as you might be telling yourself in this moment, you would not be afraid to take a small piece of time to engage the challenge of a simple few paragraph of words. But you are a slave to the lower levels of the mind. You live with a fraction of the discipline you are capable of. You obsess over planning because you don't have confidence in your future self to decide. You are in a constant state of trying to figure every-thing out. You move your attention from upcoming worry to upcoming worry. All the while, the gift of the present is being taken for granted—every moment lost a travesty and insult to the being of potential intelligent and soulful action that you are capable of operating as.

Yes, it's bad. Really bad. If you've stayed with me this far, the weight might cause you to short circuit; but there's no need to lose hope. Why? Because it's also much better than you've ever imagined it to be. The change itself is better, easier, fun. Come with me further. Get through the fire and emerge transformed.

The real reality is that tomorrow is impossible to pre-dict. We know this, but do we really? If you consider where you were just a few years ago, is there any way you could have possibly predicted the things that have come to pass? Consider—nope. Life is unpredictable for all of us. Those are simply the rules of the game and we can't be afraid to look at them. Plan if you like, but do it because it's a fun ac-tivity to engage in—not because you actually believe you're capable of controlling much more than your attitude (which is a lot).

It has always been and it will always be true that we can do more, accomplish more—together. Helping should be seen as an opportunity to have a meaningful life experience. And if everyone would just start to subscribe to this theory—that life becomes more meaningful when we're trying to help—Earth would instantly become a far better place to live. This is true, and truth is always the most solid structure to stand on (even if no one else is). All that purpose we're scrambling to find—it comes from helping. It is completely in our own self-interest to do so. How much purpose can we get by continuously only helping ourselves, our group, or our tribe? Not as much as if you set your sights on helping everyone. That is what we should teach to our children in school.

How much purpose can we achieve if we continue to believe in this illusion of separation? Can't you see how boring that is—how limiting and false? As long as you believe in an enemy, you have poison working its way through your veins. What's the score in that game you believe is real? How are you doing—how many points are your people up by? Will you keep playing for your side—your country, your religion, until the day you die? It's a horrible travesty—every one of us that dies still believing there was some sort of score being kept in the game of human against human.

I'll go back to where I started. The key to happiness is to discipline yourself to be in touch with your senses. Plain and simple—slow down enough to find pleasure in interacting with the surrounding physical space. If you view your body as a machine and your mind as a tool to be trained, you will see how simple it is. Therefore, train yourself to see as objectively as possible. All you have to do is your best no matter the circumstances. It doesn't matter if you're ever completely successful. Deal with outcomes, and then do your best again. That's all you've got to do. Being easy with yourself is your most important job. It's really pretty simple, and once you see it, you can just; ahhhhh, relax. Because none of this is a big deal, and you must not fall into the trap of taking any of it too seriously—most importantly yourself or the past.

Stopping to relax and be appreciative shouldn't imply that you're lazy—it means that you're smart; it means you're giving yourself what you need to do better. You are not falling further behind in some imaginary race going on between you and the outside world. There is no race—no permanent record. In fact, taking the time to just be, and be thankful, is a much deeper and real kind of winning. Although we tend to think that it comes from external gratification, 'happiness' is a far greater matter of the internal. That is the last secret step that we all need to take.

Here's the truth—we've all already won. We are the success of the generations that existed before us. Their work has already provided us with more than enough wisdom, experience, and fulfillment of material needs. The last step in winning is realizing that we've already done it! Then we can progress, because what else is there to do? Then we can feel into our bodies and notice all the sensation that is always happening—see that it's healthy to connect again and again. Don't turn your back on it—I promise that avoidance is the very factor which creates illness. Instead, be with it, use it—embrace the change.

TWO HALVES

aya woke up much like she did any other day—a little cloudy, with one foot still in the dream world and one beginning to dip more fully into whatever this one is.

She considered the simple ways in which people caught themselves up with their waking lives after sleep; the words they didn't quite make out, but still felt nonetheless. *OK, right, tomorrow—back where I left off. Yup, got it. Well, I guess I might as well continue right along then. What else is there to do?*

One of the first tracks she'd usually grab onto, was the mental roadway which looked to build herself up throughout the day—trying to focus on gaining comfort and confidence, by allowing subjective thoughts to float into her mind naturally. In the morning...*OK, this is my start—how does it feel?* Before bed...*this is my ending—how does that feel?* There was carryover of course (anything learned was never lost), but going to sleep was a certain kind of ending and waking up a beginning. She was a person of systems, of routine. This was the gist of her core track:

I'm meant to simply improve myself as a creature. This thought stabilizes all of my experiences. Religions that have the day of rest written into their law definitely serve the importance of this concept. Sometimes it's the simple days... where happiness and growth are most easily found. It is not for us to know when a miraculous day will come about or what might cause it. We have to be open and ready for it when it does though. So often we plan ahead instead of being here. Only the truly secure person has nothing to do and therefore can exist and grow much more rapidly. There is a sustainable peace that comes from dropping anxious worry and making it a practice of determination. Once attained, it remains there. Even if you've forgotten the substance from which you drew it, it floats around within you still having its effect.

Maya loved to sleep and dream. She couldn't deny that sometimes she felt as though she lived more in her dreams than while traversing the waking world. She'd often dream of fantastic adventures with nonstop obstacles cropping up and vital decisions needing to be made throughout. *If I make those decisions in my dreams, does that make them any less real? Maybe it's my body's way of telling me what I'm capable of and serving my thirst for action and drama while I'm asleep? Maybe. Could be.*

For a time, she felt uneasy about letting herself completely go in her dreams. Something inside of her was worried that she might do something she wasn't proud of. But then one morning it hit her...*I don't have to be afraid of that. I'm still myself even in my dreams, and I have to learn to trust my dream self too! Even if I don't have quite the same control, it's still me, still my mind. I have confidence in it.*

She considered if perhaps there was a larger lesson to be taken from dreaming. *In a dream, you don't really know what you're going to do... you just watch yourself do it. Maybe that's actually not so different from what I'm trying to achieve in my waking life as well. Maybe that's how I should view decision-making—observing with less judgment. Trying to improve, but not berating myself for not trying hard enough either.*

She probed further—*there's something else about dreams. As if meaningless distraction doesn't exist to the same degree. Purpose seems to be more clear, no matter the circumstance. Culture, or simply myself, often prods me to forget my real goal toward continually getting stronger in maturity and spirit while awake. I hate that I forget. So much.*

A decent percentage of their time together was spent with physical touch. Maya often wondered why the healing people gave to their pets was generally greater than what they gave to other humans. *That's why the popularity of massage has risen so much…but we don't get them as often as we pet dogs, scratch their heads and rub their faces; patting another human on the back is often felt to be a big deal. The touch from an outside source gives the body a reminder to relax and connect. We're meant to connect…to feel united. I think you would find a drastic difference in the disposition of a dog who has been loved through the healing of touch and one who has not. I think you'd find the same for a person. I don't see why it would be any different.*

From the start of their relationship, Maya and Peter had fallen into the practice of healing each other with touch. There'd be silly touching like squeezing the other's waist from behind while he or she was cooking; or passing by in the hall and gently shoving the other into the wall (by all accounts Maya was much more aggressive). But of course there were also plenty of deep hugs, back rubbing, massaging of the scalp, and playing with the hair. No action was really ever felt to be wrong—there was far too much trust for that, and they didn't take their bodies so seriously anyway. Even when they made love, they tried to allow the idea of performance to exit the equation. *Who am I performing for?* Maya would think. *You're a part of me.*

Then there were also games, which connected them in a different kind of way. Often, they would venture to the Ping-Pong table in their garage to let out some movement in the mechanical smelling room. They rarely kept score but reveled in the joy of long rallies and the exhaustion of continuous motion. Stopping to keep score, they felt, distracted focus from the joy of action; energy had to be transferred toward remembering numbers and caring about who won, instead of the pure sensation of swinging an arm in perfect yogic motion. It also disallowed for continuous play off of the floor, the walls, and the ceiling. They preferred that as well.

The couple enjoyed playing all sorts of other games too. Strategy and action, they knew, were healthy for the mind and good for the spirit. They had an entire closet filled with board games, and were starting to run out of space. Maya felt that it was a pity that unless you developed great confidence doing an activity at an earlier age, most adults were hesitant to pick up on new rules or strategy. Their minds were often too tired to start fresh. *Why? Because they care so damn much about being good,* she knew. *They haven't fully developed the maturity to embrace progression, and see that being skilled comes after being really shitty; and that it doesn't matter. Practice makes practice,* she thought. *Embracing 'beginners mind' is so important to squeezing the most juice out of life.*

Sports and games are needed perhaps ever more for adults. All the built-up pressure is begging to be expunged. But games have to be played without falling too deeply into an obsession for success or personal reinforcement of worth. That does the opposite of bringing on the needed relief. That is just another example of the ego getting in the way of maturity—forcing its way into a place where it has no business being. No matter who you are...what you're looking for is to be consistent whether you're first or last. It's such a fine line, she knew.

She loved watching her partner walk it. Peter played the roles of amateur and expert with equal amounts of brilliant and relaxed humbleness.

On this seemingly regular morning in the transformative month of May, Maya rolled herself out of bed, let Izzy out, fed him—also hit up the loo herself, before crawling back under the sheets for a few moments of additional comfort. She pecked her loving partner awake with kisses and small nibbles that made him grumble. Then Peter rolled over on top of her and wrapped his legs and arms around her to give her a good solid morning squeeze. He whispered nonsense into her ear, making up words that had absolutely no meaning at all: "Arkumpilebush...zarkish...klinderhop...swabblesilly...yilsoy...yip-yip. How do you like that last one babe? Maybe that's what we should have named Izzy instead—Yip Yip!"

Strange man. She stuck out her tongue, lifted her head up, and licked the inside of his ear.

"You're a real sicko, you know that?" He said in an accusatory tone—wiping his palm over the side of his face and unwinding himself off of her.

She looked at him and shrugged satisfyingly.

Most of the time, being together was simply an attempt at trying to have as much fun as possible. That was it; whatever it was worth (and it was worth much). Sometimes that perspective was lost, but as often as they could, they tried bringing it back with random behavior of humorous levity.

But they did discuss what the goals of their relationship were openly and worked as a team to achieve them. They were capable of being humorless for a short time, and knew that it was all about jumping between levels. In fact, their silliness made room for an appropriate amount of soulful seriousness. They both knew it was vital not to form an addiction to any particular way of being with each other. *Communication is everything. That's the only way intimacy is possible—without the honest pipeline of feeling closed off. A time for this and a time for that.* They could be corny often, but for a moment every day, usually when they parted ways, they made sure to speak these words with sincerity:

"You're a good person. I promise you. Knowing that truth, allow yourself to take action with relaxed confidence."

They had both improved greatly as a result of hearing the words of this practice.

Even within their work, they tried to go about it as calmly as possible. With the writing, with the school, with all the people that now heard their voices—they committed themselves to the belief that progress is best made with ease, not stress.

They both saw how simple it would be to turn away from large ambitions that others viewed as unrealistic—to focus their attention on making the most of their time with each other. *But this work is actually what makes our time together all the better,* she had realized early on. *That's what they don't get! They could have it too if they learned not to exhaust themselves with nonsense.* Peter and Maya were thankful to life itself for converging their paths. Their work was only them trying to pay it back. It was fair. And luckily, it brought them even more joy.

Sometimes people would ask them if they were afraid for their lives—being as outspoken and controversial as they were. Many folks believed in the tentacles of conspiracy, and as a result, lived under an umbrella of safe conformity. Peter would usually respond to them by saying, "Life itself is inherently a risky journey. Sharing your thoughts and speaking your mind should not be more dangerous than anything else. And it wouldn't be if we all practiced being genuine more often. What am I doing that's dangerous? If you're not being the change, what are you being? I guess the problem."

Many agreed and began to see how much purpose could be found in simply speaking your mind. But waking up on this particular day felt slightly different to Maya. Something in her mind told her it was going to be more impactful than most.

Going through some old notebooks the day before, she had found something Peter had written that she hadn't stopped mulling over since. It was two simple lines scratched onto some lined paper which caught her up and held her. It read:

"I've loved my family, I've loved my friends, I've loved my partner. Of course I still do and always will; but at some point I have to move beyond even all of that. I need to start loving everyone—start loving the energy of life on this planet."

Wow! This man never ceases to amaze me, she thought. *He really is living by his own standards.*

Yesterday she hadn't been sure what to make of it, but waking up today, the answer crept into her awareness. *If he can feel that way, so can I. So can all of us. It's right, it's the real path. Grouping ourselves into competing tribes makes no sense anymore. Tribes are OK, taking care of your own circle is OK…competing against others—believing you have an enemy…not so much OK at all! Detrimental to everything in fact. Can't have it. Why? Because it's not truly healthy for the self.*

Maya had grown up infused with respect for her ancient and resilient tribe, the Jewish people. *It is smart to know where you come from—it gives you information about yourself.* She had been taught from a young age of both the atrocities committed against her clan as well as their many accomplishments; she had never stopped taking pride in her affiliation. She sometimes worried about the harshness of their history—she felt perhaps that too many had been scarred by all the hatred experienced—*are still experiencing.*

Fear has become too prevalent a motivating factor for directing most in our tribe's lives. Too many Jews live in anxiety over what the rest of the world might do to them, and it makes the separation go quite deep—makes the problem even worse. After all, it is reasonable to become tense and worried if experience gives you a right to do so. Still, we also need to know better. For a well-developed individual, there's never a time not to take the higher ground. Have pride in what you are and where you come from while still connecting to anyone and everyone. The lesson is not to have secrets; it's not to fall into the same trap of separation. Our bond as humans should be stronger than any of our religious bonds—has to be.

Her mind took her to thoughts of creating a group of their own—a group with this philosophy. In a way, they already had, but she felt it needed more structure—a stronger container. *What should the foundation be?*

Lying there in bed with Peter, all those thoughts mixed together to boil up her motivation.

"I want to be serious now stupid. Really wake up."

He turned to look at her with a messy head of hair, a scruffy face, and an innocent look in his eyes. But she watched the transformation as he opened them wider to shake the sleepiness from his face. *Those are the eyes I want. Good!*

"I've been thinking. Listen, maybe we should start a new religion." She waited a moment to see his expression of shock before continuing on. "We already have the following to do it."

The sides of his mouth turned up in an appeasable smile, and he puffed out a dismissive amount of air through his nose. "Please! Beautiful lady, thank you for having so much faith in us to do something so large and crazy; but I think another religion is the opposite of what people need. They need fewer laws. Religion takes people off the hook for using their own judgments of morality. It dilutes their individuality by saying, 'Some outside force understands me better than I do.' I don't like that—probably never have. People should be constantly working to figure out what they believe for themselves—then following their own discipline."

"I know that, smarty-pants, but what if we worked that concept into the religion itself? Don't people decide to be in a religion anyway? If they think they don't, then they're just fooling themselves. Promote that—own choice!"

She grabbed a pillow and smacked him in the face; then placed it under her round bottom to prop herself up a bit higher. She felt all of a sudden worked up with passion that can only come from having a clear vision.

Peter still lay there looking and listening—not believing she could have this much energy so early in the morning. His love for her actually hurt him. He liked to think he would be all right on his own, but he wasn't so sure anymore. She was too damn smart—and cute; meant too much to the health of his heart. He loved when she got like this perhaps the most. *This is what a person's best self looks like,* he realized. He drank in her words as she continued on.

"I know I'm not the first one to say this, but what if we created a religion that was different? We could make it not have any laws— or better yet make all the laws only suggestions. And keep reminding everyone that that is exactly what they are all along the way." She wagged her finger at him as if that were super important. "Choice itself has to be the focal point—similar to school. Make it clear that everything is optional and work that into its code. The drive to decide what's right for yourself will be what makes our religion more appealing for modern society. The old religions have been asking for stiffer competition by making such a lousy product, and failing to adapt in an ever-changing world of insight and information. They have history and tradition on their side; but we'll have the common sense of the new age—much more powerful. It's not a business, but it's an excellent business model. 'Take what you choose from us that makes sense to you. If it doesn't, don't take it. You can still be here; be a part.' You know what I mean? Look, I was thinking about it last night before I fell asleep, and this morning it's becoming even more clear," she continued. "I really think we can do it. If we're serious about all this change, then this could be our next step. Don't give a fuck, right? We can't be afraid of losing what we've already built Peter. It all just happened to us anyway. What if I didn't decide to walk into the bar that night? What if you hadn't decided to work there? Most people don't understand how random life is, but we do! That's the best part. We have to use it. We should create a religion because it might be an important and fun way to spend our time and because we're in a position to do it. That's it. If people laugh at us—what an interesting life experience that'll be. Who cares? We're too old and mature for the bullshit of not doing what we think makes sense—what we feel is needed. It's what children want to do, but don't have the resources for. It's what adults have the resources for but choose not to do. We have to be the combination. We are the adults that haven't forgotten how to enjoy risk. This is why we haven't had children together. It would change that, although it probably shouldn't. I read something you wrote yesterday. Strangers need your help as much as anyone Peter. Have you forgotten that?"

She's hitting me where it hurts now and making too much sense, he thought. She continued on even more fervently. "People are so thirsty for structure; don't you see? A bit more of the right kind of encouragement—rules that make sense. They cling to the old ways because they haven't discovered a better option. Brilliance can be taken from those ways, but they are still old—crusty and extremely improvable. Now is as good of a time as any for creating something new which serves our thirst to connect with the spiritual. You have something, Peter. You know it. Maybe the both of us do. We're in this position for whatever reasons that are beyond our knowing. But we still have to use it to go even further. Much further."

She took a much needed breath.

He wished he had been recording her words. *How can she say all of this a few moments after sticking her tongue out and licking my ear?* He shook his head side to side and then drew his hand over her face. He slowly pressed his palm down into the mattress as he sat up, leaned over, and kissed her one long hard press of the lips that gradually grew softer and softer. It seemed appropriate. He concentrated on sending his energy of love into her whole being while their lips were together. *It's a very special thing to find someone who thinks so highly of you,* he reminded himself.

Peter felt that he had already been given more incredible life experiences than he could have possibly imagined having. He literally had nothing to lose, and in that she was absolutely right. He simply had to decide if he wanted to take on this monumental journey that he knew would drastically alter his life. Creating a new religion was something he had briefly considered at one time or another, but hearing it come from her made it that much more conceivable.

Encouragement and support are very powerful forces, he thought. *People do need structure—a system. A framework to give direction and secure individuality. A network for promoting our best selves and supporting us in our quest for relaxed action. In a way, modern life is too complex to handle without a system for harnessing. I know that. Especially considering the plethora of varied stimulation we're constantly being bombarded with. We need an anchor. It is OK for us to acknowledge the huge amount of weight we've been carrying around, and will have to continue carrying. An outlet is necessary to squeeze out some of that mentality of toughness which has been so dramatically infused into our bones.*

Peter had grappled long and hard with understanding religion— what it actually was and why so many people were such heavily devoted subjects. He was also vastly interested in why so many others resented their allegiance. Although it seemed to be a dividing force, he felt that much of the division came from misunderstanding. *If I open myself up to seeing that everything is just a smattering of different things, I know that— almost always, something of value can be taken from even that which I despise. Maybe especially from that. Open up a box, take a piece out, and decide whether or not it's useful. Just because I don't like one piece, doesn't mean I need to discard the entire box.*

Truth splits. People who are not religious do not understand how someone can be so fanatical and sure of a truth without proof. People who are religious cannot understand how anyone could possibly get through a day without releasing themselves to a higher force.

By not choosing sides and instead cutting through to truth with a sharp objective knife, Peter broke it down. When he looked at people without religion, he saw something missing for them—faith, meaningful purpose, love, spirituality, discipline. When he looked at religious people, he saw arrogance, chosen servitude, and sacrifice to a force beyond the logical mind—he saw a mistrust of the self and a lack of a belief in the natural power of human individuality.

Two sides—something to be taken from each.

As he became aware of his fear, saw sensibility, he realized there was no need to feel silly about having such a large ambition. *That's what she was prodding me towards. After all, change has to start somewhere. Why not here with us in this bed right now? We understand how fear and self-consciousness prevent the world from improving. We're not smarter than everyone else...but we're also just as smart. We're smart enough to know that without purpose...life is lacking.*

More answers came. *The whole point of the religion should be to uniquely make improvements to the planet in order to best serve oneself. Best serve oneself in order to best serve the planet. Enlightenment comes from balancing work on both ends.*

"All right," Peter said as he opened his eyes, and reengaged his partner out of his meditation of thought. She was used to his long moments of contemplation, and she let him take his time. She knew that if he didn't work things out on his own, it wouldn't be possible to get his full endorsement. She wasn't interested in appeasement.

"You're absolutely right. We do need a new code. A religion for the time we're going through," he said. "But it can't just be something spiritual, it has to be even bigger than that. Logic must be involved. You want to think big—everything packed into one. Think gigantic!"

"Hmm," she considered. "Yes, I think you're right. How about a system of morality?!"

"Nice! Yes, that's it. Simple, simple."

"A code of life. That's what religions are, but their morality is past due."

He looked at her and realized something. *Although we're doing this together, the flame is stronger in her. She has the drive, the will, and the ability to spearhead this effort...and it will take so much work. If there has to be a leader (which there usually does), it's she, not me.*

"And that's the name. That's perfect; code for life—Life Code!"

"Yes, but that's the code, not the name of the religion," she shot back after a moment of contemplation.

He thought for a moment and agreed. Something else was needed that encompassed the entirety of what it would be. *Something lasting.* And then it came. *There's probably already a group with this name...but who cares? We can use it too. You can't patent one of the three components of time.* His eyes sparkled as he spoke the words. "I think I've got it. How about Futurism? We'll be Futurists, Maya."

She brushed her fingers through his hair and kissed his forehead gently. "Yes, I love it, I love you. It'll do."

LIFE CODE

Whenever they took on a new project, they would balance time working on it together and time working on it alone. When progress was made individually, it would then be brought to the table of teamwork to be fleshed out further or kept exactly how it was. They were becoming better and better at taking abstract thought and turning it into something that practically functioned.

Their work on creating Life Code came down to three main factors: thought, meditation, and action. *To create something...first you need an idea, then you need to meditate on that idea—then when you are ready, confident action can be taken in order to solidify. All three factors are vital.*

Simplicity! A simple system in a world of complication, Maya concluded.

She felt that obligation had as much to do with the downfall of religion as anything else. *Of course...when people feel compelled to do something (as if there isn't even a choice), there is more of a chance that they'll do it. But that notion belittles our individual ability to break things apart, and decide what is in fact healthy and logical (which is really one and the same). It demeans each person's grasp on their own life.*

The concept of perfect, of all or nothing—buying into external systems completely...is based on self-deprecation and laziness. It is something that cannot be advanced because it has taken away the responsibility that we have been given to be present, and to trust ourselves. It accomplishes the immediate goal of finding an answer to hold onto, but leads to further unseen dangers that come from allowing the part of our mind which deciphers...to grow weak from lack of use.

She went further. One of the best things she had gotten from Peter, was his father's wisdom regarding the two categories of people: The ones who thought, and the ones who thought but tried not to. Realizing how much she enjoyed to think completely changed her life. It was as if a massive door opened that she had wanted to walk through her entire life but had been warned against. She meditated, she thought, she decided—she loved the abilities of her mind.

Our whole existence is based on understanding—even understanding that there are things we do not understand—cannot. Discipline is a worthy aspiration, but discipline simply for its own sake—no, not at all. That's what religions tend to be. We must embrace the power of our individual minds—not hand it over to some external source for judgment because we have deemed sitting with the immensity of our situation to be too much of a burden. It might be complex and heavy, but the work in the direction to see more reality is our responsibility. Running away only leads to more grievous future breakdowns. Plus...it's not so bad if we're willing to admit that it's more than okay not to know it all.

These were the reasons why Maya made sure to make it clear from the start that Life Code was only a guide to help navigate the waters of life and connect more with our own answers. *A structure to help keep a person healthy...if one chooses to use it.* She never wanted anyone to abide by anything they thought better of. Deciding to use only a portion of Life Code and leaving the rest was more than all right. In fact, Futurism respected and promoted it as being a part of the work itself.

But being against just to be against, to stand out...watch out for that. It's attention seeking behavior. You have to try to know why you're behaving as you are...and be satisfied with the answer. Otherwise you simply don't have an opinion yet— so leave it open. Give yourself time to gather more information before you grasp onto the first answer. I have seen way too much of that in my life—the need to make decisions before it's necessary.

Spirituality—connecting to the energy within the body; had to first be acknowledged for the incredible force of potential that it was.

Maya knew that had to be crystalline in clarity from the beginning. To move away from religion and not have spiritual moments of life was a sad and cold existence that unfortunately a growing number of people were turning toward. Maya believed that was as dangerous a path to walk down as any, and one of the essential reasons for the creation of Futurism. *The path of inflating the capacity of humans to complete understanding creates even deeper problems. Its rigidity of control breads danger. Still, I don't see why an even better alterative cannot be created. All the truths of science and nature should push us more in the direction of letting go to the absurdity of life…not make us more ego driven. It's a doctor who pulls a diagnosis because he or she is too insecure to admit doubt. The more knowing of science, the more we realize how limited is our knowing. Spirituality is natural and necessary for anyone who does not have all the answers (which is all of us). But somehow our self-obsession prevents many of us from letting go, accessing these highest level of being, and growing into our truest forms.*

She wasn't so famous yet that she couldn't lose herself in public; but sometimes Maya was recognized when she was out and about. People would want to take pictures or just say hello. Once in a while, they'd have a question. If she were being honest, she had to admit she had always felt as though she would gain some sort of fame in her life. Even before meeting Peter, intuition led her to expect great change as an inevitability coming her way. She didn't think about it often, but the feeling that there was a larger role for her to play of leadership—it hung around. After she met Peter, that spider sense tingled more strikingly. What course it ended up taking, she never could have predicted.

Even after what happened at the Canadian border, Maya was still not averse to using cannabis from time to time. *Can't allow fear to run my life or prevent me from doing what I feel is right.* To pretend her experiences of being high didn't have an effect would have been ridiculous. *Every experience feeds off of the previous one. There may be a payoff, a harsh comedown, but that's to be weighed against the positives…like anything else.* Her life encounters using this type of medicine mattered a lot. Sometimes just lying on the carpet of her living room, putting on some music, rolling around into different yoga postures; examining stuff like the legs of chairs and coffee tables was a totally awesome and powerful experience. Playing with her dog, Izzy, thinking about life, and making extremely intelligent connections that didn't have to be forced—she loved to do that. She used the time to grow in the ways that she wanted, not to escape from discomfort.

She took a deep inhale from her colorful pipe as she stepped into the park on this particular morning. She felt that cannabis was a useful tool to counteract all the years of brainwashing she had experienced within public education. *Making us forget how lucky we are and always feeling pressure to keep up with a phantom, which promotes endless deficiency—desiring acceptance so badly that we close our eyes to what we actually want. This medicine helps me truly get rid of it, and I am ever so thankful for its presence.* Considering the rapid increasing pressure being placed on the law, she was not the only one who felt this way. *The stuff fights cancer for crying out loud, and helps veterans experiencing PTSD! What further proof is needed that it has medicinal properties? The government bans research done on cannabis because it can't get out of the way of its own ego; and it's afraid to admit what it already knows. Wow is our judicial system in need of a course on 'M and J!'*

It's miraculous medicine that gives me hope, that's for sure…as long as it's not abused. But what isn't dangerous if you have too much of it? Very few things I think. It saddens me as much as anything—all those taking it too far…forgetting to love all varieties of the self.

However, you want to really identify what an addiction is…how about the addiction for trying to impress others?

Oh to be beyond that, she thought—*accept the inevitable and never-ending play that is always happening; liked, disliked, liked, disliked. Ah, so. Yes!*

She continued her day walking along a path surrounded by greenery, and fell into her typical spiritual routine. *Every day I need to find gratitude again. Feel it. Need to remember what's important…what I actually care about. Getting high isn't an escape. There isn't a more reality or a less reality… just different parts of the same game board to see.*

She took a seat in the middle of a large field of grass. *What am I aware of?* She looked at the people walking on the paths around her in their colorful gear, watched friends tossing a football, caught the agility of a squirrel jumping from branch to branch on a nearby tree. *I don't care about visual appearance or how others rank me. It doesn't mean I don't ever consider it, but 'care,' is too strong a word for those fleeting concerns over what I do not control.* She was growing stronger, shedding layers by the day—increasing her grit. *I do care about what I do with my time. I do care about using what I've been given to make things better for everyone. This is what's serious—this is what I want to spend my time thinking about. First step, untangling my personal self. Again and again and again. All the time. Back to the now—back to letting things be as they are. Watching time go by as an observer of acceptance. Being interested in what might happen.*

What's really the best part of religion, she asked herself suddenly as she found her mind taking a sharp left turn. After all, she had a purpose to the day. She could think about not only what others could, but also what no one else ever had before. She knew that. She felt blessed by her belief in her own individual uniqueness of thought. Not as better—but definitely unique.

Her mind was able to become so still that it infiltrated to the very core of subject matter. She had a great belief in her ability to unravel seemingly complicated entities and break them down into manageable pieces of organization. *All you have to do is think rationally, allow life experiences to guide you, and believe in your power of discovery. In the current age of self-suppression, most people don't have enough belief in their own individuality to think they could make a discovery that no one else has yet! That idea itself is detrimental to invention and to the progression of our species. The mentality that everything has already been thought of, because there are so many people and so many minds…that mentality leads to a feeling of helplessness, a feeling of deep insecurity and lethargy—a feeling of powerlessness. Most especially because it's so false. By allowing that thought to have merit, we strip away what we have to offer and turn ourselves into primordial beasts obsessed and worried about survival, and scraping by day-by-day. What does it matter if two or even twenty people make the same discovery? Does it make a good idea less worthwhile or brilliant?* She thought not. *Oh, the balance between being humble and grand. Who will teach us to walk that line? Someone had better.*

The answer that finally came to her about religion was so right and sweet that it made her smile broadly. As she sat there in the grass, focusing on flooding her body with feelings of gratitude—and as the sun rose higher into the sky, she thought…*Yes, this exactly! The best part of all religions is taking the time to pray! Every single one of them. Prayer, surrender. All the other nonsense piled on top has covered up the truth of what has been their treasure of substance throughout all these years! Take Judaism for example. One of the oldest religions. Perhaps what has allowed it to survive for so long is the fact that there is a blessing to be said for anything and everything. What a way to connect with gratitude!*

But that very idea can be plucked out and utilized in a more modern fashion. Just because I feel one aspect is brilliant, does not mean I have to become a follower of that book of law.

Prayer is a meditation, and it's also a chance to give thanks to the higher power of nature—to be grateful for our circumstance of being alive, not worried about surviving or controlling too much of life. Taking the time out of my day to say thank you, and to really mean it and feel it in my bones—is perhaps the most imperative factor in being happy and having a successful life. Religions nailed the human need for that.

Maya looked up at the sky. It was clear, with different shades of blues running throughout the entire spectrum. The sun shone down on her, and she basked in its energy. She stood up, moved around, stretched her limbs in varying directions that felt good. *There's nothing as valuable as this*, she thought. Then she set herself with a firm, clear goal: *take the practice of prayer from religion and use it with full knowledge of why it's important—not to pray in order to obey a set of commandments but with clear understanding that it will help us achieve happiness—which is what we all want. Part of the problem is that people don't realize or give much thought to the fact that their goal in life is to be happy. That needs changing too. If we remember this as a goal, our actions will be drastically reprioritized. We will feel the need to keep our souls at ease and our emotions in check. We have to see it as our responsibility. No work that brings income should ever overtake the duty of our happiness. Work is meaningless without that. Suffering does not lead to happiness at the end of it—nope not at all. That is one of the biggest lies of all time. Happiness is achieved by finding grace within the suffering—a different hue of happiness. Only then can we turn into the properly mature race of love that we are meant to manifest.*

What a successful trip to the park it was for her. She clearly saw how history was written in just these types of miniature moments of individual connection to the source. With all of this work done, and her thoughts clear; the religion of Futurism began to take form.

The question was; whether or not Life Code could be taken seriously enough without fear hanging over, ever present—with no sense of compulsion from threats of ramifications. It was the first great test to see if the power of reason could equal the power of fear.

It took some time for people to become aware of how strong they could simply decide to be. Eventually, with the help of Life Code—more and more moved into that place of increased freedom of the spirit—realizing how to foster their determination. Futurists would take out their LC's from their purse or back pocket and find a deep well of support in the form of words. Ideology could be extremely impactful, but a daily practice of positive action was even more so. That was where Core came in.

Simply, Core was a set of daily proclamations. The three guides were to be read when you woke up on the morning, at some point in the middle of the day, and before bed. Those were the rules if you were a practicing Futurist.

Core was set in stone, but Sub-core was continuously added to and modified. There were blank pages in the LC's, and Futurists were encouraged to create their own Sub-core as desired.

Although there weren't any divine ordinances, Futurists took great pride in seeing how deeply they could commit to their Core. In fact, it was clearly seen that if they had any chance of succeeding as a movement, they would have to honor their choices and devote themselves to some kind of united group effort. The tendencies of history were working against them; the reason of a better system and the access of modern technology was with them. The rapidly changing technological advances of the modern age had brought about a new field of play that only few could see. History did repeat itself, but things were also drastically different from ever before. Futurists were fed up with the status quo, used the advantages of the current times, and understood that if they were going to be the ones to alter the greater habits and direction of their species, it was going to be through their conviction and knowledge that risk and exposure were absolutely necessary. Without overcoming the aversion to risk, everything else was hot air.

Thankfully, rather quickly, becoming a Futurist became a trendy thing to be. That was appropriate as trends always seem to be the step required before participation from the masses takes hold. The difference between the progressive religion of Futurism, and many other movements of the past; was that substance and compassion were focal points. A good deal of pressure was put on friends, family, and coworkers to join. How that pressure manifested itself was up to the individual Futurist; but improvement and choice were what the messages contained. Many simply handed a friend a booklet of Life Code and invited them to read. Others sat down and explained about how having belief, and a system of freedom was so helpful to feeling better daily.

It was natural for people to want to share a transformative path of healing that worked for them. Overall, Futurists did not have to promote bringing others into the fold very much; people just did it, and came when they saw.

For most of course, that first step was the hardest, as skepticism toward new things was more pervasive in modern society than ever before. After all, everyone was being 'come onto' all the time. So many humanoids kept themselves in little bubbles of intimacy. To demean Futurism, these folks began throwing those ignorant stones of fear by spewing out vague word associations. "It's just another cult," was the most common ritual form of destruction." However, it was pretty laughable considering the entire premise was based on doing what each individual person felt to be right (even if that meant choosing not to be a Futurist). No cult or religion in history ever promoted that level of personalized freedom.

But so it goes with blind aversions. Opponents are often not reasonable with their attitudes; and therefore, not the ones to focus on. They were simply the ones that easily could swivel their gaze in any direction of destruction. They loved it.

Because the current gaze of culture promoted instant criticism of the unknown—they did as they were subversively told and tried to bring down Futurism as soon as it got too big for their liking. These people lived in an igloo of primarily things they had discovered as children, and cringed at the thought of lifting themselves out of the safety of their immaturity. They cared more about social standing and stigma, than they did rational action. They were the non-thinkers— the survivors.

Regardless, this time, they didn't come close to succeeding. Too many people began seeing the true power to train themselves in the ways of their choosing. So much work had already been done even before Futurism had begun—viral motivational videos, yoga, meditation, improved diets—much had been changing. Joking around in life was seen as well and fine, but for those that were ready to join something that could truly support—Futurism had targeted that which they had been waiting for. They engaged their time with a new path that made all too much sense. Self-critiquing had gotten too far out of hand, and it was time to rein it back (or at least alter its form) with the support of a new kind of community— a code which gave direction and allowed individuals to remember their 'regularness.'

Little booklets were made by the thousands and promoted through Maya and Peter's vast networks of exposure. They were not flimsy things, but glossy pages containing the meaningful words of Life Code, Core, and Sub-Core. They came in all different colors. The standard set of words was only six pages long. They were to be cherished—if chosen to be.

Life Code

1

Relax and set yourself at ease. Discard distractions and bring your full attention to reading these words. Close your eyes, take a breath, then lift your lids slowly to see a refreshed world from the masterpiece of your own cornea. Go ahead. Now you're ready.

2

Instead of having faith and confidence in the decisions that flow through me in a natural way, I can continue to chase this sickness of obsessing over the standing and worth of my personal being. Will I? That is the question.

Although I might sometimes fall back into my habits of the past, it is my goal to live a life of progression. I am different now. I move calmly and confidently through this mind-blowing journey, undoubting of my growth.

If I continue in constant worry over what I have to do and how I am perceived—allowing stress to dictate many of my actions; I will remain being what I have already been for far too much time—hurt, exhausted, and ill.

No more. The fact that so many have shared in this illness does not make it any less severe or harmful. This, I must fully realize— and then carve out some time to feeling appropriately sad about it. However, 'appropriate,' and 'some time,' are key words.

I do not know exactly how it came to be for us to exist amid a culture of such immature and shortsighted behavior. Regardless, I accept it as a part of our path. I will no longer deny the deep reality of how we follow. I will acknowledge the depth of the confusion toward taking truly individualized action.

Following blindly with the herd has turned the herd into a dangerous force of powerful mindlessness. A force with no direction, no purpose, and no real strategy. Having no strategy is perhaps the biggest cause for legitimate fear. I am not referring to the strategy of a country, I am referring to the strategy of the human race.

I become fully aware of truth in order to have resolve and strength. No more slipping by and getting through days. I seek to be honest concerning my own desires.

There is, in fact, a much better way; I can begin the process of healing myself—of allowing the vessel that I control to reach toward its potential. How? By existing deeply content in the stable realm of gratitude.

3

My religion's job is to empower me to see my life honestly and creatively—not to chisel away at my pride and belief in my own ability to draw rational conclusions. If I do not trust my own sense of what is true and real, what have I become—what is left of who I was born to be? The force of creation did not make us all different, so that we would aspire to be the same.

What I think, what I believe with certainty, should be held above all else—with steel assurance and constant affirmation. I do not mistake the things I only know halfway for certain truth—that habit is a manifestation of a sensitive ego. I am confident and honest—especially in my unknowing.

If there comes a time when I do not agree with these words, I will no longer say them. My words mean something to me.

Challenge and change will continue to be worked into my life, as they are both imperative to living successfully. I accept this fact and often seek out risky experiences with realistic safety. They help me to grow, and growth is my goal.

Any way I desire to be is acceptable as long as I do not intentionally harm others. In fact, giving love to others is the best thing I can do for myself. I know that—I remember all the time. My higher mind sees this as the main purpose of my life. Of course, in order to become better at helping others, I must make the being I find myself residing in as healthy as possible too. THAT is the secret balanced relationship between the self and the external world. We play off of each other, and both sides improve.

I am a soldier of the mind. My control extends as far as I believe.

As I move into my higher being, I see that there is no hesitation in my actions. The well intentioned are free to flow through decisions of life without pressure and with joy. If I allow it, if I accept myself—my entire life can be an experience of satisfaction and meditation. I can see each challenge as an opportunity for growth. I can do it. It's up to me. It's not too hard, but it does take practice and the holy kind of work. Work that is enjoyable.

4

Becoming what I believe takes forever and never ends. Knowing is not the same as believing…but it is close. I have already taken many of these steps. Now my work is focused on becoming and incorporating the wealth of knowledge that I have already accumulated into my actions.

The purpose of my spoken word is to help—not to play into games of inflating my status in the eyes of others. Before I speak, I ask myself; is it necessary, is it helpful, is it true? Most importantly—is it an improvement on silence?

It is not my business what others think of me. I am a regular type of human and have nothing to hide. I was constructed how I was constructed, and I am only here to appreciate and cultivate the creation of life that I was born into.

I choose again and again to be a soldier of happiness, of ease, and of love. A soldier, because a soldier is dedicated to their cause and understands the necessity for repetition. Happiness, ease and love—because these are my clear goals.

Life is amazing—I know that as truly as anything else. I am incredibly fortunate to be a human being moving my body about on this magical planet. For certain, I will fall out of this perspective of gratitude. Why? Because we are naturally beings in fluctuation. That is more than all right. I will simply be sure to come back often—knowing that the more I do, the more it will become a part of the substantial me.

5

Core:

- *I will never understand how lucky I am. I admit it. I operate first from this premise of truth. It's OK to say it. It's OK to know it. That is the best way to move closer in my work.*
- *I am never afraid to try my hardest, but I also acknowledge that there are a great many forces beyond my own determination. While trying, I give honor and respect to forces beyond me.*
- *Helping another is an opportunity to spend my time well. My intentions are directed toward making positive change in the world. Improvement is where purpose is found. I need purpose as much as I need water.*

6

Sub-core:

- *I listen to music and allow it to inspire. I dance often, as it is impossible to reach the highest planes of happiness without the glory of spontaneous movement.*
- *I focus on my breath, feeling the energy flowing through my body, and believing in its healing effects as it works its way into all my nooks and crannies. I take time to connect with my body and experience the power of that connection. I send energy of love, compassion and forgiveness outside to the world; and I have certain belief in its effectiveness.*
- *I use my mind to reflect. The process of reflection allows me to handle every situation better than I ever have before. It's my duty to reflect. I am not afraid of looking honestly at my own tendencies. I see my actions with limited ego and with the simple objective of improvement.*

CONSEQUENCES

Maya Sol set about accomplishing her goals like a technician. As the number of members grew, she became more fluent in the uses of available technology to help their cause. The influence that it had on their growth was extreme. Communication was key, and never before in history had so many imaginative resources been available. Twitter, Facebook, Instagram…the Futurism app, and their website itself. Modern technology allowed Futurism to be an ever-changing creation. It was both a religion and a technological entity in itself. New suggestions could be posted, discussions had, and even community voting took place.

Many of the experiences Futurists were having, were shared on the app. In this way, members had an arsenal at their disposal of things to say and do if they needed ideas. The Futurism app also had a tool that allowed members to create missions. You could complete the task yourself, asking for helpful suggestions—or you could offer it up as a mission for someone else. The app quickly became a network of purposeful help. With this support, more and more people began to realize that they had spent years convincing themselves of their own busyness, based on old crusty ambitions. They had not been taking the action they truly wanted, they were taking action that was the most easily measurable.

What they wanted to be doing with their time, was utilizing their brains to improve life in whatever ways imaginable. For almost everyone, the action they wanted to take most, was to help make improvements to systems they felt were under functioning. Futurism allowed participating humans to sharpen and focus these desires. Answering other Futurists call for help was extremely fulfilling activity for a Saturday or Sunday.

My neighbor, a mother of three, just lost her husband to cancer. She's in desperate need of direction. Can someone who has experience with loss help?

I work at a grocery store that is throwing away a third of its produce that is perfectly edible. Can someone find a proper procedure for getting the food to people who need it?

The help sometimes took on more complicated forms. The discussion boards on the app and website were vitally important to the sustainment of the movement.

Asking for a hand has become a lifestyle for my friend. I think the best way for us to help him is by not giving help. He needs to learn to do things for himself. Know of any strategies to make him see that he is capable of actually enjoying the process of taking on something new?

My mother feels that the world is against her and can do nothing but look at the negative. Her whole life is one big pity party; but it's not a whole lot of fun. She won't listen to anyone. She stays inside and doesn't let people in. She's been hurt too much and doubts her strength. I'm thinking that maybe an external force might have better success than someone close to her? Anyone willing to take a crack at it? Make a new friend? Have an experience?

It was finally becoming clear that quality individuals had allowed psychos (those among them who were most confused) to have a great effect on their behavior. Ideas such as "Maybe I shouldn't meet this person I don't know—he or she could be dangerous," decidedly had to be suppressed. It was time humans moved themselves beyond fear in order to accomplish what needed to be done. Instead, Futurists addressed the fear by asking sensible questions; "Doesn't having a cellular device allow for much greater safety than previous generations ever had before? What kind of risks did my grandparents have to take? They got on ships and sailed away to unknown lands. What am I capable of with the tools at my disposal? Should I not be able to do my part in helping the world improve? Am I really going to let fear and fitting in stop me?"

If there were people needing help, the fear of one's own being (if the risk was truly minimal) could not be allowed to supersede taking rational action. That was the stronghold of belief. The idea of taking necessary chances began to be encouraged and embraced in the community of Futurists. If a situation truly was deemed "dangerous," most likely another Futurist in the area would gladly lend a hand to accomplish the task, or it wouldn't be done at all. In a big way, everyone needed permission to chill out about their own choices. This structure gave them the community to do it in.

In the course of a year, the movement grew to places all over of the planet. This included those that were war- and poverty-stricken. Even in areas where people had far less—the push toward seeing beauty in life and lending help, to help the self; could still be promoted. They too were fed up with the affliction of focusing completely on external factors to support a quality outlook. Soon after food and shelter, it was freedom of the mind that people most sincerely yearned for—even if they had never realized it before.

Overall, Futurism was a sharp needle that popped an expanding balloon of nonsense that had been building up for a very long while. When it finally exploded, energy and action came pouring out.

Like those belonging to most other religions, Futurists felt an allegiance toward one another. That was to be expected—but more importantly, as a result of being Futurist, they felt more of an allegiance toward their species as a whole.

Perhaps one of the most defining qualities regarding the success of the movement was how many wealthy people were brought into the fold and redirected. They contributed their valuable resource of money. They too were thirsty for purpose and meaning beyond the game of acquiring more and more materials; and many jumped on board when given the right opportunity. They realized what they were searching for could be much better attained by tapping into their own creative capacities. By asking, "What is my heart's truest desire?" they took the time to allow their hearts to speak, and they began to see that acquiring greater social standing wasn't really all it was cracked up to be—that it failed to attain the more permanent forms of happiness. Evidence of this could be seen everywhere; on television, in the news, out in public—wealthy people as sad, immature and stressed out as anyone else. It was the masses that believed if only they could reach those sought after rungs of power and attention; everything would be different. It wouldn't. As a result of nonsensical envy, people failed to see that the wealthy were in deep despair. They were told, and believed, that money was the goal of their lives and the path of success. Their addiction to acquirement was as serious as any; and the fleeting gratification it gave them toyed with their mental sanity. With money and power, they were more prone to cling on to the hope of harnessing the reins of life. With the ability to purchase a plethora of things, it was slightly more believable—slightly; but just as fraudulent. Sickness, for example, did not have an opinion on wealth.

The lies that the wealthy were living with ate away at their core little by little until they turned into the monsters that they feared to become. When the reality of life's inexplicable nature smashed them in the face (as it can do to everyone), they were far less equipped to stand firm and emotionally handle these situations. They complained and whined about life not being fair when disaster struck, and their lack of understanding was a sharp stone of pain piercing their protective coating of greedy and senseless behavior. They were not philosophically grounded. They had become weak from overvaluing the power of materials and undervaluing the power of giving. Futurism was for them too.

Action...action is key; Maya had identified as being foundational from the start. Any Futurist could post something that interested them, and others who felt similarly could combine efforts. A popular form of effort was simply to go out and promote their message of importance. Futurists set themselves upon the cities of the world in swarming hordes of positive energy. With them they displayed, and snatched for themselves, the greatest symbol of all time: on signs, shirts, and even painted on their faces—they bravely displayed the two humps and singular downward point of a heart. There was also the Flame of Futurism—unique in its structure of two 'F's' linked together.

Still, many who experienced this activity in the streets resented it. It pressed extremely sensitive buttons and lifted them out of the cocoons of their typically structured days they had decided were as satisfying as life could ever be. But it also made them think, and that was the whole point—and the importance of the tasks. With words, and simple conversation, they were forced to face the reality of their own melodrama. They saw well-dressed people, similar to themselves, with symbols of love, purposefully being vulnerable and outspoken.

"Do you know how lucky you are? Nope, guess not. You look pretty stressed out to me. Hug? We're in this together brother."

"Are you being thankful today? You know you're living in a paradise, right?"

"No more messing around. Grow up already. Enough of your childish nonsense. It's about *you*, not *them*."

It took a brave Futurist to say something like that. It tended to really piss people off. Still, maybe it was worth it. It was up to each Futurist to decide which words were appropriate for the person presented before them. The hierarchy of leadership was barely visible. Futurists were only encouraged to say what they felt.

They put themselves in teams for everything. The ability to organize faster and more efficiently helped build an increasing storm of momentum. Some teams went around asking, "Can I help?" and prowled the streets doing good deeds. Other teams danced in groups on corners, or shook strangers' hands, and offered to give hugs. Most importantly, they looked people in the eye and smiled, made connections, and weren't afraid to stand outside and see what would happen. They asked how others were doing and meant it. They went out and were the change. They were doing the work that had to be done in the world.

Some instances people tried to take advantage of them; but those occurrences were rare as Futurists stayed in groups, and if ever were in a quandary—voted with a simple round of rock-paper-scissors.

Most of all, these were awesome individuals. Futurists were the kind of people (if you were like them), that you wanted to hang out with. They attempted to help each other along the path of self-acceptance and saw this as the most substantial work. Along with their colorful hearts, Futurists also used a single word to signify something larger that no one really understood completely (which was perhaps the point). It was a word taken from Frank Herbert in his masterful book series 'Dune.' The word, *siaynoq*, could be described simply as— "honor and remembrance to spoken sincerity."

And that was it. That was all of it. It was time to put away the bullshit and start being sincere.

What Futurists had sincerely intellectualized and transformed— was the truth about trading. Trading good deeds that seemed one sided made as much sense as trades of instant gratification. Futurists realized that they didn't need to know right away how they were being rewarded. Simply by creating a world of more helpful action, they were doing the best thing they possibly could for themselves; in order to promote a healthier environment in which they were a part. It wasn't too much to think about it. The truth was right there if one took the time to grasp it. No matter how much they impacted someone else, their actions were totally selfish—and they never claimed otherwise. They trusted that their rewards would come back, and then they watched as it happened. Futurists took helpful actions instead of having long meals, instead of going to ball games and watching movies. They did those things too; they just also spent time practicing their new religion.

Going into public and meeting other Futurists and strangers, was what many parents began doing with their children. It was important for them to show their offspring that it didn't make sense to hide from strangers, and that often interactions with strangers were as entertaining as any other activity. They also told them that they were a part of everything and therefore had to go out and make things better. The children understood and loved engaging it. It wasn't folky or idealistic. It was very clever.

As many other religions had done over the years, communities used each other as support to quell their fear of awkwardness in not following traditional social norms. They didn't give in to the mockery in the media over trying to create a utopia (a cause that was bound to fail of course). They weren't trying to create anything specifically— just taking the suffering of the world seriously and then doing their part within this span of life. They were finding purpose by taking on bites of their own choosing. Very sensible. There was no pressure— softness was key.

With time and continuous growth, the number of people who doubted Futurism as sustainable began slowly subsiding. It seemed to be the right time in history for breaking through with something of this nature. People were waiting. Like any other movement, the more people envisioned victory to be possible, the more contagious the following became. This was exactly what so many wanted and had hoped for—even if they hadn't realized it. If they were being honest, the collective consciousness was only afraid of being let down yet again. How many times had they tasted hope, only to have it crumble under the weight and influence of the confused pessimists? Not this time.

DOUBT

O h how people clung so tightly to their fistfuls of coolness. The opposition was ever present. But something was different this time. What? At the disposal of Futurists was an understanding of what doubt itself actually was. One day, Peter posted on the homepage of the website words that never left:

Doubt is death. As soon as you doubt the possibility of something, you take away from its potential to be created. You have in fact become the very force that will contribute to the destruction of its possibility instead. Question; but never stop supporting what you feel is a reasonable desire for an outcome.

This time around, doubt was not to be underplayed in its true function as a disease. It was a pull toward pessimism—toward the act of settling. Doubt was a load of hogwash. No one secure enough to understand their limitations held any delusions in regard to knowing what may or may not come next.

Mikey Clark didn't know either. He was at a rally one day in St. Louis. He'd been to so many before. His idea of being a good Futurist was going to all the major functions across the country, and lending whatever kind of support he could. He wanted to feel the pulse of what was happening on the front lines.

All the while opponents would come to their gatherings and create a new kind of get together for both sides. It was so funny to think about it—*two groups of humans playing at being angry with each other,* he realized one day. *Who the hell decides, "This is what I'm going to do today— I'm going to go try and prove some points; convince some people who feel the exact opposite as me."*

But that's just what I'm doing too, he admitted to himself. *And I like it. I'm not going to stop.*

Well, he thought, in accepting the surrender of his instincts—*at least I should really prove my point well, shouldn't I? OK then…what's the truest point I want to make?*

What he chose to do, was use his own demeanor to show the worth of Futurism. He couldn't think of anything better to do; rather than to simply be the best example of his own particular form.

He chose to go right into the fire in order to achieve it. And it worked. He had been experiencing more success in the past four months than the two previous years combined. What did he do? He crossed the lines. He decided to stand or wander into different places within the oppositional forces. He wore a shirt with the Futurism flame displayed proudly over his left chest muscle. The back said in bold large letters: "BEWARE OF CHILDREN OVER THE AGE OF THIRTY."

Mikey let them talk to him, to yell—he embraced the feelings that came when the words were poured on; but he made a vow to never argue back. *Notice when the level from below tries to pull you down with its ego attacking shark bites.* It was the point of the whole challenge to him. *Don't use words of debate. That isn't the reason for your action. Barely use words at all. And if you do…make them helpful and powerful. Make them an improvement on silence.*

So he would listen and look at those who despised Futurism with the greatest amount of genuine openness they'd ever seen in their lives. In many cases, he was the only person these people ever saw who didn't want something from them. Mikey was just there—palms open and completely exposed as he moved or stood still within the crowd. He looked, he tried to understand, he harnessed his intuition.

What Mike was doing wasn't phony. He accepted himself so deeply that he opened his heart to facing fear. It allowed him the strength to wipe spit off his face and then ask the mucus launcher for a hug. He challenged himself *that* far. Even if this person turned around and walked away; those who were around saw—and it affected them. How could it not? Don't we all have the ability to acknowledge true human majesty of control when we see it?

Often the opposition were Christian fundamentalists who opposed Futurism in the largest numbers. But Mike also found it was the easiest to connect with them. They usually saw right away. Most of the time the encounters ended with nods and handshakes. It was a result of the work he had done personally. It was the look on his face that wasn't possible to fake. *Any emotion can be reasonably masked besides love*, he discovered. His features were stoically present with a thirst to simply connect in a place where connections are the most difficult to be made. It was a way for him to do his work. *I just need to look them in the eye while I manifest true vulnerability,* he told himself.

His reputation had grown, and today there was a man in the crowd who had heard a story. The tale was about a silent Futurist effecting one of the faith so profoundly that it caused them to turn their back on Christ.

Jesus had given so much to this lonely man in the crowd. He had been destroying himself for many years, until he had been saved. As soon as he heard the story, he knew instantly that this Futurist was the devil—and that it was his duty to remove this manifestation of Satan from the Earth. He knew that Satan would always come back, but he also knew that it was the path of believers to continually throw him back down to Hell where he belonged. He convinced himself it was his personal responsibility to play this major role on the path toward the second coming of resurrection. *Carrying no weapons and using intoxicating words is exactly the sort of thing the devil would do,* he thought.

There was no possibility that this man could accept Futurism as a harbinger of change. For him, his change had already happened.

There was no openness to new paths of transformation; his path had been found—and it was a great tunnel of distraction.

So he went up to Mike Clark, and stabbed him with a large hunting knife. It wasn't a group attack, or a shot from a gun. It was the fluid motion of pulling a knife and stabbing a thing which made you feel so uncomfortable. After all, immature and un-prioritized mental delusions can cause humans to act extremely impulsively. The weight of the mental conflict and frustration with lacking control, caused one person on one day to forget that no God of creation would ever desire the irrational action of murdering a stranger.

Mikey died right there on the spot, and the crowd of vehement anti-Futurists surrounding the scene grabbed this murderer—held him down; and gave him to the authorities. In those last few moments of life, Mikey looked up at all the strangers trying to help him from the cool concrete surface of a crowded parking lot. He held his belly and then gently allowed his arms to fall off to the sides. He spoke the most aggressive words he'd used so far during his experiences across the lines:

"Stop focusing on your differences," he told them. "I can love you too if I want."

Mikey had known that what did happen, could. If he hadn't seen that possibility; he would never have been able to do what he did. He had no desire for it, but also felt that if he was to go down, that this was exactly the type of sign he'd want to leave. He hoped that his story would be told—one of full commitment toward taking passionate and reasonable risks. If other people chose to take advantage of his display of vulnerability…*well that was their problem*. He just hoped that if his time was up; the memory of his actions would ignite further changes in the right direction.

Mike Clark was the embodiment of the 'peaceful soldier.' *Soldiers die*, was the last thought he had. It gave him strength in the passing. *But, we all do.*

The truer truth is that the whole drama really didn't have anything to do with a battle of religious beliefs. This man who took the action of murder actually loved the story of what Mike Clark was doing. In different circumstances, they could have made an impressive team of heroic brothers. The man wished for the power to spend his day walking up to others and proving to them how good Jesus made him feel. But he hadn't manifested the idea himself, so he turned it around—called it the devil's game; and decided to hate instead. The difference between unification and animosity seems to often rest on quite the precarious edge.

A MIDDLE STEP

Maya had never given a speech to half this many people before. She stood with Peter and a few others in the Columbia University library behind the podium waiting patiently. Her parents and grandmother came to support this moment of her exposed leadership. Seeing Juliet gave Maya feelings of both pride and nervousness. Although she was fully conscious of her adulthood, Maya still felt a slight childlike urge to impress her family. She couldn't deny that. But she settled herself down with mental tools of grounding.

Being nervous just means that I care. It's natural to return to childish ways around people who have given you so much time and love I think. Use the nervousness Maya. Sit with it and allow it to heighten the present moment.

An audience of thousands flowed out sideways like a liquid onto the streets of Broadway and Amsterdam to either side of the monstrous campus; they waited for her beyond the doors. They stood packed into every crevice of the bizarre roman-like layout; filled with statues, different levels of concrete creativity, and patches of greenery.

Even more important than the number in attendance, however, was the fact that her speech was being broadcast to anyone with access to the Internet or a television. Much to their discomfort, the networks which claimed to facilitate 'the news,' had no choice but to bustle their way in with their cameras and their 'objectivist new coverage.'

Maya looked down at the cold glass of water in her hand and considered how it must have felt for Mikey to pass on. They were all still dealing with the tragedy of his unexpected death. She noticed the beads of condensation on the sides and the round shape of the bottom of the glass. *It's amazing how the mind can jump so easily from one thing to the next.* She looked at her hand and inspected the features that allowed it to mold itself to grasping almost any object. She was being in her body. *What I do today is dedicated to you Mike. Give me some of your strength please. It's not easy what we're doing.* She took one more sip and watched her arm move to place the glass ever so gently in the center of a coaster on the brown coffee table before her.

The prep room she was standing in felt slightly odd. There were racks of coats surround this ordinary set up of furniture. She smiled thinking that it was somehow perfect. Then she turned, opened—stepped out of the door, and up to the microphone waiting for her at the top of the marble stairs. She took a moment to gaze out into the beautiful crowd of faces—allowing her eyes to open up to the light. Below her were ancient stone steps that made their way about fifteen feet or so down to the main grass field. She saw that it was currently brewing with a great many colorful humans. Blue blazing hearts and yellow flames were proudly displayed everywhere. She was not above everyone else. To her sides were higher levels also filled with spectators, as well as a great many people standing from the balconies of the surrounding buildings. Their height seemed to hold the space below in a sort of motherly nest.

Maya lifted her gaze to look up above even all of that. She acknowledged the power of the sun as she tried to often do, giving her life as well as composure. It was early August, her favorite time of year. They had been working hard to set up this event for more than three months now. She looked out at the three separate monitors displaying the beginnings of the words she and Peter had knitted together. She was focused. To her, this was too important not to fully give it her all. *Don't hesitate*, she told herself. *Go.*

So she plunged forward in true form—parting her lips and beginning what would become widely referred to as... 'Maya's Future Speech.'

"The future of humans," she began and then stopped. "Let's take the time to consider it. It isn't as hard as you might think to create some logical hypothesis and propositions regarding the future of our planet. But to do it, we need to make sure we have two things settled—and both of these entities exist within our minds. The first thing we need, is a belief that the strength of love will eventually outweigh everything else. Without this belief, know that you are already far behind logical perception, and cannot make any kind of worthwhile prediction." She waited a moment for the harshness of her words to subside. "The second thing is faith. Faith that in the end, no matter how long it takes—humans will eventually turn toward doing what is logical.

"These two factors, which are closely linked—combine to allow us to set off imagining, and therefore creating; an even better future." The crowd erupted, and she was taken back by the noise. Never before in her life had she experienced anything like the current sensations within her body. *The desire to be validated goes deep,* she quickly thought to herself. Then she settled down.

"You see, what we decide to imagine, has a tremendous effect on the direction that we'll end up going. Can you see that, and can you believe it?"

She paused. Swallowed, then said with a still feminine, yet slightly deeper voice: "In the future we will be radiating beings of understanding and love. We will train ourselves to be far stronger mentally, far more appreciative—than we are now. This will happen, and it's important for us to stop doubting it, or thinking that the words are some lofty, unrealistic fairytale. At some point, it will be a common well known practice to admit that our minds are our best asset. It's already happening. This is important, because with that assurance, we will embrace the process of training them toward a fuller degree of use.

She then waited patiently as a good orator will do. Most Futurists already knew these things, but hearing her say them was nonetheless invigorating. Plus, like any other mass of people, the group fed off of its own energy. Then she stepped back into her flow. Unlike many other crowds, this one subsided their cheering in a fraction of an instant. They knew what it meant to listen—what it meant to allow a speaker to determine their own rhythms.

"Avoidance is not the same as 'presentness.' Avoidance is fine, and necessary much of the time—but it isn't the same as feeling the need for nothing. Everything changes second by second. Therefore, we must fully acknowledge the good seconds. They go away before we've realized that they've left."

"The next step in our evolution is to take our collection of experiences and value them more highly than our collection of material objects, titles, and certifications. Experiences can be very, very simple—yet amazingly satisfying due to our ability to enter into the moment. Experiences of letting go of the self, enough to feel. Experiences of giving, of helping a stranger. Experiences of sitting outside on a beautiful day and taking it in. These will be prized and seen as opportunities for growth—not as sacrifice. No more sacrifice! In our future, sacrifice will finally be unveiled for the myth that it is. There is no such thing. There is only a mentality that eats away at our souls by confusing our direction. Experiences of help, have great personal value to be taken. People of the future will not feel guilty for feasting upon them. Many of us have already begun to follow this practice beautifully." She stopped again to focus on her inner ear and listen to sound. Sounds of the wind, sounds of the street, sounds of the hands and the voices. The microphone boomed as she joined them with her own.

"In the future we will train our minds not to worry in the same ways as we do now. We will come to accept and embrace the tremendous and unpredictable forces of life and nature. We will even be better at celebrating death. Much better. We will have more faith in ourselves and more appreciation for the times in which we are living. We will be humble concerning our abilities to distinguish right from wrong. We will do our best, knowing that often the best of intentions can still lead to disaster. This is what the mature adult knows; life—filled with uncertainty at its foundational core. Still, there is no other choice but to go forward with our best intentions, and most sincere motivations.

"In the future, we will see hardship as an opportunity to reach new levels of growth. We will constantly remind ourselves that we are often mistaken in knowing what our path should look like. You don't believe it? It's true. We will be far more accepting of all our experiences—for one reason and one reason only: because they happened. This does nothing to prevent us from trying to make what has yet to come as positive as possible; we should do that. But Futurists quickly put the past where it appropriately belongs—in the past. With no anger, and not much longing for it to have been any different. That terrible learned habit of judging what we think we deserve—it disrespects all we've been given.

Giving a speech was art. It was making music. Maya knew that. She chose her moments—allowed the universe to determine her pace and pitch of voice as she moved along through it.

"Powerful forces of fear and guilt will finally be acknowledged and understood in the future. They will be counteracted and attacked with a force equally strong, if not much stronger—the force of gratitude. It is in the absence of gratitude that we truly have reason to feel ashamed. Does it really make sense to convince yourself that you are a weak animal with nothing to offer? Does it make sense to spend our time obsessing over ourselves, our appearances, and our personal lives? Does it make sense to try to be the best in a game where no one cares or keeps score? No, future humans will not operate themselves in such fashion. They will acknowledge the work needing to be done in order to wean themselves off of their own spoiled behavior. That kind of unending pressure—those things we tell ourselves about how good we are—they're not the truth. They're taking away from our time with gratitude."

She paused again, found another glass of water on the front edge of the podium, and took one nice big gulp. She smiled at the absurdity of the position she now found herself living in. She looked in front of her. Eyes were wide; people were paying attention. She had now passionately worked herself up into a healthy state of 'not giving a fuck,' and was eager to jump back in. As a result, she felt herself obtaining a higher level of mastery over her own words and tone. She was allowing it to be more fun, and that was what she wanted most. *Fun and importance at the same time...what better combination is there?*

"Freedom," she said and stopped with a jolt. "Let's be honest. We sort of have it now—some of us more than others, don't we? But, in the future, there will be much more freedom for all of us. Loads more.

"Now you really laugh. But I'll tell you why. Because more freedom is the only practical way for us to continue living together—for us to evolve into something better; for us to even insure our survival. It's the only way. There may be many disasters ahead of us before we figure that one out—but I hope we can do it without them. It is only through personal choice that we can be brought together. In the future, laws will be changed, and people will be much freer to do what they wish with their time. Humans will acknowledge the right each person has to make choices for their own body. It will be accepted that there is no other way to better live in a community, but to extend the cord of safe choice—out as far as possible. We cannot ask for freedom ourselves and then deny it to our neighbors because they make different life decisions than we do. Instead, we must believe in the philosophical concept of freedom more strongly than in the rest of our opinions. We can encourage, we can argue, we can try to sway; but we can't use force—and we can't use the law as a means of using secondary methods of physical might to enforce our opinions of lessor importance." *Whoosh...that was a lot to get out.* "That is, with the exception of physical harm being done from someone onto others. Then, and only then, will the future population step in with the might of government. Punch holes in this theory if you like, but there is no stronger foundation of logic." *They'll argue later on in order to defend the abhorred status quo—and therefore distract us from the necessary changes needed to be made. I know that. Can't be avoided I guess. My only hope is for enough people to see through this silly game of nitpicking that sucks our focus away from the real concepts that matter. The game of destroying new ideas to maintain the comfort of the known.*

With these thoughts in mind, Maya decided to pull away from her scripted speech. She had told the teleprompter operator that she might do this, and he paused the words on the screen for her to return to later.

"There are far too many of us who have taken on the mentality of trying to plug up the holes of a sinking ship that we are on—trying to live in the past for as long as possible." She spoke these words from a place of real feeling. "These people have already damned our future within their own mind; they have lost faith. They've allowed their intellectual pride to supersede the acknowledgement of their limited sight. They don't realize that our only choice is to be constantly constructing a new ship, not maintaining a broken one that is eventually destined to go under. The past wasn't better. It was just different. A new ship is the only way—a ship built with the energy of faith itself. If we lose faith, everything crashes down into the abyss of fear based action. Instead, we have mature faith which is in tune with the nature of existence—in tune with how it must be. Our faith will be attacked. But even when it is, can we still see reasons?"

Closed eyes and deep breaths are key. Don't forget to take them, she told herself as she did so. Then she moved back into orating her scripted lines.

"I'd like to take a few moments to talk about something that many are averse to discussing. It is, indeed; appropriately sensitive. I'd like to talk about parenting. The most vital responsibility any of us can choose to take on is demonstrating a good example of human behavior to a youngling with vast horizons—as parents or as teachers. The concept of freedom is as important to successful guidance as anything else. In the future, parents will have a much improved understanding of this—before making the choice to foster another human's creation within their belly. Again, how we did things in the past is accepted; but great improvements can be made going forward.

"While guiding, a parent must allow and accept the reality that their children are in fact—not in their control. This is simply the nature of the circumstance. That said, within each of us is the potential to take both wise and unwise actions. The right influences can make all the difference. Guiding is art; and forceful proselytizing is lazy. Future humans will teach their children to stop putting unrealistic pressure on themselves. Our children will be more OK with not catching every joke, and every word of every conversation. They will give their minds peace by allowing them to take what they will from being in any experience and leaving it simply at that. They will be smart enough to accept that some days we are sharper than others—that we are creatures in constant motion and change—and that we must embrace and hold on to the best moments when they come. Future parents will be much better at improvising. There is something to be said for having plans, making them tight, and then doing something else completely different. Our children yearn to see us do this—to embrace the spontaneous energy of our levity. Not all the time—but once in a while. The rarity of it, is what makes it special.

"But to allow yourself? It's something that few adults, especially with children, are able to do in a healthy way. We take our lives too seriously, and it is disrespectful. The children; they know it."

Maya Sol took a short deep breath and blinked twice. She readied herself for a strong ending.

"We keep it secret," she continued calmly. "How crazy we are— the things that we do and the stuff that we think about. If we were sane, first we'd learn that nothing needs holding back—that there isn't a right or wrong way; just the guesses we take in any direction. If we acknowledged that, we'd all be a hell of a lot more thankful and secure. It's become far too socially acceptable to bitch, to worry in our minds—to move so fast that we can't keep up with all the things we're doing. Together, we must consciously support each other to change that.

"My friends, believe that good change is coming our way. Difficult, but also good. Only when we stop to clear our minds do we see that these changes can only occur inside; inside each one of our own personal vessels. Again, not lofty—very real. If we are truly committed to improving our beings, then we will start by giving ourselves the right kind of rest, the right kind of exercise, and the right kind of personal acceptance. These groups, labels, and divisions we have created will not suit our future selves. They were created out of fear and were perhaps necessary for generations past—no longer. Can you not see that your best friend could just as easily have different color skin, speak another tongue, and belong to a group you consider to be your adversary? There are both assholes and awesome people in every single race, country, religion, age and gender. I promise you. I'd love it if we started wearing T-shirts that said: 'Don't generalize. It's pointless. Think about yourself instead.' In all the ways that we can combat prejudice—this is most effective. By acknowledging how senseless the entire platform of discourse is.

"When you're immersed in the fog; you can't see anything else. As a result of maintaining such unhealthy places of being, many remain fearful and emotionally underdeveloped. Insecurity disallows for seeing the actual person standing in front of you. Instead, it's easier to categorize groups of people—that way we don't have to bother with really being present. It might be easier; but it's also a way of the past.

"Truth: we are all part of the same species that inhabits this planet. We are much more similar than we are different. Look at others and see so much of the same that's within you. Living in peace and trying to improve the world is logical. How do we do it? That is the question. The answers are found with patience and logic—not anger, hate, or a need to make overarching judgments that might be true a certain percentage of the time. Be silent, or come up with something better to say. Even if there is some truth in labels, it is not worth our time to discuss them. As long as there is one person within a group that breaks the mold of your generalization, you must accept that you have been unfair to them. You have made their life unnecessarily more difficult by perpetuating a falsehood. You have become the obstacle to this individual's ability to get a fair shake. You would complain if it happened to you.

"Breathe in the air that gives you life—acknowledge that you're a small part of something much larger. Do not disrespect those who cannot move by taking the wonders of your own body for granted. Often those who are terribly sick and dying have insight into the travesty of not finding time for appreciation. At the end, they finally see how much of their lives were wasted on worrying about nothing. The place of acceptance they finally come to is so sweet and pure that they're able to let go of what they are without. You'd give up all the materials in your procession if you only could experience the bliss within their mind for a flash an instant. It would teach you for a lifetime. Can we learn without losing it all? That's the question I'm interested in. How amazing, what an honor it would be to those with less; if we harnessed the magic of perspective. If we improved our ways on our own—now; without the harshness of despair. Simply because it was smart to do so. What if we fell in love with the process of change—of looking and observing our tendencies without the distracting forms of judgment? What if we were simply curious observers who practiced stopping ourselves when we dropped into lesser ways of being to notice and therefore to shift? What if we knew that kindness to the self was our way up? The present always tries to pull us back—what if we allowed it to?

"It is hard to take the first steps. It's hard to go there on your own. Having a structure is essential, and so is having belief. That is the point of our newly formed religion for all. These are the ways of a Futurist—to be taken and utilized if you want; if you choose. No one is telling you to do anything. There is only an invitation that you can feel blessed to receive. There's a part of me that wishes religion wasn't necessary; but it is—just not the kinds we've had.

"In the end, love and gratitude—like a body of water growing in strength—will eventually break through the dam of fear. This is the flow of humankind, and it cannot be stopped. Why? Because it's the most logical conception that exists in the entire multiverse—that's why. Because it's what we're meant to do. You can join this flow now or wait until it sweeps over and past you. Rest assured, love is coming for you no matter what. Thank you."

With that, Maya turned around and walked back into the room with all the coats.

ALTERNATIVES

David sat looking out the window in his room. He was now forced to concede that this nursing home would be the final residence of his life. *This will be my last bedroom,* he realized.

He sat in his familiar chair with wheels attached to it. He had been wheeling himself about this expansive building going on three years now. David had just returned from the common room where the other old frail humans in his community spent most of their time. He sat there watching television with them often, but nothing had ever been on that screen of projected images like the content he witnessed today.

A single woman giving a speech said things that I've never heard anyone say before, in a way that people just don't say them. At least not during the course of my life.

What was happening? He wasn't sure, but something that he hoped he'd be around long enough to see more of.

As soon as this lady had finished speaking, and stepped away from the podium, David felt like he had been punched hard in his gut. In that moment, he thought that he might throw up—he quickly carted himself back to his room. After staring at the toilet for a good twenty minutes, he finally gave up and hoped the feeling wouldn't return.

Currently, he sat looking out onto a small patch of grass with two miniature pine trees on the far end of the green rectangle; directly on the other side of his window. In the middle of the grass was a set—small brown metal table, four brown metal chairs surrounding. In all his time viewing the space, he had only seen anyone sit at that table once before—even though it was quickly and easily accessible to all the residents. He looked out of his window onto that same scene every day—those empty chairs. They seemed to him to be somehow significantly sad—unused.

In this current moment, however, what he was seeing didn't quite look the same as usual. It was hard for him to describe the change to himself. *The objects seem to be shimmering with an expression that they don't normally give off. Curious.*

Typical days for David Keegan were fraught with a myriad of painful sensations. Getting from the bed to his wheelchair was the most common challenge—but not a simple one. In order to do so, he had to sit up in bed (already a great feat), grab one arm of the chair, lock the wheels, and push off from the dresser using his other hand with all the strength he could muster. He would stand for a moment, praying for his wobbly legs not to crumble under his weight—then quickly swing himself onto the seat. But it still wasn't over. Then he had to attempt to lift his bottom again and try to adjust his pants to some sort of normalcy. This was his reality. His waist itself was an elusive beast, and no pair of pants ever fit him properly.

Most days he couldn't control his bladder. Sometimes going to the bathroom was more painful or more difficult than he could bear. Usually he just let it out into his adult diaper, and sat with it for long periods of time. In order to combat the problem, he took only a few sips of water daily, so that his mouth was dry and he was constantly dehydrated.

That David spent the majority of his days in bed was no small wonder. He felt that many of his body parts weren't even in their proper places, let alone able to function as they needed to. He wondered how he had possibly lasted this long, in this way.

Needing another person to clean his own waste was something he had not come close to being prepared for. *It really is true that a person returns to being as helpless as a baby if they grow old enough. The only difference (and it's a big one) is that I've had the experience of being independent. That experience matters.*

It was no exaggeration to say that he was ready for it all to be over. *Can anyone really blame me? Not until they've lived in this diaper,* I think.

Sometimes he would lay in bed listening to his lips repeating the phrase over and over: "I want to die, I want to die, I..." He'd wait a moment; "WANT—TO—DIE." The nursing staff didn't seem to care very much when they heard him. Assisting him with his request wasn't an option for them. Overall, they didn't know what to do; so they did nothing. They'd pester him about suicide protocol, until he took back his words, and said that of course he wanted to live. *Playing the crazy forgetful role always seems to work. What a silly game.*

David had been a successful man in his younger years, or so he always believed. He was an accountant for the state and had even testified before the Supreme Court once. He was admired by his peers and often sought out for help and advice to solve larger problems. He had a beautiful loving wife who took her job of caring for him very seriously. He had an extensive social network of friends, along with positions on boards and councils. He had been able to retire early and had a pension that allowed for a very comfortable lifestyle into his later years. He had grandchildren whom he was able to help raise. He knew countless facts and a wealth of history—had plenty of talents and hobbies. David was a good boy and did all the things he was supposed to. But that had been before—in that old life. None of it changed the reality he was experiencing in the present. He now felt he was locked in a small cage of cruel helplessness. Most of the nurses hated their jobs and used any chance they could to ignore what needed being done. He'd press his buzzer that was supposed to bring someone—often no one came.

The home had one or two social games offered throughout the day—usually one of them was bingo. He hated bingo. "No skill, limited fun," he'd say.

The food that came out of the kitchen was some of the worst he'd had in his life—and he had served in the second half of the Great War. He didn't know much about nutrition but had a sneaking feeling that a diet composed mainly of sugar and carbohydrates was not optimal for elderly persons experiencing so many bodily challenges. *And they say we're advanced medically?*

He had begun to question whether perhaps he had somehow failed in his life and deserved this sort of ending—*a horrible one*. What other sense could he make? There was no way he could spin it that felt right. Shouldn't he at least be granted quality substance to ingest at the very end? *Where did I go wrong?*

Again, in the moment of this day however, everything seemed to be flipped over on its head. Not just the look of his outdoor setting, but his feelings as well. Right now, his mind was active with a deeper kind of thinking—the kind he yearned for and hadn't experienced in so many years. *I still have my mind. What that lady said…it's true. I can't deny it any longer. In my ninety-four years, I haven't heard anything like it. She said all the things I've been trying to say for so long. I couldn't put the pieces together, take the time, or find the strength. The best I had were a few bursts of clarity that were almost immediately snuffed out shortly after experiencing them. Why didn't I hold on to those? Why was it so difficult to be the way I truly wanted? Perhaps it has something to do with what being a man meant to me? We're supposed to accept the game and thrive at it…not complain about the rules. Our deeper thoughts are not supposed to be shared. A man's emotions are meant to be held in check in order to provide the image of a deceptively hard exterior. A man is personal—he does not cry or question the system. He only succeeds in it.*

But who made up these rules? Maybe no one. It's like when you're a child in school and think that the teachers and principals have eyes everywhere and know exactly what they're doing. Then you get older and realize that they probably had trouble seeing what was right in front of their faces. They were struggling to hold on to their semblance of structure just like everyone else. And yes, they were delusional too. They were good at pretending…actors really.

And so was I, he thought. *Perhaps there isn't anyone behind the curtain—perhaps it's all of us assuming that there are those who know better—the notion allowing us be lazy.*

After experiencing the joy of putting all of these thoughts together, he had an insight. He finally realized that he was allowed to think about whatever he wanted. *Who's going to stop me? I have all the time in the world—nothing to do. Be revolutionary!*

He gave himself the freedom to ask deeper questions and then try answering them. He had no reason to fear entrance into the darkness of reality. What he found was that it was so easy to go there; that it was in fact what he really wanted. *It's a healing place to be. If they can't do it with their drugs…I'm going to do it myself!*

With that, he dropped into emptiness. Then pure knowledge sprung forth out of the void. With space, with time—more words came.

Could I really have been another way? Could I have been thankful during the days I had freedom of movement, freedom of friends, freedom of money? Could I have been happy and helpful and honest? Those are the ways of being I actually liked, but I always felt that I was only allowed so much of them. It would have been strange for me to have gone against the grain—awkward even. Would it really have been any better to have been different? People would have talked about it too much, because that's what they do…talk about other people. They would have thought it strange if someone went around speaking about how great being alive was all the time. I don't think they would have really even let me. If I took risks, let my body move freely the way it wanted, and didn't care what they thought…they would have put me in one of these kind of places much sooner. They would have thought I was malfunctioning—called me crazy. I had to hold back my whole life from being the way I wanted when there wasn't anything wrong with me. I'm sure there are many others who feel the same but are locked in these invisible sadistic chains. What a sad and terrible story! When I was a child, I was free…but that was the only time they ever let me be. Even then—they started bending me early with the ways they knew I had to be. Maybe if there had been some support, I could have broken through. Maybe if everyone else wasn't constantly competing and complaining. A little support like what this woman had said would have made all the difference to my young self. Maybe the world really is changing now. Hope? Perhaps. I certainly could use some of it.

Then David realized what he had been for the majority of his life—it hit him like a ton of bricks dropped upon his shoulders. *I've been a spoiled grouch. We all have. Back when my body was healthy, I spent the majority of my time worrying about my career or something...anything else to continue the addiction to doubt. I doubted whether or not I was being productive enough with my day, what injustices were being done to me, why I didn't have more money, what I was going to wear to the party on Saturday. My mind had needed something to worry and complain about. Even though my body can barely keep itself alive, maybe I was sicker then than I am now? Wow!* He gasped at both the absurdity and truth of the thought.

He felt suddenly horrible in his stomach again. He quickly wheeled himself back to the toilet and this time was able to release what felt like a lifetime of poison. He sat there with his mouth hanging open and drool falling out in a spittle to the side. He felt empty and numb as he stared at the pattern of the tile floor below him—feeling somehow more alive than he had in so long. *This floor looks pretty,* he thought.

The next day he awoke with more confidence. He was invigorated somehow—resolved to put together the pieces of what had come over him. Getting sick actually felt good, and right. It was a beautiful sunny day, and the newspaper said it would be eighty-two. David hadn't been outside in well over a month—perhaps it had been two. He put on a light sweater and wheeled himself to the closest exit and out into the fresh air. He sat himself at the table outside of his room's window which no one ever used. It was the first time he sat there himself.

He stopped, he breathed, and he thought. As a dying old man, David felt he had a right to see depth; now there was no one that could argue with him. He had lived enough of life to know how much of it had been wasted on nonsense. *We don't have to wander about all day saying thank you, but at least we can take a few minutes to smile and consider how miraculous it is once or twice every twenty-four hours. That would make sense. That would help. Yes. What are we rushing on about that's half as important as doing that? Nothing.*

In the vast majority of his days on Earth, there hadn't been even one of these moments of appreciation within them. In fact, it was probably a very countable total number for all his days. He thought about money and finally understood what a slave to it he had been.

Money doesn't stop you from getting old. What is its value compared with physical health? Nadda. They took it all away from me to pay for this shitty place anyway. I finally fully realize it now when I wake up daily ready to die. What a terrible laugh. Somehow my heart keeps beating and my eyes keep opening, but I'm numbered. The only reason I don't take my life is because I'm too scared. I'm still a coward. I still don't know how to end what I want ended. My body asks me to, but I can't listen.

He was furious and sad at the same time. He couldn't believe he had fallen so hard for the trap of normalcy. The most difficult part to handle was that deep down he had known the truth all along. But instead, he had chosen to follow the judgments of both everyone and no one at all. Somehow, following—being accepted—seemed more important than what actually made sense. *How? I wanted people to like me. I never really knew whether or not they did. I spent most of my time either trying to do what I was supposed to, or feeling guilty for enjoying myself. I never learned how to truly relax, and so I still can't do it when there's nothing else left to do. What a waste. I deserve this place—this situation. I deserve it for not having any resolve. It doesn't matter how many others don't either…we all need to be ashamed of ourselves. Those of us who haven't found time for appreciation have disgraced the gift of being human. Without thankfulness, there is no point.*

He saw now that that perspective was where love itself came from. He was flooded with a new feeling that could only be acquired through deep understanding of what it meant to let go of it all.

He sat outside at the simple unused table and prayed for surrender.

GENERATION GAP

Going to see her grandfather was not something Amanda had ever really enjoyed doing much before. When she made the trip, it was out of obligation—filled with feelings of guilt. After all, she got the creeps from being in that place. The smell alone made her feel depressed and tiresome. But in the past, she had always gone with her parents, and they had made the decision for her. For the first time in her life, she made the visit by herself. No parent or sibling—just her deciding that this was what she'd do today.

As she walked the halls, she kept her gaze nervously straight ahead. She could feel the eyes on her, as if it had been months since they had last seen a person under the age of thirty. Tubes and mechanical devices of all sorts hung from ears, mouths, and noses. *Who ever thought to put all these people in the same place? Is it to hide them?* She wondered.

Amanda had graduated from Gratitude two weeks earlier. At her school it was an option to graduate from being a student any time before one's twenty-fourth birthday. Although she could have gone through the ceremony years before, she had chosen her time to be at twenty-two. The whirlwind of her life felt somewhat unbelievable to her. She could still remember that little girl trying to get all A's back in the public system. *A freakin life-time ago,* she thought.

That image was faded now, and sometimes she wondered if it had really happened at all. Being a grat was simply too significant of an experience for her. It gave her skills and a relaxed sense of being that transformed her into something different and new...*something vastly improved*, she knew.

Although Amanda had learned many practical tools for handling anxiety, still, the question remained: *what do I want to do with my time now? I fully understand the freedom I have...but what to do with it?*

Perhaps these thoughts led to the choice of now taking the time to form a relationship and prioritize a man who had given her much love. *I'm a grown woman—capable of bearing burdens and converting them into purpose. No more time for running away from aversions.* She had learned that running toward the uncomfortable—and facing it—was actually the smartest strategy to take on. The first day was awkward of course, and she and David didn't really know what to do with each other. However, Amanda came back the next day, and the following one after that. In fact, quickly she realized there wasn't anything more valuable for her to be doing than bringing herself to this place. As she had been taught to do, she re-assessed the merit of experience within her mind, and came to her own conclusions.

She'd usually bring a book or a notepad to do some writing in case grandpa David was sleeping, or not in the mood for conversation. He thanked her for coming all the time and looked her in the eyes in a magical sort of way that let her know she had made a sensible choice. Days turned into weeks and weeks into months. When she told people what she was doing with her time, many of them seemed impressed. The truth, though, was that she was taking at least as much as she was giving. It wasn't simply about her grandfather alone. It was being in that place, being a part of the community of elderly as a whole. By witnessing those in the final stages of their lives, she felt her maturity growing rapidly. She had an awareness of time and death, an appreciation for her young healthy body, that couldn't possibly have been more profoundly achieved any other way.

"Shouldn't schools take field trips to these places?" She scribbled down in her notebook. *"The young need to see the old, and the old need to see the young. Is there really anything else they're doing that's as important? Boy oh boy*

does the lack of sensible and creative leadership go deep. These two groups of people could really use each other. There is no better purpose for the elderly, and no more humbling one for our youth...than to be exposed to each other."

Sometimes Amanda would help put on her grandfather's shoes, help feed him, or rub his back when he complained that he wanted to die. Being there felt so appropriate and necessary. Her other plans for action quickly took a backseat.

David's credulous mind made a connection between his breakdown after Maya Sol's speech and Amanda's arrival. *Could it be that the energy I sent out from my insights, then led Amanda coming here? No, no way. That's a silly thought. Don't do that you superstitious man.*

The truth was that he had no idea why all of a sudden he was blessed with his granddaughter's presence. He didn't understand what had changed. It was the kind of life turnaround that he had most certainly given up on expecting to receive. In a way, he made sure not to become too invested in her visits. He had been in assisted living for almost ten years now, and no one had come to see him daily, or even weekly! A monthly visitor was a reasonable expectation; but even that was inconsistent. *She's a capable young woman bound to take off in any direction at any time,* he told himself. *How much longer will she want to continue visiting her miserable, dying old grandfather?*

After half a year he finally gave way that she was committed. Sometimes if he was up for it, they'd play chess together. Although his mind no longer worked optimally, David had been an extremely formidable player in his younger years. That skill wasn't easily lost, and he still made all the automatic moves that come from enough repetition. At first he toyed with her the way he did with most others—he'd even let her win a couple times purposefully. But pretty soon he realized that he was having the kind of sincere competitive games that he hadn't experienced in quite a long while. She picked up the strategy with alarming quickness. When she lost, it appeared that her ego wasn't affected in the least. In fact, he noticed that he had a much more difficult time at keeping his emotions in check when defeated. When she won, he would naturally develop a bad taste in his mouth and fall into a worse mood. His granddaughter would smile and laugh and comment on how well he could still play—then ask if he wanted to go another round.

Sometimes she would bring in her guitar. Although she didn't think much of her talents, Amanda felt singing to be an extremely uplifting practice. To express the sound of her voice was as valuable to her as anything—more. On the days he refused to wake up and listen to anyone—her music seemed to be the only cure for snapping him out of his depression. *Sound is the most powerful of forces*, she thought.

But most times they would simply sit together having basic conversation—being polite and asking questions. He couldn't help but prod her about what she was planning on doing with her life—about how she was supposed to make an income and find a husband. David had been asking those kinds of questions for too long to stop now. He was starting to see that he didn't really know another way of engaging people socially. Anxiety was a part of him, and he deflected it onto others.

"Don't worry," she'd tell him. "It'll be fine. I don't need that much money to be happy."

"Yes, but you have to make a living."

"I will."

David worried about her though. He didn't know if this was the right place for a young lady to be spending her time. With every visit, however, he became more and more impressed by the character of her ways. *She might know better than me—be stronger.* That was an idea he did not easily consider. For a long time now he had safely assumed that he was the smartest person in any room. *The way she deals with all of my moods, the way she speaks to the nurses, the way she smiles at the other residents—memorizing their names. Most importantly, the way she's able to hold a gaze and calmly allow her grandfather to investigate her face. Good*, he thought. *Be better than me. I want you to.*

There came a moment one day when he realized he had been do-ing the same thing to her that he despised in others—the same thing that had caused him to make so many of the wrong life decisions. *She seems to be somewhat immune to my prodding, but perhaps it's more difficult than she's letting on. Why am I trying to turn her focus toward fear?*

He tried harder to change this tendency of his more than anything else he'd ever done. Perhaps it was his own determination, or perhaps it was the support of the booklet 'Life Code,' that she gave him (he'd been using the words for daily support). Regardless, he was successful.

"I want you to know, Amanda," he mustered up the courage to say one day, "that you can and really should do anything you want with your life. I mean that. I've spent far too much of my time on matters that really weren't very important at all. I can tell you is that I see now in my last bit of time the reality of how we're supposed to look at it. It can be hard sometimes and also challenging, but that's only more of a reason not to be clueless. I don't know if you've decided what you want to do with your days, but know that if you want, it can be something special. It can be really good."

She smiled as if she were fully aware of the impact that those words could have. She smiled as if she was happy for him to be able to say them. "Thank you," was her reply as she slowly inclined her head and closed her eyes. After a brief moment to herself, she lifted her lids, looked up; and made her next move on the chessboard.

A few months after his passing—from the information some family members attained through testing their DNA; Amanda discovered that David Keegan had never been her biological grandfather after all. Her grandmother had been artificially inseminated, and told no one. *Two years of my life spent prioritizing time with this man.*

Somewhat shocking to her—it changed nothing.

PART V

POLITICS

A ROCK

How deep do the problems go? Maya asked herself one day as she was out taking the Izzer for a stroll. He was such an unbelievable creature, this little dog. So obedient—so eager to please. He never strayed too far from his watchful human guardian, but still found great enjoyment in the freedom that the allotted proximities provided. It might have been a bit silly, but Maya drew faith from her successes in training him. She never had to put Izzy on a leash and never had to call him more than twice—*well usually.* Although she certainty was aware that she had found a top notch prize, there was no doubt that her nurturing also played its role. *I have achieved greater success through love and positive reinforcement than I ever could have with fear of physical dominance, and punishment. It clearly works much better. Similar to the way we decide to feel in regard to the possible results in expressions of good versus evil. Contrary to popular belief, the power levels are not equal.*

As she stood in the park watching her little side-kick hop around and play fiercely with the other dogs, Maya took the time to consider where they currently stood in the progress of their movement. *Once momentum is picked up, you have to continue feeding off of* it, she knew. Futurism was a powerful force taking shape and creating community; however, the old and current system of politics was so firmly entrenched that it frightened her appropriately. *Something more is needed—so many steps still left to take.*

She reflected on how many movements of the past had lost steam and faded from memory due to their inability to identify the most worn out cogs of the wheel; and focus on fixing that which most urgently needed reassembly. *Without bias, without anger...only with precision. So, Maya...think big! What needs it the most?*

In terms of the political structure, the first thing she identified was the voting process. *Bad leadership is at the core of every one of our issues. I don't know if I can think of a larger target to hone in on. There is a plethora of well-intentioned, massively intelligent, and wise citizens with guts and grit (pretty much all the graduates from our school)...but they are not the ones who are holding these offices of power and decision making. They are not the ones going on the journey to become politicians. The ladder is not set up for them to climb the rungs—therefore they're not. It doesn't matter though. These types of people are capable of anything—climbing ladders that are set up for them or not. Practical intelligence has no bounds. We must feed the right people into the system. I'm sure of that.*

She quickly stood back for a moment and took an aerial view. *Oh how I love when the answers come. Our future leaders need to be given a ship and a direction to propel their talents forward. Futurism must give it to them. It can.* It became clear to her that the skills necessary to win election in the current system were not close to those most essential for being a good leader. In fact, she thought that they very well might have been in opposition. In her opinion, it was a problem too great to be ignored any longer. *Improvements will be severely limited until a solution is found for our leadership conundrum.*

She was on a roll now and continued. *Individual leaders are far more important than the platforms of political parties. We must begin to see that. Everything flows down from the top. Voting based strictly on party lines is death to our hope of finding the most needed trailblazers; I know that. People should not care what political positions their leader take nearly as much as they care about the character of the individual offering up advice.*

Take work as an example. If you resent your boss—feel that they aren't suitable for the position—you will never perform to your potential. End of story. Doesn't matter if you watch the same news channel, if you both believe in larger or smaller government. If the person at the top is fraudulent or weak in their self-esteem, the whole system is destined to be as well. Character is the key. Top down.

Izzy's decision to make a squat caused Maya to take a break from her contemplation, take out a bag, and perform her enchanting owner's duty. When she got back to her spot along the fence, she didn't skip a beat, and picked up right where she had left off in the avenues of her mind. The way she saw it, the major issue in politics was that people were not really getting to know those who were being elected. Instead, they were voting based on the promises of an agenda coming from those that may or may not have been honest. *If their end goal is getting elected (not making necessary change), then they might be willing to say or do anything to reach that end. You always have to identify what the end goal is for a person. Many of these people don't understand the truth about process, the truth about phoniness. Honoring promises doesn't matter very much if the promises themselves are used as bait for reaching a plateau. People who are honest do not tend to understand the workings of a deceitful mind. THAT, is a major problem.*

She zoomed out further and saw a deeper issue from the opposite end. *Most people invest their time in watching the happenings of an election not to create an improved world, but rather in order to be socially interesting. Wow, this is a hard truth! What people want more than quality change is to participate in conversation—to debate with their friends and family—to have smart opinions. Because of this reality, many of us only search to acquire talking points rather than to develop a true understanding of the seriousness of our role as a voter. Our eyes are only partially open—lacking in objectivity as a result of our own insecurity which still thirsts to prove something about our own intelligence—endlessly.*

She took out her phone and wrote down some notes. A strategy was manifesting itself. *There is all of that, plus the general feeling of helplessness that is so pervasive.* This truth scared Maya perhaps the most. *In a way it's not our fault. After seeing so much of the same type of repetition, it's hard to imagine what real change even looks like. It's hard not to feel that the system is rigged against us.*

That most people ignored local politics but heavily invested their time in concerning themselves with national elections was further proof to her that most citizens did not in fact have a conscious desire to focus on rational change. Instead, the whole process of election was yet another layer in the same ego game. The majority of the population was too consumed with their own personal standing to do what was needed in order to become the change themselves.

Regardless of local or national elections, Maya realized that people were horrible at identifying what actually made a good leader. *Politicians give manufactured speeches that reek of safety and phoniness, yet few seem to care, mind, or take action to stop them in their tracks. The words of candidates often connect to the lowest parts within us and do little to address any real directive for citizens to take more personal accountability.*

They do not even tell us to be easier with our thoughts, to take care of our bodies, or to have courage enough to change our habits. Instead, they speak of the greatness of their past, puff up their audience with compliments, make fantastic claims about what they'll do, and perpetuate the avoidance practice of continuing to point the finger. All the while contributing to this destructive illusion of separation. What a sick game we've allowed to spiral out of control, she thought.

As the days kept rolling forward, Maya continued fleshing out her ideas to transform the political game. She remembered the value of a team and thought she knew the perfect person to partner with for this new project. She gave her old classmate a call.

"Marty, I have something I'd like to discuss with you—can we meet up?"

"Of course. How about a hike tomorrow? I'll take the day off."

She thought to herself, *there are not many things a friend can do to make you feel as worthwhile as instantly dropping everything when you need them...especially when you know they're one of the busiest people in the world.*

Maya and Marty met the following day at the base of a mountain not far from the estates of Revolution. Summer was finally cooling down, but most of the trees still held the majority of their green.

Hiking was a favorite activity of hers—similar to driving; the goal was simple and clear—*get from point A to B. Use the time in between however you like.* She loved that.

She couldn't deny that when the two of them were together, phero-mones were pervasive in the air. Maya knew very well that she and Marty could have made for a solid intimate partnership. She had known this long ago, but he had been with Stacey since the time they first met, and she was not one to engage this particular brand of disruption. The fact that she loved Peter so completely, but could still feel this way—did however, cause her to question the practicality of a society where monogamy was the norm. *I understand the need, because it gives us security…but I still think it's a weakness. If we truly love the people in our lives, should we not want them to have other experiences of deep connection with others besides ourselves? Furthermore, if we're willing to look more closely, does the concept of monogamy not completely derive itself from the energy of jealously and sacrifice? I don't mean emotional monogamy—it makes perfect sense for two partners to commit themselves to forming the most intimate team possible. But why can't we experience feelings of closeness with others as well? I don't see how one necessarily has to detract from the other. Whatever. This is one thing I don't need to take action on. I just think it's interesting to think about and question the foundation of. I searched for a long while, and then I did find something even better than my hopes. I found him, and it's led to incredible amounts of goodness. You can tell when any event is a significant addition to your life, when you clearly witness 'a before' and 'an after.' I certainly do.*

So I'm not complaining, I'm just wondering if maybe the next generation will be better able to sort out appropriate sexual behaviors. In the logic of my mind, I know that my own complications only stem from the brainwashing that's been done. Because of that…I leave it alone. I leave it alone because I have perspective and realize that within a grateful mind…getting everything you want doesn't matter much. I choose not to focus on the vain practice of monogamy, and allow it to be a passing thought. Depending on your current condition, some paths are best left untraveled.

As she was hiking, Maya told this to herself immediately before taking on mental movement into other areas of thoughtful intrigue. After an hour or so of moving through dense forest, these two friends arrived at an open clearing. They sat for a moment atop a large slated rock gazing out into a deep valley before them. Often Maya felt that the most enjoyable activity in the world would be to wander about inspecting different parts of nature throughout her days. *What could be better than that? It's too peaceful and beautiful to ignore—the uniqueness of the earth surrounding.* Her eyes floated to a far-off peak barely visible on the horizon, to the intricacy of the leaves on the tree right beside her. She closed her eyes and dipped herself into the void of calmness—drawing on the tools she had spent so much time cultivating. *Everything's all right. This is exactly how it's supposed to be. Making change is best done in a relaxed and determined state of acceptance. When I feel into my body, then I remember. I fall contently into that flow.*

She turned her attention back to Marty. He was resting on the rock beside her with one knee pulled up into his chest and his opposite leg stretched out comfortably over the edge of the cliff. She felt ready to begin.

"Let me ask you something. Why do we have such unsatisfactory political leadership, Marty?"

He blinked his eyes as he swiveled his head ever so slightly in her direction. "Yeah. That's one of the big ones, isn't it?" He hesitated, unconsciously shifting approach, then said; "What if I start by letting you answer? I'm not sure I'd know where to start, but I do know you well enough to guess that you probably have somewhere you'd like to be going with this. Correct? No need to squirm your way in with me. Go ahead Maya. Tell me more."

She smiled shyly knowing that he was right. *Fair enough…well played sir!*

"OK, the way I see it; we have to do something to help people pry into the real character of those who run for our political offices. Somehow conventional practice has allowed these candidates to hide themselves; while at the same time appearing to be out in the open. It's not the polished exterior that's important for us to see, but rather their true character and personalities. They place themselves out of our reach by making the container so phony, and we allow them to do it. What if we didn't anymore? We're capable of getting to know them just like anyone else. But we need more information—the right kind. The public has been confounded and kept occupied with too many other issues and worries to see this. Distraction keeps us from making the assessments that really matter. The only solution I believe, is if we make local politics somehow more entertaining to follow. Can we do something to help people be the change without requiring too much effort; and also by giving them something in exchange? Politics has always been entertaining; but maybe we can improve the level of theatre?"

Marty considered for a moment as Maya watched and noticed the changes to him that were most likely a result of teaching so many hours at Gratitude. His responses reinforced her assessment that his maturity and patience had increased to new heights.

"Yes, I think those are excellent points," he projected with the same ambiance he'd answer one of his students in. "The two-party system of this country is preposterously disempowering. We give our leaders access to change, yet we restrain the good ones, by making them comply with restrictions and adherence to a set of standards. We want them to lead, but then we take away the only thing capable of actually allowing them to do it well."

"What's that?"

He was glad she asked with practically no hesitation. "Their individuality. The ability to make mistakes and be wrong once in a while. For leaders to show us their humanity and their transparency. We need to allow them freedom to change opinion to meet the situation—not be fearful that they might step outside of a confining box they've already agreed to unrealistically live in. This is exactly why we must focus on electing the person rather than the platform or the party. We do the same thing with our associations. Many of us hold ourselves back with opinions that we've previously formed—not allowing for the freedom to discover more truth as we get older. We've clung to ways for so long we're scared to lose them. In this way, we put a cap on our growth potential."

He was silent for a few moments. He picked up a small pebble and rolled it around in his fingers. "Most importantly, though, we need to get to know who these people are. Yes, you are definitely right about that. That's what it ultimately will come down to. But we are also just beginning to realize that we have to be able to rank values appropriately within our observations. We are slow, Maya. The ego makes it so by failing to acknowledge our limitations and believing we stand higher in the grasps of control, stability, and progress than we actually do. It'll shock the world when we open ourselves up and finally admit how much further we can travel."

She looked over the horizon and took in the truth of his words. The implications made her smile sadly. Then she jumped right back into the stew of word exchange. When she had been younger, she probably would have listened for longer—marveling at wisdom coming from another. But now she was more in touch with her desire to participate herself. *That, and a lot of practice being around Peter.*

"Hmmm, yes, that's true. But there is also more to it than just the slowness. Presently, most of our leaders are infatuated with caution—always afraid of making a misstep. Therefore, they make so many more of them. They congratulate their ability to avoid flames instead of using their own personal fire to blast away the garbage. That's what we need. Leaders who can brush away bullshit, again and again. Then Futurists will stand and say 'yup, he's right. Stop trying to sidetrack him.'"

"Or her," Marty cut in.

"Yes, right—or her. Stop trying to sidetrack me with bullshit!"

He laughed.

"It's amazing that such idiocy, such fearful behavior of the ego, has survived for this long," she continued. "Do they not realize that life is unavoidably risky? Not only that, but it's possible that fear is currently more prevalent in politics than it's ever been before."

They sat together for a few minutes contemplating the weight of the challenge before them. Then Maya began summarizing what they already knew in order to pick up momentum.

"Here's what we've got so far: We need to make well-thought-out decisions about whom we elect. After we do, we must give them the support they need in order to explore their own individual beliefs— ever changing. Do we want leaders holding to their previous truths, or keeping their eyes open in order to develop deeper ones? The way it stands now, most of them are just struggling to maintain the status quo. They haven't yet realized that desperately trying to hold on to what you have is the surest way to lose it."

She waited a moment and gave Marty a chance. He took right up with the opportunity. "Yes, to make change you have to set yourself on a clear course of improvement and then light a spark of motivation in order to go there. It's as simple as that, and has everything to do with our relationship to memories of importance. But fear and a lack of faith in the power of good, make for timid humans. Anyway, back to the matter at hand. I know you better than this, Maya. I know you have a plan. I don't think you would have come to me if you didn't. What's the course we're setting? What's the fire of motivation we're lighting up? Share please," he said with a smirk.

So she told him her idea. "A reality TV show made specifically for politicians." It was perfect for his background and expertise—after all, Marty Linden was the duke of reality TV. He was well versed in the power of it to hold the viewer, and even cause deep and fanatical obsession. As she explained the details, he found himself falling in love with the concept; and inwardly berating himself for not having come up with the idea sooner. *So it goes. Creative conception is a tricky thing.*

Together, right there on that flat rock, the two of them began laying out plans—building off each other's insights and progression. Luckily their magical cellular devices allowed notes to be easily taken and saved. Marty began cutting through the operational challenges like a master sculptor. *Where, when, how, why, with what money?* He had trained himself to stay focused, almost as if he were the lens of a microscope. He constantly moved himself back into greater perspective, and then forward into little bits of focused detail.

Never once did they question the possibility of it actually occurring. They had already moved passed that once they decided it was a good idea. When they had—there was only the manifesting left to do. Therefore, the process spread out in detail from their certainty of success.

KYL

The first season of 'Know Your Leader' was held in Atlanta, Georgia. The framework for the show went as follows: Seven people living together in a house for six weeks. The prize— support in their bid for mayor of the city in the upcoming election.

Like in any other reality show, all the things that came with living in a house with strangers were available to the cameras: how they took care of themselves personally, how they worked, what they ate and read, how they handled their relationships, how they interacted with their own children over the phone…*everything.*

But they also did have a solid goal that would exemplify their abilities as a community leader. Each contestant was given $15,000 to affect the most positive change he or she could in three months. The parameters were broad, but that was the point. They were free to be as creative as they liked with their time and money. It wasn't an immense amount of cash, but it was enough to do some significant work; if spent wisely.

Contestants built new social forums, charities, and bartering programs—made additions to parks, and established methods of neighborhood communication; anything they thought to be in the direction of improvement for the communities of Atlanta. The public watched them throughout this entire process—watched how they took initiative and how crafty and well intentioned each contestant could be.

Perhaps transparency was asking a lot, but Maya and Marty both felt that a truly honest person should not have anything to hide. *This is the price that must be paid in order to hold such an important job,* Maya thought. *In truth, there isn't even a price. People with secrets are never the ones you want leading anyway. The guilt eats away at them in strange ways. You make a commitment to yourself or someone else…then you break it, and then you feel guilty. Why would you ever want to do that? There's no reward aside from very surface-level stuff. Forgotten is the fact that guilt is the worst feeling in the world, and causes brutal forms of separation.*

The first few seasons, contestants were not well-known names. Many of them did not even apply to the show themselves as it was acceptable and even encouraged for others to apply for you. Of course, you had to accept being nominated. But Maya did not believe someone had to be good at making extraordinary claims about themselves in order to possess the necessary skills of leadership. *In fact,* she reflected, *maybe there's something wrong in a process where candidates are forced to advocate so arrogantly for their worth. Often the best leaders in history have in fact proven to be quite humble in character—confident in their perceptions, but uncomfortable and smart enough not to give much time considering their ranking among others. How did that truth get so lost over the years?* She wondered.

The audience was guided to vote on the answer to two questions: "Which person have you grown to respect the most?" and "Who do you think would make the best leader?" They voted at the end of the season, and the winner was backed by the full influence of Futurism in the next election. Not only that, but viewership alone promoted the contestant's careers more than any traditional campaign element might have been able to. Like other reality TV shows, people watched because it was interesting, and then voted because of their emotional investment to the characters. *Story has power.*

Excitement stirred to see if the winners could make it to the next level. The popularity of the show was immediately successful, and the contestants were of high quality. There wasn't really a comparison between someone who had his or her name printed on a bunch of signs—who gave mundane speeches; and someone whom voters were able to see truly interacting with all aspects of their lives. In a way, this brought about the stunning realization that for years the population actually better knew their celebrities than their chosen leaders. Contestants on *KYL* may have behaved differently than they would have without a camera, but they were still presenting their true selves— and that made all the difference. The public didn't just see them in a debate or in interviews; trying to hide their humanity. They saw them live. In fact, this soon became so obviously necessary that years later people questioned how there was ever a time when we allowed those making decisions for the masses to escape the necessity of showing us who they really are.

After the winners of the first few seasons all won their elections, old-time politicians had no choice but to acknowledge that there was a very real threat to their cherished system. Legally there was nothing they could do, so when they were up for re-election, they made the other choice; they applied to *KYL* themselves. Most of these stubborn old timers were too afraid to enter the fray, but some took the chance—they had to. They had watched too many of their colleagues lose their seats to no-names with independent party affiliation. As they had done throughout their lives, they were willing to try anything to hang on to their power. Most were unsuccessful and finished at the bottom end of the voting, but a few transformed into something more venerable. It was certainty engaging for the audience—that was for sure.

Maya had been gifted with foresight, and *KYL* cut straight to a major source of the problem. Once again her belief that any problem was solvable with enough creativity and resolve held true. Not many people would have thought reality television able to break apart and open up the political system that was so incredibly entrenched. But no other person was Maya Sol. She had belief, and belief was everything. Like most things, the change did take some time—patience was foundational. But slowly, the right leadership was beginning to move itself into place. Through the years, hope continued to build upon itself.

LAW

*T*he law, Peter Sol considered from the chair behind the desk in his office, *is just like someone with a fragile ego—it refuses to acknowledge imperfection or admit that its power has limitations. THAT, is a very dangerous force to contend with. Our strategy must be rock solid—our discipline impeccable.*

The petitions and rulings had been coming down for some time. *The law is after us,* he thought. *That's no good.* He pushed himself to move past that. His father had taught him the power of strategy. *Maybe it can be made to be though. Use the reality of the situation and move from there Peter.*

The law was demanding that Gratitude shut itself down. After all, they were not quite abiding by the guidelines set out by the state and national education departments. They didn't require their students to take standardized tests, and they didn't even demand that they study the common core of subjects; the ones that the education department had decided were most beneficial for the mind of humans to learn during their prime years of growth. *Don't they understand that I can learn more about what actually matters from reading 'the Gita' on my own, than I can from sixteen years of traditional schooling? I guess they really don't.*

How little do they think of themselves that they have to rely so desperately on tradition? Don't they understand that it was simply the best that other humans of the past were capable of at that time? He wished they didn't have to take it so damn seriously. It gave him the feeling that something else might be behind it.

Perhaps this attack was a conspiracy by certain agencies to slow Futurism down by shifting Maya and Peter's focus away from their movement. *Perhaps*, he thought. But Peter wouldn't allow conjecture to distract him. *The reasons don't matter all that much. This is simply an obstacle placed before us to contend with. That is all.*

He made every notice they received visible to the entire school community. Tension began to build. Eventually a session was called for and a vote taken to determine the best course of strategy. Luckily, they had been preparing and even expecting for something like this to happen from the outset of their creation. They quickly established community desire, and then sent their intentional action from there. Communication was essential. The first step they knew, was to begin having nightly meetings.

They started out by playing within the rules of the game—writing letters back to the California State Education Department. They tried using reason as best they could—giving the opposition the benefit of the doubt. They explained that if parents didn't have the ability to choose how to best foster the growth of their own children, what freedom did they really have? After all, all of the minors at Gratitude had permission from their guardians to be attending.

"Is this not the home of the free?" Their first letter began. "We prefer not to be analyzed and put into spreadsheets. We prefer to learn what we feel is most important. Is it not our right to choose what information to plant into our own brains? How are we causing harm? There is no doubt that Gratitude is a safe space. Can you shut us down merely on the basis that we are not complying with your standards of how to educate? You see, for us it's the other way around. We feel that the standards established by the education department, are in fact detrimental to the health of children. Is it not our right to form that stance and take the best action for the benefit of those closest to us? We can give you plenty of specific reasons if you need supporting evidence to our assessment of your harmful creation of an institution. "More to the point—should citizens support the law if they feel it conflicts with their moral beliefs? Are we supposed to ignore what we have taken the time to figure out in order to be in compliance? Should we homeschool and take our children out of the support of a community when a better option has found its way into our lives? "Yes, you might say—the law is the law." Well, we disagree. We're not breaking all laws and have no desire to break any of them—just the specific ones we consider to be detrimental. To us, this is the action of a true American.

"We wouldn't be so opposed to taking state mandated tests if they actually measured something at all worthwhile that could be put to good use. But they don't—and they aren't. Now you attempt to rip away our own solution to your disaster. You demand we change our ways, but you do not offer us an adequate solution. You should be stepping up to face our questions, not the other way around. Instead, you play at games of elitism—attempting to force us back down below you. We can't have it."

They didn't receive any answers. After all, they were writing to an establishment in such disarray, that they didn't even know who was in charge of replying to this sort of thing. Still, more automated notices for closure continued arriving in their mailbox.

"You have thirty days to begin taking steps toward adhering to the law. If you do not, further action will be taken to ensure that every child is not deprived of an education that allows for the opportunity to be successful."

They don't even understand the meaning of their words! Peter thought. *Perhaps not this particular conflict, but a future battle will come down to our ability to define that one word—'success'. That's what this is all about after all. They stand by a system that is a broken relic of the past. They not only refuse to adapt…they're forcing the whole population to live in the past as well. Unacceptable; completely unacceptable. Their definition of success is elementary at best. We absolutely cannot give in.*

As time moved on and the harshness of the letters increased, the community of Gratitude took a vote they had been putting-off for as long as possible. They voted overwhelmingly to allow the system to "use their force." They saw no other worthy alternative.

As they dove into strategy, Peter and Maya tried to see both sides of the situation: "Negligence is their only argument with legal legs," she told him. "Remember, we have to beat them at their own game. Perhaps if proof of negligence can be determined, then that is a space for the law to enter. However, that is certainly not what is occurring here. At Gratitude, we identify the habits of the mind that will allow each individual to determine how to best optimize his or her time in life."

"For crying out loud!" Peter replied. "We guide them to find their own purpose—and we do not take on the inflated viewpoint that we know what's best for them better than they do. That's negligent?! This is nuts."

"You're right—but they're serious Peter."

"I know."

What Peter was smelling, was the scent of corruption—most terrifying due to its defiance of logic and disinterest in any kind of moral path. *They can find something if they want to. They're quite adept at using the law to serve their own terrifying ego needs. I don't know if we can ever win through the court system. It's simply too corrupt. The media is the only method to counteract it which I'm aware of. Media exposure is going to be perhaps our most powerful weapon.*

Peter was well aware that Martin Luther King Jr., and therefore a great step for human rights, would not have been accomplished nearly as quickly without the basic invention of the video camera. The proof was right there for everyone to see on their home television sets—unarmed citizens being beaten by those who were meant to protect. *Little did the civil rights movement know, however,* Peter thought, *that the education system they were trying to gain equal access to; was absolutely no prize at all. It was merely another disguised set of chains created by everyone and no one. Regardless, we fight to break those shackles now.*

Gratitude had not been initiated with the sole intent of causing commotion, but it wasn't to be denied that there was always a feeling of great change that hung about in the rooms and corridors. The possibility of revolutionizing education and improving a system in desperate need of reformation was something they courageously engaged.

Although Futurism was rapidly gaining members; opposition to the movement was growing just as fiercely—the two sides were on a collision course. Maya had only given her speech a few weeks before the first letters from the C.D.E began arriving—and perhaps this was a move to quickly strike back against their growing tide of influence. It was common knowledge of the link that existed between the movement and the school. The issue of whether or not Gratitude would remain open somehow seemed like the breaking point in a larger, much more universal battle of public debate.

When the day for the law to take action came, television and internet representation swarmed the grounds of Revolution in their large vans and SUV's. The Council of Leadership decided to allow the media to access any part of the school—to see everything that they took pride of inside. Also if they wanted; to politely ask for interviews with grats, guiders, or parents alike. The only condition was that if someone didn't feel like speaking to them—that they'd politely accept, and move along; not harass.

The cameras captured everything. Not only the brilliance of the design of the physical structure of the buildings (which was impactful to the audience who had never seen anything like it and were watching at home), but also the forces of the law; as they stormed onto the beautiful grounds with warrants and badges, grabbed children roughly as they were listening to music in their GPs, puzzling, meeting in study groups, or working alone in the notebook room. It was shocking to most people watching that such a beautifully created space; could somehow be in violation of the law. The evidence didn't add up.

During the meeting of the previous night, the council had decided it would be up to each individual member of Gratitude to choose their own action—that violence was off limits, was of course implicit. The limitation of physical force was one of the first lessons every grat learned. Aside from that, however, each member of their community was free to act as they saw fit. Most students allowed their bodies to go limp and be heavy as they maintained stoic faces (among their own younger leadership, it was agreed that this was the most sensible form of noncompliance to effect viewers at home). Others, however, cried and flailed their arms—held on to railings and benches; pleading to be left alone. Still others walked strongly with their heads held high as they cooperated with the requests of the authorities.

There were also a great many who tried to somehow lift the officers out of their own tunnel vision with words. "Please, please—you're hurting me. Stop it!" Some screamed as loudly as they could and didn't stop. This was perhaps the most brutal aspect for viewers to witness. All the fictional movies they'd experienced hadn't prepared them for such a real life episode of disarray. Regardless, the media drank it in for all the entertainment value it was worth.

Although effective in that sense, none of it did much of anything to prevent the movements of the great and mighty authority. The police-force was a machine that had turned its setting on 'use of physical force,' before they had even begun taking action. They were all pumped up with motivation from their superiors. Therefore, they could only see their objective—and were not taking responsibility for the operation of their own bodies.

But one did. Perhaps the most influential moment from the conflict, was the photo of a single policeman off to the side—cap thrown down on the ground next to him in the dirt; head in his hands. Brad Henly couldn't do it, and therefore his name lived on through history. Chain of command could not overcome individual interpretation in this instance.

Parents asked many of the other officers who had come nowhere close to the conclusion that Brad had made: "Where are you taking my child? To their house? You can leave them right here instead with me, and it will save you the trip. I'm his mother!"

A father was recorded to have said, "Does it really make sense for a big strong man like you to be lifting an eight-year-old girl away from her studies? Think for yourself! This makes no sense. Screw your job. Are you existing in such strenuous personal waters that your only desire is to survive? To do that you have to keep your job? What a travesty. Get your shit together and be a man. You're capable of much more than you realize—sir!" Unfortunately, the cameras didn't capture this man being slammed in the face with a nightstick.

The police continued pulling children away and handing them off to the storm troopers waiting at their converted armored school buses (there was something ironical about this as well). Little girls and boys sobbed as they were physically manhandled by much larger humans that they had never met before. They didn't understand, and it was far too much trauma than they deserved to experience.

They're doing a better job than adults ever could, Peter thought to himself as he stood next to Maya and Daniel, watching children he loved being taken from their community. The majority handled their bodies with incredible amounts of self-possession. The ones who didn't cry or struggle somehow made him feel the most sincerely sad—he hated the idea of children needing to become adult-like before they had to. Somehow it felt like losing to him.

They stood outside just under the entranceway of the bronze sun. His arms hung loosely to his side, and he felt the touch of Maya's hand on the small of his back. It took all his self-discipline to simply watch. *They're peaceful warriors,* he told himself as he saw and rationalized. *Gaining strength from this experience to carry with them for the rest of their lives.*

Although it was a rationalization, he also believed there was truth in it. *Acquire value from struggle. Have I not done the same throughout my own life?* He held onto that belief now with desperation. It was the only way he could cope with the present situation. *We have to have faith when we're challenged. We do not ask for it; but we can still use it.*

"Let them show the true colors of the beast they've sworn allegiance to," he posted on his twitter account moments before the first police car had arrived. The blackness was being seen.

Although the event created further division and much debate, the majority of viewers were appalled by what they saw. The height of exposure and coverage the event received surprised the media most of all and initiated a great many more Futurists. It raised many questions that had been avoided or glossed over for far too long. The 'Grounds of Revolution' became a major event in American history. The scene was disturbing enough to demand extensive debate and consideration. It finally showed the government for what it was—a stubborn and uncreative bully afraid to lose power it had no right holding to begin with.

DEVON

The collaboration between the department of education and law enforcement was mediocre at best. After all, they weren't used to working together. Not much thought had been given to what would happen in the swaying's of the media. So much work had to be done simply to acquire the necessary warrants to move the children off the campus. Perhaps they thought after one strong act of force the scale would tip—that the parents would break and that would be the end of the mess. The leaders of the opposition were very wrong.

Every single grat went back to their school the following day. They just went back; it was as simple as that. For some reason, no one thought they would. In their meetings one parent had said: "If they don't stop us, why shouldn't we? Let them repeat their behavior again—multiple times if necessary. Put it on them to figure out what to do." The community mischievously agreed.

The educational department now found itself in a serious bind. The attention was on them, and they were finding the brightness of the light not much to their liking. They couldn't repeat the same scene daily. Even though they might have the legal right, they were afraid that taking these children from their homes and fostering them would prove a worse public episode than what they had already fallen into. What could they do? They couldn't afford to lose another media war;

they couldn't give in—but the limits of their power were being pushed to their maximum. They had to do something.

Devon Pearson sat with the secretary of education on the back patio of his mansion on the southern tip of Florida. Devon had three boats, sixteen cars, and two other houses besides the one he currently found himself in. He had inherited ownership of a large trucking company in his twenties, which gave him great financial security for the entirety of his life.

He was now fifty-one. His wife, Anna, was a retired model yet to hit her thirtieth birthday. That she was more than twenty years younger made little difference to him. *No matter what people say, seeing a man with an attractive young woman increases his standing,* he thought. Anna had given birth to their first child a year and a half before. Thankfully for him, she had quickly brought herself back to the level of fitness he expected.

Not that it had ever held much interest to him, but Power Trucking now sat far down Devon's list of priorities. *That company is for hacks and pencil pushers to run,* he decided. *I don't even have to do anything, and the money will continue flowing in. In fact, it's probably better that I don't.*

What held Devon Pearson's attention now was politics. Soon he hoped to sell the company and fully immerse himself in his game of interest. He didn't want to run for office himself (he laughed at the thought of how limiting that would be). No, what he wanted was something much more subversive. He wanted to be the man behind the scenes. The one few knew about—the one who held politicians in the palm of their hand—like Don Corleone.

Throughout his youth, his mother had made sure that Devon attended the best schools the country had to offer. He was not the most attentive student but rather deemed himself, 'a wizard of personal relations.' In his sophomore year of college, he became president of his fraternity by pitting three upperclassmen against each other. By expertly manipulating rumor, he made room for the unknown entity of himself—with only 27 percent of the vote. He decided afterward that it would be the last election he would ever personally run for. It was too messy for him—he didn't like giving speeches and displaying himself before a crowd.

He laughed at how easy success had generally come to him throughout his life. The way he saw it, people were very simple to understand. *Give them attention by playing into their interests…set them against each other by making them believe they've been slighted or underestimated. Most importantly, make them think you are powerful and know better than they do. Then give them reason to take on tasks that will increase their standing in your book. That will be your proof of their loyalty.*

Therefore, he currently had four assistants all vying for the position to be his right hand. Little did they know, he had no plans to ever decide upon a winner. He would just keep it going, and knew that he could.

Money was his tool for accomplishing all of this. Devon gave away more gifts than anyone else he'd ever known. He allowed his workers to use his boats and jets, sent them to dinners at the most expensive places in the city, and vacations to brilliant resorts. He didn't ask for anything in return. *Give someone a gift, and they become in your debt. They can't help but feel that way. Don't tell them they are, just know it to be the case. What's even better, they don't usually realize the shift that's occurred in their own allegiance.*

Devon wasn't always a devious person. As a child, he was quite adept at creatively using his time for enjoyment which harmed no one. But as he grew in years, he found himself pretending more and more to be depressed about life—in order to be included socially. He wasn't stupid. His natural observations showed him that his social standing would never rise unless he started picking out things to complain about and make fun of. Soon, he became the first one to criticize the hell out of those who weren't around. These were often people he considered to be his friends—those who had even just left the room. He did it so well that people clung to spend as much time with him as possible; fearing what he might say about them if their presence was missing. Of course they never said it aloud—but they felt it. For a while, it was indeed acting; a path he saw to victory in a social game.

But soon the need to impress other humans outplayed all his other desires. His acting became so natural, that he embraced it; and forgot all about the pleasant child within.

In the past few years, Devon Pearson's name became one spoken about more frequently in small circles of the political upper hierarchy. It was for that reason that he found himself currently playing host to his countries secretary of education.

"I'm telling you, Mr. Pearson, this whole affair is one big mess. The news doesn't know the half of it. Our strategy has fallen apart. From what I can tell, we don't even have one. We just bicker and pretend like we have it all under control. That's the way it's always been. There's no real leader in this. Well, I guess I am; but you know, I just don't really have a knack for this sort of predicament."

The secretary took a look at Devon's face with a pleading expression. When he received no reply, he continued. "General political strategy has always tried to keep the conversations regarding education to a minimum, or simply to use it as a talking point—an easy pathway toward the appearance of empathy during election. Target and tag with labels of care. We all believe that it can be improved upon, but we're not going to actually talk about how of course. It's easier to just give it blanket support, promote it—and move along with other interests that are easier to discuss."

The secretary sipped his vodka lemonade before proceeding with the bullet points he had marked off previously in his mind. There was no real order to it. They were clumsy arguments that led nowhere. He had become so adept at appearing to be smart, he now convinced himself that he actually was.

"It would be one thing if this were a charter school we were talking about; but the way this place has been set up—it can't be allowed to stand any longer. Plus, everyone knows about it now. The public is satisfied with our system, as long as they don't go getting big ideas in their heads. Look, I know you've seen what's been going on. I'll admit there's a part of me that wishes we hadn't taken that kind of action. But they were pressing our buttons with all those damn letters. Maybe it would have been better to allow the place to continue existing as quietly as possible. I don't know," he said sadly. What's done is done—right? I've got more and more petitions coming in every day asking for money to create these ridiculous kinds of institutions. We have to smash this movement down now before it picks up any more steam." He made an aggressive gesture with his fist. "Sooner rather than later I think. It's a pivotal moment. Let me get to the point—can you help us Mr. Pearson?"

Devon had become known for his ability to systematically disassemble his enemies—putting an end to games before they even started. His proven success was the reason for this meeting.

"I believe I understand your predicament secretary, but one step at a time here; let's slow down a bit. What you must understand, is that always, always—there is one person that holds everything up. If you take down that person, the rest crumbles. Pick the scapegoat, but pick them wisely. That is all you need to know, and that is all we need to do." He reclined back in his lounge chair and interlaced his fingers behind his head as he appeared to comfortably give off his opinion. "Trying to get every student out of that building was a mistake for the ages. What were you thinking?" He asked pompously. "You should have posted officers at every entrance and not allowed them in to begin with. Better yet—close off the roads. Most importantly—keep out the media! How could you not see that allowing those snakes in would be a disaster?"

The secretary fought to defend himself. "Yes, we considered trying to get there early enough to stop the commuter kids. But how about all the boarders? That was our problem. Plus, we couldn't legally deny the media access. There was really nothing to be done."

Pearson gazed at his guest shockingly. Then he moved forward. "Alright, I disagree—but that doesn't matter. There's too much attention on this to hope for it to fade; at least not anytime soon. For now, we have to continue allowing the silly place to stand. Let them think they've won a victory. To answer the question you came here to ask—yes, I'll take this on. I don't want my name anywhere near it though. I contact you, and then you take the action. However, you have to understand one thing: From this point forward, what I say is done—IS DONE. Without question."

The secretary considered briefly and then nodded and reached out his hand to seal the agreement. He had known this to be his choice before making the trip down to this mansion. He had done his research—he knew with whom he dealt.

TRIAL

T ime moved on. The leadership at Gratitude had a feeling there would eventually be reprisal—and they were right. The logical choice for Devon Pearson and his team to scapegoat, of course Peter Sol. They searched hard to find something in his past to dismiss his credibility and shame his name. There wasn't much. His writing on drug use was something, but it wasn't a lot. Rapidly the public was beginning to have differing opinions on the issue, and they couldn't press it too much (especially in the state of California). Regardless, they went after him with their charge of action against the government—by founding a school in noncompliance of regulation.

As soon as the trial began, Peter saw that he had no chance of winning. It didn't matter how many Futurists were outside the courtroom protesting in support. *It's too easy to put down any one person within this system.* The judicial powers against him were far beyond his own; and locked together cohesively. They piled up claims that were too rooted in law to overcome. "If students refuse to take the exams, then they are acting against the laws currently in place. It doesn't matter if you agree with them."

That was where the line had been drawn, and Peter refused to walk over to the other side of it. *We must fight against anyone who attempts to remove us from our sensible freedoms...even the law,* he felt. *It might seem like it isn't a big deal to comply—but it is. This is how they get you. The first movement of bending is required for an eventual break. Our habits are everything. If you have no desire to take a certain action, better not to move toward it at all.*

When it came time for the defense's closing arguments, he saw no reason not to let out his own personal opinions. *Those who will listen will hear. Might as well use this chance. The media is perhaps as important as the court room now anyway.*

He stood before the judge with his hands behind his back. His words came out at a steady pace as he attempted to combine his emotional charge with as much rational opinion as possible. He told himself, *I'm talking to everyone, and to no one at all.* "I understand that there must be some kind of oversight. Our children do need to be guided in a healthy manner as they develop. I agree that of course there have to be restrictions to prevent neglect and harm—a set of standards. I do not argue against standards themselves, I argue against the standards that we as a country have put into place. It is no longer bearable for us to deny that the current education system is inadequate for the time in which we are living. I am astounded that more of us are not outraged enough to take action on the matter. Quite frankly, it does not provide a healthy or positive atmosphere worthy of our better selves. Children sit in classrooms disinterested and miserable—learning to despise reading and writing; unknowingly stagnating their bodies by not giving them enough movement within their days. The health care system cannot withstand these standards. We have tainted the natural love for learning and exercise that all humans are born with—and it is the saddest truth I have witnessed in my life. We give it little attention because they are children after all—and have no power. This should shed light onto our cultures tendency to churn its' wheels in progress only when powers force it to—when disasters strike, and not proactively.

"There isn't anything particularly wrong with the core subjects being currently taught around the world; but they certainly are not the most important subjects for children to learn. That is, in order for them to become functioning, thoughtful, healthy adults. You know this. Everyone knows this. If you open your eyes to see, you will realize that an overwhelming amount of us are struggling greatly just to survive the time of our lives. What a travesty! For this, I do place a good deal of the blame on habits developed during childhood. Of course, it is not the only leak in the pipe—but it is the one I believe requires the most immediate fixing.

"Gratitude is a place where students take on learning from the standpoint of already feeling full; not endlessly empty. We don't want their only choice to be competing against their peers. We know where that leads.

"I have no desire to flout the law. However, when citizens feel that a law is immoral and harmful—should they really continue cooperating with it? Think about that before you point fingers. When citizens see and create a better way, should they not follow the path of that creation? Is it not our duty to take action that we feel to be moral? Morality or law—we must choose which is held as a higher authority within our own minds. Personally, I cannot accept the law above my own judgment. If I don't have faith in what my mind decides makes sense—what is left? Then, I am a robot.

"Quoting Thomas Jefferson, the third president of our country and writer of our Declaration of Independence, "If a law is unjust, a man is not only right to disobey it, he is obligated to do so." We should not simply believe it because of whom it came from, but because what President Jefferson said makes sense. It has been proven many times in the past that the laws of government are not always up to the standards of the time; and are in fact quite fallible. Consider slavery. How long did it continue to be lawful while the greater percentage of the population knew in their hearts of its wrongness?

"It is of course reasonable that laws are flawed. They are a system simply made up by imperfect humans. However, we are constantly evolving entities and our present intelligence should not take a back seat to those who came before. In many ways, the current population should have the greatest insight into the realms of morality. That we forget what we are capable of, or the opportunity we've been given; is a sad truth.

"Ultimately, when laws are not logical, citizens will break them. Perhaps not in the moment, but eventually. If the government expects its people to obey simply because it has power—well then, now we have entered the realm of becoming the kind of state that we claim not to be. Instituting this unsteady relationship where government forces it's laws down it's people's throats is destined to implode. This kind of system exists to create short term wealth for those at the top scrambling to get as much as possible before their senselessness is uncovered.

"You might argue that if we don't abide by all the laws, that it will create disorder. Let me ask you. How about a little faith in people to do the right thing? You don't have it? Well then, I believe in your mind; we've already lost. Get out of the way. Why? Because you have fostered the belief that humans are more evil than good.

"There is no success for a group of people unwilling to engage doing what is right. Counting on law to control us has no chance for creating sustainable co-existence. It's a fireworks factory in which a thousand fuses are lit. You may be able to stamp out fifty or a hundred fuses, but there is no denying that the building will ultimately go up in flame. School is the place where we can make our streets the safest. Laws do not keep us in line—they are proof of what we already believe. They are a byproduct of our own mental health and clarity.

"Traffic laws are a great simple illustration of how the law has vast room for improvement. Let's consider what it's like to be on the road. If you stop at a red light and there are no cars coming in any direction (if you see that for sure with your eyes), does it really make sense for you to sit and wait until that light turns green? I mean, come on! Does the overall safety of the road not already completely depend on the scrutiny of our own wits?

"Robots, which the law often tries to turn us into, cannot adapt to emergencies which cause us to break the law. Does it not make sense to draw upon our own logical inferences and promote them even further in order to make the safest roads possible? I believe it does. The same is true with school. Why don't we penalize what is dangerous instead of what breaks the law? Are they not two separate things? How little trust does our government have in our own common sense? How drunk are they on their belief that they can control the uncontrollable? If we're more concerned with getting nabbed by a cop (and many of us are), than driving safely—it makes the road a much more dangerous place to travel on. I don't want drivers constantly looking down at their speedometers for fear of getting pulled over. I want them looking at the road ahead and deciding for themselves what speed is safe. Try to make us think less, and you'll get what we sadly have—more terror than anyone can handle. This is the source of the problem—going against the grain of what it means to be human. This is why we need to become philosophically grounded in our own personal moralities—this is why we need to change our schools!"

Pause, breath. As an afterthought Peter added: "We also need to allow our police officers to use common sense—not put them in a box of regulations either. In many ways, they are doing the work that most of us wouldn't have the courage for. Their jobs are as difficult as any. Common sense is the only way for them to do it best.

"No matter how many times we use words to brag about our freedom, it doesn't change the reality of our situation. What does it matter how much our freedom compares with that of other countries? That is a part of the same childish game of comparisons that our current public education is grounded in. You do not look at someone who is lower than you in order to make yourself feel high. Do you? I hope you're wise enough to move yourself away from that.

"One change of focus will cause everything to fall in a better direction. Only through education can we teach our population how to attain a higher level of individual morality—a higher level of common sense which will help everything. It will take time, but the next generation does not have to suffer the same senseless experiences as we have had to during the days of our youth—being locked up with tyrants and confused adults interested in maintaining or increasing their own personal standing. We can make things better—we must. Are we the generation that has the resolve to become the fulcrum which stops the wheel of fear? Maybe yes, maybe no. It certainly isn't easy, and you might not have faith; but there's a chance you also might be hearing what I'm saying."

Predicting little chance of legal victory did not prevent Peter from feeling like he had been punched when the verdict was read. It was hard for him not to be angry, but sometimes he also gave in to anger—realizing it was not always such a terrible emotion to have. *Anger has its place just like any other emotion. I can use it as a very formidable tool moving forward. They care about what they think is right for themselves more than they care about what is right. Small-mindedness. I need to focus on the larger battle for public opinion. That's what these words were really all about anyway.*

The court tried to give him a slap on the wrist and hope he would go away. Gratitude would be closed indefinitely, or Peter Sol would face further charges that could see him in prison. *That's what they really want...not me, but Gratitude closed. They're clawing back against the deep blow our school gave them. They didn't think we'd be so darn good at defensive tactics.*

The judge stated, "If that doesn't end it, then I'm sure the state will bring charges against whoever tries to open the gates of that school again. Each state provides a curriculum, and that curriculum must be followed. The court appreciates your efforts and the sincerity behind your words; although many of them slid away from relevancy in this particular case. Regardless, the institution named Gratitude does not follow mandated guidelines—it must be closed until it decides to abide by them."

ANOTHER WAY

Ever since his second year at Gratitude, Miles Carson had made the decision to commit himself to becoming one of the most formidable experts on law. Therefore, he planned his moves accordingly. One of the first most obvious, of course, was going to a University and getting himself a degree. The fact that education could cost so much astounded him. *In order to get better jobs, you need to be qualified. In order to be qualified, you have to pay incredibly high sums to be given the chance to acquire them. Unless you are wealthy, you are now trapped in determinations you set for yourself as a teenager due to your unyielding debt. You have to scrap in order to grab the freedom you were originally handed as an inherent right. How does that not give the wealthy—who already have better access to resources, far too skewed of a position? How does this not trap the poor? Is this not extremely unjust and also detrimental to a society whose goal should be to lay down a path of righteousness for its most credible citizens to step forward upon? Can the law, which is a doctrine that proposes its adherence to logic, not remove itself from this lunacy? It's bad for all of us. Money should have no place in learning. If there has to be a sorting, a ranking...merit is the only factor in a society which strives to reach its highest potential. Otherwise we become a culture which suppresses its own talent and therefore holds everyone back.*

Beyond that, Miles didn't much see the necessity for law school in its current conditional format anyway. He went, he participated, he did his time; but he simply wasn't impressed. His own assessment would be that there were far more optimal ways to acquire the necessary information. However, he had to accept that he wasn't in charge—that he wasn't the one laying the stones. He had to focus on what he could control, and the practical turns needed to be taken on his own road toward a larger goal. Therefore, he thought he might as well squeeze the experience for whatever it was worth. Although he loved his freedom, he knew there was a place for some conformity as well.

Another major decision he made was to distance himself from his grat team; the D.T.'s. He felt it best to test the waters of life solo for a while. Although he knew that in many ways it made sense to stay in communication with them—help out as best he could on any of their current projects—he needed a break. *Time away is important. I know it. Have to do it—not permanent.*

His most honest fear was the close proximity of so many inflamed in the indulgence and addiction to competitive behavior at college. *It's so hard swimming against the current of social regularities,* he recognized. *Not a force to be underestimated in the least. The ego thinks it can stand firm, but the vigor of the water often knocks over your own resolve with ease…as it continues right along the bottom of the river.*

He quelled his aversion by turning his blanket of truth over to the other side: *How many times have I learned from unforeseen (yet needed) lessons of getting knocked down? It would make you think I should look forward to them. Sometimes we take the most from our experiences of being weak. No matter what they throw at me, I'll never stop believing in the logic of working together. My own personal belief in the power of teamwork is so grounded in certainty that it can withstand any rapids. I've been trained well. Come at me with your great social pressure of separation—but I won't lose a grip of my truth.*

Another ally of his, was his pure love for ingesting words; that had been developed decisively as a boy. It allowed him to dive into pages of legal studies, without the burden most other students experienced in their personal prodding's toward long hours of forced concentration. And anyway, he had been preparing himself for years by reading similar content during his personal studies at Gratitude. In fact, he had filled out notebooks with his own individual assessments of many historical court cases and read the biographies of a number of famous and esteemed lawyers of the present and past. He was as prepared as anyone might be to take on the required knowledge of law school.

It was his own disdain for the manner in which people tried to teach and learn in this new institution which brought the greatest challenge to his focus. Years at Gratitude had trained him to zoom out and take note of the larger picture of circumstance. He couldn't help but do that now. In many ways, his opinion once he experienced it, was even more depressing than what he thought he'd find (and he had prepared himself for much). *They really try to make it as boring as possible. They treat their students as if it isn't at all likely that their mind might have an opinion worthy of the entire class for deep consideration....that it isn't possible for them to break into an area which no one has gone before—isn't possibly to enjoy. The whole entire thing is based on a hierarchy, which, although humans find comfort in...is not grounded in a productive process worthy of the time we are living. "Get through the tough years, pay your dues, and then maybe we'll acknowledge your qualification enough to allow you to speak. Maybe if you wade through a similar torrent of shit that we had to—we'll finally be willing to turn on our perceptions and hear what you have to say. Then we'll watch in delight as you speak the words we have pressured you to feel. All for the sake of appeasing the insecurity of our sensitive egos." These are the exact disastrous forces working against progression. I know them.* Miles wrote them down.

Carson exercised his need to be creative, by always coming to his own personal conclusions on a vast array of moral dilemmas; even if he wasn't asked. The history of the law itself did fascinate and impress him, but he also saw no reason his own grounded code of morality wasn't supposed to decipher its personal position all along the way. The biggest difference he could see between himself and the other students was that he searched to find his own answers from an internal source. He didn't expect anyone else to provide them for him. He had learned during his adequate years of schooling, how to be detective-like in his searching for information. *Lose the swirling opinions of your own imagination...what do you have left to contribute? You can't become an expert by following only the ways of others. That's a lie. An expert stamps its own name on the package, and stands by it—simply because each of us know what we know. This includes the lessons and truths we take from others. Balance. It's like spending time alone and spending time with friends. It's not that one is better, it's that there is quality experience to be had in each. But taking the opinion of someone else and seeing it as accurate…that's just another method of forming our own opinions anyway.*

Early on in his studies, Miles saw that he would not allow his personal flaw to be—underestimating the genius given down from the past. *The current methods of the law do have to be respected, abided for the most part…and also appreciated. That's important. In many ways it does know better than we do. But there is also so much room for improvement within a creative and confident mind. This kind of mind always goes forward, not getting stuck in the trappings of nonsensical thinking. Instead, a creative mind harnesses the opportunity of time in order to search the past to find solutions of creation. The moral and mature human sees it as his job to do so.*

So Miles searched for this healthy balance. The ideas of the minds he was studying, gave way to even more of his own. His mastery over ethics deepened as he continually invested in the positive conditioning of his own brain with as many different perspectives as possible.

After he was finished reading cases, and during, he would stop to ask…*What do I think? What's right here?* He felt responsible for best utilizing the tools he was given. He loved the process of allowing his mind the time to search for answers.

He thought about so many things. He'd sit and watch as he found himself considering subjects such as 'situational humanity.' *The difficult part of living in a bustling city, is that it's so easy to take on the mentality of feeling small…to scratch and claw for your own personal share. After all, there's only so much right? In a city, you can see the challenge of great numbers with your own eyes. But the problem is that it's guided us away from tapping in to our inner most powers of comfortable individuality. It is okay to feel special. We all want to be. Good thing for us…we are. In fact, I think we have to love our own peculiar creation to bursting amounts of gratitude. Then we're ready to work with others to do the same thing. Divine…it's all about seeing ourselves as divine*. The opposing and flourishing viewpoint he saw while studying at his accredited university—it broke his heart. He knew it was wrong.

History itself was like large pieces of fruit he devoured in order to satisfy his urges of understanding. He was fascinated with the circumstances of the founding fathers most of all. Since as far back as Miles could remember, he had always had an affinity for George Washington's humility—in his non-party affiliation, and in his creation of limited terms of office. But as he gathered new information with his developing objective mind, he saw that Washington was only doing his duty. He truly did not wish to be a monarch; was a tremendous military mind, and saw himself as ultimately a simple man. However, he wasn't the greatest leader of his time. As Miles weaved through historical documentation, he saw that that designation was firmly reserved for two others: John Adams and Thomas Jefferson. It was really these two men who were the most significant fathers of a new system of government on the land of the Americas. They, were in the possession of minds with philosophical morality and creation that was truly revolutionary.

In a completely just course of event, Miles felt it would have been Adams elected as the first president of the country. He, more than anyone else, put his honest views on public display. He was a little fighter who argued with every ounce of his might. He was a fantastic lawyer who at first achieved notoriety by defending British officers accused of murder in Boston. He sought to prove to England that Americans were civilized by the very substance and worth of our own system of justice. However, what he found out, was that in order for that to occur—a father who seeks to gain respect of his son, and become aware of the point in which his child has proven his adulthood, is required. Through circumstances that followed, Adams began to see that equality would never be given out willingly; that English leaders were not wise enough for that. He saw that equal standing had to be taken—proved one time, for all to see and acknowledge; as America showcased its mature standing.

But Jefferson's person (along with his writing) was the proof of Adams argument. He was a man who saw beyond the borders of national lines, and therefore wrote a proclamation revolutionizing human understanding of basic rights. Jefferson did the real work of revolution. He had journeyed out with his soul to swim in the waters of liberating free thinking and grasp onto his own sensible conclusions. He tasted the beauty of living, and his accomplishments were the result of his relationship to life. The strong legs of our foundational table, which are the words of our declaration, are due to the personal desire of his 'inventors mind,' which formed a healthy addiction to the sensation of solution. To understand him, is to understand what America is all about: *Independence. The soft guiding of worthy leadership,* Miles concluded.

The piece of information that astounded Miles more than anything else he came across in his studies, was that John Adams and Thomas Jefferson died on the exact same day. Furthermore, that day was July 4th of the 50th anniversary of the country they created. He wasn't sure what was a more fascinating piece of reality: This occurrence, or the fact that it wasn't widely known or spoken of. *How can I just be finding out about this now?* He was not a conspiracy theorist, but... *of all the life happenings needed to be recorded and expounded as being of sensational coincidence...how is this not one of them?* He questioned.

Perhaps what allowed Miles to gently engage in his interactions with other people, was the fact that he was a serious lover of animals. The connection Miles had to his four dogs made him wish his life was spent interacting with a vast array of animal species. *Will we ever progress enough so that we better incorporate animals into our daily culture?* He didn't think he'd live long enough to see that, but he hoped for it anyway. *Should school not teach basic abilities to interact with animals and grow our own food? Learning must take place in the wilderness,* he thought. *This is one advantage our ancestors had over us...they were more intimate with nature. Although they didn't realize it was what they were doing...they had more gaps of space to meditate. We have to bring that back. We need to become little yogic wizards who can tap into our wiser ways of being.*

The more Carson saw of how things actually were, the more he worried about animal life on the planet. The rampant killing saddened him often, and he sought to become exposed to the history of the developed relationship. *Will we ever learn how precious our connection to other species can be? They have lessons to teach us if we stop being so thickheaded about our own particular talents. The killing does not bother me as much, even, as the waste. This disrespect proves the state of our barbarism I think. Perhaps we went off-track when we stopped using horses as our primary mode of transport. What a cool relationship between beings!*

He learned about the history of mankind's encounters with land and animals through the great fictional writer, James Michener. Through story, Michener displayed for Carson how money and the ego had been equally guilty conspirators in the obstruction of these relations. *It all comes down to the same thing...immaturity. Fur traders, buffalo and eagle killers, cattle ranchers—they all got drunk on the emptiness of disconnecting our connection to being a part of a larger whole. They didn't want money as a tool to experience greater freedom, they wanted it to be envied; on that never ending reach toward external acceptance. What a travesty—humans so addicted to their thoughts of ranking, that they lose control of what is.* Through these stories, he learned how gluttonous ambitions toward achieving unnecessary amounts of wealth, had blinded humans to the possible value of daily interaction with animals. *Those who work to acquire wealth that they have constantly been dreaming of, do not one day have the ability to say, 'now I have it. Now I can relax and bask in the enjoyment of what I worked so hard to get.'* No, he realized, *the mind doesn't work that way. Always fear can find a way to hold onto something—anything. It will, and it does.*

Miles continued on his path of learning through a wide variety of exposures. But he never stopped grounding himself in his own life circumstance. The fact that Gratitude was now closed, was a fork in his wheel of letting go to the flows of life. He saw no way around his desire to take the most aggressive action possible. He knew it wouldn't be successful though. Therefore, he did what he could to focus on the depth of the problem within his mind—exhibiting tremendous patience and maturity. Needless to say, it gave him great motivation to fully grasp the terrain of the situation. If he was sure of anything, it was that Gratitude was a place that should be operational. *How did everything ever get so lopsided? My school is a brilliant glowing light that can help ignite us toward a more advanced place of human training. The law closes that down? For heaven's sake Thomas Jefferson...help me!*

He remembered the child back in public school who knew himself to be at a critical point in determining the direction of his road. If that sequence of events hadn't come to pass, he was certain he would presently be standing in the skin of a very different type of man. His experience at Gratitude was precious, and the fact that others were being deprived of it sent frustration into the hollows of his bones, and determination into the soul of his heart. *Use it, use it Miles*, he often chided himself. *Fix this thing from the inside out. That's all you can do.*

When he finished his three years of standard law schooling, he decided to focus his energy of attention on the criminal sector. He worked for years, fighting to prosecute and give adequate penalties to those who had taken up criminal activity. More than justice, he did this in order to learn what was necessary for his own training. By the age of thirty-two, he had experienced countless tough battles over sentences that would have tremendous implications not only for the life of these particular individuals, but on the future of the law itself. Aside from a few early losses, his record was brilliant, and each case was a stepping stone toward victory in the next. No one had a memory quite like his—he combined its use with his deep understanding of the law to give him a great advantage in court. He realized that the law was adaptable to almost any argument.

Although anyone who was watching his career would consider it to be a thriving success, the greatest value of his accomplishments came from his own personal and meticulous notes at the conclusion of each sentencing. He compiled his own assessments for how adequately the law had matched any given crime; and used their lessons as the bedrock for his continuous learning. He wasn't so much interested in what the punishments were (if that was the focus of his concentration he would have exploded in frustration at the inept prison system long ago). He was interested in the assessment of crime and all the factors that mattered within categories of morality. *That is worse than this—this is worse than that. Sorting it out is dirty work…but someone has to do it.*

Continued success as a prosecutor meant that the fish he went after grew larger and larger. He loved taking on targets that few believed could be defeated; then slashing and slaying his way as best he could toward victory. An important asset at his disposal was his lack of care in his record. *Winning and losing is nothing compared to lessons taken from real challenge.* As a result, his record continually improved.

After many year of practice, Miles came across a case that caused him to have an epiphany into the capable bandwidth of the law. A defense lawyer he knew, made him aware of a man suing the school system of the state of Oregon where he currently practiced. His colleague laughed at the notion: "Who committed the crime? The government against itself? Right—like that's ever going to fly. Anyway, thought you might be interested in taking a look at this. Maybe it's something your crazy mind will decide to go after."

After he ended the call, Miles studied the case in detail, and found that his friend was accurate in his perceptions. *That's right. The law is inherently biased in matters in which it has a mutual interest. If you sue a school of the state…the judge in all matters of practicality…will also be the defendant. Still, the system claims to be above even that. Its objectivity is said to have no equal. Let's see if it can adhere to its own standards.*

Although the attempt to sue the government was thought to be challenging beyond imagine—it had already been done, Miles knew. *Just in ways more concretely wrong than this. After all, there are plenty of very troubled individuals who have violated their students with physical and sexual abuse, police officers who've committed murder.* Yet the angle he'd be working from in this particular case was even more fragile. *Which makes it more important. I need to prove that these circumstances are not so very different. The system must take responsibility for these disastrous situations that occur under their watch…the entire scope of them. You don't send your child to school expecting their bodies to deteriorate.*

It had come earlier than expected, but this particular case was the opportunity Miles had been waiting for. He used the process and his position against itself—claiming that in his defense of members of the state as prosecutor, his duty was to support their safety. Therefore, he didn't allow the case to be filed with a defense attorney. *This is a prosecution for a criminal act. I will represent the law on the side of the plaintiff as a citizen of the state who has been wronged…the state will provide another lawyer to defend itself from the other side. That's how this is going to go down—the state arguing against itself.*

The plaintiff had grown up in grueling poverty, and therefore ate both breakfast and lunch at public school for over two hundred days, every year, for eighteen years of his life. He had developed early signs of diabetes by the time he was twenty. Miles found old food menus from his school and called upon eyewitness testimony from workers who had experienced firsthand the horrific conditions in the kitchens and cafeterias. For a child in that situation, there was no other option—no way for them to maintain a healthy diet. The vast majority of what was served, was clearly below nutritional standards. As Miles saw it, this situation was proof, that the institution had certainly failed in its promise to provide a safe environment for developing minds and bodies. *Children who are expected to be given an adequate amount of food to nurture themselves—are instead born with a deformity and beaten down again and again by an institution more caught up in the politics of money than what is actually right. Without a healthy body, it simply isn't possible to succeed on any level of substance. This will be the main lever of my argument,* he discovered.

Miles considered how different his schooling at Gratitude was. Not only was the food in the cafeteria extremely nutritious, but every grat was outstandingly environmentally conscious. They weighed food waste at the end of every meal, and it was a fun game to see how low they could make their combined weight. They each carried with them their own unique set of utensils and plate ware: Fork, knife, spoon, bowl, plate, cup and even straw. There were art classes where students could create their own personal sets for themselves. It was one of many fun ways for grats to establish individuality. He smiled thinking of himself waiting in line to rinse off his personalized 'Wheel of Time,' inscribed set.

Miles smashed the defense of the state with ignoring basic knowledge of health standards available at the time of the transgression. He brought financial records of money spent on technology never implemented in the classrooms—money that could have easily been used to increase the quality of food that the cafeterias were offering. "The system has failed to prioritize that which is obviously most important. Better food is not even necessarily more expensive, so you cannot hide under the blanket of inadequate funding." He argued further: "Of course, life cannot be equal for everyone, but we have to at least try to give the neediest a decent chance; shouldn't we all be able to agree on that? Not because it's nice, but because it's the smartest action for our society to be taking. It's what our country is founded on—great minds rising up from anywhere to benefit everyone. If you do not believe in this, then you are not a real American." Carson took a deep breath and concluded his thoughts for the court. "Food should be as formidable a way to help our citizens reach their potential as any; if that is indeed what we want. Without the necessary fuel, we do not function properly. This is not a matter to be taken lightly anymore."

Surprising to almost everyone, his client was unanimously victorious against the state. The plaintiff was awarded $24 million dollars to be paid half by the state education department, and half by the federal government. More important than the money, however, were two other factors: The first was that public-school cafeterias never looked the same again—a culture was shifted, and healthy living began to be promoted with greater emphasis. The second resulting factor, was that Miles gained a significant boost in notoriety which allowed him to move into the next stages of his career.

The greatest lesson taken for him was that sometimes people force upon themselves blind and unworthy trust in that which is actually most important...*their schools! Why? Because they don't have the guts to ob-jectively see.* It was the only way for Miles to rationalize the population's lack of outrage in what the system of education actually was. *Perhaps I underestimate the difficulty in looking at hard truth which has the ability to overwhelm. However; even though it might seem easier not to open these doors to begin with...we must engage the overwhelming. The future of our children is reason enough to cast our sight on uncomfortable foundations. And anyway, it's only too much for what we think we can handle. In truth, we desire most to engage in the challenging. Improving that which matters is where life purpose come from. I can't wait until we all finally grasp that,* he decided after the case had concluded. *Only then will the real progression flow forward as we find the ability to take an honest account of our own community.*

THE STRIKE

Amanda Keegan paced back and forth in Peter's home office. She had been staying with the Sol's for over a month now working furiously on their strategy. Emotionally she had never been able to accept the decision to close Gratitude. The school had simply meant too much for her. Therefore, she was the one spearheading the revolution that was about to take place in school systems all across the land. The results of Miles recent victory gave them great support and momentum.

"I just don't know if we have enough yet," she mumbled half to herself and half to Peter. *She likes to be sure of things from all angles,* Peter thought. *This one has a difficult time taking chances. That's good. That's what we need….the best game plan possible.*

"All these parents say they'll support their children's actions—but when push comes to shove, I'm not so sure. Too many people have broken in the past. The pressure that will come will be more than they expect or have ever experienced before chance must be taken."

"You're right, of course," Peter replied, "but we've now accumulated higher numbers of endorsement than ever before. Sometimes you have to take a leap and see what happens Amanda. We can't wait forever. Decisions we have yet to make could prove to be more important than all the planning we've already done. If now isn't the time, then when?"

She felt he was right, but still; she wanted to swing the momentum a bit more in their favor before everything began. *Not just yet…one more piece,* she thought.

So Amanda did what she knew how to do best; she wrote and posted her writing in 'Responsible Minds.' She became fire itself and sent it out to the millions in their community awaiting direction. *What we are attempting is indeed monumental. We can't forget how important this is.* She titled her work 'Serious Business.'

Serious Business

The time we are living in calls for us to tap into a bit of anger. Yes, anger. Not violence; but the steady anger connected with determination. I try not to get worked up because there is a stigma about it that implies a loss of control. But now I see that there is a time for relaxation, and also a time to give it all we've got.

With the attitude of thoughtful fury, we can create change more quickly. Fury that is simply used to motivate and keep our focus steady on the changes we demand. Fury that shows the opposition how serious we are.

Being in full awareness—it's time for us to get a little pissed off.

If you open your eyes to evaluate fairly, you will see that there is a whole lot to be furious about. You can even be angry at how many angry people there are out there; with no real direction or purpose behind their anger. That's OK. However, the situation which stirs the most fury within me—the thing that frustrates me to no end, and I feel should frustrate you as well; is our current system of learning.

I'm furious that we have mandatory regulations in place that are so incredibly archaic. I'm furious that the system that has the ability to make more positive change than any other single element, instead brainwashes perfectly moral people into feeling that they aren't good enough. It brainwashes people into feeling that they are destined for a life of competition. Truly, it brainwashes us into having unnecessary anxiety and never-ending ambitions to be accepted. It has brainwashed most of us into spending our precious time living on this planet in distraction and fear. You don't have to look very deep to see. This is serious business. Our future hangs on the balance of how we foster the growth of our children.

The idea that "suffering is a part of life" has created more suffering in the world than anything else. Proof of how widespread this concept is can be seen directly in the institution of education itself.

"I know you don't want to wake up to go to school, but sorry, kiddo, in life you have to do things you don't want to. You don't want to take this test, do homework, work on this project, sit silently for hours at a time? Sorry, there isn't a choice. This is our way of limiting your growth and indoctrinating you into our system of painful existence. Get used to it, OK? Soon, once you're addicted to this feeling of suffering—you'll willingly choose to place yourself into similar situations throughout the course of your life."

How often do parents use this logic of accepting suffering to educate their children? Why in a life that's so precious and furiously fast should we spend our time doing things we don't want to be doing? Perhaps we decide to make commitments out of responsibility, but shouldn't they be our own to make? A life of compliance eliminates individual decisions and therefore causes us to suffer.

What we are doing is getting humans into the habit of trusting others to decide for them how best to live. This is nonsense. This is extremely dangerous and has led to more unnecessary depression, torture, horror—than anything else in the world.

No one else has any idea what's best for you—how could they? Should we not be teaching this concept in school? After all, most of us don't even know what's best for ourselves! Often we pretend that we do, but that is so very different. Those who truly know, don't talk much, don't force their views onto others. The best among us are usually the quiet ones—the ones who avoid conflict and only speak when they have actually worked matters out quite securely and repeatedly within their minds. It's time for this group of people to gain some bravery and do what needs to be done already. We must realize that there's no one else who'll do it for us.

In order to create the right kind of system, we have to be able to take a huge step back and open up our observations of logic; ask the right questions. To begin with, what's the point of school? What are we trying to do? Is it just disguised babysitting to maintain the workforce, or are we attempting to help our children foster their development of happiness? From what I can tell, the system has no real goal aside from perpetuating its own importance. Children are not learning in order to acquire a love for it, but rather to get into college and get a job. But 'career' and 'college' are just words that bare the illusion of success. Don't we all know this? What is success really? You can have a great job and a great résumé, make boatloads of money, have a family—and all the while be suffering terribly internally—keeping dark secrets, hating yourself, and fighting against unseen enemies. How many times do we need to be shocked—finding out contrasting information about those we thought had it all together, before we believe?

We think we know what'll make us happy, but most of us have not a clue. Most of us are so set in our ways that we can't see how much better it can be. I have experienced another way; so different. I've seen what better looks like, and I want you to see too. You deserve a life of gratitude; same as me.

Her words made a difference. They hit the ones who needed that little extra push before taking on this monumental cause of change. Amanda and Peter chose the first day of November as appropriate for the children of the world to begin their strike against the system of education. It felt right (enough time into the school year to experience the extent of the burden, but also the freedom of summer not so distant in memory). They tried to keep revolutionary action as simple as possible; all those who made the choice to join would simply not participate in their dull studies. They would continue abstaining from doing classwork, homework, and taking tests until school agreed to at least discuss with the leaders of Futurism the possibility of making greater changes to their system. All they were asking for was a discussion. They eventually got it.

The revolutionaries were mostly comprised of high schoolers, but also contained a good percentage of middle school students as well. The younger ones, of course, weren't yet developed enough to take this on; although many still supported in their own ways.

Futurist adults, however, were the centralized and organized body the was the handle of the hammer (the children were the head). Futurism enlisted all the tools of marketing to promote the cause; beginning months in advance. Television ads, billboards counting down the days until the start of the strike—a swarm of social media. It made it difficult for anyone not to know what was coming.

Although the teachers' union, administration, and many who had no plans to give up the standing they had suffered to get, tried hard to push back; they were no match for the amount of energy sweeping in upon them. They didn't have the time or methods of communication to game-plan well enough. Over the years they had immersed themselves in so much red tape that it made change, and communication, a long and arduous process leading to very little productivity. What they had at their disposal, was the same boring tools. They scraped together threats of detention, expulsion, and blemishes to personal records—bad letter grades. This time however, their attempts at playing at fear and a mentality of ego separation had become too recognizable. Once understood, these tools were only a somewhat productive method for swaying the weakest. People began to understand that if they could stand firm now and break through this barrier—everything would improve. They understood that there wasn't much of a choice. Supporting parents told their children, "if you don't do it...who will? I believe in you." The kids absorbed the concept, and most of them experienced more exciting purpose than ever before in their lives.

The first day of the strike, over two million children around the world absolutely refused to participate in regular classwork. They went to school as usual, they sat, they read books and journaled (if they were allowed to). They listened to music or made art, but they did not participate. For the first time in history, it seemed that children had enough support not to be intimidated by the illusion of power that system adults tried to hang over their heads. These adults feared opening the game of control, and children quickly saw their own position of strength. Through the communication enabled by the internet, strikers supported each other and agreed not to give in to the threats they knew would soon be coming. They promised each other they'd stand firm and be more mature—have more conviction and resolve than those who were attempting to maintain the status quo.

Most student revolutionaries began to feel that they were now a part of something that was big and meaningful. They didn't want to remain on the outskirts of a cause that might actually triumph. Therefore, day after day the numbers of revolutionaries grew. Nightly YouTube videos were posted by both children and adults instilling resolve not to give up—to continue with the cause until a better system was created. When those on strike were asked by their teachers or principals, "Why don't you participate? You've always been such a good kid and a leader to your classmates."

A usual response to this blatant flattery was, "Change the structure, give me the freedom I deserve, stop forcing me to take tests—then I'm sure I'll choose to participate. I'll go back to being that 'good kid.'" Unfortunately for many in opposition, this type of manipulation had been well prepared for.

"Remember there are no rules to how we do this," Amanda guided her community in her own video. "If you want to participate in class, by all means do so—but do not feel pressure or compulsion in any way. It's your right as a human of this planet to do with your body what you like—as long as you are not intentionally harming anyone else. They can't force you to participate. Remember that grades and test scores mean nothing in regard to your own personal value. What you have inside matters a billion times more. Even if you choose to answer one question while in class, you can then fall back into the role of noncompliance. There's no 'being broken.' That is another aspect of their devious tactics. We all take steps backwards. Do what you feel, but consider what makes sense. Start over as many times as you like."

The old school media—a force that fed off of disruption and conflict—was all too ready and satisfied to jump into this tasty battle. They took videos of classrooms where only one student still paid attention to their teacher. It was interesting footage to say the least; and for perhaps the first time in history, the nightly news was engulfed in the topic of education. The pressing question—*what'll happen?*

Students, parents, and administrators were interviewed on talk shows. There were plenty of debate panels. Former students from Gratitude were in high demand, and most spoke extremely passionately about their experience at their old school—of a better way already put into place, but locked down for inexplicable reasons (the public still had those images of children being dragged out of their beautiful school firmly held in their minds).

Although the media took both sides, as time went on, they found themselves beginning to lean more and more in favor of those in peaceful revolution. After all, a simple conversation didn't seem to be such a lofty request—*was it?* When the voice to hold a conference between the leaders of opposing groups became loud enough; things really started to swing in the direction of change.

Everyone seemed to have an opinion on the ways in which school needed reforming—arguing back and forth on what was truly realistic. In a sense, that was already achieving success. The real conversation had finally begun.

The strike was bold, and boldness always seems to be necessary for shocking people into shifting their focus. It wasn't easy for the leaders of the old system to give-in to negotiation. The foundations of their seemingly indestructible walls had been built up over so many years. It was almost impossible to agree to knock them down and start over again. Money was a tremendous factor and as ingrained in their system as anywhere else. Too many standardized-testing prep courses, too many textbooks, and too many jobs to be lost. They were worried that Futurists would demand far too much.

Regardless, after a full two months of only increasing pressure, the leaders of the governmental system were left little choice. What could they do with schools where only twenty percent of the students were agreeing to participate? It could only get worse. They had been successfully backed into a corner. It was time to lick wounds, gather what they could hold onto—and move forward into the unknown.

THE UNEXPECTED

O n the second day of negotiations, something happened that shook the world and diverted its attention toward an event which demanded it more urgently. Peter had just returned to his hotel room after a run around the Washington, DC, monuments. The fact that he was now in the capital participating in discussion with the secretary of education was a great indication of progress itself.

He took a shower, started to get dressed, and flicked on the news. Entertainment channels disguised as news tended to overuse the term *breaking*, but for this—it was indeed warranted. What he saw horrified him. It was something he had never wanted or expected to see. However, Peter Sol had grown to expect the unexpected. Still, it didn't make it easier. Today he didn't feel like taking it. He harnessed anger and sadness the way Amanda prescribed. He pledged to himself: *This time I'm going to do everything I can. It's time to take the next step in utilizing what Futurism has built up. No holding back.*

The worst terrorist attack yet to occur in the nation's history began on a rainy day in January in the multicultural city of San Francisco. At midday, over fifty heavily armed terrorists all began simultaneously unloading their weapons into busy areas of pedestrians all across the city. It was a horrible, well-planned attack in its efficiency. The public was stunned. It was not just a singular day, but a continuous nightmare that lasted for almost a week. When the police believed they had eliminated the entire threat, another bubble of extremely confused humans with poisonous conceptions of justice, would pop up in a different location—then another and another. The prolonged continuation made it more heartbreaking and challenging to bear than any other previous attack. Helplessness was felt deeply among the majority of the population. The city had no choice but to lock itself down. Even so, the terrorists could not be diverted from their cause. They went into private homes at night, into homeless shelters, and large apartment complexes—killing vast numbers of strangers. They were using creativity for the most destructive purpose possible.

The coverage of the media of course stormed forward as it always did—placing its attention firmly on engaging this battle; and how the country could possibly strike back militarily against the fundamentalists. It seemed that when faced with conflict, only force could be seen as a possible means for problem solving. Little focus was given to the real reasons behind why these groups were recruiting more and more members successfully every year; little understanding that the idea of wiping them out by means of violence was becoming more and more unlikely. *How can hundreds of people (many of them citizens of the country where they are committing these acts) be willing to do what they're doing? What's really going on here within these confused minds?*

These questions are rarely asked, as thirst for violent revenge overwhelms and outweighs all other calm perspective and level strategy. Peter saw that the whole problem with addressing terrorism by military means, was that terrorism was constructed exactly for the purpose of not being vulnerable to the effects of traditional physical might. Although he was sure he wasn't the first to realize this, it seemed governments were unable to think outside of boxes imposed by old history, and develop more creative solutions for the present time.

In the wake of the tragedy, strong pressure was placed on Futurists to give up their strike on education and return to a state of normalcy. After all, didn't these issues pale in comparison with that of self-defense?

So went the logic of much of the public; but Peter thought differently. He was sure that this was the exact time to open an even larger conversation—and hold onto the ground of progression already made. *Perhaps not during, but shortly after. We can't be afraid to address our larger problems here.* He dreaded the obstacle this imposed on their built up momentum. *Perhaps it came be used effectively,* he wondered.

His appearance on television three days following what was hoped to be the final bubble of violence was one of the most highly viewed programs of the year. Both supporters and opponents tuned in to see what Peter Sol had to say. There wasn't a debate or much of a production at all. He sat down at a polished wooden table in a simple room, opened up his notebook, and began to read words.

Many found that they were growing quite sick of traditional commentary and coverage—thirstier for something in the media with more substance. A week of being glued to the television made this even more apparent to the public. What they truly wanted—was greater vulnerability of opinion. Peter gave it to them. The media constantly underestimated the intelligence of their viewers; he did not.

"I invite you to close your eyes and listen," were the first words he spoke. "I'm not going to look up at the camera very often because I don't think *who I am,* is so important—given the subject matter. Words, ideas—are more important. The light coming through me trumps my individuality. Regardless, it's up to you what you choose to do with your own eyes, your own mind. Let's begin.

"Can I flow through life powerfully? That is the question I am interested in. Because unfortunately it takes much power not to get pulled down and sucked into the ego games that those who are tragically ill are submerged within. Have no doubt—their goal is to pull you down to their level. Why? In order to prove to themselves how terrible everyone is—just like them. Can you see? The reality of our time is no different than imagining a make-believe zombie apocalypse. Except that it is more challenging since those who are contagious appear to be in the same health as anyone else. They are zombies in disguise. Regardless, those who have been bitten, unknowingly—mindlessly, spew at us their contagious venom. It is that severe. And it takes an incredibly healthy immune system to repel these attacks. It takes such a deep acceptance in the variety of normalcy of the self; to travel to the place of ego battle—see that we are there, and use it still for growth. Each time we defend, we get better at defending. Until we are able to laugh at the absurd notion of victory."

Peter was talking about terrorists, but also a perversion more widespread even than that. He was talking about the thing which causes terrorists to do what they do. *The thing that is everywhere. I hope they see that,* he thought.

"A successful community works together, and the whole planet of Earth should be seen as one big community. It should be seen that way simply because that's what it is—that's what we are; even the ones that are so far from seeing it. Is this you?

"It is not a small community I'm referring to, but it is one nonetheless. You can dislike this concept immensely, but it doesn't prevent it from being firmly true and real. There is no escape from our connectedness. The only thing we should be competing fully in; is seeing who can love our time of life the most—to help our community."

Peter took a long pause. *That one is an entertaining conception to think on. It's a fun game of appropriate competition, if our mind is in need of one.* He shook himself away from this thought and continued.

"There's no smarter or smartest among us. There's only different. This is not a message to be scoffed at. No one is bad, but many of us are indeed extremely confused. Some to the point of taking violent actions, and others to self-destructive measures. Others to the point where the need for revenge clouds the presence of all the rest of their accumulated wisdom.

"Allow me to be personal for a moment. My sister was murdered by one of these very confused individuals—a terrorist who was also a part of our community. There's no getting back at anyone for what's happened in the past. Trust me, I've been there. There's only the kind of revenge that helps to make a better world—a world of less occurrences like the ones that just happened. Violent revenge clearly hasn't worked. What are other solutions?

"To answer, I want to talk now about our jobs, and not the ones that have anything to do with making money. Let me ask you; when will we realize that our primary job is to simply focus on bettering the being which we control? Is it now time for us to finally see that we have been distracting ourselves—that we really should have been grounded in this truth of attention yesterday? Contrary to popular habit, our job is not to analyze the worthiness of ourselves compared with others. It's not to change others either—for better or for worse. That's their job. Our job is to become the best self possible; and then hold an iron clad grasp in the certainty that positivity will naturally spring forth from living in that space. And not one of us is ever at the finish line."

He sat with it—allowing the space of silence to work its magic for a few moments. Peter was in love with spaces of nothing.

"Support on this path is crucial. Rediscovering our community is essential. Falling into perspective, we can see that there is nothing that requires more of our focus than supporting ourselves and others to be our most authentic versions—and to do our own work. You and I are children of peace. But sometimes children of peace get soft and forget that there is also a need to be strong—very strong. Through our inability to be strong with our peace, we have allowed matters of little significance to distract our attention from the things that desperately need it.

"A pressing example of the lack of strength in the ways of our culture is that we have not yet found an adequate solution for combating violence. Although it might be hard to see, the best way to combat violence is not with violence. Perhaps in some instances, but not in the large majority of them. Forceful conquering is a way of the past to be chiseled into our history so that we learn what not to do. Our power of physical force might be necessary in very well-considered ways—but ultimately it is not the larger key that will unlock the door to a greater arena of peace, progression, and strength that we yearn for. Violence is a Band-Aid of a solution. There are more permanent cures at our disposal. Physical force should always be the last-case scenario—mainly because it's an action that's proven many times to have negative ripple effects far into our future, and well past our limited vision. We don't stay away from violence because we want to be nice; we stay away from it because it's self-destructive.

"The truth is that there are only people that need our help. The ones who want to kill us probably need it most. They have sacrificed their experience of being gratefully alive, and therefore they have made themselves into something on the verge of no longer being human. We must pull them back from the abyss by displaying for them truer examples of human evolution and justice. To squander the gift of living is the definition of insanity itself. It's what comes from believing that life is boring or hard—that allegiance to a system beyond our own logic is wise. It never is. For this reason, we must be grounded in our philosophy.

"I'd love to give my full support to the government of my country. However, I cannot. This does not mean that I am unpatriotic. In fact, I believe the complete opposite to be the case. Blind allegiance is the last thing any wise government should want from its' citizens. Is our country wise? That is the question. I believe my country has failed to see that it has lowered itself to the level of those who believe in the conception of 'enemy.' It has been caught in a trap. We do not have to play at war merely because it has been declared upon us. We have simply to defend ourselves while working toward helping those in need (including those who believe that they hate us). How can we help them? By focusing on not falling for their trickery. Is this not how we teach our children to deal with conflict; 'be the bigger person?' Should we not practice the lessons we preach?

"The mature person does not have enemies, and the same holds true for an entire tribe. If it thinks it does, then it is not mature. It has not seen reality clearly, but rather played too far into its own need to pound its chest and brag about how superior it is. We all know that those who fill the air with loud words of their own greatness, tend to be covering up a deeper deficiency of spirit. Furthermore, those who take on this practice of boasting—often try to push us into the same tendency as well; and it works. Therefore, many of us take on the practice of bragging when we have no interest in bolstering ourselves like that.

"Most importantly, do not fool yourself into thinking that the root of the problem exists in the mind of a very distant stranger. The root of the problem exists within you. Yes, don't run away. It is our fear and self-doubt, that prevents us from having the clarity to discover progressive solutions that are easily within our grasp. You're not too tired or weak for it. It's our fear and sloth that prevent us from prioritizing love and finding healthy new openings. The change we need to make will take time, and there will never be an immediate solution. Many of the bad habits that have been cultivated have strong roots, and it will take years beyond the time of our lives to pluck all of them up. Luckily, in many beautiful ways, the change is already happening—has been happening. Being OK with existing in the realm of change is enlightenment itself.

Peter took a few deep breaths— calling his parasympathetic nervous system into action. "However, it's our schools that if rediscovered will make these positive changes happen with the greatest haste. We cannot allow these lower forms of violent action to distract us from our own work toward changing a vital system which is in such need of repair. Yes, what happened in our loving city of San Francisco is despicable, horrid—a testament to the rampant sickness of humankind. The solution, however, is not to make ourselves sick as well. Do we not want our children to have the ability to solve the problems we haven't yet been able to figure out? The sooner we allow them to believe in their own answers—the sooner they'll provide them for us."

Again he chose to let his words sit in the air. He didn't want to overwhelm those who weren't particularly adept in arenas of auditory learning.

"Reflect on all the people you know, and then consider the absurdity of trying to rank how smart each one of them is. And for what purpose would you even want to do that in the first place? Is there a point to it; aside from inflating our own ego's desire to have an opinion? I hope you agree that the topic of who's better is fantastically boring as well as incredibly unproductive. Let's move past it already. Our children need to be spending their days more wisely than this. Trying to rank them by levels of intelligence is so incredibly ridiculous and harmful to all of us. It's a heavy burden to see this. Is grading itself not an example of competition taken too seriously? You have to get on board. The train will leave without you.

"Consider this issue of terrorism. One of the worst acts in human history has just occurred. Will most children honestly discuss it in the current school system we have in place? Almost certainly they will not. Very few teachers have been infused with the freedom to engage such a sensitive, yet vital topic of conversation. But children of course will have been exposed to what has happened—they will know about it. Are we really going to sit back and take a chance that every parent will handle these deeply philosophical moral issues appropriately in their own homes? Parents who have been raised in a culture based on unrealistic and rampant fear themselves? Parents who believe in enemies, and who are scrambling to stay afloat—scrambling for survival, and often psychologically ill? Parents who are too scared to open their eyes to how fantastic life is, and how fortunate they are? I think maybe we should not do that. I think it's a pretty lousy method of investing in our future growth. I believe school is exactly the place where these conversations must be had.

"Every study on education has agreed on one conclusion—the quality of teacher matters. Our teachers must be the most respected, highly paid, highly trained, highly evolved members of our species. And then we must place around them the most optimal environments of support. We must do this. We can't wait any longer. There is no other job that's as important to our combined success. We all must become interested, and even obsessed, in this subject matter."

Peter stopped and looked up from his notebook into the lens of the camera for the first time. "Thank you for listening today. I'll be back tomorrow for a little more."

He was aware that only so much could be integrated at any one time; and he wanted to leave his audience considering what it meant to be a teacher.

He was a man of his word. Peter walked into the studio the next day at the same time. He moved to the desk, sat down, opened the same brown leather bound notebook, and began reading once again. The number of viewers (which was already outrageously high), doubled the second night. For many, it was the only thing they wanted to talk about in the space between his two sharing's.

All his life, Peter Sol felt as if he'd woken up into a world outrageously confused and out of whack. He felt he was trying to grab people by the shoulders and shake into them awareness of what was obvious. But he also felt that he had been given a great gift—and he knew gifts were meant to be shared. Therefore, he spoke slowly and purposefully.

"Those of us who see and know must finally admit that we have allowed ourselves to get sidetracked—pulled into a direction we had no intention of moving toward. Still, that's OK. There's always time. One of the lies that the little voice whispers into our ears is that it's too late or that we have no chance. True wisdom has everything to do with moving away from clinging to what has already occurred.

"There's no need to shame ourselves for what we've done or how we've been spending our time. All of that is merely part of the path that has brought you to this point. It needs to be accepted—more than judged. Judging can be productive, as it leads to growth—but only under the larger umbrella of time acceptance. The destination is indeed the present, and we come back to it again and again. It's time for us to finally get rid of all the wasted worry we've been carrying around—the negative thoughts and unrealistic fears. What is it that you've been doing? Does it matter? Does it help? Is it what you want to be doing? Are you scared of engaging these questions? Ah, so!

"If we really want to be serious about growing to new levels; if we want to be serious about our opinions having value—we need to take on practices that make us alert, aware, and satisfactorily confident. Daily practices. If we are strong in the mind and body, we can accept ourselves—and then become the natural artists of love that our evolution calls for. Artists of love consciously consider where to move and how to use their bodies. They flow with intuition because they are deeply aware of their inherent 'regularness.'

"We have to get better at solving this problem of violence *now*. I will of course never say that we deserve to have our physical freedom taken away—that's ridiculous; but this destruction can also be used as a calling to see some of our own failings. Why shouldn't it? Is this not the most rational practice to take on? These events can in fact become useful tools which shed light on all the necessary changes that we've been tiptoeing around—that which we do control."

Peter knew that he had to be extremely sensitive in regard to what he was about to say next. *So often words are misinterpreted and taken out of context.* Luckily he was simply reading now. *Stick to the lines on the page,* he told himself. *Trust the time you've put into creating this.*

"This is a hard pill to swallow—but if we were more righteous with the ways we lived our own lives; if we lived more with love and gratitude—these terror groups would have a much more difficult time recruiting members. Many of these confused humans live minimalist lifestyles. They gain empathy by calling attention to the commercials for cars, food, and diamonds that are placed directly after news broadcasts of the terrible acts that they have just committed. They point out that our sports channels get better ratings than our news programs. They mock us for the amount of time we obsess over our looks and how quickly we move on from one distraction to the next. They see the makeup, the hairstyles, and the cosmetic surgery of the people we put on television to report on them. They take guesses at the amount of time we take in choosing what outfits to wear.

"We don't have to celebrate them in order to believe that they might have some valid feedback for us to use. You might not want to take that on, but it's an honest point. You might say that they would always find things to criticize us for, and that could be true—but I'd rather consider each point of morality in isolation.

"Let us not fool ourselves—if there is a war that does exists, it's one of ideas and reason, not physical force. If we believe in the concept of freedom, we must show proof by living into it more sincerely. Start by giving people the right to do what they wish with their own bodies. Start with giving more freedom to our children."

It felt good for him to say all of that. So good. When he continued, he drew his voice from a much softer place:

"Does any of this mean that we're bad? Does any of this mean that we deserve to have our lives taken away? Please don't be absurd, and please don't shift your attention from what actually matters. A mature person learns to weigh levels of right and wrong—to have perspective. None of our faults exist on the same hideous plane which takes away the life of strangers. Terrorists like to argue; "your governments do the same thing by dropping bombs on our communities." Let me respond by saying this: Who's being the bigger person now? My friends, beware of anyone who ever attempts to justify their actions by crying out: "Well they're doing it too!" It doesn't really matter to me if it's true or not. Wrong is wrong any way you slice it. Now I will address those who think they are our enemies.

"Dear terrorists, my sadly confused fellow human beings. WHAT ARE YOU DOING?" Peter said the words as a parent enraged with their child.

"Your actions accomplish nothing. Truly nothing. You'll never stop us from loving freedom. You'll never create a big enough explosion unless you take out yourself and all those you love as well. Oh well then.

"But we know what this is really about. No matter your strategy, this isn't about winning at all. You're not trying to win, because you can't. And the more we become artists of compassionate, yet absolutely efficient and lethal methods of self-defense—the sillier you'll begin to feel about how you've chosen to spend your focus.

"But anyway, like I said—this isn't really about winning at all. You think you walk into a crowd and blow a bunch of people up and achieve anything? Nope, you achieve nothing. *This* is the truth you are so afraid to look at. Look! Your lost lives—they meant nothing, and you have gotten nothing from them. Anyone can see that it is objectively horrendous for your own communities to do what you do. The sad truth is; you're too weak to find a more productive form of bravery. Your vicious anger impresses no one. Do not even pretend that you don't care about what other people think. Don't you ever say that—you liar! You care more than anyone. Why else do you think you're about to do what you do? For you, this has everything to do with impressing others. Don't ever say that this is religious. It's the farthest thing from it, and you know it! Although your actions are entirely about finding social acceptance—still, no one cares—and you are a failure. Grasp it! You make things worse, but time still moves on. You're already an atrocity of the past. Although it doesn't matter, mankind is ashamed of you. Future terrorist—can you turn away from your path instead? That's real bravery, and much harder. Doing the right thing, even when no one else will recognize it. That's the juice of life. That's really letting go of what other people think."

Almost finished Peter. He was starting to feel exhausted. He dug deep and continued to sharpen his sight on the words in front of him. This time he spoke with smooth fire in his voice.

"Yes, bad deeds will continue to happen; but we cannot let them shift us away from hope. Resolve! We must use these atrocities as fuel to set us more securely in our own direction of growth. Allow your will to build up the way it wants. Think clearly—use your own words. Our planet is begging for us to stop giving so much attention to our separation. We are separate, but we are also connected. Life is too unpredictable and our time too precious to be fearful of thinking big. There is nothing worthier of your time than thinking big. You have no reason not to. These are things we all already know. But we need reminding—again and again and again. If you take the kind of action which believes helping others helps the self, I promise that you will somehow receive back all the meaning and progression you've been searching for your whole entire life. I don't know why it works that way, but it does. It's awesomely amazing. It means that the universe is on our side. But please don't feel pressure to come up with some masterful answer to solve everything. But if you want to—sure—with ease. However, there's a one-degree shift we can all make that will naturally have a ripple effect we can trust in. It's so simple, and it's really enough."

Peter took a deep breath in through his nose as his shoulders and chest rose and fell. He quickly looked up at the camera speaking now the words he had memorized.

"Slow down my friend. Watch your speed of action. It's our thoughts that cause us to be so tired all the time. The food too, but not as much as the stressful kind of thinking. See that we are more addicted to thinking and doing than anything else. Observe yourself getting pulled back into fight-or-flight mode—needing to do as a result of flashing emotions of insecurity. Slow down and focus on simply breathing; feel your senses and body—see how you really want to be, as objectively as possible. It is beautiful.

"We've all been moving around so fast, not taking enough time to find the glory of stillness. It's making us truly sick. If we slow down enough to feel, we can train our thoughts to be the kind we take pride in—can be the kind of presence we're striving for. First, you must believe that your mind is yours to use however you like. It's the most incredible tool that we've been gifted with. It doesn't matter how it compares to others'. It really doesn't. Your unique creative capacity is endless. See that you already know everything you need in order to awaken your potential."

Peter Sol brought his palms together in front of his chest, closed his eyes, and inclined his head forward once.

"The light in me honors the light in you," he said. Then he slowly pushed the chair out behind him, extended his legs, lifted his torso—stood up and left.

UNIFICATION

R egardless of the great many challenges, the movement swelled. Increasing numbers of humans made the decision not to spend their whole lives feeling anxious about the future—not to distract themselves in the hope of never having to see the reality of the human predicament. Instead, they chose to dive into the realm of the honest search for truth—knowing it to be the only way. They chose to consider the immensity of Space and our little dot of a home existing somewhere within it—often. They pushed their bodies to feel love, to find joy and to see the blessings of experience. They realized that it was their duty to do those things, if they were serious about playing their role.

So many were. A continually growing majority decided to accept that the norm was an insane set of standards to live by—that striving to fall into the category of normal never ended; and led to an almost certain destruction of the spirit. People who had true belief in their worth did not go around constantly searching for validation—had no need to convince anyone of anything, or pump their lives full of material clutter in order to present an image cloaked in childlike safety. Human beings' personal relationships and understanding of themselves finally went deeper than the sum of the imagined opinions of others. The need to constantly be evaluated was an addiction that the population, together, were slowly supporting each other to get the hell away from. The process would of course be a slow progression through generations—but there was movement on the path of greater cleanliness; and progression was the perfect place to stand. There was no denying that it was a time of mental revolution. It electrified the masses.

Negotiations concerning the structure of learning continued moving forward. All the schools throughout the world did not instantly turn into Gratitude (although Gratitude itself was finally permitted to reopen). To all the students who had spent time there, it was a great moment of both relief and victory. It was felt that nothing would happen to close those doors ever again.

As far as the greater school system went, more and more changes happened steadily, yet still at a turtles pace. This became possible as simultaneous improvements to the political structure took place. It was certainly about time that the population began feeling more trust and allegiance toward their own leadership. It was something that countries were longing for—more than they had even realized.

But it was the unconventional religion of Futurism, and the substance of Life Code, that stabilized itself as a personal tool for growth that everyone could use along their journey; no matter the external factors. Many souls that were parched for connection—were finally able to quench that thirst via an invitation into the practice of letting go to a self-conceived higher force of practicality. Unlike other religions, Futurism did not feel a need to define or understand what that higher place was. It was simply necessary to know that it was important to release to some larger force.

Futurists were encouraged to use the tools at their disposal: "Take the time to listen to music and move your body to it—even if that means not moving your body at all. Read books and learn from those who are sincerely tying to share with you what works for them. Don't be in a hurry—clear your mind—relax. Let it be the only thing you do when you carve out necessary time for it."

There were many others who graduated from Gratitude along with Miles that didn't take on monumental court cases and had no desire to place themselves in the public spotlight. Many of his classmates often resorted to a quiet kind of living—becoming masters at appreciating the simple things through their training. They were akin to the hobbit folk from 'The Lord of the Rings'—so focused on their immediate surroundings. They tended to read a lot, spend their time working with nature—peacefully enjoying the process of passing the time they were allotted by remaining minimalistic. Gratitude had promoted the idea that it was for each of them to decide whatever felt right to do with their time—and for many, the logical choice was to gently appreciate the immense range of simple beauties. They were mentally free enough to feel lucky, and not enter the realms of mental comparisons. It allowed for satisfying days spent lying around with their pet animals, feeling like kings and queens of the world simply because they had comfortable safety and health. The difference between them and so many others, was that they knew how to love their circumstances to bursting. It was for this that Gratitude had given them the tools and preparation for.

Miles was like them—he could sit down in a field of grass with the rays of sun energy beating down upon him, and feel as full and complete as any other human on the planet. However, unlike many others, he felt the need for peaceful rebellion in his bones. He seemed to have no choice but to actively do as much as he could—a devotion and a need to make things better on the largest scales his mind could imagine. When Mikey was killed, he vowed to use his friend's memory to ignite him with higher levels of the majestic juices of determination. He could think of no other effect he'd want his own death to have on those left alive; and he sought to pay his fellow revolutionary with the same respect.

Beyond even that, Miles was a creative visionary. He simply couldn't allow his visions to go unattended. Gratitude had been an institution that advised him to go after what he wanted with ease and strength. He had taken that message straight to the heart of intentional improvement. Miles completely embraced the notion that going for it and taking risks which felt intuitively correct, was a fantastic way to spend his time. *I feel blessed and full with the experiences of life,* he'd tell himself. *Anything else to come is just icing on the cake...therefore, knowing that, I can more effectively go after the icing of my choosing.*

Ever since his days founding philosophy club, Miles had continually allowed himself to travel deeper and deeper into the halls of rationality. He even used logic to discover the need to let go of trying to figure everything out—tapping into feelings and intuition and allowing them to be as valid as any well-constructed string of word logic. *It's obvious to any serious truth seeker that there is a logic behind letting the self act out intuitively.* This was very important.

Miles would manage his time going back and forth between using his thinking mind, and then not using it at all. He watched as he flowed between these states, seeing how the empty space led to more productive thinking. He was a reflector and often asked himself, *could I have done something different that I might try next time?* He didn't play with better and worse—he wondered at alternatives, took mental notes on hypotheticals, which then influenced his future actions. He played with possibility and would often search his mind for unique perspectives and ways of interacting with others. His friends started calling him "a social experimentalist." Miles wouldn't say that they were wrong. *In fact, that might be exactly what I am,* he thought. Often he would feel himself beginning to say a certain thing, and then consider, and therefore do—the complete opposite. *Social situations are opportunities to have fun with less of a filter—for us to not really care so much, and therefore grow our bandwidth of self.*

He saw paths before him and had to choose. He did it knowing that any path was fine. By doing this he learned much about people and also found an incredible amount of entertaining experiences to be had as well. He also saw that being unpredictable was fun for others. He got a kick out of making their experiences sharper with his unexpected questions. Instead of regular conversation starters, Miles would allow the randomness of the mind to grab at words chosen quickly in the moment for no particular reason: "How many times a week do you eat ice-cream cake for breakfast, three—or four?" They'd look at him like he was out of his mind, he'd look back at them with a completely straight face.

"Probably more like six or seven actually."

There it is! Enter the game of ridiculousness…I love it.

"If you had to pick a color to describe the day—what color would today be?"

"Maybe pale orange."

"Yeah, I was thinking the same thing. Either that or pale green. Let me ask you a question, do you have discussions with your dog about the joyous feelings of urination and how we should appreciate the little things in life, or do you save that for your cat?"

"Are you high on drugs?"

"No, not at all. I probably should be. Thanks for the compliment. Well? You know it's supposed to be good training to have conversations with your pets right?"

If he had someone fun to work with, the conversations would go forward from there—expanding from their humorous shock, and continue back and forth between absurdity and the stealth infiltration of honest opinions.

The more absurd the better. What do I care? Miles found strangers to be extremely amusing in their individual reactions. Most of the time, his bizarreness actually set them at ease and allowed them to better showcase their own personalities as well. *You just have to learn how to pry it out of them—with the right mixture of kindness and peculiarity,* he decided. *As long as we don't offend, we tend to have a pretty long leash. Even if I do, I did so unintentionally. Gotta love risk. Most importantly, I like to make others feel comfortable by sincerely being whacky myself.*

As he got older, and as a result of his tendency to experiment, Miles became more actively aware of the widespread and chilling mental suffering that engulfed the innards of his fellow human beings. His practice of being outlandish allowed him to see this variance more acutely. *People are so damn uptight for no reason.* When it came down to it, he felt that he had no choice but to continue getting more serious about his own ability to help others heal. He aspired to find a continuing amplified balance between personal strength and softness in order to do it. What he transitioned into was a bulldog of honest proclamations. He was a man who openly admitted to dealing with fear on a daily basis and therefore becoming that much better at using the fear to motivate. His confidence drew from his acceptance as being a regular functioning human, and his humbleness from the understanding of the limitations which that implied.

He often interacted with others lawyers, financial analysts, and salesmen. Many of these were friends of his. He often liked to ask, "What would you like to be doing with your time most of all?"

Many would respond with all sorts of creative answers: "I want to be working on music." "I want to be starting a project I've had in mind for a while." "I want to be an entrepreneur." "I don't know—anything besides what I'm doing now. I won't be doing it for much longer though." They'd shake their heads; "No, definitely not for much longer." Years would go by and they'd still be doing the same thing. It connected Miles with a deep and necessary sadness that he knew he had to face.

The most powerful feeling in the world, is realizing that you're not doing anything wrong. And if you are, it's not exactly wrong...just misguided. Guide yourself back; no matter what it is, and learn how to forgive mistakes as a consequence of your humanity. Mistakes are inevitable. The mature person does make less though—because they know they are secure in their intention. As we improve and become confident in the goodness of our actions, others witness our sincerity, and then perhaps use our example to move to a sincerer place themselves. This makes all the difference.

We have to be stronger in our beliefs than in anything else. By forming the habit of repeating to ourselves what we believe to be true and most important, we discipline ourselves to hold on to this derived strength. Then our core beliefs easily overwhelm any fear, doubt or struggle that will inevitably present themselves along our path. Take the time to work out what you believe Miles.

When Miles had this thought of further developing himself, he instantly knew that he had to make his own list for what he cared about the most. He was astounded that he hadn't ever thought to do it before. *How can we possibly continue moving through life without consciously taking a few moments to prioritize? We don't do it because we move so fast—so much fear day to day. Something so simple, but unparalleled in worth. Yet what percentage of people record what they truly care about the most? You are allowed to be anything you like Miles!* He engrained the words into his being. *Who would have thought that'd be such a revolutionary notion?*

He remembered the day sitting on his couch as the words poured out naturally from his heart of truth and onto the pages of his journal.

I care about feeling good, and I care about letting go. I care about trying to exist as naturally as possible—whatever I choose to decide that that means. I care about concepts of liberation. I care about choosing to turn myself into something better in order to do my part in helping the world. I care about allowing myself to better accept fluctuation and cycles as ever present in this experience of being human. Most importantly, I care about getting serious about my relationship to love—loving and helping other people as well as all parts of nature, including myself. I definitely care about that, and want to care even more.

It's good that I'm making this clear, that I've written this down. I feel different now.

—M.C.

PLATFORM

C arson's best attribute was that no matter how much negativity he was witness to; he never questioned his certainty in things continuing to improve. It was, in fact, impossible to persuade the man to let go of his positive faith in the overall direction of humanity. He knew there were examples of progress to be seen everywhere. His optimistic focus lubricated the gears of his motor, and pushed him to do all he could in order to bring about maturing change sooner.

When he got back to together with his team, it was like experiencing the feeling of an enhanced super power for him. Amanda, Duncan, and so many more. Not only had he done a tremendous amount of maturing and accepting of the self—so had every member of the Dramatic Triangles. It was like wearing a new set of arms that were all willing to be used toward a selected goal. The loss of Mikey, one of the founding members of their team, was a severe blow of course. He was a magnificent leader and team player—in both words and actions. Their only practical choice was to honor him by pushing their evolution further toward their individual potential; further toward achieving their current goals within the political arena. They knew with certainty that it would be what he wanted.

Eventually they felt Miles was ready to participate in the eighteenth season of *KYL*. They developed strategy and followed through on precise action. Miles allowed himself to both passionately and securely interact with team members. It was a joke to consider doing what he was attempting on his own. That most people didn't have these sorts of teams in their lives, perplexed students from Gratitude. Grats didn't understand how so many people would work up all this cohesion under different settings, and then not try to utilize potential advancement of idea through teamwork. They noticed that most humans would say goodbye and walk back to their lonely lives which contained an old core of trust they had established back when they were brave enough to create relationship; severing the new connections and feeling uncomfortable about them for some peculiar reason.

It simply didn't make any sense to grats. Their whole time at school they were taught to do the exact opposite. *Search for connection. Search for new teammates in life.* It was a whole other way of looking at human interaction. They enjoyed it as much as they could—as a practice. For those stuck in an archaic system, the inevitability of loss seemed to be constantly held in their belly's through so many experiences of life. *Why?* Grats would wonder. *How can you get the really big stuff done? I guess they don't know how to open their hearts to exposure. They are not standing healthy in their bodies,* they realized. *They are sick. We have to help.*

When the D.T's picked a project, everyone combined effort to creatively think about what they could do to achieve said goal. They had long sessions of debating higher strategy. Then, they'd independently get to work; in a solo fashion or in smaller groups—knowing how to create needed jobs for themselves and communicating effectively all along the way.

Miles would take on work himself, or hand off tasks that could be accepted or declined by other members. In fact, anyone could offer tasks they developed themselves, but thought could be better achieved through the talents of another member. It wasn't lazy—their functioning was beyond that. Instead, they often saw it as an honor, as usually the match had been given thought and was something the team member cared about. And anyway, it was often just the sort of challenge that particular person enjoyed taking on and spending their time with. Still, the D.T's were not at all afraid to push each other—and then push back. That was their method of settling on solutions in a healthy way. All of their ego relations were at an extremely calm level. They could look at criticism, and simply see validity or not. If one brought a complaint, the other listened. They didn't instantly fall into attack mode the way so many in the outside world did—which often led to skittering around action of avoidance, until the eventual ignition of a drama land mine.

For any grat, it was about being constructive—nothing else. If they felt the taste of ego sensitivity; then they simply called each other out. They did what they talked so much about doing. They were the children who had trained themselves to think on another kind of level. And so they were the ones.

The team combined effort to push Miles steadily up the rungs of the complex and often horrifying political ladder. First he became a simple councilman, then a mayor, and then a congressman in the state of Oregon. As they continued, the team was better able to understand the depth and effectiveness of a successful campaign strategy. *To connect people, to unite...communicate!* They boiled it down: *Get your voice heard, and then make it count.* In order to win a vote, they had to make it so any given community came to know their candidate—and then was impressed. The impressive part was easier, the exposure more challenging.

It was the season the team had been waiting for, and it seemed to come about with perfect timing. They'd be lying if they said that they weren't excited about it. For many grats, the creation of their school itself made this event somehow destined to occur. Regardless of the immensity of the particular task—they stayed determined and remembered their training. *Trying as hard as you feel like for whatever cause you believe in is a great way to spend your time...none better.* Their current goal: make Miles president. That was it. Could they do it? Why not?

KYL was the perfect method for publicity, and there was unanimous agreement among the D.T's to take this next step. 'Know Your Leaders' had been the number one show on television for the past five seasons; and for the past two, second place wasn't close. Even though the team was quite familiar with the creators, they still had to prove their legitimacy in order to get in. Miles' accomplishments mattered, and they, along with his present disposition—gained him acceptance to the most highly coveted season.

Carson was at the steady age where confident life experience has the potential to combine with just the right amount of youthful vigor—the early forties. If you wait too long, the hottest part of the fire is no longer present. If you start too soon, well, too much fire can overtake patience. That and the development of discipline. Humans are more like flowers than anything. It's not that being in your prime is better, but there is a certain point of peak energy that does exist within the span of a lifetime.

As he participated in *KYL*, millions of viewers became witness to the ways of Miles' personality. And that was what the team wanted—what they knew would actually matter the most in the end. *My character itself is valuable,* he told himself objectively. *That's how it should always be, and that's how I'm going to make it. No titles, résumé, or any events that I've gone through. Just me. Standing alone for whatever I am currently worth along my developmental track. No deception.*

So he moved through his days in front of the cameras; increasingly showing respect for the opinions and expertise of the other contestants, while simultaneously displaying proof of the confident value in his own thinking. He expressed belief, taught kindly, and asked many questions.

He woke up in the mornings the same way he had now for the past eleven years. He walked to the mirror and said, "Can you love living so much that it scares you today?" Then he'd meditate for fifteen minutes, set to a timer—making himself as still as possible until the alarm sounded—then he'd do his yoga for as long as he felt, before setting off for the rest of the day to do whatever work he chose to take on.

The competition was electric, and Miles was impressed with the quality of those going through this experience with him. *Anyone who wins will be a serious upgrade to what we've had going. That is a very good thing which gives me hope. Marty and Maya have done an excellent job finding the right talent.*

He often sat back and observed intently—jumping into discussion when he felt he could add value, but otherwise remaining rather quietly relaxed overall. When Miles did speak, though—others had a tendency to perk up and listen. If they weren't paying attention, he could usually tell. He'd stop, wait, and give them a chance to re-engage before continuing. It was a part of his practice not to speak to phantoms—it led to the receiving of much respect. That, and the fact that he was already a pretty famous dude.

While on *KYL*, Miles had to discipline himself not to fall too deeply down the rabbit hole of self-comparison. *I wouldn't have started this campaign if I still had any doubt about how my abilities as a leader stack up against others. Regardless, the public can make their own decision. I'll have no qualms with their choice, as long as I feel they have gotten to know me well. I have to show them that I'm able to break down my own personal walls of doubt and limitations,* he thought—*while at the same time remaining confident in my honesty...that is all.*

He went deeper in his consideration of personal obstacles. *The greatest obstacle of all—the one that denies that they will always exist. Humbleness is the key to quality leadership. Admit to the depth of the unknown,* he often told himself. Although other people often remarked on how great of a listener he was—Miles knew the truth. *My attention might be more adept than most others, but that doesn't mean anything. I have great reason to be humble. We all miss so much,* he knew. *Listening is a great example of it. We hear songs, pretending to others and ourselves that we have just taken the length of vibrations in at steady rate, when it's time to voice our opinions. Not true—we hold back from what we can easily know. The mind fluctuates. Be humble—admit to the attention discrepancies of the mind moment to moment... and become that much better at listening. This is the key.*

In this way, Miles developed the skills to be confidently humble. For those few months on the show, the audience watched him go about his daily life with balanced vigor and ease. *Balance, the middle path,* he reminded himself all the time; *be steady with your own self-care.* His morning moods, what he ate, his reaction to social situations, and how much he enjoyed learning new things—it all took on a feeling of 'groundedness.' They saw his humanity, and he was not afraid of showing it. After all, that was the true brilliance of the show. No other means of campaigning could have come close to comparing in effectively forming an allegiance to a person. Viewers were able to take their opinions from any part of the game. People can say what they like about television; but it is indeed a very comfortable position to be scrutinizing from.

Of course it was a bit awkward having the cameras constantly surveying him. However, Miles did believe that people had a right to know him if he was questing after such an important position of power. But aside from all of that, he saw it even more simply. It was a great opportunity for him to engage in the personal practice of becoming more comfortable and vulnerable no matter what the setting or situation. *Isn't that what should make a good leader anyway? Camera, or no camera…it doesn't make one iota of a difference; you get the same thing.*

Therefore, he made sure to limit his self-conscious feeling even when he had the urge to dance around outrageously in his PJ's. He didn't let his thoughts go to the place where he was considering if people thought he was acting out on purpose—just for them. His credo was to be natural and trust himself. He danced freely—to all sorts of different types of music. After all, he had done it every day of school while at Gratitude, and continued the practice after his graduation. As a result of his professional level of ambivalent attitude on the matter of movement—his dancing sessions during *KYL* became legendary and fascinating pieces of entertainment. He gave many other people inspiration to begin getting the daily cobwebs of stiffness out themselves. Although he most definitely was trying to win the competition; he used the exposure for a wide range of purposes.

Although there were set episodes that aired during prime time, they also had television and web channels dedicated to broadcasting life in the house around the clock. Miles and his team (along with everyone else), had the opportunity to use the constant surveillance to creatively strategize improving their relationship with the audience. After all, *KYL* was seen as preparation for service; where there aren't rules for how broadly you can attempt to effect change.

Gratitude's preparation worked perfectly in this system, and the entire D.T team thrived engaging creative strategy. It was slightly odd that Miles was the only one on stage, but that was simply the role he was playing within the team. They all did work. When they had hang-ups, they asked for help immediately (after giving the quandary an honest shot at fixing themselves). It was seen that knocking problems around brought about solutions; either from the asker or the listener. If two couldn't figure something out, then they'd grab a third—and so on. This was how their efficiency worked—with respect for opinion and consideration of spoken words.

Miles oldest friend Patrick, had the idea for him to give a nightly yoga class to the viewers. "They can either do yoga alongside a very good and qualified instructor for free—or just watch and listen to you while you teach. We should showcase this talent. Either way, it'll give viewers good insight into your personal spiritual practice. It'll be even better than your dancing!"

Patrick didn't have very much persuading to do—the whole team knew when to recognize an idea of merit. Then, they'd pounce; developing detail. Part of that detail was to alter the form of some of these sessions. They noticed that Miles led best when he didn't have to use his words to tell everyone where to put all their body parts. Therefore, they chose to keep many of his classes as simple as possible—promoting personal ownership of the body. They put on music, let Miles both move and speak with great abandon.

He thought of yoga as simply moving the body in ways that felt good and beneficial. Miles led simple postures and movements. He wasn't into the kind of yoga that attempted to turn the body into a pretzel in order to take cool photos and impress. Not at all. To him, yoga was a sanctuary from all of that energy. He saw that it scared people into not stepping foot into the studio to begin with. *Way too much of that elsewhere in life,* he thought and often said. *Leave my yoga alone! It's for everyone.*

Health of the body was the clear goal, and he felt it best achieved through the lens of 'non-judgmental awareness.'

Not only were the D.T.'s best able to clearly exemplify his philosophical messages during this time, but viewers saw proof of his beliefs through his actual athletic forms of freedom. Only those with very limited insight had trouble connecting the progressions of the body, to work done within the mind. *That we elect leaders who don't know how to take care of the health of their bodies is laughable. How can we expect them to take care of the health of a whole nation then?! We have an age requirement, basically a marriage requirement, as well as religion requirement for years and years, and a requirement to fit into a box of one of two parties of course…yet our population doesn't demand for the prerequisite of health! Unreal.*

Sometimes he said these sorts of things during his virtual classes. He might not have in the outside world, but openness was the premise of *KYL.* Miles was allowing himself to be an open book.

One of his friends told him that he was likely to be assassinated by an obese person who took offense to his discriminating stance.

"The point isn't that we should make a rule to only elect people who are in perfect health," Miles had responded. "The point is—that so many parts of our system don't make any sense."

"I know that. But I'm not sure they will!"

Regardless of the criticisms of the few, through his own spiritual and physical practices, Miles taught thousands and soon to be millions, how to relax into the acceptance of their own individuality. He did it with balancing direction and invitation—offering throughout, and always telling people to decide for themselves. He was becoming the kind of leader, and true Futurist, he wanted to be.

The greater the progress I make; the faster more of it seems to come my way.

THE PRESIDENCY

In the final episode, an opportunity was given for all candidates to stand behind a modest podium and give a short speech. It was the last chance to impress the audience and sway opinion—after everyone had gon, viewers would take on the responsibility of voting electronically and deciding the winner. In fact, *KYL's* system was said to be more secure than the governments, in terms of applying, "one vote per person." It boggled the minds of the creators that it took hours and even days for the government to count votes during elections. *KYL* did it immediately that night.

"It's math!" Marty Linden had said. "Math and computers combined—that equals instantaneous. How does the public let them get away with it?"

Miles embraced the weight of circumstance, so that when his turn came, he allowed it to excite him. He considered the moment to be far greater than simply the culmination of his performance on the show. He considered it to be the start of a new sort of political discourse that he had no plans of letting go of. He chose to wear a simple plaid button-down shirt, loafers, and dark jeans. Together the D.T's had agreed it to be the most effective. It wasn't a message of insult—it was a message of priority. They didn't give it really too much thought though. It was the cherry on top of an explosive message that was now about to pour forth from his vocal chords.

Most other contestants wore the expected dark suit with a red or blue tie; or the highly conservative single color dress (attempting to look as previously presidential as possible).

Before the speech Miles reminded himself why he was doing this. He was doing it because as he grew in years, he saw more and more proof that nobody knew what the hell was going on. Not that he held all the answers himself, but ever since philosophy club he humbly embraced the role of leader—he honestly felt that the world could use someone like him. Others could take his place, but they wouldn't be him. That was all there was to it. He had his blind spots, but he could set the population on a straight path toward better accepting the truth of unknowing. Ultimately, he was tugged by compulsion to bring himself to this place.

With age, Mile's voice had deepened, and he had worked to develop and promote the natural frequency of it. In fact, he had filled a whole notebook back at Gratitude dedicated to studying the power of voice itself. He was well aware of its importance. *The way you say a thing matters as much as the words.* He remembered that as his overall conclusion at the end of his study. It was that and his yoga which overcame his nervousness.

His face housed a finely trimmed beard and he wore glasses framing a set of considerate eyes. As he took his steps up to the podium, he elongated his spine, lifted his shoulders up and back—noticed the natural energy flowing through his body with the breath, and stood up even straighter. He was not a particularly tall man like Peter, but he made up for his lack of height by how solidly he held his body.

Out the window behind him was a view of the properly imposing Washington Monument. Miles tuned into his heart and allowed it to speak for him. His words began soft but rose and fell at his intuitive discretion.

The D.T.'s had decided to begin first, by going after the foundation of the old structure:

"Did you know that Democrats and Republicans argue about one single philosophical topic?" He began. "What's the issue they argue about so passionately throughout the course of their careers? Freedom! Freedom boils down the whole entire thing. Let me explain...

"Democrats have become more and more insistent in their advocacy for social freedoms. Republicans, on the other hand, fight for the freedom of capitalism. When Democrats are backed into a corner, they say, 'But what about a businessperson who swindles—who's greedy? We can't just allow this person to move about making decisions unchecked. In this instance, we have to limit freedom!' Republicans combat this with, 'If you don't give opportunity to succeed in business, you will be limiting the amount of creativity and economic prosperity that has the potential to be created. Freedom is the best course of action for any successful economy. Don't set a narrow path for people; allow them to set their own path, and you'll get something much better. We can't allow the misguided few to make it worse for all of us, can we?'" Miles was truly enjoying what he was doing. Anyone could see it. This was his jam—this was what he got up for in his life.

"But Republicans do not truly believe in the concept of freedom either (only in regard to the specific issues they've agreed upon). They do not advocate for individuals to have personal freedom in all aspects of their lives. When they find themselves in the same position on the issue of drugs or a women's right to choose, or often homosexuality—they are the opposite of libertarian, and proclaim: 'We can't simply allow citizens to ingest any substance they wish—substances that may cause them to behave poorly and commit crimes. We must prevent others from having the opportunity to make this choice! We can't let women choose what to do with a physical part of her body. Even though a growing potential human is attached to her—we know better than she does about what she's created. Homosexuality; well that's just gross. A man was meant to be with a woman!'" He continued passionately.

"That our leaders fail to see their hypocrisy—that they take up either side of the same argument so fervently is somewhat disturbing and should lead us to glimpse how mildly developed they are in the realms of stable logic. Many of us are addicted to argument instead of actual beliefs. It may not be for the common citizen to feel such responsibility to censor their own hypocrisy—however, our leaders claim to be the most righteous among us. It's disturbing because it proves how ungrounded they are morally—how confused they are in what they actually believe is right. My friends, beware of any leaders that make their positions about being a part of the right group—instead of the work needing to be done. How sad it is, that it's become the norm."

Miles had gone off the cuff, and added that last part in intuitively. *My words, my choice.* He looked back up at the teleprompter and continued.

"The problem with seeing sides—with trying to fight—is that as long as there is an opponent, progress is limited. Members or supporters of either of these parties often think to themselves, *if only my party were in control everything would be different.* But they fail to see that the sides themselves are the issue—fail to see the heavy addiction to fighting. I can tell you one thing for sure; as long as we see it as a fight, we'll drown in our own hopes for the impossible. The way the game is currently being played, it's unrealistic to believe that there can ever be a winner.

"Let's return to the concept of freedom. Take a moment to ask yourself, 'Do I believe in it?' Yes, you might say. 'Well, sort of on second thought.' Perhaps when it suits you, right? In a probable reality you have one foot in and one foot out of the philosophical door of freedom. If we'd like to make headway most rapidly, I don't believe we can continue to balance ourselves on this edge of fogginess any longer. We must be grounded in our philosophy, and form a more stable relationship with our understanding of freedom. Our Founding Fathers knew this. That we claim we are free (or freer than others) does nothing to mask the reality of our continued path toward increased regulation. The Declaration of Independence was not written solely to identify the rights of Americans. What made it such a powerful document was the fact that it argued for the liberation of the entire human species itself. It argued; that once we are born, we are entitled to basic rights of freedom." Miles was picking up steam now and driving at a pace.

"Regulation, is, and has become, our way of quickly attempting to solve problems on a very surface level. I advise you to consider our history in order to become witness to the repercussions of limiting freedom. Great care must be taken anytime we choose to deny it. Perhaps there are times for freedom's repression, but those situations are few and fragile. Their fragility is the exact reason behind the need for quality leadership. However, no one is allowed to be off the hook, nor should a sharp mind desire to grow dull. We all have a responsibility to figure out what we believe, and our collective health is the only true measure of our culture." He puffed out an exhale.

"So, let's get to it. Where do we draw the line of freedom?" He was giving people what they wanted, and most of them didn't even know it. "Here's how I break it down: First, freedom to harm the self is a freedom we must allow each and every person the right to. We might not like it, but we can't deny the reality that each of us has charge of our own physical being. Attempting to deny that right is pointless, and the law should never try. If one of us wishes to end his or her life, or make it more painful—although we are free to persuade that person otherwise, we must acknowledge his or her right to make decisions for their own body. It's about time we come to grips with the limits of our control. We do not have to promote the act of ending life early, but we should not try to force another person's body to our will either. Whose right is it but the individuals, to decide if they have had enough time?

"Now let's address the other side of the coin—the place where freedom must be taken away, and the very reason for the creation of the law itself. It is only within this one simple area: When freedom is used to harm others, then we use force. Crime, which the law assesses, splits into two branches. One is unintentional harm, whose details must be scrutinized in order to consider basic negligence. The other is intentional harm, which also must be assessed in order to weigh the severity of the action to determine the punishment. This is what the law should be used for, and only this." He was picking up more and more speed of well pronounced speech. He was a musician allowing his hands to fly.

"What the law has become instead, is an overstretched rubber band that is tragically worn-out. Our police officers are overwhelmed with the number of unrealistic rules they're trying to uphold. We need to help them by making their work more manageable. Taking away freedom from the general population turns otherwise good-natured people against their own government. It makes the job of police officers much more difficult. Harsh restrictions should never be viewed as a recipe for success. It is action taken from fear—it leads to shaky ground that is likely to crumble. Again, there are plenty of historical lessons that provide us with adequate examples of leadership choosing to inflate the possibilities of their own power to control. Disaster ensues every time.

"If you open your eyes, you will see that in many ways our behavior has caused us to enter very dangerous territory. You might be too tired to look, but it's your duty to look anyway—and then also to not become a pessimist.

"This next one is tricky, so hang in there with me." He took a nice long deep inhale, followed by the freeing release of a natural exhale. "One of the most disastrous examples of this is adults attempting to control the sexual relations of our youth. In many ways we are less fearful of violence than we are of our children finding acceptable persons of their own age with whom to find pleasure. It's natural, and it makes sense—yet it makes too many of us cringe. It's a great example of how we have over inflated our attempts at control, and therefore infiltrated areas which are none of our business. Who are we to say what's right for them, if they're not causing harm? What are we so scared of? Our culture has a dirty little secret; except it's not so little at all. We are incredibly immature in regard to physical intimacy. If you don't have faith in your children to make quality decisions to find partners and feel ready, then you're not doing a good enough job communicating—most likely because you've been brought up to avoid these issues from your own parents. It's as simple as that, and someone has to be the one to step up already and do what's right. You don't have to look very deep to see how this suppression has caused widespread confusion and irrational behavior. People don't understand what's behind their feelings—and it's a huge problem. HUGE!"

Miles grabbed another quick moment of space and then said slowly and seriously, "What the fuck is wrong with us? We cringe at that word and find it necessary to bleep it out. A word! Four stinking letters. It's someone's job—probably multiple people's job—to prevent children from hearing that. Are you serious? Come on. Grow up! You child masquerading in the body of an adult. One of the most serious obstacles that holds us back, is getting trapped in the time drain of silly detail. Have the ability to prioritize what actually matters. If you do, you'll see that swear words belong at the very back of the line on the list of topics which could use your attention. Realize how we've allowed the laws of ancient religions to have terrible effects in our present culture. These laws were created by humans who were scared and confused. We now know better than they did—believe it! The actual problems are way too severe to be tiptoeing around your archaic aversions to your own truths. Have you lost sight of them? Get it together—keep your eye on the ball!" Perhaps Miles best attribute was that he could challenge profoundly, while at the same time somehow keeping it light.

He took a sip of water. When he came back to speech, he had added vigor and fire in his eyes. He was feeling the weight of what he was talking about. He didn't care if people agreed, and he didn't care if he was tired either. *Transparent vulnerability,* he told himself.

"I wish it weren't real—the extreme amounts of needless suffering. I really wish it were all a delusion of my own mind—my own need to be critical and set myself apart as unique or special. Without caring about being corny, I can say that what I honestly want the most is for everyone to get better at loving each other. I have enough confidence to simply state that as fact. Why? Because I am certain of my own desire for it. I desperately want this game of considering how we stack up against others to end already. It's boring, unproductive, immature—and we don't have time for it. Too much needless suffering is everywhere, and it's the saddest thing in the world. No matter what type of person you have a tendency to befriend, you must ask yourself if you truly wish all members of our species well. Even if you don't like who someone is—would you want them to grow into a better version of themselves—become more genuine? If yes, then realize that you don't really hate anyone at all. Give that reality to yourself and allow it to take effect. The deeper truth, in fact (if you can wipe away your hardness for a moment), is that you do in fact love everyone. We choose leaders because it is the best way to organize ourselves. However— the story, the focus—shouldn't be so much on these individuals; but rather on what they are able to do. The problems, the improvements— they're bigger than all of us. When we obsess over the fogginess of our personal goodness, we put a halt to our progression—our focus shifts to matters of lesser importance, and then we stop improving. That practice has been promoted far too successfully in the subversive layers of our culture." He was blowing people away and treating it like it was nothing.

"Do you know that fear itself is an insult to the amount of experiences you've been gifted with? We can be, we can do, whatever we want with our time. Not being aware of the extent of our freedom holds us back more than any other factor. The freer and more accepting the mind, the more positive solutions come about—the more wisdom is discovered. If you have chosen responsibility in your life—to take care of other beings—remember that responsibility is a choice as well. We like to complain, but it does us no good. Wishing for the life of another person doesn't help us. It's childlike in nature, as it fights against reality. Illness of the mind is a rampant epidemic that should make us cry every day as we work toward healing our self-destructive behaviors. I'm sorry to give you all this hard truth, but someone has to. Do not be afraid to see the depth of the contamination of your own habits. Avoidance leads to negative explosions of frustration. Avoidance sets us up for disaster. Instead; love the growth, and see how far you can progress from the place you currently stand. As you begin owning up to these truths, you will start to see that it is not mature for us to cheer for revenge when we assassinate others—I don't care how disastrous their deeds. We don't cheer for the uglier side of what we must do. A true adult does what needs to be done—softly, gently, and with grace. A great man or woman and a great country are sharply stable on their ambiguous path toward improvement. They are humble most of all.

"It's understandable for a child to accept the flaws of a system; but it should not be so for an adult. We need to be stronger than our children—need to show them what strength really is. We stand back and let this competition prosper when we absolutely know better. Competition is a tool to be used productively—not a way of life. We took this land we stand in simply because of the invention of the rifle—a weapon of death and destruction that only a fear-based, competitive culture could conceive of. Did we achieve victory? No. What is the value of a life lived with anxious hatred? One span of life filled with genuine appreciation is worth more than a million lived in fearful distraction.

"We are indeed quite ill with fear. It's time we admitted it. Our ancestors ripped away the lives of those they unnecessarily made their adversaries. They killed those with the strongest immune systems. The people who threatened them by not being threatening. A Native American culture, which was so beautiful it didn't understand the very concept of owning land. Native Americans who did not have the ability to conceptualize killing animals for any reason aside from necessity. They didn't set up concentration camps for their fellow planet inhabitors in order to prove their own might—didn't eat flesh without considering where it came from. They were a much more secure kind of human, who opened themselves up to the mysteries of life. With fault for sure, but also with much wisdom.

"This is simply the reality of our past, and true adults aren't afraid to view it and learn from it. It is indeed a horror—not only our past but also our current ways. But we are only trying, and trying produces mistakes. The solution is not to feel guilt. The solution is to do better now and accept the laws of imperfection. Can we adopt lessons we missed the first time around? Doubt in our ability to do this, is by far our greatest barrier.

"The wise are able to see something else amid the sadness. They see that the past must be accepted completely. For one very logical reason: Because it's gone—because it happened. That's why we call it the past. If we go further, we see that life is often beyond our understanding. However, we can know that guilt over what has happened leads to stagnation—that acceptance can lead to a future where our actions line up more appropriately with our beliefs. Most of all, we don't take our trying too seriously; but we do try as hard as we like. My friends, of course it's OK and even righteous to feel pride. But that should simply give us strength to focus on doing even better. Back and forth we go between pride and progress. Take your time to feel proud, but then let it go and fall into humbleness. Know that ultimately it's no big deal whether you're complimented, criticized or even if other people don't see what you do at all. Let me ask you: Are we the generation that has the courage to surrender to the fluctuations of life? I hope so. Believe!"

And with that, Miles Carson's time on *KYL* was up.

PART VI

THE AGE OF INDIVIDUALITY

BASIC INCOME

With an abundance of support and energy from his victory on *KYL*, Miles launched his bid to become president. For the first time in history, a candidate chose to make education the primary platform for their political campaign. This was something Miles had made the decision to do long ago, and now he was finally given an opportunity to follow through on his self-imposed promise. He was obstinate about it throughout the entirety of the process. On occasion, he refused to even discuss other matters until they were established to be secondary in importance to the drastic shift needing to take place in the system which fostered the growth of future generations.

The public accepted. The strike, as well as the well-remembered disaster on the grounds of Revolution had prepared them. They bent, and then they broke in his direction. What else could they do—refuse to recognize the positive ripple effects that had the possibility of occurring with a more sensible system of child rearing?

When people stopped to consider it, it was easy to see how creating better humans overall, was the best form of action to prevent the continuation of all the things they were fed up with. When he debated, Carson used Gratitude as the foundation for the worldwide learning environment he proposed:

"You might not agree with me on all of the particulars, but at this point, that doesn't really matter. What's most important is that we don't get sidetracked and lose our perspective—that you join me in believing that reforming our schools should be the first priority for my presidency; that it's the key to unlocking the door to a permanently better future. It won't immediately solve all the problems, but with time—so many of them. The true adult has the discipline to be patient with change. If you agree with me there, that alone should make me the candidate you support."

Momentum from the show and the strike continuously multiplied, and Miles Carson became the first independent candidate to win the presidency of the United States. The people had spoken. They were done messing around with the old two-party system, and Carson was the Futurist who proved that current times had to make way for significant modification. The continuing changes to education were messy as hell—especially during his first two years in office. But the team Miles put together was a resolute, focused, and brave bunch. These were the qualities needed to overcome all those so firmly entrenched in trying to hold on to their investments in the crusty old system. It was quite difficult, in fact, reasoning with humans who only had interest in clinging to their personal sum of processions and status.

"The underdeveloped child inhabiting the body of an adult is the most serious obstacle of contention for our current age," President Carson had stated in his inauguration address. "We cannot allow them to run things any longer."

He had four or five people he trusted completely and allowed great freedom to lead large branches of organization. Many of them were a part of the D.T.'s. Duncan became his official chief of staff, Amanda his secretary of education, Patrick his press secretary. Marty Linden was integral in showing him how to establish his pyramid of communication all along the way. His former teacher, and newly appointed secretary of treasury, infused Miles with the highest regard for organizational tactics.

However, perhaps the second most important role went to the leader of the Futurist movement. Maya Sol ran as his vice president. Now being an older, well known and stately balance to his young, brash, upstart self; it was a wise choice. Although Miles was always involved in larger decision making, for the first year and a half Maya took on the brunt of the general workload, as he focused his efforts on changing the public school system of their country.

Not to be outdone by her younger supervisor, Maya used her position in a revolutionary fashion. The first thing she did was work to throw away the electoral college. It was a system which had originally been established for the archaic reason that the masses could not be communicated with. That was clearly no longer the case within the current technological terrain. She was fed up with a non-democratic form of government continuing to claim how great its democracy was. Maya appealed, "A democracy is one vote per person. Everyone counts the same. If you want to do something different; use another word, not democracy."

In the election preceding theirs, the most horrific disaster many feared had in fact occurred. The candidate who won the electoral college and therefore the presidency had been crushed in the popular vote by more than twenty percent. How? By winning every single decisive state by the narrowest of margins, and then getting blown out in the rest. It was unlikely, but possible; and it happened. The winner of the popular vote had lost elections previously in history, but never with such a tremendous disparity. It mattered not—the law had to be followed of course, and that candidate who received many millions of less votes—become the leader of the country. It was yet another example of people being too lazy to make obvious needed changes to a system—until disaster struck. Now that people had witnessed the degree of injustice, they were finally ready to change the law. *When will we learn to reconstruct our systems before we are pummeled in the face by their obvious ineptitude? I wonder,* Maya considered.

ABRAHAM GORDON

With the help of the majority of the public, Maya Sol tore down the electoral college from within. Once she succeeded, she was invigorated with strength to tear down multiple other structures that didn't have a logical foundation as well. She had gotten a taste for many victories of spirit, and she saw no reason not to attempt more with her newfound position of possibility. As vice president, she began investing her energy heavily in two other matters of importance. The first was promoting the development and uses of solar technology. *The sun should be able to give us all the energy we need. It already does anyway. The ways in which it can be more efficiently harnessed, however, is never ending and must continue as a top priority of any administration.*

The other issue which cemented her in the history books, was the matter of agriculture. Weaning people off of their purposeful distraction over what they ate was like taking a favorite toy away from a child—even though it had been coated in lead-based paint. No one really wanted to talk about their eating habits, but Maya forced the issue upon the public. A great deal of kicking and screaming went down of course, but she no longer allowed the subject to be swept under the rug. There were too many disastrous implications to unhealthy diets, and she felt a call of duty to keep the light shining brightly upon even that which was most uncomfortable. Keeping up with the demands humans were placing on the meat industry was causing more harm to the environment than any other single factor. To produce one hamburger required an incredible amount of water. *It's funny how we consider something such as water to be expendable when it is not; not funny at all though,* she thought. *Can a thing be cheap yet still be precious? Of course! Can a thing be bountiful but still be magical? I don't see why not. That is indeed the case with water, air and the sun. All free—all as important as anything. If we don't acknowledge preciousness where it exists, everything gets tangled up.*

Is it so hard to see that future humans will say… "oh yeah, we should have had a different relationship with water—shouldn't we have?"

It was a mess of a problem, compounded by the social competition to see who could avoid thinking big the most. Maya often wondered at the notion people used to justify their behavior. They'd say to themselves: "Well I could kill animals if I had to." *That very well may be…but you are not in the wild surviving currently…are you? Stay in the here and now, please; and with your actual circumstance. Without being backed into a corner of hunger, could you really hold down a struggling pig and slit its throat? Do not imagine hypotheticals which take you off the hook! Have you not seen the minds ability to justify anything? You are living a life of luxury, and within this life of luxury there are plenty of reasonable options of food that our ancestors did not have. Thanks to improved technology and cultivation—human ingenuity; you can still find extraordinary stimulation of the taste buds without eating intelligent and emotional life. Take it on once in a while as you wean yourself off…but let it be a treat. Start with less and see how it feels. We should all be able to agree that less is a good idea. Gentle with change as we accept ourselves as products of our life-long habits.*

She couldn't force people to eat a reasonable diet, but she could use the power of money to shift things around. *Is that not the exact thing the tool should be used for?* Somehow, in some strange mess of priority and value, meat consumption had become as cheap as vegetables. Maya would go to restaurants and notice that the meatless options cost virtually the same, if not more, as their animal counterparts. *How can that possibly have happened? Do we not value life? Just because we can convince some humans to commit mass slaughter daily…is that truly the path to a sustainable future?*

What had happened over the years, was that those who were down in the financial dumps, had become used to a diet composed of mainly meat and unhealthy foods. *Why wouldn't they choose it…it costs the same anyway,* she thought. *Change the prices, and we change the health of the lower class. That is, of course…if we want to. And yes—we do!*

She saw a time when fast food restaurants would have a menu which was half vegan and vastly lower priced than the meat alternatives. It was one of the ways regulation could in fact be used sensibly. *Should those who kill animals not have a limit on how many lives they are allowed to take daily? Sometimes capitalism does need to be reigned back in by the government…if the population is not up to the challenge of handling their freedom morally.*

Maya realized what she had to do in order to achieve this: *It has to become financially worthwhile to eat fewer animals. End of story. Possibly because they are living, breathing creatures with personalities…possibly because we torture them while they're alive …but also because our planet cannot take on such a dramatic waste of the magic matter of water anymore. Thankfully less meat is actually better for our bodies anyway.*

Even twenty years earlier it would never have been possible for her to win these battles. But politicians now were a much different sort of breed. They didn't feel entitled to battle back against their superiors simply because they were of a different party affiliation. They gave their opinions, but they had respect for the wisdom of authority as well. Neither major party had the same kind of power that it once had. A bubble of Democrats and Republicans tried to unite against Carson's administration at first—but that challenge had been lost before it started. The groups had despised each other for too long; it was easy to stick a wedge and divert their focus. If politicians continued on with their funny business—with their corrupt aims of personal power; they'd be bounced out of their seat by some young Futurist with a budding reputation for determined organization. They knew it, the public knew it—so they towed the line.

Without the brilliance of multiple creative minds forming a countless number of solutions daily, the shock to the education system might have imploded. Every individual on Carson's presidential team was seen as a vital limb necessary for the optimal functioning of their engine of transformation. They broke off pieces of progress and handed them off to each other in methods of exceptional teamwork. Much of the progression toward redesigning schools had to be done during the summer months—breaking down the walls of cookie-cutter classrooms and transforming these buildings into comfortable places of learning. Although the layouts of the buildings physically needed changing, even more had to take place in the structure of the schedule, and the content of the curriculum itself. The administration planned further and further into the future—taking on realistic steps toward changes one year at a time. By Carson's second term in office, no public school in the nation looked remotely similar to the way it had just a few years before.

Although fixing school was his primary reason for becoming president, Miles didn't stop expanding his scope of observation. When he was certain of the productive course that the new education platform was on, he handed oversight off to Amanda and turned his attention toward more aggressively helping the battles Maya was engaged in.

The president would constantly practice meditating and recording his thoughts. He used these times of spiritual practice to solve problems. He also used cannabis and openly advocated its effects in working to spiritually heal the planet if handled wisely. He was often seen lying on one of the many sofas in the White House creatively considering deep philosophical matters for practical reasons, as he puffed away at his hand held vaporizer. He had moved past the guilt and associated stigma indoctrinated in his youth. There was no doubt he was using the medicine to increase both the physical and mental well-being of his body. This wasn't during his time on the clock to be sure. In fact, previous to his term, the presidency was viewed as a twenty-four-hour job—creating a bit of an issue for him. *No presidents ever got drunk? What a laugh at that*, he thought.

So Miles changed the law making it so that the president was also entitled to having time "off-the-clock." Of course he'd help out if needed and do his best in the situation he found himself in—but he didn't see how him using cannabis was much different from previous presidents getting drunk (except that he was certain his practice was drastically more productive).

During this time off, if there were any national crises or emergencies, Maya would be the final one to make any decision. That was the failsafe they created, and he was absolutely fine with it. *It actually makes more sense and should always be the case*, he thought…*that leaders agree to terms which acknowledge their own humanity. Expecting superhuman eventually leads to burn-out, and a performance of lesser quality.*

Miles often had deeply personal meditative sessions, and allowed answers of significance to come to him. This was how he zoomed out and saw the larger picture he was put in power to see—in a flow of openness, with a notebook beside him, and trust in the intelligence of his own mind.

Contrary to popular belief, the economy isn't the most important element of a successful nation, he thought to himself one day—*but it is a vital one. Income inequality is a tremendous issue, but we have to be very careful in how we attempt to solve it. Complete fairness is a laughable attempt at controlling nature and should never be the end goal. Still, the suffering experienced by many due to a lack of finances in this world is certainly nonsensical and is most definitely holding us back in our evolutionary growth. Education can help, but that will be a slow progression. We can do something now that will lead to more immediate change. How can we really make things better and somewhat more fair?*

A reporter once asked him: "How do you have such a good memory President Carson? You often pull facts from a wide variety of areas, and rarely give misinformation."

He replied, "because I don't worry about how much I remember. Whatever comes up in the moment—great. Whatever doesn't—no problem either. When we pressure ourselves, we cut off our flow to the answers we've already discovered. If I forget, I forget. It's time we stopped trying to hide when we don't know. We humans have an unhealthy addiction to trying to endlessly impress."

A president speaking these words had very large implications for the ego games of the general public. It was fantastic for people to see the leader of the land so comfortable with the unknowing.

The economic decision Carson developed during one of his spiritual sessions ignited him on a newfound charge—the B.I. system.

The institution of basic income was not communism or anything close to it. It was, however, what the name implied: A basic income for everyone. No unemployment, no extreme poverty, no complicated governmental agencies—simply a basic entitlement given as soon as a citizen turned eighteen.

It may have been expensive, but it was actually in the countries best interest not to stress its population with the burden of survival. The greedy power players thought it keen to keep the population consuming—it was not; they were very wrong. The goal of B.I. wasn't to level the playing field. The larger focus had to be kept in mind. It was created to help all of human society. Any person was allowed to work to accrue as much monetary funds above their base amount, of course. But every citizen was entitled to their own individual allotment—whether employed or not. It was not enough to spend frivolously and get away with it, or solve mental disorders—but it was enough to be reasonably comfortable and hopefully decrease overall stress for healthy humans. Fraud of course would be prevalent for a while, but that was a solution for schools to combat with their teaching of morality. The basic amount given wasn't changed based on the size of a family, and it wasn't changed based on the living expenses of a state or city. Those were choices each person made, and citizens had to learn to be accountable for them. Turn eighteen, receive the same amount as every other eighteen year old in the country for the remainder of your life. That was it. It wasn't that difficult to make things much more fair.

"The government is like a parent who is constantly learning how to better nurture the development of their child," Miles wrote and then shared with the public. *"The liberal rock star cries for complete freedom, but they have to also be shown the value in some conformity. Let them wander when they're young and make the choice to come back to your presence and wisdom. Have enough confidence to know that you have tools which are valuable to them. Then they will have chosen your company, and the fact that the choice was made will make all the difference. Tell them, "freedom is how we got to a place where we choose to take sensible care of each other. We've chosen to help make life less brutal and sufferable with our combined experience. Never underestimate the value of a team. Yes, trial by combat can produce an effective warrior, but so can our connection to love. Know that the trial is there for all of us regardless, as there's no such thing as a life without suffering. That interpretation only arises when we try to compare each other with the over-inflated justice of*

our minds. Children will see the truth as they experience it. A government's relationship to its citizens is very much the same. Tell them, "I'm not going to do everything for you, but I'll give you some stuff. Go! Adventure on! Those of you who now have money, access to medicine, and confidence of spirit that's been developed in the nourishment of a healthy education system...go! Those who have been taught to use their thoughts for good...go! Make the world better. Investigate your potential. Why? Because there isn't anything else for us to do! We know it, and we're waiting for you to see.

"We give them the most intelligent safety net, and they move from that place. We know that the optimal functioning of our net is something that can always be improved upon...so we improve it endlessly. This is how a government strives to evolve its own people."

It was difficult to implement, of course (through the tangle of the legal process), but President Carson now had enough supporters in both the House and Senate to pass their plan into law. Taxes rose, but all from the top 20 percent, who in some kind of unfathomable way had been able to accrue 85 percent of the country's total financial wealth. They had so much of it that they didn't even know how to productively disperse it. Although freedom meant everything—this particular aspect of it was not sensible for a culture that fessed up to its interconnectedness.

The B.I. system was a parent stepping in and saying: "You're out of control if you don't see the advantage to using what you have to find purpose by doing good. What else is important to you? Looking good? Get over yourself, my child. It is your right to continue with your material addictions if you choose, but it also our right to change the tax policy required for living under our roof. If you take illegal action in retribution, it is also our right to bring down the hammer of our own capabilities. My position of experience, and the wisdom in my heart, tells me it's time for you to accept your responsibility to mature."

Spending hundreds of thousands of dollars on automobiles and parties didn't help the economy—it threw it into a disproportionate mess. *Making more, spending unreasonably, and hoarding what you've accumulated...that's just a childish game taken too far,* Miles realized. *It's something that's been passed down from the days of Alexander Hamilton. He influenced Washington to hold money over all else...just as the British had. In the ways of our economy, we were not revolutionary at all. The reason Jefferson despised Hamilton, was because he understood how much more there was to the game than money. Hamilton was an amateur player of life...disguised in the successful illusions of a simple minded past. He cared about his personal image above all else the way so many power addicts do. Jefferson on the other hand, was a direct link to an existence of far greater quality. The only problem was that too few believed in his example. After all, it is much easier to quantify a large house than a satisfied heart. But which of the two is of greater value?*

Many of the über wealthy, as expected, fought against the proposition adamantly. They even threatened to leave the country. Miles knew, however, two important truths: One was that there was a very long distance between threat and action, and two; reacting under the fear of threat is never an intelligent path of leadership. He wouldn't go there.

The bill passed. Some Americans left. Very, very few—and not enough to matter.

The changes were immediately dramatic. His team worked through the logistics with grit like championship focus. Although an uncommon sight; when homeless people were now seen on the street, there was no longer a question of whether they were lazy or had drawn a poor lot. They had been given a basic income, and for some reason had chosen not to be mature enough to handle it (that, or they simply enjoyed living on the street). Either way, it changed the nature of the relationship strangers had for each other—and overall deepened the connection between citizen and government. It also caused more people to question: *"What is an adequate, basic lifestyle? How much do I really need? Do I actually believe there is enough for everyone to be comfortable?"* The simple inquiry into these questions was revolutionary in itself. It was a foundational rock of philosophy that Americans should have rooted into the ground when they had first founded their government. They should have seen the need to do it through their education. Either way, they were doing it now.

Of course, so much change did bring difficulty. With changing perspective and structure came the reshaping of many industries of business. But *this* was where the brilliance and need for the B.I. system really came into play. This was where Miles had drawn together conclusions of sense while meditating. It was him thinking three moves ahead.

B.I. provided the best safety net possible for allowing tremendous structural systems to be brought down and rebuilt with new found practicality and effectiveness. It made way for a US economy to soar well into the future by giving a higher standing of importance to the term 'cutting edge.' *We take a half a step back in order to make great leaps forward. That is the only sacrifice we need to make. But it's not truly a sacrifice, because we find great personal benefit in participating in sensible, well-thought out behavior.*

As a result of B.I., the whole philosophy behind work itself was re-shaped and molded into a much different entity. Allowing citizens to choose jobs they really wanted and think as creatively as possible was easily the smartest decision for any team of people to make. *That is... if you seek to optimize the ability of your people, and therefore ensure the highest levels of innovation. Any philosophy against this is grounded in a basic distrust for the human ability to find joy and production simultaneously together. We can't have it. Doing work can be as satisfying as anything else. The jobs that few want to be taking on...such as cleaning toilets or being around garbage, will instantly become better paid. That's the way it should be anyway. No matter the B.I., there will always be those who seek to acquire as much money as they possibly can. It will rearrange our system in a more sensible fashion.*

It was no longer looked down upon for adults to take a few months off from their jobs and consider what they might like to do next in order to maximize their time of life. The fear of being viewed as "lazy" became seen and understood for the pressure that it was to scrap and grab at things before you decided what it was you wanted to be doing. *Productiveness cannot be forced onto someone,* Miles knew. *That is trying to lead others at the hand of a whip. Usually it has the opposite effect in the long run. The desire to be productive in an individual's own particular way must be owned...THAT effort usually coincides with feeling that we have reached toward our potential. If we allow the opinions of others to supersede our own, everything starts to crumble. Then we maintain brains that are utterly confused by what is happening. THAT wastes our gift of life.*

MAN V. MACHINE

As president, Miles pounded away against the idea that sustaining jobs was a reason for making economic decisions. *It's a childish perspective on problem-solving.* No matter what the world might be like for people if they lost their jobs, he felt that it was not rational to provide any kind of job unless it actually needed doing. He went on news shows and debated this point fervently.

"President Carson, how could you possibly suggest an overhaul that would leave so many people out of work? People need more jobs, not to have them taken away. Even with the B.I. program established, if we make the industry changes you suggest—in many cases citizens will be making a third of what they had before. You can't just take someone from rung six on the ladder and move them swiftly down to rung three!"

Miles considered for a moment—choosing words in his mind before responding. He had decided not to play into the typical games of aggressive argument where neither side opened their ears very well. Therefore, he asked: "What are your answers?"

Nothing—stutters, shock, uncertainty. There is a phantom on the other end of the line who is grasping for breath in the defense of his ego, Miles thought. *Let me help him.*

"Ben, listen to me for a moment and relax." He was talking to one of the most liberal voices in the media. "Pardon my bluntness, but the truth that you are seeing here resides in shallow waters. If you allow it, I will try to take you into my perspective. I know that your viewpoint comes from a place of care, and that's good. But there is often a larger picture to see beyond limited hardship."

Engaging in this kind of dialogue was like donning a favorite shirt for the president. That was what made him a great leader. He listened well, internalized—and then allowed the correct response to calmly and naturally arrive from the enjoyment of what he was doing.

"Let me tell you the truest secret to a stabilized economy. People can only have jobs if there is work needing to be done." The president held up his hand to stall his interviewer's interjection. "Now listen and wait for me to finish. Meeting actual need is the only level we can operate at as a government. Luckily for us, there will always and forever, be plenty of jobs to be performed by human beings. I don't care how large our population gets, or how advanced the technology—I'm a firm believer that this will always be the case. To give a person a job simply to keep him or her occupied or maintain his or her standard of life is a recipe for disaster and despair that I simply cannot allow for. I don't care what they've convinced themselves of, people don't do well when they're getting paid for work that doesn't have a necessary function. Countries don't do well either when that happens. People might think they want to get paid for doing nothing, but they don't. Lacking purpose (which is gained by inserting your individual gifts and capacity out into the world), slowly eats away at a human's sense of worth and value—which is far more dangerous than being out of work. Can you see how we have inflated the importance of money beyond all else? Ben, money is our reward, not our objective. This is most important. Pulling one over on the population by keeping secret truths away from them, will never ultimately work. The next generation must see and believe this in order for us to progress—this generation. We don't have time to allow each other to spend so much thought concentrated on obtaining money; unless we have something *really* important to do with it. Do you follow?"

Ben stared back at him dumbfounded.

"To answer your question even more specifically—yes, you can go from rung six to rung three on the ladder, or even from rung twenty to rung two. Countless humans have proven that truth throughout our history. Many of us are still proving it now. New heights of joy, presence and purpose, can be drawn out of difficulty. Natural disasters, horrible bad luck, war. We don't take on unbearable hardship willingly of course, but we can still utilize it when it suddenly breaks its way into our lives."

The reporter was about to respond, but the president felt the need to cut him off again. *After all, he receives plenty of airtime sharing his views when I'm not around. He can bash me when I leave if he wants.*

"Listen, it doesn't serve us to think ourselves weak and to forget our strength. Should we really be going through this wonderful gift of life getting by and holding on to the safety of only what we've already known—staying in a survival mentality instead of one of adventuring? Does it make sense to fear going out in open water to discover what we're each truly capable of? I think it does not. The evolved children of the next generation will be much more comfortable with seeing this." Miles snatched for himself a much needed breath before continuing to spew forth his motivational discourse. "Can we become them now? Because it's people not reaching their potential that holds us all back the most—not a lack of jobs. Once you go down the rabbit hole of trying to create functionality where it doesn't exist, you are going against the very foundation of what has made human beings successful throughout the history of this planet. You think you are helping them with this stagnation, but you are in fact clipping the wings that will allow them to soar higher. It's my job to see past that—to make the decisions that have the greatest chance of strengthening everyone. I plan on continuing to do it."

The interviewer sat with the words for a moment. He had inflated himself up and put Miles down in his mind before this meeting so that he could feel comfortable going toe to toe with his president. *I won't back down so easily,* he thought. *Give him a little and then attack from another angle. You can do it...your career is on the line.*

"OK, I see that Mr. President, but what about all the advances in technology that have the ability to replace the work humans have been doing? Do you think we should just eliminate all those jobs too so that robots can sweep in on us?"

"Yes!" This was when Miles would start to feel himself getting a bit frustrated—when he knew he wasn't being listened to. But he quickly cooled himself down and realized that it was an opportunity to explain our relationship to technology even further. "Don't make things more complicated than you need to. If a robot can perform a task better and more cheaply than a human, then by all means—employers should have made those changes yesterday. Ben, when did you lose, or have you never been taught—the possibilities of human ingenuity? This idea that humans could be overrun and left with nothing to do because of advances in technology amounts to a preposterous fear and insecurity that needs to be stamped out immediately. It's a figment of our imagination—a joke and an insult to the amazingness of the human mind. We must stay connected to our roots while at the same time continuing on with the moral progression of useful technology. We must make time to consider, and therefore take strides of understanding—on both fronts."

Miles let it sit for a span of space before continuing—Ben seemed to currently have nothing to say.

"But it does bring up a good point. Maybe we have to change the kind of work humans consider doing. We have to realize that we are capable of specializing in an infinite number of things that robots would have no chance of being successful at. Plenty of great science fiction writers display this truth to us. There are certain functions that robots perform brilliantly, but overall, nothing can compare to the elasticity of the human brain. The first step is letting go of the fear which doubts our capacity. After all, it was humans that created the robot! Have we not taken the time to acknowledge what an incredible feat that is? I think we should."

"As far as the B.I. program goes—I agree that it will be a very challenging time for a while. Change is never easy, but someone has to be the one to take the first step. There is no better way for us to be spending our financial contributions to our government than by helping people stay afloat while we go through the process of redefining our priorities in order to create an always improving future. Furthermore, we help ourselves, by giving others the platform to reach higher levels on their own personal pyramid of potential. It's equivalent to closing the store to do some remodeling—not ideal, but wait until you see the changes! A basic income is exactly what's needed for the present time of transformation. Without it, we have no chance of rocking the boat in order to make the necessary repairs. Maybe one day everyone will voluntarily take on all the needs for our society, and there won't be much room for government left at all. I hope so. But we aren't there yet. And anyway, the government is an entity of our own creation. We don't need to feel guilty about having one, or using it in the ways of our own choosing. Luckily, there are more than enough resources —if we are willing to scale back a bit on our gluttony regarding materials and experiences of endless instant gratification. If we're willing to open up to the truth that much of what we're looking for is inside. Not a hoo-hoo notion— solid reality.

"I believe that a basic income will naturally create the most affluent economy the world has ever seen. This is my belief. It is essential to keep our systems simple. Perhaps people will be lazy for a period— perhaps some of them for the remainder of their lives. However, we are going through a revolution at the moment, and there is no perfect answer. The psychology of fearful survival is thankfully losing its hold on many. This movement contains people of all ages. People who don't want to feel nervous anymore—people who are sick of being too scared to tap into their best selves—people who have come to realize that finding purpose keeps the soul healthy, and that acquiring a great deal of objects is a pretty lousy investment toward that goal of higher priority."

WHAT'S HAPPENING?

Many intelligently predicted changes came to fruition. The schools brought about a different kind of person that arose from never being asked, *"what do you want to be when you grow up?"* Instead they were guided: *"Be present in life because it's happening right now. Make decisions about your future calmly while appreciating the place where you currently find yourself to be."* The change made a world of difference. As a result of the massive overhaul to the demeanor of children—schools themselves were given a new responsibility. They took on serving a function so desperately needed: Protecting, and creating; the *right* kind of news.

What better organization to take on this role? Children, after all, have a natural ability to commit themselves to justice and see the totality of a landscape with less bias. Their unaltered lenses (although lacking experience), tend to catch more beauty, which the adult population desperately needs in order to be appropriately and consistently grounded. Many awesome adults collaborated and added value to production of course, but children were the ones who now made the decision: *What to broadcast—what to open up to the public in the precious few hours of time that we have?*

Children working for the news, scoured the internet for valid information with more speed and accuracy than most adults could match. Younger children made essential contributions, but it was the teenagers who anchored and balanced the values which they grabbed from their uniquely sandwiched position. After all, they were the ones caught between two worlds—and could therefore pull value from either side.

Needless to say, much of the horror which had previously proliferated the news, began to take a back seat. News was a technology of communication which had been used inappropriately for far too long. The government under Carson's presidency created a new media outlet run primarily by those under the age of twenty. They dubbed the network, 'What's Happening?'

WH did have commercials, but aside from paying the wages of their employees, the rest of the funds were filtered back into the education system. The ads, however, did have to follow a similar pattern to the content of the news itself: All products had to be deemed 'morally responsible,' which basically meant the enticement of healthy and useful tools, instead of superficial excess. There was a committee formed in order to make these decisions, and a vote taken whether or not to broadcast commercials for every single potential product.

In order to find the right humans to join the *WH* team, they operated on a platform of: Talent above ambition. The team found that often those who have the tools to successfully fill out applications, do not necessarily possess the highest capacity to perform the actual work. The problem mostly stemmed from an American love affair with personal determination toward pressurized dreaming. It was also a laziness toward the engagement of common sense. The truth, children knew, was that generally the most talented people are uncomfortable with marketing themselves. They also knew that societal problems caused so many people to exist deeply inside of their own personal determinations; that these folks failed to allow themselves to witness the surrounding impressiveness of what was happening beyond the ego. *WH* searched to find people who weren't like that—the members of the network decided to push themselves to constantly be on the lookout for jaw dropping talent. Discipline was needed too, but talent most of all.

As the years went by, the older news networks became so clearly outperformed that people stopped watching them in order to acquire a higher level intake of worldly information from *WH*. What could the old media stations do to stop it? This was capitalism at its finest. They tried to replicate the same methodology (being the plagiarists that they were), but few adults were willing to give up their positions of power, and young sets of eyes were the key to *WH's* lasting success. No matter how specifically others imitated, their broadcasts simply didn't have the same flavor of authenticity.

The consumer had confronted greater quality, and few were interested in going back to their former allegiances. The average citizen was beginning to lose interest in the disease of fear—it had become old and unproductive. They wanted to know about all the interesting things that were currently happening around the planet, and not only from the narrow tunnel of negative human behavior. Instead, they desired to know about the news from a morally grounded source, and witness the capacity of humans to be decently creative.

Furthermore, the public began to thirst for an outlet that didn't take light of its own role toward the creation of an ever-improving future. *That, most of all.* The old networks could no longer get away with taking part—while simultaneously claiming that they didn't have any responsibility. The new network knew their role and took ownership of their own subjectivity.

WH wasn't only a global channel, it also had stations and programming locally; connected with surrounding schools. They broadcast news concerning their communities, which of course most people had a natural inclination of interest and investment. *WH* often threw out questions like this at the end of their segments: *"Ask yourself, 'how much time do I spend getting to know what's happening far away?' Ask yourself, 'how much time do I spend getting to know what's happening, here, around my physical environment? Are you appropriately appraising your balances of attention?"*

A new bedrock of questions was formulated to guide the direction of information to be made public: *'What is necessary for people to know about?' 'What will inspire them?' 'Are we expressing reality properly?'*

WH defined themselves as: *"An agency that uses real-life events to guide and support the population in a beneficial direction."* Oh, how different it was from the older platform. The media had developed rules for what was considered "newsworthy," and children were the perfect group to explode out of that limited container of crime, disaster, and cut throat politics. The news, in fact, had become a precise example of the habit toward not fixing known problems (or even recognizing them), until something had broken. Then they would stand back and say "oh, how terrible! Let's watch and do nothing."

Instead, *WH* put together programs which chose to cover a very different arrangement of planetary occurrences. A few were: *'Random acts of kindness.' 'Lessons from professionals.' 'Evaluations of human habit.'* Breakthroughs in science often headlined their news, as the leaders of *WH* agreed that humanities understanding and connection with nature was imperative beyond all else. It boggled their minds that the other networks often kept silent when incredible new discoveries were made.

In large part due to the transformation of the news, slowly the two-party system of the United States began to dismantle. *WH* had representatives from all parties come to many of their debates during election time. They also did a scramble form, which paired each candidate up with another—for a separate, more personal debate. The true character and professionalism was better squeezed out this way, and more effective candidates jumped into positions of leadership. Talented individuals moved forward into the political arena as they felt that they finally had an opportunity to win a competition that was at least set up with a semblance of reasonable parameters.

Years went by, and a sense of unity began to be felt more than ever. Greater numbers traveled and saw proof that humans everywhere were far more similar than they were different. It made little sense for vicious accumulation of material to be an end goal when there was so much simplicity to be enjoyed. *This* was the mentality that *WH* advocated for. And it changed the world.

AN OFFER

Although a great many were now immersed in the need to maintain their positive feelings toward the direction of mankind; multitudes still were not. In fact, the rapid evolution of humanity threatened the hell out of a large percentage of the population—the split was severe. The iciest opposition consisted of those previously rooted in the familiarity of old systems.

Not all of them, but many religious followers were vehemently opposed to the breakthrough conceptions of Futurism. These were humans who believed that it was not up to current humanity to reinvent a wheel that had already worked for so many generations. However, for many species, logic is the breaker of all chains. If anything can cause leaps of progression—it is the force of common sense. In many ways, it is the glue that binds the magic of the planet.

Still, it was tricky. The religion of Islam, especially, had a philosophical dilemma with the amount of freedom that Futurism promoted. The growing number of their followers who had begun using Life Code to enhance their days was not a reality their leaders were willing to turn their backs on. Their holy book (which although filled with many useful practices of discipline and messages of wisdom), did not contain much of the vital and imperative attitude of 'live and let live.' Many did not wish to see the truth of how forcefully it plowed its way against the direction of tapping into intuition—but it did nonetheless:

Either you're with us, or you're not. If you don't follow the path, you're punished. This is the way. This is the only way. Do not trust your mind to decide…trust me above it! Trust these words to be greater than you.

As a result, the most devout followers did not possess the necessary tools to question the validity of a movement such as Futurism. They didn't take the time to adequately engage the philosophy and decide how they might disagree within their own personal realm of opinion. It wasn't possible to see that a great percentage of their lives had become about engaging in unnecessary competition between groups of humans on this planet. Their own morality was tucked away underneath a bombardment of commandments. Simply, if it was not Islam, it was blasphemy. The book said it was so, and so it was. Heated discourse would have been welcome. Terrorism—not so much.

But Islam was most certainly not alone in their opposition. Most religions were filled with similar doctrines of competitive separation. Logic preyed on this hollow promise of contentment, and as a result, these organizations continued to lose members in droves. For the honest, free thinker of the new age—more was necessary than a life spent simply trying to break other humans to their own point of view.

The outlook most Futurists took was: *Go ahead, do your thing. Just leave everyone else alone with your physical force. Be confident enough in your personal discovery that you don't need to use anything besides words to sway others. If people are not swayed…then let them be. If you believe in a creator, then it should be enough to simply bask in the amazement of controlling the majesty of your own personal body.*

Regardless, the leaders of the old religions took on the mindset that they only had a short time for one last major move of power to tip the scales back in their corner. They knew they should have come together sooner—but years of oppositional concentration had caused their union to delay itself until their predicament was overwhelmingly beyond repair. They quelled their animosity by activating the outlook: *My enemies' enemy is my ally…but only until I destroy my 'main enemy.' Then YOU will become my main enemy once again. My state of mind, as a result of my horrific conditioning, requires that I will always have an enemy. Please bear with me as I waste a great percentage of my life by forming an addiction to the feeling of hatred. I'll die having done nothing in the ways of healing this planet. Why? Because I was too petrified to enter the realms of personal logic and love. I was too petrified to free myself from the games of human competition, and I was also too weak to stop feeling sorry for myself.*

The halfway, insincere union between ancient religious forces was probable reason for their failure. Still, they tried to draw out whatever they could from the threat of extinction.

Devon Pearson sat in the back of his limousine reeling with contentment. He had just put the finishing touches on a commercial that was truly a masterpiece of propaganda. He did not consider himself to be particularly religious, but he did bring his family to church on the major holidays. That a conglomerate of religious influences were the ones depositing funds into his many accounts mattered not a bit to him. He loved money and was so satisfied by the accumulation of it, that there was no need to stop and question if the carrot he was chasing was worthy of his attention. Money was an excuse for him to enjoy the activity of competing against the new wave of Futurism. He never allowed himself to go any further than that.

The strategy he implemented was not so different from the vicious political campaign he was used to spearheading. However, contrary to his usual attacks on individuals, this time he set his sights on assailing the very foundation of Futurism itself. He considered that there probably had never been as much money or resources spent to disintegrate an opposition in the entire history of the planet. Not only was he backed by religious institutions—he was also supported by many of the most powerful universities, as well as the most affluent media and food corporations.

Devon had told the powerful men who had come to him for help what he knew for a certainty: "You win by understanding that this is all about only one thing; public opinion. Nothing else matters. Do not forget the power of fear to persuade the masses. It's the tool we use all the time, and it's a formidable one. People are not yet too far beyond your reach to remind them that these changes are unrealistic. Shift enough minds in your direction, and then allow them to do the work for you. That's all that I can suggest. Give me funds and I'll do what I can."

He lived thinking that most people were suckers. Devon's differentiation as being better than everyone else was his key to feeling good in life. For him, it was all about having the inside scoop—about taking advantage of others so that he could get more power and money—it was about manipulating the masses toward personal gain for himself and his small circle of 'winners.'

He would have used violence against the leaders of Futurism if he didn't think that the current situation wasn't already well beyond that. *Even if we take them out…we can't take out all the writing. Damn technology! Plus, there are way too many of them now. Even if I could get Miles Carson out of the way, the others would become even more of a pain in the ass.* Therefore, Devon used money instead—used the media he could still control. His team launched so many advertisements degrading Futurism that it was difficult to watch television, or travel the pages of the internet without coming into contact with his little pieces of anti-Futurist rhetoric. Most told stories—family members and friends who gave accounts of their loved ones breaking off relationships as a result of their allegiance to this ridiculous religion. All they had to say was that relationships ended—they didn't need to go further, to explore whether or not this was healthy for the person they claimed to love. They left out that they had been the ones behaving like assholes for years. Whether or not blind loyalty had the potential to be a poisonous and destructive priority, was not an inquiry up for contemplation. Fear of loss was the essence of their shallow argument.

All segments of propaganda began with the flashing of seven words:

"THE TRUTH OF FUTURISM. THE LATEST CULT. Have you been effected?"

This was followed up with honest and kind looking people invoking rhetoric: "What's wrong with our ways of doing things—with the wisdom that's been handed down from the past? Why do we have to change everything?" Images would flash with symbols of Christianity, Judaism, and Islam molding together in harmony—pictures of ancient civilizations coming together in prayer.

Priests, rabbis, or imams would then come on the screen explaining the importance of heading the advice of books of the past. Sometimes a group of leaders would hold hands together claiming that this was the start of a new age of old religions: "We understand the mistakes that have been made. Together we have learned to combine our efforts and appreciate our differences. Come follow the ways of your ancestors…it is not too late my friend."

Devon was very satisfied with the results so far. He supposed that with enough pressure, he would break the public in his direction—or at least perpetuate a never ending war. *I don't need them all. Just enough of the ones who vote.*

The only thing that was unsettling him was that the leaders of Futurism did not appear to be fighting back against his massage barrage of blows. He knew they had the resources, but they seemed to be mischievously allowing themselves pummeled through his devices. It made him wonder—but not enough to stop continuing to land punches with all his might. And anyway, it was too much fun for him. He lived deeply within his own game.

An average spring day in the early month of May saw Devon Pearson's limo pull to a stop in front of his apartment building in midtown Manhattan. It was not too hot and not too cold—there was a slight easy breeze in the air. Pearson stepped out of the door, looked up toward his building, and was shocked to see a familiar face staring back at him.

Sitting comfortably on the steps leading up to his doorway was the current president of his country. Devon looked from his left to his right and glimpsed secret service agents standing actively in their stoic positions on either end of the street. He gathered himself up quickly and got rid of the shocked features from his face.

"Hello Mr. Pearson," Miles said as he stood up from the cracked steps. He was wearing loose grey jogging pants, sneakers, and a plain light-blue shirt. "I was wondering if you're free tonight?"

"What's this about Carson?"

It was the first time they had ever met in person, but Miles was behaving as if they were long lost acquaintances.

"Care to go on an adventure with me? I'd like to invite you to the White House tonight. I give you my word to do you no harm. Feel free to let others know where you're going if you like."

Devon thought to himself, *maybe this is the blow back I've been waiting for. Well, let's see what he's got. Perhaps I can gain some information to finally finish them off. It's not his style to physically harm. I'm sure of that. More likely he underestimates me. I can deal with that.* The enticement of going to the home of the president, plus his curiosity, caused him to oblige.

"I will let others know. Can you give me about fifteen minutes to gather some things?"

"Of course. Take your time."

It was only when he stepped through the side entrance of a White House door, that he questioned for the first time whether or not he had made a mistake. *After all, this is the man who finally brought a halt to my success in closing that damn school,* he remembered. Devon felt the weight of the man's achievements standing in the place where he now found himself.

At the same time, his mental habit of arrogance made it hard to imagine himself being swayed away from his view point by anything at all. So, as he continued his way through the impressive halls and rooms reconstructed by Truman, he chided himself...*one day I'll be here again for a very different reason.*

Finally, they arrived at the inner sitting room to the presidents' personal quarters. The sun had recently set, and the light was growing darker by the moment. Surrounding was an elaborate setting with fine furnishings of quality craftsmanship. However, the whole set-up was clearly not as ostentatious as it was capable of being.

Sitting on the floor lifted off of some cushions sat two other individuals both unfamiliar to Pearson. Both were dressed in loose fitting white linen clothes. Both held dark faces of similarity. One was an aging man and the other a young woman. Beside them, he saw, was a smattering of musical instruments. The entire scene was causing his brain to become more and more perplexed and wondrous. *Wasn't I just getting home—about to watch some television for the rest of the night?*

"Allow me to introduce you to Palu," the president gestured at the man, "and his daughter Gai-eesha." Both looked up and inclined their heads in greeting at the newcomer. "They are from Brazil and come here from time to time to hold ceremonies for me."

"Welcome," the older man said. "Please, please, sit."

There were thin blankets laid out on the floor, and Devon found his spot atop a piece of green and brown fabric inlaid with writing of a language he was unfamiliar with. Carson did the same nearby— stretching out his legs and making himself comfortable.

They sat together for a few moments before the president finally spoke. "The first thing we must do, is see whether or not you choose to take this journey with us. Palu, if you would please—some context.

Pearson saw how the man's charm and confidence had allowed him to move up the political ladder so swiftly. Still, he didn't like him; just found himself forced to grumpily feel a tinge of respect.

The man Palu spoke with a focused, steady pace. There was a part of Devon's mind which told him that he was supposed to immediately run out of the room as quickly as he could, and never look back. Surprising to himself, he couldn't seem to lift his body off the floor. Instead, he listened. He was placidly aware of his own intrigue.

"Whether or not you choose to believe, there are powerful medicines to be found in nature. Most particularly in the rainforest." Palu spoke with a husky voice. "In fact, about twenty-five percent of all western pharmaceuticals are derived from rainforest material. About seventy percent of plants known to be active against cancer cells come from the same place. The rainforest is dense with life unlike any other region on the planet, and is undoubtingly special in character. All you need to know in order to make this decision, are two pieces of information: The first is that you will be drinking a brew made with all natural ingredients of the rainforest—vines, leaves, and shrubs mainly. The second, is that it is known to possess psychoactive and transformational characters."

Palu allowed the information a moment to sink in before continuing: "This is not an easy path; I must tell you sir. The body will feel many sensations that it has never before experienced. Not all of them will be pleasant. In fact, purging is quite the common occurrence during ceremony. Know, however, that we refer to this process as 'getting well,' and believe it to be very much the case. It is likely you will face feelings of difficulty, but also extreme feelings of elation as well. It is a journey into the vast unknown that is life itself, and therefore contains appropriate amounts of variety."

Palu abruptly came to a halt and gently placed the palms of his hands over the tops of his knees. Then he closed his eyes in meditation.

President Carson turned to look at Pearson. His face was a mask of relaxed composure. "So there you have it. This medicine is called ayahuasca—maybe you've heard of it. Regardless, you have been given enough information to make your decision I believe. If you choose not to participate, you will be escorted back outside and taken home. I would apologize for using up your time, and hope that this encounter would remain only between us. In fact, I would hope that to be the case no matter what your choice. If not, well, I'll just have to live with my propensity for engaging in risky behavior. I guess it's gotten me this far."

Miles waited another moment. "Okay. It's time to decide Devon Pearson. What will it be?"

Devon looked at the three other people in the room. Then he began to stand up very, very slowly. When he got to his feet he said to Miles, "you're a real crackpot aren't you? Not just a little bit, but the full-fledged real deal. I didn't know quite the extent until this moment. I can't believe you brought me here thinking I would agree." He laughed. "How did we ever allow the integrity of this office to stoop down to the likes of you?! As to your offer, nope, not at all. Please take me home now. Thank you very much and not at all."

As he turned his back to leave, it was a feminine voice that spoke up and held the future of Devon's life on the balance of a choices edge. "You don't trust yourself very much, do you Mr. Pearson?"

He would not have allowed the words to affect him so significantly, but for the fact that his wife had spoken virtually the same exact ones to him earlier that very morning.

"What the hell is that supposed to mean?" he said as he rotated his head around violently.

The woman Gai-eesha replied coolly. "You stay in your bubble. You're scared of life I think. Yes, this is so." She had no idea who he was. She was only perceiving.

Carson sat watching intently. He felt the weight of the moment, and its call for him to presently find comfort in the role of spectator. "Listen, I'm not going to let you bully me into being tricked," he spat.

"There you have it," Gai-eesha interrupted quickly before he could pick up steam. "'Being tricked?' Who is tricking you? We do as you do in this ceremony—drink as you drink. We told you everything—honestly and openly. You allow fear to overcome opportunity as it presents itself in your life. Have you experienced a ceremony like this before?"

He looked at her blankly.

"Then why do you think you're entitled to hold such a strong opinion of it? You don't know. Until you know, you are not permitted to have an opinion. That is a basic truth I teach my children."

Gai-eesha was not old, but she wasn't young either.

"Listen, I've heard of people having permanent damage from this kind of stuff," Devon replied more softly. His indecision was starting to be felt in the unsteadiness of his words. "No thank you." He said shakily. "I don't need it."

"Not from ayahuasca you haven't. I have not come across anyone, and I have sat with thousands—my father with many more than that. Even if people decide not to participate again, they are all glad to have had the encounter one time. This is the truth. If it is not the exact truth, it is the almost truth that anyone should feel comfortable living by. The potential far outweighs the non-possibility of any kind of 'damage,' occurring. In reality, community centers should be hosting these ceremonies for everyone, all over the planet—to safely explore. Ceremonies are for doing personal work—and it's not always pretty; but it does have to be in a supportive environment. I do not always desire to drink the medicine myself. Sometimes I have no wish to engage with the spiritual on a particular day. But it is my work, and it is my duty to continuously get more well.

"From what I hear, you are a man who is quite capable," she continued—swiftly changing the direction of the conversation. "What are you so afraid of? Are you really going to walk away from this chance—in this place?! I have found that most people are afraid at the idea that they might lose something if they let go. They fail to see that it isn't possible. You might be changed afterward, but you can never forget the self that has already been created. I promise you. That part is always there to come back to. You'll just see it differently, and maybe decide on another course. Still, you'll have the choice. Relax for a second. Think, and then decide. If you still want to leave, OK. I've said my piece."

Devon looked at this beautiful woman, with a smooth face and deep knowing eyes. He couldn't help but feel as though he wanted something that she had. He wasn't able to exactly put it into those words, but that was what he felt. More than the sexual attraction, it was the certainty with which she held her body, and the sincerity with which she spoke her words. It enticed and challenged him to examine this decision a bit more scrupulously. It was as if she knew more about him than he did, and that irked his pride. Suddenly he knew his answer. *I can't have that. I'll always wonder, and it'll eat away at me. No one has to know about this...but I'll do it. I'll walk into this trap.*

"Come on then," Devon grudgingly replied. "You win. Let's go. Show me what you've got."

MEDICINE

Devon engaged in the motions of the ceremony disdainful-ly; the prayers, the sage and the tobacco. Palu lit a fire and said more prayers while sprinkling ash into the flames below the chimney. The shaman then finally poured the first small glass of brown earthy liquid for himself, lifted it with two hands, and drank deeply. Then Gai-eesha did the same, before himself, and lastly the president partook in the ritual.

It did not taste good by any means, but it also wasn't as unbearable as he had expected. Then, they all simply sat back and relaxed for a while. Devon was given his own space and encouraged to get as com-fortable as he desired. The room was mostly dark with the fire provid-ing the majority of the light.

The first thing he noticed from the medicine, was that he felt more tuned into sound than he was used to. When the instruments were played, he found that he was quite present to the melodies. When silence was provided, he became deeply aware of the layers of sound.

Other than that, an hour or so in, he wasn't feeling much of any effect at all (aside from a bit of tingling in the belly). Therefore, when Palu offered up a second round, Devon promptly came forward with haste. *If I'm going to do this, I'm going to see what it's worth.* This time he brought the full amount of liquid into his mouth and swallowed it all at once.

He went back to his space and continued to pass the time. However, he didn't need to wait long before he was hit with a newness that crept up on him with impressively cunning stealth. He began experiencing pictures of vast, sporadic images when his eyes were closed. He saw shapes and colors as in a kaleidoscope. The realness of it overwhelmed him—as images of fairies and castles molded in and out of his perception. Devon immediately became aware that he had never experienced anything remotely similar to this feeling in his life. He watched what was happening in disbelief. He became so completely interested in the visions of his mind, that all his other concerns promptly fell away.

Surprisingly, he found himself strangely in control—playing with his thoughts just as he had when he had been a young boy. He brought to mind a snow globe, and then found himself moving around within the circular winter world as a tiny little being within his mind. *It's so real...so amazing!* He shockingly told himself. Inside the globe, he ran and hopped over a fence with fluid ease. Then he was faced with a large gingerbread house standing before him. He saw his tiny body walk up to the roof and take a big bite out of the brown deliciousness with red frosting on it. *Wow, this is some crazy shit.*

Then the whole visual disappeared and moved onto something else entirely. *Wild!* He then found himself existing on yet a new platform of creative thought. For the first time in so long—thinking was playful for him.

He considered how interesting it would be if we placed small cameras on the foreheads of animals, and caught the world from their vantage. *What a great idea for a television channel that would be! Constant streaming life through the eyes of different animals.* The experience was reminding him of how creative he had the potential to be (he had forgotten almost completely).

Presently, his mind easily found itself capable of viewing life from all sorts of different animal's vantage points—a feat of imagination requiring a great deal of patience. He pushed further and played with variety. *Here's a squirrel jumping inside the trees of a forest, here's a giraffe looking over the fence at humans at a zoo, here's a dolphin racing through the ocean. Whoa this mind of mine!*

Finally, Devon opened his eyes and looked out into the room surrounding. He saw Miles sitting upright with his eyes closed swaying gently to the music played. Carson sang himself, and Devon was taken aback by how beautiful he found the presidents voice to be.

He looked at the man and saw 'the regularness' that was present for the first time in his adversary. He had never taken the time to notice before. *Like me?* he questioned.

Then Devon began to feel a familiar sensation creep in that was a sharp contrast to the previous moments he'd been living in. *Guilt.* He quickly scrambled back, trying to remember all his reasons for hating this man. He struggled to keep up the guard of defense that was usually so easily held in place. *Don't fall into the trap*, he told himself. *Don't do it!* But he couldn't help to see what he saw; which was confusion. He was open to honesty in a way that was inescapable. An honesty which proclaimed loud and clear: *There is no trap. You do not hate this man.*

As a method of avoidance, Devon stepped back further into his mind. The material was riveting for him, and his inner desire yearned to explore this new feeling. Therefore, he glimpsed a larger perspective on the very same thing. He saw how his mind continued to predict what it might say to other people. He saw how important that planning was to him—how big relationships were in his life (the conflicting ones most of all). He saw how much time and energy was taken up with consideration over how to make other people think highly of him. Although he pretended extremely well, he saw now that he had always known the truth. *It's a lie*, he thought. *The amount that it matters—it doesn't.*

The only reason he finally grasped this obsessive addiction, was because he felt more relaxed than ever before in his life. He gleaned that it was possible to actually drop the planning. He saw that there wasn't a need to worry because intuition was in fact his best weapon.

Suddenly, he panicked at the thought—seeing the degree with which the thing he had opposed opened up real answers for him. He wondered whether or not he had the ability to follow this new path, or that perhaps his insights would fall away from his memory. *I have placed the restraints on myself so tightly.* The insight caused him to cry— seeing for certain what he had done to himself by fearing the actions and interactions of his future so continuously. He had forgotten about 'before.' He was only here now.

Devon followed this internal session by promptly 'getting well.' He finally purged for many reasons well beyond the power of words to describe. He grabbed for the small white bucket nearby and released the contest of his belly into its depth. It was all the built up crap expunging itself from a place it wasn't needed any longer. He felt the disaster that was the configuration of his face—all worked up and twisted. *So ugly*, he thought. *So what...what does it even mean to be ugly? What do I care? All I want is for everyone to leave me alone. Stop thinking so much!*

He found himself on the cusp of transformation—between the solidity of a known old world, and the brilliance of something new and frightening. As he continued to purge, he saw dark images all around him. He imagined that this was some kind of devil's ceremony he had joined; and continued getting well, knowing of the falsehood of his thoughts. He purged knowing that he was doing that same thing again—playing it safe by putting down others and lifting up his ego for a brief gasp of superiority, which normally sustained, but could not do so now. *These games of comparisons are such a big part of my life. Can I really be rid of them? I don't want them anymore!*

He kept going. The release felt so bad and so good simultaneously. He was shocked at how much he had to get rid of, but knew that none of it could stay inside any longer. Devon purged and purged and purged some more. He loved it. He loved it for its realness. It was the most beautiful experience of his life. His mind flickered quickly, as he sensed the presence of a body coming into his personal space.

Gai-eesha approached, and without much notice of a change in consciousness, all his attention now focused itself on this new interaction between himself and another. He felt such deep gratitude as he watched her replace his bucket with one that was fresh and clean. She looked at his face and saw the tears on his checks and the mucus around his nose. He saw that she was crying too.

"I'll get you a tissue," she said.

Devon extended his arm impulsively to grab her wrist as she was turning away. "No, stay. Please stay."

She nodded her head as she reached out and gently clasped his right hand in her left. Devon saw the thoughts come together in her mind so clearly: *Priority. He needs me in this moment. If I leave even for an instant…everything will be different when I return.* Although he had just met this woman, surprisingly, he didn't feel uncomfortable holding her hand. There was no need to take it away, or to keep it there. But there was more. She encouraged something in him. *You can be with this moment*, she seemed to be saying with her eyes. It was a thought so new, so shocking in contentment, and so opposite from his usual tendency to run away from the uncomfortable. Right now he couldn't care about what might happen—he was too happy to be experiencing the feeling of extreme cleanliness.

He looked up into Gai-eesha's face and saw the bleary image of an old woman morph in and out of focus. *What is this? What am I seeing? This medicine is still working strong.* He surprised himself by thinking of it as medicine. He felt no need to turn his gaze away. He knew that she didn't care, and he was beyond social awkwardness. He just kept looking at her face right in front of his; as peacefully as he had ever peered at another human's features before—fantastically observing the reality which was occurring before him. What he saw reminded him of an old Native American woman, grizzly and wise. It was so real, and somehow seemed to be impossible. She looked to be almost hollow—as a ghost. He would have liked to believe he was existing in another world, but he wasn't. He was as present as he had ever been. Then she spoke: "You are not alone brother. God is with you inside—always. You are divine. Believe. You're not alone. Don't feel that. Untruth."

Normally he would have taken solace in the role of his male machismo and skepticism at such language; but he found that he couldn't do so now. Her words were too close to what he needed to hear. He didn't want to feel solitary anymore, or to pretend that he wasn't. Devon was sure he had played that role for far too much of his life. He saw now the depth of its un-serving, and he glimpsed the possibility of feeling the continuous presence of company.

Finally, he began to understand why they had referred to the purging as 'getting well.' He breathed in large heaps of air that tasted like bliss. He released his hand and leaned back into the softness of the pillows. He closed his eyes and relaxed so profoundly that he began to cry again for how much it was needed. *What have I done to myself?* He wept—loudly and well.

Meanwhile, Miles was having his own experiences across the room. This was his ninth ceremony in the past three years, and although every time was drastically different, he was learning how to use his previous encounters with the medicine to sink more fully into the next one. Currently, he felt the working effects powerfully. He didn't resist the desire to purge, but he also felt a pleasant yearning to keep the medicine within for longer. Breath was his friend and he used it to relax himself into an 'openness of being.' *Try to hold on and you lose it all. Allow the mind to be like a child on the playground,* he told himself. *It searches the terrain—whatever it finds...it's content with. The child is only interested in seeing what might happen next.* Then he closed his eyes and allowed images to come.

Miles saw himself strolling along rolling hills—little bumps of land above a small town. The ground inhabited both live and dead grass. All surrounding, about every twenty feet or so, were short little cherry blossom trees with wild bare branches scattering out in all angles of artwork. He continued moving through the landscape, walking consciously—feeling no desire to be any other place. Above the green and yellow of the grass, and the brown of the trees, stood a pleasantly formative overcast sky. As he dove into his mastery of possibility, he noticed his mind lifting his body up into the vertical space above the ground. *After all, anything is possible within the imagination,* he remembered.

Miles hovered in his mind—looking out onto all the features below and allowing the wind to gently move his body side to side—forward and back—up and down. Then, he played even more dramatically; picturing himself tumbling and twirling into the clouds—stretching out and holding all sorts of varying postures of freedom. There was no weight at all—only enjoyment. As he decided to carry himself up even higher into the sky, he brought his chin to his chest and cast his gaze down into the mist of the clouds now below his feet.

Suddenly…*Oh look! The birds are here!*

There were elements of his imagination he considered before creating, and others that were just created spontaneously—out of a place he couldn't see coming. The presence of birds was the latter. He knew he was imagining it all, but it didn't matter. His usual filter was tucked away somewhere in a place of unconcern as he experienced the full weight of these visions.

A black raven came near and circled around and around his body, rising and falling from his head to his feet in spirals of prayer and protection. Then the winged creature came to hold its position directly in front of his face. It flapped its wings in a calm motion, and the two of them looked back at each other with a piercing steady gaze. Miles took in something within that flare of time. He felt a message being clearly transmitted from this ancient bird and into himself:

"Everything is shit," it diffused.

"Wow…that's what you have to say to me?" Miles thought back.

"Before you argue," it said, *"open up and try it on first. Taste the fullness of the thought. Notice the effect of the feeling of letting all care go. I am just riding along with you through this journey, and I have a message to share. Still, the message is shit too."*

Miles tended not to use such negative language; but feeling the concept of 'everything being shit,' had the effect of making him smile and feel largely freer. *"Yes, I see your point. Everything is shit. Please continue."*

The raven happily complied. He realized it was telling him exactly what he needed to hear. *"Conclusions, conclusions, conclusions! You constantly search for answers that you've already found my friend. Everything changes. So fast—for everyone. In less than a second, your mind has taken you to a whole other place of seeing. Not only now…always! Stop deceiving yourself from this truth."*

And just like that—poof, it was gone.

Without questioning Miles took in the significance of the message. It was not that it made him feel uncaring; it was that it made him feel appropriately small. He was not trying to see what he wanted; he was trying to see how it was. *A relaxed uncaring that leads to more of the right kind of action,* he thought. *Stop searching to be wise. Remember how much the ranking of your wisdom doesn't matter. Remember how much your position of power is nothing.*

Then Miles intuitively decided to invert his body so that the crown of his head was facing down, lightly touching the clouds. His toes were pointing up toward the flaring sun. He began allowing himself to fall steadily—through the coolness of the clouds face down. The moment when he came through the bottom of the ice crystals, and the earth opened up to his vision, he felt himself smiling so sincerely that his chances of forgetting this moment were nil and nadda. Mountains, a lake, forests and small buildings sat together in overwhelming splendor below. Then, like superman, he flew back up high into the atmosphere and then down toward the ground once again. Anything was possible in the depth of imagination. It was the coolest thing about being human.

His body flew in glorious curves of abandon. He repeated the process that seemed to be never ending in satisfaction—up through the top of the clouds, and back down through the bottom of the white bulbous substance. Finally, he crossed his legs in the air like a monk, and gently floated himself all the way back down to the center of the grove where he had begun this particular adventure. Miles took a moment to integrate the experience on the imagined land, before opening up his eyes back to the truer reality of the ceremony occurring in the place he now called his home.

Throughout the rest of the evening, lessons of wisdom continued to fire off—as if by not caring about it, more was brought his way. The president felt as though he could reach out and grab a hold of a countless number of thought anchors at any time. They flew through his brain, as a result of his deep belief in the goodness of his constructed circuitry. *In a similar way that we go back and forth between the feeling body, and the thinking mind...we switch from concentrating on our individual experiences and our connection to something larger. Back and forth, back and forth...what's happening to me, what am I a part of? Yes, that's it.*

Words continued to flash out in startlingly clear composure. He scribbled them down in his notebook as soon as they came into formation. He knew that by recording, something was being sacrificed—there was no doubt about that. Yet, he felt compelled to transcribe—*even if something is lost, something else is gained.* He inspected and sat with each string of sound meaning for a time. He thought that anyone could make use of them. He wrote:

> *Allow yourself your full bandwidth...all the unknowing.*
>
> *We need environments which give honor to our fluctuations.*
>
> *Move forward and shake off whatever just happened...it isn't as important as you think.*
>
> *Protect your mind from nonsense thoughts.*
>
> *Once I gave up trying to get, I was given everything that I ever hoped to want.*
>
> *We're so fucking scared of the emptiness...there's nothing to be scared of. In fact, the emptiness is God. Everything is God.*
>
> *I am allowed to have fun and be happy. I am allowed to accept myself. I have seen how good I can be. Now my work is to believe it more often. When I don't believe it, I commit violence against the self, which is God.*

This seemed to be most important of all. It was deep, but he knew he had to settle into the honesty of that truth. It was the most real thing he had found. *Self acceptance.*

Miles looked over at Devon Pearson crouched over a bucket with Gai-eesha by his side. As soon as he saw the expression on Pearson's face, he felt content with his actions toward bringing this man here.

Often we seek to solve our problems by taking away instead of sharing. Because of our lack of patience, we do not fully explore the possibility of creative solutions that might be incredibly effective. An ayahuasca ceremony is not always the appropriate solution, perhaps—but bringing others into places where we feel love…that's the best we can do—promote ways that work for us. What else is there?

Miles saw that Devon was struggling and currently experiencing convulsions. He was crouched over himself; banging his head against the floor. He remembered who he was dealing with—that this was a man who had taken countless disgraceful actions in his life. *What else is there to expect when you finally face that enormous pile of ugliness? That's why they run…because the weight has been piling up so massively.* He considered letting the man work through the pain on his own, but when Devon let out a scream, Miles decided it was too much. He stood up and walked over to his adversary and brother. *I can do nothing, yes…but I can also do something.*

He bent his legs and crouched down to meet this man on his level. As soon as Devon felt the touch on his arms, his head lifted up and he looked at Miles with fire in his eyes. Miles stared back in calmness and reached one hand out to clutch the back of Devon's head. The brutality of the situation had already been cut in half through these few quick movements. Miles had taken a risk, but the medicine was in him too. His strength was real, and when Devon saw his face—he knew what it was to be with another.

"It's OK. I know. It's OK. You're here now." Then Miles stood up and walked calmly back to his space to engage with his own meditations. His objective was achieved.

EVOLUTIONIZED

I t was hardest for the people of the United States to come to grips with the fact that they no longer had to try being better than any-one else. After all, they had been so far deep into the lifestyle of competition between humans. But it was also a culture that caught on quickly when slapped in the face with a harsher reality. Once they had their major shift, the wave broke all over the world. It was not that they had to lose their competition, it was that they had to start thinking about it differently. Less people walked around completely consumed with the conception of 'I.' Human beings pushed themselves to move their flowing desire for progress toward balancing the 'I,' along with the 'we.'

Perhaps the greatest feat in the history of humanity (in large part due to the evolution of 'the news'), was the gentle, and well-disciplined process of disarmament. It was, in the end; the dream of efficiency itself, which blossomed into an entity strong enough to overcome the desire for forceful retribution.

Along with this grounding logic, came the idea that the process would not only move at appropriate intervals of slowness, but also— that a single government body would always maintain a defense force capable of repelling any bubble of violence from terrorists. Overall, there was growing faith that these idiotic disasters would become less and less as the greater society of humans continued moving in the direction of improved mental health, logic, education and love. As this occurred, the government promised to continue converting its own supplies away from violent material.

Opponents would argue, "do you know how many technological discoveries have been brought about due to military influence?"

Heady Futurists would respond, "So have airports. It's not the military or any other structure that brings about new discoveries, it's simply the human mind and its desire to make things better. That will never end. Violence isn't necessary for our innovation."

However, there were more complexities which paved a way for this new road of less physical violence. In exchange for the United States transforming the largest supply of military equipment into other uses—almost the entire rest of the planet agreed to adopt English as its official language. There was much dramatic debate of course, but overall it was agreed to be a pretty reasonable exchange toward the investment of a joint and beneficial planet for all. Having a common language would allow for greater travel, connection, and trade. Trade, was widely believed to be the healthy basic platform for human interaction. English had already become the langue of the planet in all but title anyway. It was time to make it official. Other languages and cultures were still of course free to maintain themselves with as much vigor as they wished, but no one could prevent the progression of sensibility, and one set of sound communication universally understood.

WH covered the transition of these fears, as well as those of the next layer. Through many formative debates, it was generally concluded that humans never need to prepare for defending themselves violently against outside intelligent sources from Space. The government could have enough physical might to overcome other weapons that existed on this land; but they would not continue advancing technologies of violence to defend against abstract unrealities from extraterrestrials. To presume that intelligent alien life would come to us, sprung out of a culture that wasn't interested in peaceful cooperation; was a conception grounded in fantastical and unrealistic possibility. It was something for the movies—not for a practical, mature thinking mind.

A fear based mind, simply wouldn't, in actuality, evolve into the creation of technologies allowing for complex Space travel and transportation. Only the conception of teamwork and trust could do that.

This was the higher level of belief that was beginning to catch on in popularity. One of the many great new age debaters argued, *"only the energy of loving progression has the ability to advance technology to its highest possibilities. If we go out further, we do so in peace. There's no reason to think that any other life wouldn't do the same. Humans murdering other humans as a result of emotional upheaval is a way of the past. It's over—even if it's still here right now. Peaceful trading is the only interaction that's sensible."*

Eventually, the leaders of 193 countries came together with the hope of merging themselves beyond the archaic foundations of the United Nations. In the beginning the merging happened slowly, but then rapidly expanded as the general population began believing in the necessity for it. It was agreed that the creation of one world government was inevitable and far too rewarding an opportunity to get bogged down by fearful worries. When enough people began considering the reality of our situation within the grand universe—the separation made little sense.

Healthy functionality of the planet required unity. Yes, there were known dangers to putting so much power, so much decision-making, into any one body of organization. But danger, it was understood, could never be completely eliminated. The best solution was to simply handle it with as much foresight as possible.

One of the greatest concerns of the new structure was making sure that responsibility was placed into trusting hands. The system for vetting had to be improved upon. Democracy, it was agreed, was the best method for accomplishing this—true, popular democracy. Not alternate forms which billed themselves as such, or democracies that secretly tried to manipulate its people into not voting. Democracy, which used all power of influence toward encouraging its citizens to step up and play their pivotal role.

Events like the Olympics were still heavily competitive and a tradition continued well into the future. After all, old geographical lines were a fine way to create teams to demonstrate athletic prowess. But it was realized that the type of competition appropriate in sport was not acceptable in more serious life matters.

So the progression went. One world government was created through the most impressive logistical feat of all time. Every citizen was given a personal account that only he or she could access online. *WH* ran a campaign that inquired, *"if banks can effectively protect their clients, why can't the government?"*

Having an individual 'citizen account,' created a much greater feeling of unity throughout the population. Not only could citizens vote on elections through this platform (and the comfort of their home, or on the subway), but also on any number of issues that the world government opened up to a planetary wide voting (which they did as often as possible).

It was about time that the highest levels of technology were put into the hands of the people who understood that communication was everything, and that the population was wiser than leaders of the past had wanted to admit. Of course there were never-ending details of concerns, but that was the work for the leaders of the time. Creative humans were happy to find purpose in taking on the nitty-gritty minutiae of making a better future possible.

Perhaps the most important part of the process was that people everywhere began focusing more on improving their own local communities. They gave attention to larger elections, but it was secondary to the amount of focus they gave to finding the right people to lead their surrounding areas of land. New community centers that humans actually went to, began popping up in large numbers. Much of this was due to the organization and project planning of Futurism. These were places to connect with other humans and use the variety of intelligences on hand to get grounded morally, physically and psychologically. In this way, small circles of positive change spread outward until the entire planet was led by those actually capable of carrying the responsibility.

The police of local countries still operated, but were also unified under one all-encompassing system of law. The laws of the planet, in fact, made everything much simpler and safer. After all, it was the sum culmination of the best aspects from every previous system.

The job of 'lawyer,' was virtually eliminated, as every inch of the world became monitored by satellite cameras. Judges had less difficult decisions to make, as proof of what actually occurred was almost always accessible to their jurisdiction. Perhaps the cameras were indeed the ultimate form of Big Brother, but some of the flows of technological power were too useful not to be implemented. Locks were placed on all video surveillance and only opened up when a specific location was reported to have been the scene of a crime. The old population would doubt the ability for this process to be taken on responsibly, but the new one had far more faith in a system comprising of individuals who had come up through the ranks—and fully understood what it meant to be a professional.

For a while crime continued, but slowly those obsessed with personal circumstances became aware of the effects of harmfully developed habits. Schools taught this. They also began teaching self-defense as a true form of art. It became accepted that being prepared did nothing toward the promotion of more violent behavior. Eventually the truth was seen that the truly confident body had no reason to utilize its skills of action unless it felt it necessary to bring about justice. Terrorist activity had brought about the realization that it was everyone's responsibility to act with the utmost common sense during situations of emergency.

It wasn't long before there were stories of three children tackling the legs of a shooter, while two others struggled to take his weapon away. People would stay calm, hide in corners, and then jump out to take action when the moment was felt to be right—risking their own lives to protect freedom. With the changes to the institution of school, came the ability to implement effective techniques of communication during emergency.

When the threat of terrorism began to subside, weather disasters became the real point of attention and concern. *It is unacceptable that we distract ourselves from the unknown reality of the weather,* many humans began to advocate. *There is no excuse in expecting the government to save us. We are too many. It takes every ounce of human ingenuity to plan, and we are all responsible to learn.*

Even more impactful, was the government's new practice of distributing rewards for good deeds. The program focused on the psychological power behind positive reinforcement. It was not a lofty notion; it simply worked. The only catch, of course, was that the good deed had to be reported by the receiver, or by a spectator. Deciding on appropriate rewards was the perfect job for future humans, and an example of a task that could never be adequately performed by robotics.

A petition for rewarding random acts of kindness was submitted in a short self-video, or SV. These SVs became a major staple for 'news content.' It was known that this practice would infuse the population with a sense of hope and good merit that people were now searching to seep their minds in. Witnessing the great actions taken by others was inspiring and also quite entertaining. As jealous envy began to be acknowledged as the destructive force that it was, motivation toward living naturally became the norm.

The rewards program, however, soon became secondary to the duty citizens began taking on in being more conscious of their own 'self-care.' The most mature members of the population didn't feel the need to be rewarded for doing what made sense. If they received rewards, super—if not, the experience of meaning was more than enough.

Past humans, of course, would consider this new world outlandish and unrealistic. However, that was indeed the kind of pessimism that had prevented these changes from taking place far sooner than they had. In a world where logic reigned supreme and citizens were encouraged to enjoy the gift of life, it made little sense to limit the personal freedoms of others. Those who continued to do so were targeted as confused and simply had to be rehabilitated. They too came along with time, and caught up quickly with exposure to more logical environments.

Overall the change became an exciting process to take up and be a part of. After all, what better cause was there to see within the course of a lifetime? It was joint purpose everyone could take part in—it was a piece of fruit on a tree branch that the population had unknowingly been trying to grab throughout its history. The only thing preventing their hands from taking hold of it, was the belief that it was well within their reach.

DECIDED ENDINGS

The feelings of recent events hung in the air like a cloud of cold truth. *Certain experiences make way for permanent change,* Maya Sol thought to herself. *Days can be so different.*

It had been more than fourteen years since she had finished serving her second term as vice president. She enjoyed her retirement immensely, but had not stopped taking on roles and playing her part in the vast array of pivotal events occurring across the globe. Still, she was not prepared for the challenge she had been faced with just this morning.

They had come to their arrangements quickly—putting details together in accordance with Daniels requests. In harmony with the alteration of the constitutional rights regarding euthanasia, came Daniel's feeling that he had had enough time existing within his current body form. The concept was simple; he would broadcast his last moments directly after the new law was put into effect. He would be the first to take advantage of his new right, and he would be an example. Not as a brutal form of entertainment, but as a valuable piece of basic self-freedom to witness. It was an appropriate celebration; a calm and decided end—as opposed to a panicked and unpredictable struggle. Afterward many followed, but Daniel Sol had set the bar high for how to end a life.

"It matters how we do this," he had told them. He wasn't in a hospital bedroom. His ninety-seven-year-old body sat on a bench in front of a fountain in Princeton, New Jersey. Around him were his family, friends, along with a camera crew. A former wrestler of his came up to introduce his brand new infant daughter. Maya held in her memory the vision of Daniel's old, wrinkly, dark hand, reaching out to lift and separate the little baby fingers of this brand new humans' extremities. *That is an image worth keeping*, she told herself. *A human about to die, inspecting with fascination the newness of creation.*

Although Daniel's body had trouble moving, it hadn't completely broken down on him yet. Still, it was obvious that the man was in physical pain. He leaned back against the bench as the brown painted wood creaked with brittleness along with his body. The sun was bright on his face, and the sky was fully blue.

"First, I want everyone to relax," he said clearly. "Know that this is my moment. I'm taking it without any feelings of guilt. And what I want everyone to do, as I prepare to leave this world, is just one simple thing—I want you to feel comfortable. Nothing more or less. I want you to simply be yourself with confidence. If you want to speak, speak—but only if you feel your words will be an improvement on silence. I want you to believe in your own natural goodness, and I want you to send out all the love that you have to offer. Do not get ahead of yourself, pushing others out of the space and failing to acknowledge their presence. Watch and listen, but also feel for the right to display your own brightness. Most importantly, I want this to be a party. Not only a celebration of my life, but a celebration of life generally. Please give this to me in my last few moments. I humbly request it."

Amanda Keegan spoke up after a brief respite, "I remember back when I used to visit my grandfather at the nursing home. I can see him now—so old, shriveled and beyond his senses. He was about your age, but in far worse shape. I went to the head nurse and asked her, "If someone in your care asks to die often—if they are in so much pain and feel that that they have had enough time—is there anything you can do?"

""No," she had told me flatly as if she had already considered the matter a great deal. "There's nothing I can do. As long as some of the days he gets up to eat, then he's well enough." That's what she said! Even worse—they never even asked him. Never asked if he wanted help to end his time how he wished and when he wanted. Instead, they ignored it as if deciding yourself was some kind of diseased subject matter."

Amanda stood up from her spot on the bench, remembering the conversation and speaking to the camera with spirit. "Who are we to tell those in pain how precious life is, when we are not bed stricken ourselves—when we are not living within their bodies? No more. I just wanted to say thank you to Daniel Sol. For his tremendous courage to be revolutionary at the end."

"Words in harmony with silence," Daniel replied. "Thank you Amanda. I agree. Only a few years earlier, I had to watch my brother go through the same thing." Daniel closed his eyes and spoke out loud to his brother. "Brian, you who taught me the value of well-rounded strength—you who were too smart for your own environment. This is for you too. Thank you to all who have taken action which has paved the way for me to do this today. It is an incredible blessing to be able to say all of the final words that I really wish to speak. It is a blessing to be able to pick the day, pick the place. Thank you."

There was music playing his favorite songs, and Maya watched as Daniel drank in the sounds with happiness. There was a certain electric weight in the air felt by everyone; knowing that this was the last little chunk of time of someone's life—and that it was exactly the way he had decided for it to be. It went beyond the depth of sadness. It was something more. It was sadness combined with justice.

Maya recalled Daniel taking a break from humming along to a song, leaning-in and whispering: "The melodies free us from pain and teach us how to feel—now. You can never get enough music Maya. Being played in the background was one of her favorite Bob Marley songs, 'I'm still waiting.' She felt what he meant. Then he said, "Make sure he's listening to enough music please." That he was referring to Peter was obvious.

"I will," she reacted.

Eventually, when he felt the gathering was at its peak crescendo, Daniel called everyone in close. "Here's the deal. We're all going to walk over to that space over there." He pointed to a large open area of grassy land. "I want everyone to find their own comfortable spot and lay down on your back if you would, or stand if you prefer. Either way, please focus on feeling the heat and energy of the sun. Then we'll all just be together quietly for my last moments of life. When I feel ready, I'll take my pill. When you've had enough of your meditation, leave to continue onward in confidence with your life. Please remember, there is only one question that counts: 'What do you want to do with your time?'"

It was telling of his character that at his end, he was still concerned with making improvements for those he left behind.

"Accept the self and do it. It will most likely be awesome. The worst thing that happens is that you learn—learn to respect life enough to let go of your fears. To respect life!" he said with gusto. "Do you do it? If not, why? Think of all the faith you have had to have in order to be where you are standing—trusting in this crazy process." That he was speaking also, to those beyond his physical proximity was apparent. "We are born into this," he said. "There is nothing to take credit for. If you're looking for that, you must enter into the world of deep spiritual soul work. Look to your potential, and don't turn your back on it. That's the real work."

With a hand on his son's shoulder, Daniel lifted himself from the bench and found his place on the grass. As he closed his eyes and felt the sun that he loved so much, he spoke his final words, and took his last few breaths. The microphone clipped to his shirt was catching the sound clearly.

"Be easy with your chasing. Too much chasing just to chase going on. If you have to chase, at least chase what you've really taken the time to decide that you want. In life, just like in sport; if you are not relaxed, you're much more likely to cause injury. Stress leads to disease, I am certain. Stress is disrespectful to life. So stop stressing and start appreciating. People say that I'm relaxed; they always have.

But I've wanted so badly to be even more so. I can see now how the label of being too much of something held me back from defining my own levels of appropriate. Once you've had a real taste of surrender, you see that there isn't anything better than relaxing into the flow. Surrender to both the good and bad days my friends. It's only a matter of how well we're able to utilize the capacity of our minds while we experience both struggle and comfort. I want public school, every school, to have classes dedicated to 'getting stronger.' Simply students sitting, standing or lying down and thinking to themselves—repeating as a mantra over and over: 'I am making myself stronger with the flow.' Even for a few minutes a day. Oh how wonderful the effects—holding our minds focused on one thing has tremendous implications. Do you know that?" He allowed the question to hang in the air before turning toward the personal self.

I choose to use the same technique now, he thought as he allowed his body to be heavy and connect with the ground beneath him. *I am making myself stronger...being with the flow. Even the flow of my own decision.* The words circulated his inner world—as he felt an energy burst with the true trying power of the statement. Then Daniel Sol calmly lifted his fist to his mouth and swallowed the contents within.

HEROISM

Maya, Peter, Marty, Duncan, Patrick and Amanda stood with Miles at the large window taking up a good three-quarters of the wall. They peacefully observed the mass gathering of people amid this particular hunk of land before them. The window was tinted so that no one standing below was aware of their presence. Duncan, who was somewhere toward the middle of the group said, "Yesterday I was at a party and this guy I was talking to claims out of nowhere; "I never get stressed. What do you make of that?!" Duncan didn't allow anyone to answer before continuing, "I told him that of course everyone stresses—that the idea is simply to have less and less of it. He seemed shocked that I would refute his claim."

Miles laughed. "I'm glad you set him straight Dunk. Did you ask if he ever practiced observing his complete range of emotions?"

"No, that would have been a good one though."

"It's a little funny how we try to run away and convince ourselves not to see reality sometimes," Amanda chimed in. "I mean what kind of thing is that to say anyway? How engulfed can we be in our own labels? So much more fun to admit to the never-ending changes I feel.

Miles continued to look out into the crowd on the other side of the window. Many of the people below swung huge flags displaying images of the sun, hearts, or the flame symbol of Futurism.

Beyond the massive field filled with humans, sprouted an enormous bulbous silver structure which immediately filled Miles with happiness and pride as soon as he took note of its presence. After all, it was a rocket unlike any that had ever been created before. The space traveling edifice he was looking at would carry a satellite capable of providing virtually free solar energy to millions of more people on this rock they called home. It was the culmination of approximately fifteen years of planning.

Along with it being the day for a tremendous step in energy progression and innovation—it was also an important day for another reason. Today, was the inauguration of the president, and the establishment of the first unified world government of the entire race of humans. Nothing more or less dramatic as that.

Although Carson had considered turning down the newly created position, he was still young enough, still had energy, and still believed in his duty to effect as much change as possible while alive. He accepted the nomination with this steadying justification.

In his mind, the position did not give him a right to represent all aspects of nature—but he also knew that his decisions would affect the circumstances of a wide variety of life on the planet. *Humans are the most intelligent, which pushes us in the direction of leadership. Therefore, we are responsible to use our given traits to make conscious decisions for everything.* He saw it as his personal responsibility (and the intelligent human populations' responsibility), to safeguard the entire planet with as much quality decision making as possible. He chose to believe that all creatures preferred survival to destruction. That was the platform of belief which he took action from.

He thought that perhaps avoiding situations where humans were ingesting as much animal product as possible in the hope of winning competitions and then regurgitating their food in order to ingest more was a level of disrespect that could be socially dissuaded by the government. *I can do that at least. We don't need to make something illegal in order to create change I think. Leadership should mean more than that. We don't need to make it a law to put on your seat belt, but we can still have virtually the same effect by promoting it as a practice that makes a hell of a lot of sense. The government can have two jobs: Create law, and create an agenda. The agenda—the voice, does not need to be any less influential than the law. That is, with a government and leaders that people trust and respect. Tapping into social pressure is very effective. Much, much better than the alternative of force. We're all propagandists. All words are a manipulation; that's for sure. Question is, what is the intention behind the manipulation? That's the only thing that matters. My higher self, the one I take pride in...is only interested in manipulation for the sake of helping others help themselves. That is honest. If I ever manipulate out of greed, I know that it is done from the space of fear.*

Carson had been fully aware of the presence of those who promoted cocky and arrogant doubt throughout every step of his journey. He had even known about them from all the marvelous stories he had read as a boy. *Writers know,* he thought. In a very real way, his stories had prepared him for much of the opposition he had faced along the way. He considered all those who thought him naive for thinking he could infuse change on such a large scale. It seemed productive to think about his naysayers from time to time—in order to take account of his own personal progress, and keep his fire burning strong in the direction of personal advancement beyond the ego. *When you don't like me I can feel it. And I love what it does to me. It causes me to open up my heart and become nothing and everything simultaneously. Loved or hated...neither prevents me from doing what is right. My body is a vessel to be used for good. That is all. What is good? I get to decide. Those of us who put down others as unrealistic in order to escape the necessity of taking on any kind of effective action or responsibility are a tricky bunch. As if their opinions of stagnation and hopelessness are so valid that it gives them the right to spread their diseased mentality of lethargy—of not really growing up, and instead getting angry about getting older. This is the problem. To be ungrateful, to not take the time to acknowledge the gifts of experience...it insults life.*

Miles turned from the window to look at his friends—*my fellow warriors of change, my team,* he thought. *It could have been any of us standing in my position right now. Peter, Maya or Marty. Amanda for sure. Even Duncan might have the most potential out of all of us. Perhaps not Patrick,* he thought honestly…*but he plays a fantastic supporting role and I love him for it. Mikey though.* Miles took a moment to honor the memory of his old friend… *yes, Mikey would have been great.*

The point is, he continued thinking—*that it was never about one savior. I'm not that at all. I'm simply practicing my yoga which helps me see a small part of the complex set of circumstances which brought me here. For the true revolution to take place; heads of the Buddha snake had to rise up from everywhere. Had to! It was never about one damn savior. That's the element of so many stories which is shallow and unrealistic. It was about making sure that the confused human had no chance of overtaking the power of a team. The best way to accomplish our goals was simply to create a whole army of us.*

"Once we changed the way in which children developed, the old system was bound to crumble."

They all turned to look at Peter. Marty responded, "Even now, I feel that was the big leap too. Children currently being born will go further than we can possibly imagine—and that's the best part of it all. You D.T's are the breakthrough bunch."

"Exactly! Wish me luck," Miles requested cheerfully. "What I do now is for all our combined work."

Peter caught up to him a few moments later, just as he reached for the button to send up the elevator box. "Can I give you a hug?" Peter had a flashback to a moment with his father long ago. "You're a great kid, Miles."

Miles closed his eyes and took a moment to allow the best compliment in the world to penetrate deeply. He felt for the appropriate reply, and then opened his eyes. It didn't matter that he was staring at an aging man—he knew it was the right thing to say. "So are you, Peter. You're a great kid too."

Eyes stared back at Miles with the most piercingly neutral expression one could imagine. For a moment, they shared a beautiful understanding of what it meant—'being a great kid.'

As he stepped out of the elevator, Miles walked forward toward a final flight of steps leading to the exit lobby. When he moved through the automatic doors of one of NASA's newest buildings, he instantly became aware of the sharp, hot summer air. The sun was descending on Cape Canaveral, and the Florida landscape was changing color by the moment. There was a row of clouds that reminded him of ocean waves—curling and crashing down in shades of pink and white. The sky to the other side was still radiant in varying degrees of blue. *All the beauty we require is surrounding us in abundance,* he thought. *Look—decide that you want to see as much magic as you can.*

Sometimes Miles considered outrageous strategies of action—locking himself away in a basement for a few months and taking away all his basic luxuries. Why? *So that I can emerge out the other end and find myself able to fall more deeply in love with the world. That's why. It's not rational perhaps—but then...maybe it's the most rational thing I've ever thought to do. It's a remedy for the amount we get to witness beauty. Deprivation can be a valuable tool to increase appreciation. For real. Restraint is not meant to punish—it's the other way around. Restraint is meant to make us freer.*

He chuckled to himself as he put away one of the many creative thoughts that often find their way into his consciousness. Then he walked up an ordinary set of steps, onto the stage, and toward the podium.

As he moved his feet along the finely polished dark wooden platform, Miles felt nervous sensations begin to rise. He was well aware that the opportunity to share his words with this many people was a responsibility that could easily overwhelm. After all, there was a great sea of humans with seemingly no gaps in their ranks waiting for him to speak—billions more watching elsewhere. But he had great amounts of practice turning that nervousness into something he could use. *Run away and the nervousness remains a heavy weight to be dragged along behind. Embrace it and go to another level of passionate attention.*

How did my life ever come to this? he thought. He smiled as he waved—stepped up to the microphone—opened his inner ear and listened to the booming noise. *So loud! I'm like a character from an adventure story,* he thought...*but it's real life.* He brought himself into the present even more fully. *What do I want to think about? I know what it is...how to do good with my body. That is the grounding that has brought me to this point...and my mind is a part of my body.*

Miles connected to his lips. He told them, *try your hardest.* He told them, *remember kindness and speak good things.* Many years had passed since his first appearance on television via *KYL.* Heaps of experience as an orator and leader allowed him to gather up a moment like this, and inflate it with the air of his personal comfort. The sounds of his truth blasted triumphantly through the electrical currents of technology and space.

"Happy day on Earth, fellow humans," he began. "This is a really good one, is it not?" He smiled, taking in the great noise of approval—taking in what their accomplishments meant and how bizarre the whole journey had been. He looked out into the mass—focusing, taking in the moment and allowing any hint of anxiousness to subside.

It's so incredibly important to celebrate, but there is also still so much healing left to do. It never ends. I have to be strong, he thought. Then he doubled back upon his thought. *No...I am strong. That distinction means everything,* he realized.

"Starting today, everything can be better. Much better." *How about that for an opening line to a political speech?* He smiled to himself at the revolutionary course of action he was currently embarking on. *What's better than this? All about the risk. Have to risk. Too risky not to.*

"I'm referring to the blooming of a new kind of awareness that must take place at some point in time. How about now? There are only two things we must do—try, and believe. That's it.

"I will bring you in on a little secret. I have gotten where I'm standing today—because I have only one central focus of interest; doing the right thing. That's all. But the way I see it, it isn't anything much to feel prideful about. I don't want to be doing anything else, and I don't believe you should either. What is doing something wrong? Immature acts that make no sense—no thank you, I don't have interest in them. Why? Because they serve something we think we'll like but won't. Wrongness does not increase the health of the soul. It might appear to in the moment, but that's simply because we're not grounded in our philosophy.

"The more brutal we are toward the self, the more we feel entitled to obsess over the details of our own personal affairs. But self-immolation does not give us a right to forget about the community of humans we're existing in. The solution couldn't be clearer for our problems. We all have to step up and start doing the right thing more often. Why? Because we see that it makes sense for our well-being. No other reason is necessary. We see that it's our duty to ourselves and each other—to in some way make things better. It's perfectly acceptable around ninety percent of the time to try having as much fun, and being as silly as possible. That's real work too—to ease the seriousness. But that other ten percent—it isn't healthy for us to run away from it. That's our time to show up and problem solve with strength—to be the bigger person even when it's uncomfortable—to fix things that need fixing."

Miles took a few deep breaths before continuing. "If you're in the habit of taking actions you aren't proud of; it doesn't mean that you have to keep repeating them. Truth is, we're never off the hook. Feeling that you're already so far gone that you can't change—no! I'm sorry, but that's the easy way out—and you aren't allowed to live from that place. Each time we take action, we are making a brand new choice that we're accountable for. Each action stands alone for itself—separate from the trends of our past. Thinking that it's too late—that's baby stuff.

He let those last two words sit in the air for a moment. "We are all responsible for what goes on among us. In this new community, no one gets a pass. It boils down to this, and I don't think I can say it any more clearly: It's time to stop pretending that you are more upset than you actually are. Hmm, yes—that's right.

It's also time to stop projecting judgment onto others before we've taken the opportunity to learn who they really are. The insecure ego is the smaller self that demands answers now, instead of the one who asks for them to arrive.

Break, breath. Silence. *Good,* Miles thought. *More!*

"I ask you today, to creatively imagine a different kind of world. Thought is the first step toward creation, and although it's often ambiguous—it is not to be undervalued. It's going to take a long time to turn ourselves away from all the messy habits we've created. Imagining better is the essential activating phase. So, see what happens when you consider a new kind of society that promotes a different set of standards. I invite you to contemplate what it would be like if you were able to tap into your full manifestation of confident imagination. Ask yourself, 'what would it feel like to be assured and creative simultaneously—believing you mind to hold as much valuable potential as any other?"

He gave his audience time to ask the question.

"Please do me a favor now. Attempt to tap into the feeling of loving stillness."

Again he gave them time. It was the presidents stage, and he had no problem with standing there and saying nothing. He knew so many would choose not to participate in the exercise. It didn't matter. It was for the others.

"Now gently send your love outside of your body—radiating from you. All your healing energy, to the entire planet and beyond, even into the depths of our galaxy. Imagine your love to have unlimited power, and doing its unique work toward healing. Imagine your love having the ability to encourage others to believe in the power of their own. After all, each of our expressions of love is as unique as us. Why not try? At the very least it isn't a harmful activity to engage. No different from praying. Go even further though. Feel your eye balls moving deeper into their sockets. Concentrate on feeling confident and secure, and allow that feeling to flow through you and outward. Let go of all the senseless weight you've been carrying around. Breathe, heal—see what comes next. Hold onto the feeling of self-acceptance until you're so full of it that it can't ever leave. Accept how your life has been, and also how it's going to be. Connect to the nature which you are a part. Have unbreakable faith. Without faith, it is not possible for us to reach our potential. Faith that it is how it should be, simply because there is only one reality of time. No other reasons are necessary. For the human mind, there is no further search. Feel trust in your bones."

They stood there like that for two full minutes—a million people, and many others watching from far away—in silent, relaxed, healing meditation. Science was an amazing instrument of discovery, but perhaps the most beautiful part was that it admitted to the limits of its knowing. Although there hadn't been enough experiments yet done to prove the effects of Metta meditation, for many, an experience was all the substantiation necessary in order to believe.

Is it so crazy to think that energy has the ability to escape our bodies and be effective elsewhere...that our emotions send out currents which affect our surroundings? Miles didn't think so—most of the people standing with him didn't think so either. *Maybe science will always be one step behind what we already know? If we have faith, if we trust our intuition...we can stay a step ahead of what research will eventually discover. We do this by letting go of the need to create facts, and existing comfortably in the realms of personal opinion. If we don't trust, if we need others to tell us it is so...we become followers instead of leaders. We lose the self and therefore become a part of the problem.*

Eventually, when he felt the moment to be right, Miles drew his arms down and allowed his fingers to hang loose by his sides. He began again.

"What an amazing effect. We should do this more often I think." That got some jubilant cheers of *"YES! Let's go!"*

"Now I invite you to position your body into a comfortable and relaxed stance, open up your ears, and allow yourself to enjoy listening as we make progress together toward stabilizing our intentions." He took another deep breath in.

"If we open our eyes with clarity and insight—if we look at the humanity of each and every one of us—we see that there is not a single human on this planet who really knows what's happening. I easily admit that for myself. I view a strand of truth which shows me that we are all simply trying our best to figure out what to do with our time. I see that no one is an expert at prioritizing. We grasp, we try. That is all. Realizing this can be a very scary thing which jars our reality into fright; it threatens to tear down what we have already built up. But know that you can't tear it down. What you've built is always there to go back to. I think it's important not to forget that. It will allow you to travel into the uncharted waters of truth discovery. Trust your future self to know better than you do right now. That added assurance will change everything and allow the present self to relax into the moment. It will overcome the obstacle of the ego's need to figure everything out *now*—and it will free you." Wild sounds of positive reinforcement broke his rhythm. He took his time coming back to it.

"Can you stop to see that we've been caught at a time when our intelligence and our wisdom are severely out of sorts? We are confused because we know so much yet also so little. Therefore, we have become masters of distraction and avoidance—following trends because it's easier to remain a part of the herd and ignore the burden of self-discovery. As a result, we have taken on a much larger weight—a weight that questions the very goodness of the self. This is most important.

"If you are hiding, you are already playing at a game that is not able to be won, a game of panicked survival—not thrival." The made-up word generated some more whistles and cheers. The necessity of survival passed down from our ancestors has prevented us from best utilizing the time in our life. Every day, we have to work at freeing ourselves from the anxious fear of mere survival—of wearing the mentality of 'getting through the day.' Thrival happens when we firmly believe in our regular humanness. It allows us to go after what we know for certain more fiercely, and with the knowledge that mistakes are opportunities for learning. When this occurs, the total population will combine to create a new kind of culture. A culture that understands that mistakes are not reasons to make ourselves feel terrible; they are merely gateways toward improvement. This is real.

"Let me be crystal clear about something. I will never ask you to blindly accept what I have to say. I don't think you should blindly accept anyone's truth above your own. Instead, allow positive influences to infiltrate the heart when your intuition tells you there is an opportunity to grab onto something of value. Following blindly is just another way of shirking accountability, and adding to a system of power struggles. It is not for you—the progressive future form of humanity. Each of you is aware that your individuality is of value." Miles allowed his own words to relax him. "When you follow because you know the reasons why and choose—it is no longer following. Maybe you didn't see how to break down that wall of obstruction, but you've still decided to walk through the opening. There is most definitely pride to be taken in that—in following wisely. There's no cheating. We humans share and build off of each other's discoveries. Only those stuck in the fallacy of ego games become agitated when others exploit their discoveries." He was never the most comfortable talking about himself, but he knew that his audience needed to see him open up to them fully. Therefore, he spoke with careful self-control.

"I am the type of leader we've been waiting for." *Never thought I'd hear myself saying that,* he chuckled silently. "I say 'type,' because I do not see myself as anything special to get so hung up on. I say 'we,' because I have also been waiting. I didn't want to wait anymore, so I decided to become 'it.' That is the power at your fingertips. I have done enough mindful work that what you think of me, is just one of many small fleeting thoughts passing through my circuitry. What matters a great deal more, is that my words reverberate honestly—that they're effective. Rather than getting swept up in the consideration of who this body I carry myself in is—let's stay focused on the question of 'type.' Let's ask together: What kind of leaders do we want? If we do this, we can insure a multitude of worthy decision makers far into our future, and not just grasp at a single person in time. After all, that isn't a very practical strategy. Instead, we should believe that diamonds exist everywhere with proper incubation. *This,* is the strategy for our cumulative future thrival. We need to become more organized in all sorts of ways that we haven't yet thought about.

"It has not always been easy for me, but I have held my determination on a setting which seeks to positively redirect the energy of life on this planet—with limited fear. This is where it has brought me. Here, right now—to this day; believing in our cumulative worth—believing in the effects that come from speaking from the heart. I do not take credit. I am merely a vessel that truth has decided to move through."

A magnificent outburst of noise bombarded his ear drums. He smiled and tilted his head forward in humble thanks. He pressed down into his feet and stood up taller in response to the support he'd been given. *Oh how true it is that we all suffer from the same afflictions*, he thought.

"I want to go further with you. Can I do that?"

"*YES!*" Came the response.

Miles burst forward—picking up greater speed as a musician displaying his greatest ability. "Societal pressure is strong and real. It's so strong that it can take us away from what our instincts know to be right. We learn from others to distract ourselves and waste our precious time with nonsensical, low-level ways of thinking. For too long, it has prodded us to be critical and avoid feelings of gratitude that we know are necessary and appropriate. If I'm being honest, I must admit that I believe societal pressure will always exist. However, I also believe that we can move its weight in the directions of our own choosing. Society can pressure the individual into constantly discovering what is true and real for them. We can direct our neighbors with offerings that work for us. It doesn't hurt to offer. There is powering in saying, and being willing to hear — 'NO.'"

"I will offer you two of my own discoveries for you to ponder with ease. The first, is that feeling into our own bodies and asking them for answers is an absolute must. Our bodies know. The second, is that almost always, the best answer to escape depression is much more simple than we realize." He waited a moment. "What is it? You're not going to like it, but here it goes." He spoke with slow and dramatic emphasis, smiling. "EEAT LESSS!. Give it a try before you knock it."

Miles felt the air of the wind passing against his skin. *Remember to find your pace. No need to rush. Enjoy this and you will give them your best. Back and forth between light and heavy.*

"I am your chosen president. It's my job to tell you these uncomfortable truths—to lift the veil. The past shouldn't make you feel guilty, that is simply another obstacle. Go further—beyond the guilt. Find the motivation waiting for you, and give yourself what you truly crave—to gently begin the process of living in a continuous state of improvement.

Pour it on Miles. A little more.

"Do you know that we humans are unbelievably, incredibly, fantastically inventive in the ways we spend our time? Perhaps you do—but allow me to magnify the situation. There is so much to laugh at, to smile and feel passionate about. Compassion, love, support, intelligence. These are the things that can make life for all of us a more pleasurable experience. For the future human, it is no longer cool or socially acceptable, to complain about your life. Being spoiled to such an extent is a way of the past that our future children will study in order not to repeat. They will not spit insults at their ancestors, as that is merely unproductive. But they will wish that we would have gotten our act together sooner. The reality of our existence, the functionality of the human mind-body; it's far too fascinating to warrant the extents of our negative habits. That is truth. Pessimism is old time stuff.

"Future kids will be incredible. Want to know why? Because they will see that there are certain things they must safeguard against in order to experience the highest levels of appreciation. One of those things, is an over obsession with the accumulation of monetary funds. Yes, money is a very serious obstacle. How do we balance it? Future kids will know that they are free to add material pleasures they are able to afford without experiencing feelings of guilt. They will see that there is nothing indecent about trying to make life more comfortable, and allowing the acquisition of useful material to cause small giggly bubbles of delight. However, they will also know that happiness is a strange and often elusive beast. They will know that they can enjoy a purchase because they value its use, and not merely for its flamboyant social signals. They also will know that no purchase can out-sustain wavelengths of happiness which come from doing inner soul work, or from fixing problems which haven't yet been solved by other humans."

Huge eruptions of passionate noise rose up to meet him yet again. Miles allowed the energy to infiltrate the fabric of his heart. He looked out onto the faces assembled in front of him. Most were intently focused, and some had their eyes closed—trying to isolate and internalize sound, he knew. He reached for his most powerful form of voice.

"In order to move further along, we must accept the reality that we are all each other's brothers and sisters—everyone. We must give more attention to the truth of our community like existence, rather than splintering ourselves off in mental duels of 'for and against.' How could it make sense for us to divide ourselves into groups of people, according to imaginary lines drawn over land for so long? Have we failed to understand the power of teamwork?

"NO!"

"Seeing all humans as a community is a philosophical decision that each one of us must hold onto. Do you believe in a day when humans will accept it as merely sensible to play our individual part in making things better for everyone? It's already how it is! Our interconnectedness will be an obvious assessment, made and known with certainty by us all. Today should give you proof that we are most definitely moving in that direction."

Miles then allowed himself to play the role of politician and raised his fist up in the air, adding to the roar. He lowered his arm and opened his eyelids to their fullest extent. *Almost there.*

"I hope that it will make you happy to hear that as my first act as leader of the entire species of humans, I will change the name of our habitat. 'Earth' is a fine name, but it's time to give our planet something more suitable for the reality it is. My hope is that changing it will assist us in maintaining a more appropriate outlook.

"'Paradise' is what our planet will now be called. If we truly take the time to imagine a fraction of the immensity of Space within our mind—and then consider this ground we are currently standing on, or the air we are breathing—we see clearly why this name is far more appropriate. The whole planet is in fact the image of the Garden of Eden itself, and I get the feeling that it has been waiting for us to actualize this.

"Perhaps there are endings, and perhaps there is injury and suffering; but perhaps we were also never entitled to have any of this to begin with. Have you noticed how entitlement crushes our sense of wonder? It is with great sadness that we shall begin looking back on the time and years of life that so many of our ancestors spent distracting themselves with what they were without. They had, unfortunately, become addicted to the habit of fear. They convinced themselves they had to survive, while at the same time enjoying greater safety than ever before in history. That survival mentality is over and done with—this lack of perspective happened, and there is no changing the past. But it has no place in our present, and definitely not in our future. Each of us must now begin to improve our intimate relationship with the laws of time—accepting the past while moving forward in the direction of greater loving strength." He waited a moment—gathering himself and connecting with sadness willfully.

"There are still those on Paradise who truly have good reason for needing to maintain a survivor mentality—the abusive situations are rampant. When horrible drama is happening in your life, it is so hard to engage with the reality of beauty. When we're able to do it—that's when we will find the answers to work out our predicaments. We must help these fellow family members who have been pounded down into these places by unacceptable uses of force. We must find out who and where they are, and we must creatively improve their lives—immediately. It's all of our responsibility, and there's no larger source of purpose to be found in the uses of our time. Doing so helps us all. Get excited for it. First, however, you must make sure you've pulled yourself up and out. Do not pity those you help. See that they are waiting to use their hardship to bask more deeply in the ecstasy of greater liberty. If you have been through challenge and come out the other side—you know of what I speak."

"We are all crazy. Yes, it's true. What goes on in our minds is completely insane no matter how you slice it. Whether you choose to see it or not, doesn't change it from being true. Sanity is nothing at all. The closest thing we can find is self-acceptance.

"You're allowed to feel anything. You don't have to tell anyone. It's true. Now that that's straight—what is it that you want to feel? Hatred, paranoia, lack of appreciation, lack of faith?" He paused for a moment. "Nope, not for me. No thank you. Let's try the other way around." *That's right,* he thought. *Can I allow my life to happen?* He felt the energy rising within. He focused it on his task.

"I want to end by saying that I think we have somehow missed the messages that Buddha, Jesus and all of our enlightened leaders of the past have sent forward through time and space. If they truly were what we hold them to be, then their message was not for us to place their individuality up on a pedestal of admiration and nonattainment. Their message instead, was that we can each go where they went."

Miles Carson stopped for a moment before closing his eyes and speaking his final words from the most deeply spiritual place he could find.

"It is with relaxed determination that I engage my life. And it is with great pride that I honor the power of my mind and my heart to function together in harmony. I offer to you, as your chosen leader, a simple pledge: I will do what I believe is best for everyone, and I will share with you my strategies as I constantly strive for greater levels of saneness within the personal self. I will close my eyes often and remember that we are all connected. That intention is all I have to give—nothing more and nothing less. What I ask is for you to do the same."

With that, Miles turned around and lifted his thumb up in the direction of the sky. He kept his ears fixed on the thunderous cheers of the crowd, even as they gave way to the deafening sound of rocket engines bursting to life.

THRIVAL

The most influential lesson Peter Sol ever learned was how fluid life was destined to be. Somehow the process of it seemed to be both cyclical and linear at the same time. As life moved forward, he observed that similar thoughts and feelings floated around in patterns of sameness. Even now, into his later years, he was prone to the part of the cycle that was anxiousness and depression. *It never completely goes away*, he thought.

Taking into account how much he saw and how deeply he went, it was almost to be expected that life could feel at times overwhelming. No one's accomplishments or status could change the heavy weight that comes from not always being with the higher self.

It was hard to explain exactly how Peter felt in the particular moment of today; but it's safe to say that the true depth of circumstance was taking on a particularly dissatisfying shade of color. Part of the reason perhaps, was that his body was feeling rather static. *I should probably move around, maybe go outside,* he thought to himself. It was raining lightly, but he opened the front door of his newly developed home that was carved out of an old lecture hall on a college campus. It was both beautifully and creatively constructed. Regardless, he was still getting used to the change. The previous year he and Maya had moved out of their house on Revolution and handed the reins of Gratitude over to Amanda and Duncan. The two of them had finally realized what everyone around them had seen for so long—that although they were incredibly different, they had a very satisfying balance to their relationship. Just last week they had brought a new human into the world together—a boy. *Gratitude is in good hands,* Peter knew.

He stepped out into the hazy mist of wetness, took off his glasses and placed them on a small table under the overhanging roof beyond his front door. Although he knew everything was different now, the surroundings still looked pretty much the same. *Like Paradise should look*, he thought. But it also wasn't the same at all. It was very different.

The campus he was living on was part of a growing trend to convert vacant universities into new kinds of communities. Countless former academic institutions were not able to maintain themselves as enrollment plummeted. Rather quickly, a greater number of citizens became enlightened to the fraud they had sheepishly fallen into for so long. These paper institutions were not prepared for the blow—hadn't saved properly, nor did they have the ability to adapt their curriculums quickly enough. They had been greedy, and expected things to stay the same. They sold their precious land at extremely low cost.

Now, all were within close proximity of often majestic pieces of property—where nature meets the human cleverness of craftsmanship. There were new hospitals, school for all ages (even adults), nursing homes, self-sustaining agriculture, open habitats for a wide variety of animal life, plenty of community space to interact with other humans, as well as work spaces to take on new projects.

Of course, everyone rode bicycles. If they wanted to travel a distance by car, train or bus—they'd have to first walk or ride over to the outer edge of the campus.

Besides the obvious conveniences of living in such a practical space, the foundation of the construction depended on the psychological benefits of interacting more often with other humans. As much as he enjoyed spending time alone, Peter had to admit how much he loved joking around, playing games, doing work with other people— and overall being well-liked. *It's not the most important thing, but it is fun and fulfilling.* He hated drama, but loved environments that were free flowing with positive, witty, and light hearted interactions. It amazed him how easily this place was able to become that.

It was the end of fall, and Peter was feeling connected to the present mood of the season. *Not quite the winter of my life, but almost there.* He took steps to move his body about and found himself standing in a spot under a large oak tree that dominated that particular space of grass in front of his new home. Perhaps it was strange for a man to stand next to a tree and stare placidly at the surrounding area—but, he knew, *it shouldn't be. Especially in a place like this. There are things much stranger going on here.*

Knowing this gave him courage to continue letting go and ease himself into his senses. He stood there meditating as his eyes calmly swept over the land, drifting from one piece of matter to the next—looking, inspecting; without any intent.

As he found himself gazing at the intricate markings on the bark of the tree, a fabulous idea struck (as they so often do when we allow ourselves to engage fully with existence). As soon as it came, he did not hesitate in taking action. He made the decision to climb the great oak immediately before grabbing the firmest branch he could reach. Although he was nearing seventy, his body was still strong, healthy, and capable. *For how much longer, I don't know. That doesn't matter much today though does it Peter? Take advantage!* He had been a natural climber when he was a boy, and he immediately fell back into the role of carrying, and shifting his weight toward positions of safety. *Take a chance, then find stability, take another chance…find stability again.*

He thought of his father watching him do the same thing so many years earlier, and nicknaming him 'a monkey' as he told his son to be conscious of his balance. Peter smiled at the memory of a great man now gone. *In a way, he really started it all—raising Jo and I the way he did. Then again, he wouldn't have been who he was if not for his parents and his brother; and their parents, and so on—endlessly. Oh, how great is the truth that our actions our interconnected, and our experiences so much more than our own.*

It was in that moment that Peter remembered his near death experience learning how to swim as a child. He grinned from ear-to-ear realizing that he hadn't thought about it since it had happened. He smiled at the power of memory—*how could it remain intact after so long? Amazing.* He contemplated the thought of how profoundly that experience may have unknowingly guided subsequent actions throughout the long years of his life.

Peter shook himself back into the moment. Up he went—rising joyfully—scouting his next move and then making it with certainty. He didn't climb just a few branches but found himself going up higher and higher, almost all the way to the very top of the tree. As he gained height, his awareness of danger became more apparent. *But,* he thought, *if I don't trust in the strength of my hands and my feet, what else do I have left to trust in?* With that sense of spirit, he climbed until he was well into the very tops of the leaves. He found a comfortable place to nestle himself between three of the last strong branches. He had earbuds in the pocket of his sweatshirt, so he took them out, plugged them into his phone—and allowed the almighty power of music to have its say.

This is so much fun. This is what life's about...being crazy and letting our bodies tell us what they want us to do with our time. They know. We've allowed our minds to dominate too much—we need to direct it toward asking the body.

Peter perched high atop the tree like a watchful owl—gazing out onto the area of land that was his neighborhood below. *Everything is different from this vantage point. I can't exactly describe what I'm getting from it, but it feels valuable. I won't forget this feeling of being up here easily. Experiences are like that,* he thought. *You're somehow aware of the memorable ones as they're happening to you. It's a wonderful characteristic of life.*

Still, he played Jo's old game of asking, "how much can I solidify this experience in my long-term memory?" *She was right to believe that we often over-inflate the amount we think we'll remember...it's usually less. We forget what we think we'll hold onto all the time,* he knew.

His consideration of memory brought to him another glimpse. He thought back to his years living in Asia. He smiled at the thought of how stimulating his time had been there. *The landscape felt incredibly sharp and unique. The unfamiliar culture directed me to a place of higher awareness. I can pick those memories out and use them. Looking out even at this revolutionary neighborhood…it might feel ordinary in comparison, but is it really any less awesome than what exists on the opposite side of Paradise? It's just as pleasing visually. Maybe part of a healthy and successful mindset is taking what we see all the time and experiencing it as fresh and new—changing our relationship with the ordinary. Can we train ourselves to do it? Yes! Very important.*

He crouched up there for a while, looking and watching. Soon his dream-come-reality pulled into their narrow driveway on her purple speed bike. At the same time, their next-door-neighbor Harris also arrived home.

It continually amazed Peter that he had found Maya at all. They now woke up every morning and started their days with one sentence to each other. Peter would say, "I want what's best for you." Maya would respond, "I want what's best for you too." Then they'd know its truth and hold its support in all their subsequent interactions with each other and others for the rest of the day. It was them trying. It was pretty cute.

He thought about one of the warnings he had given her about himself back when they first met: "I can be argumentative," he had told her. "But know that all that is, is me getting far too wrapped up in playing some kind of game. The only time you have cause for concern, is when I'm not being open with you. If I'm not being vulnerable, there is some uneasiness to be pried out. Please push me to spill my guts when it feels right—it won't be that bad, and then we'll both feel much better I think."

She responded to him in the most satisfying way. "Peter, I think that goes for all of us. I'll watch out for your tendency to hold back, and you do the same for me. We'll both remember the levels of growth possible after a good honest purging of crusty aggressive thought. You dig?"

Peter took out his earbuds. Up in the tree, he could hear her speaking.

"How's it going, Harris?"
"Not so bad, Maya. You?
"I try not to complain."
"Yeah, same here. Have a good one—see ya later!"

That was it. *Very businesslike in their cordiality,* Peter thought. *That's all people are really after most of the time. A whole conversation isn't always necessary—just some polite words to acknowledge each other's presence before moving right along. Other times...we need to argue, or comfort—and then we have many words. But I don't think we have to consider who we like all the damn time. The inflated value of our own opinions holds us back so freakin much!*

He laughed to himself. *I could really shock the hell out of their daily routine if I gave them a shout from up here. After all, an old man hanging out in the top of a tree is not such a common sight.* He closed his eyes and concentrated on noise—trying to hear very distant sounds and then sounds that were closer to him. It was a centering practice he often fell into. *The variety of sound that is always present can be so meditative—if I allow myself to connect and notice.*

The most important thing to know about Peter Sol, was that he did not enjoy his life because that was what he wanted (although it was); he enjoyed it because he felt responsible to. That was why feeling depressed didn't sit well with him. *Perhaps once in a while it's OK to feel down in the dumps and to be with those feelings...but overall, there isn't much time for it I think. Climbing a tree like a little boy can easily remind us how much fun existing freely is. Life is only depressing when we forget the extent of our freedom—or the extent of our growth. The suffering can then be deep. There is no doubt that we must also make sufficient time to be with sadness. But it is also a net of choice, and there are more all-encompassing ones to hold ourselves within.*

With only a few branches to hold him, Peter fell into trusting the tree and focused on relaxing his body completely. There were no thoughts—only emptiness, and good feeling. He sucked it up for everything it was worth. *It's so perfect—this stillness.* He put a stop to any kind of pressure at all. 'Peaceful' didn't do justice to describing how it made him feel to truly let go of the doing. He knew in his heart that it was the right thing. It didn't matter what would happen next. *These loads we carry have to be released over and over. No matter what they are. Each time...the overall weight gets lighter and the place we go to becomes easier to travel toward. Again and again.*

A lifetime filled with 'higher experiences,' taught him the fallacy of trying to sustain 'the best.' That was why the one net he allowed himself to be gladly caught in was the one of fluctuation. There was enough truth in it to satisfy his mind's desire to deal with all the variety of differences. *Things end, and then start up again. We watch the process of the whole thing. Repetition toward progress.*

He held the current goodness he felt swirling within the depth of the center of his heart.

As he moved out of meditation, more thoughts began to trickle in. He watched, and allowed his ego's stories to happen. *I was an adviser to the first presidency of the human race. I helped transform our system of training the future generation. My notebooks have been some of the most popular works of writing in the history of writing. Even more than all of that...I have been present for it.*

So? What does it mean? Anything much?

He remembered choosing to embrace roles of leadership. At one point he had no choice but to accept and simply go for living the way he believed. He had made the decision not to deprive others of what he had to offer, and everything else had tumbled out of that one place of truth-strength. *That, and Maya of course.*

Peter did what no other person could do. And still it wasn't a big deal. *What credit is there for me to take for living with a passionate desire to make things better? Is there really a smarter way to have operated? No chance. And that's the reason I've had to share.* It boggled his mind that still so many other people didn't see it that way. *Oh, to the possibilities of how awesome and magical of a world there is still yet to be created. It's so easy to feel small considering how many people there are and how much is going on. But it's a shame and a pity not to see how big each one of us has the potential to be. There is space. Really! But do you? Are you smart enough to want that practice in your life? That's the question.* Peter beamed inside. His thinking was on point today.

Our bodies don't want us living nervous and scared, and only concerned about our own personal situation. That's the truth. Our inner nature is not calling for us to play it safe. It's calling for us to realize that we are these awesome machines to be moved about as productively as we can imagine.

We can pretend that our fear is funny, but it isn't one bit. There's no amount of joking around that'll lighten the massive mistake of falling too deeply into story lines that obsessively attempt to question the worth of the self. The self is valuable—now go do what you want! But he knew it was slightly more complicated than that.

The battle between old habits and new growth is a very even match. It's pretty scary being as big as you're capable of. The constant battle is often tiring. But we become freedom torpedoes when we surrender to what our intuition already knows. Holding ourselves back leads to such a severe reality of lost potential. If there is a creator, I'm sure that'd be the only thing to make It feel sad.

He considered the oddity of these thoughts while hanging on to a few short branches way up in a tree. He smiled, taking a look down at the green grass far below and feeling quite safe. He fell into one of his personal mantras.

By being happy, I'm doing the best thing I can to take care of myself. By taking care of myself, I have the best chance to reach my potential. I reach it by continuing to mature. I mature by accepting. Celebrate the freedoms that come from both feeling separate and connected. I am happy. Do I need to be happy all the time in order to say, feel and mean it now? No…I can simply be happy now. I can practice as much as I want to. Tell yourself that you're happy Peter. When you feel it, pray for more of it. Sanity, I think, is getting comfortable with any room of thought that the mind's personality has to offer up.

Ultimately, I want to be wise enough…to flow through the inevitable changes.

That led his mind to consider the question Jo hadn't been able to answer; the question that drove him in everything he did. In a flash of insight, he realized that he had it. He thought the answer to his sister telepathically:

The only purpose we need is to feel love as often as we can—to embody it with our movements through constant practice. Relaxed love and surrender… we don't need to strive for anything more than that. Don't you get it! The belief that there needs to be anything more is only possible if you haven't yet experienced the feeling within the body—or if you've chosen to forget the powerful experiences when they come. Perhaps we can't sustain it…but wait for it, look for it—it's bound to return.

Peter allowed himself to get more personal. His mind often drifted into analyzing general human tendencies, and then back in the direction of his own life. *Yes, I have been walked over. Many people have decided to 'like me,' and have thought that their positive evaluation is complete enough to then walk away. As if their opinion was so important that there was no interest in getting to know me any further. For this reason, many of my connections have been able to only go so far. And that is a shame. This is why so often others lash out at us with nonsensical and harmful actions. For an attention seeker…it makes plenty of sense. Conflict tends to keep the opposing party in our thoughts. We must be more serious about our love than this. We must give ample consideration to those we really like.*

Still, am I going to distract myself with all of that and get sidetracked from playing my necessary role on the path of transformation? No! I control one person's body. That being's actions are my primary concern. The only way to really enter the game is to open up and share what I believe; to anyone and everyone. Choose your excuses for holding back your honesty carefully…we're only allowed so many of them.

Those who keep their honesty to themselves remain on the fringes. They surely have more work to do in the next life.

Then Peter had a beautifully unique and brand new insight. *There are many voices, but there is always a captain. Our captains voice knows best. Problems occur when our lesser voices rebel, forget who the captain is, and take themselves too seriously. The captain questions what to do with the body in order to create positive change. The captain knows that in order to be healthy, I have to continue to believe that I'm healthy...especially when I'm feeling just fine. It isn't enough to only pray for health when I'm sick. The captain within me knows that what I do now implicates my future. The captain guides me to connect and build successful relationships on platforms of open possibility of teamwork and honest loving intent. The intuitive captain encourages me to hold my time as precious—it is the truest self, which doesn't want to be dragged along, grumpily obeying. The truest self wants to surrender to the moment—to relax and tune into the situation, and then develop a game plan that excites the desire for purpose.*

In his calmness, Peter felt very connected to his sister. He couldn't be sure of it, but something told him that she was aware of his thoughts—that she was aware that he had grabbed at an answer that could bring them a satisfied sense of completion. Perhaps they had both known what it was all along, but he now held with an ironclad first, the concept of seeing himself as a manifestation of love. *Is that not enough? It has to be enough. Be love, Peter. It's not corny...kindness is the most powerful way of being. Don't second-guess its place on the highest part of your shelf of purpose. Be more serious about it. Ever more serious. It's what the captain wants.*

He thought more. *It is so important to let go of everything that I'm trying to remember. Memories don't go away. Instead, they reprioritize themselves into levels of importance. In this way, I become more attached to the thoughts I really want to have—by letting go of all of them. Yes!*

He went back to his place of nothingness yet again. He would get all worked up with passion and thought and then remember that it was good to flow back to the void. *No thoughts—the dock of emptiness—where the I is lost for a time. It's there, always, if you're up for taking the trip.*

All thoughts have ego attached to them—they seek to validate themselves by hanging around the longest. Thoughts manifest in strings, he realized. *Again and again and again we cut the strings and find peace. Just cut the thought! Sever it right in its tracks and then hang on for the start of a brand new ride.* The conception was so clear and right in his mind. He smiled at the feeling of its rightness, and of a new found understanding. He didn't need anyone to confirm his hypothesis. *Feeling truth is more than enough for me. Even when I have beautiful thoughts of insight and good deeds...still, I know there is ego there. The ego can be used for good or bad, but regardless of all of that...it needs a break, or it'll get rusty and tired and put to poor use.*

The break is pure and sweet. Oh, to be happy with whatever it is I'm doing. To want for nothing. Oh, to feel THAT! Holding that space...what is better? The sensation of contentment, I think, is connecting to godlike energy. It's grabbing time by the scruff of its neck and holding on firmly. It's being a human who realizes that 'getting old,' and 'growing up' are two very different things. Being, here, now...it's not fucking around with bullshit. I'm realizing three things about it: One, it feels so amazingly good. Two, it takes practice. Three, it isn't better or worse. Instead...it's more of the time. That's all. The distinction means a lot. Easy does it.

He began speaking to his naysayers with brand new, clear thoughts. It was this particular room of the mind that had pushed him to be such a trail-blazer throughout the course of his life. He knew that to see the truth was also to see how much wasn't in the truth.

You think that my meditation is an escape, but you couldn't be more wrong. It is where I grow and do the work for all of us. It is in your failure to meditate which serves as the escape—running and doing in order to perpetuate the false-hood of separateness and fill that which you have decided is empty. It is in our fear of fessing up to how spoiled we've been which holds us back the most. No. None of that for me.

Do in the same way that you do nothing Peter—with flowing and consider-ate movements; all the while, accepting that you're a part of something much larger than your own personal understandings. Do—OK, great, fine. But do gentle.

THIS, is the evolution of our species, he intuitively felt. *The only thing we do wrong; the dangerous aspect of being human...is when we think that what we want is in opposition to godlike surrender. Why? Because it isn't true. We forget that all our individual ambitions are also just a part of the very same larger fabric which contains it all. Surrender to every part of it all, and then find what it is you never knew you were looking for.* He took a deep breath, allowing calmness to fill his body. *Become the part of nature that you already are,* he told himself. *And then, send out good vibes into your soul and outward. When I accept myself...all I want to do is learn—and grow. I have spent my whole life asking one question: 'What is right?' Nothing else is half as interesting to me.*

Still, even in the swirling currents of bliss, there was something about sadness itself that felt right to Peter. *Perhaps this happens when we glimpse the true depth of how much better everything can be,* he thought. *So easily! Mostly, by taking a minute to decide not to take our experiences so seriously. And then, as a result of this mindset...doing all the right things.*

I should really be writing this down. He smiled yet again. *Most importantly...*

Peter separated the lips of his mouth and spoke two words; clearly, loudly and kindly. To the tree, to the sky, to his new community, to himself—to everything and anything around that might be listening. "THANK YOU." What mattered was that he said it, and that he felt it—nothing else. The words were the true home for all his grounded strength. They always gave him the feeling of completion.

Then he began making his way down to his partner.

YOUR TASK NOW

Besides of course continuing to do all of your own personal work to help improve the planet…there's something else very simple. Share! It means everything. If these words have helped you, pass them on to others. Do not overhype, as expectations tend to do funny things. See a stranger, look them in the eye, and hand them a copy. See a friend, and do the same. Very simple and easy to play a role.

NOTES

NOTES

NOTES

NOTES

NOTES

NOTES

Made in the USA
Middletown, DE
19 January 2018